I commend Abe Kuruvilla's book to you for its intriguing proposal on how better to relate hermeneutics and homiletics. I have read, and benefited from, his earlier book, but this one goes further. In identifying this new ugly ditch, he also makes an original contribution to the theological interpretation of Scripture. Kuruvilla's homiletics rightly emphasizes the theology of the text and the importance of the congregation's response. His focus is squarely on edifying the church. This is a book on preaching rooted in theology rather than communication skills, and for this I am very grateful!

—**Kevin J. Vanhoozer,** *Research Professor*
Biblical and Systematic Theology
Trinity Evangelical Divinity School, Deerfield, Illinois

From Origen to Karl Barth by way of Augustine and Martin Luther, classic Christian interpreters have placed the sermon or homily at the heart of their practice of scriptural interpretation, yet the move from text to preaching is not a straightforward one that can simply be left to individual inspiration and the Holy Spirit. It requires a theologically and hermeneutically informed reflection, lacking in much of the more recent literature in the fields both of homiletics and the theological interpretation of Scripture. It is this lack that Abe Kuruvilla addresses in this thought-provoking and highly original book, which takes as its starting-point the "pericope"—the section of Scripture, read to the congregation, on which preaching is based—as the primary form in which the biblical Word is encountered.

—**Francis B. Watson,** *Chair of Biblical Interpretation*
Department of Theology and Religion
University of Durham, Durham, U.K.

A theological hermeneutics for preachers has been long overdue, and I am glad to see that this book provides an accessible entry-point into this vital topic. The move from the Bible—with all of its particularity and groundedness—to theological truth requires a depth of hermeneutical sophistication that can only be gained through serious study and attention—and mastering a book such as this. For too long, I have been frustrated by those who present the mechanics of preaching but neglect to provide the theological and hermeneutical understanding to make God's word come alive in the pulpit. I think Abe Kuruvilla has provided an intelligible approach to this perplexing and recurring problem.

—**Stanley E. Porter,** *President and Dean, Professor of New Testament*
McMaster Divinity College, Hamilton, Ontario, Canada

In this sophisticated and lucid study Abraham Kuruvilla draws on recent work in hermeneutics and biblical interpretation to shed fresh light on the nature of biblical preaching. He gives careful attention to the specific issues posed by the use of Scripture in the context of preaching. Kuruvilla offers a constructive account of a biblical hermeneutic, which takes seriously the challenges posed by the Old Testament, and which over all offers a valuable resource for all those concerned with faithful biblical preaching.

—**R. Walter Moberly,** *Professor*
Department of Theology and Religion
University of Durham, Durham, U.K.

Finally, a book on the hermeneutics of preaching from the Old Testament that takes the biblical texts seriously. Responding to many approaches that pay lip service to authorial intent in Old Testament texts but then quickly impose typological and christocentric meanings on them, Kuruvilla asks seriously what biblical authors were doing with their words. With patience and great skill he guides us in how we may first interpret biblical texts to discover their intended meaning, and then he explains how the message of those texts is authoritative for Christian readers. This is the best book on preaching on the Old Testament to come out in a long time.

— **Daniel I. Block,** *Gunther H. Knoedler, Professor of Old Testament*
   Wheaton College, Wheaton, Illinois

This is a magnificent work, showing us how to move from the *then* of the text to the *now* of the audience. . . . Kuruvilla repeatedly demonstrates how paying attention to the details of the text leads to the underlying truth that spans all generations. His discussion of how all parts of the law—civil, moral, and ceremonial—are applicable today is worth the price of the book. You will understand your task as a preacher as never before and find yourself with a renewed excitement for it.

— **Donald R. Sunukjian,** *Professor of Preaching*
   Chair, Department of Christian Ministry and Leadership
   Talbot School of Theology
   Biola University, La Mirada, California

It is one thing to talk theoretically about the necessity of biblical theology in developing one's hermeneutic, and quite another actually to do it on a passage by passage basis as preachers must do in their ecclesial settings. Kuruvilla addresses this omission in current discussion and fills the void by showing how biblical theology, interpretation, and preaching fit together to serve the edification of the local parish. This volume makes a significant contribution to the ongoing conversation between the disciplines of hermeneutics and homiletics.

— **Kenneth A. Mathews,** *Professor of Divinity*
   Department of Old Testament
   Beeson Divinity School
   Samford University, Birmingham, Alabama

Rarely does one find such a clear, careful, and comprehensive description of the goals and methods of biblical theological hermeneutics as we have in this volume by Abe Kuruvilla. The fact that the discussion never loses touch with the urgent task of preaching makes this volume not only provocative but virtually unique in the field.

— **Thomas G. Long,** *Bandy Professor of Preaching*
   Candler School of Theology
   Emory University, Atlanta, Georgia

Too often practical preachers skip over theology and hermeneutics in sermon preparation, arguing that they have little time for theory. However, this well-researched book challenges preachers to develop a theological hermeneutic that is not only essential for the preaching task but proves immensely practical. Focusing on pericopes as segments of the biblical canon, this new approach invites preachers to see projections of God's future world that make vital claims on Christian obedience. A challenging book for any preacher who wants to go deeper, and that should include all of us.

— **Michael Quicke,** *C. W. Koller Professor of Preaching*
   Northern Seminary, Lombard, Illinois

PRIVILEGE *the* TEXT!

A THEOLOGICAL HERMENEUTIC FOR PREACHING

ABRAHAM KURUVILLA

MOODY PUBLISHERS

CHICAGO

© 2013 by
ABRAHAM KURUVILLA

All Scripture translations are by the author.

Edited by Philip E. Rawley
Cover design: Thinkpen
Cover image: Shutterstock #57903223 / #62554042
Interior design: Smartt Guys design
Author photo: Dan Regier, DTS

Library of Congress Cataloging-in-Publication Data

Kuruvilla, Abraham.
  Privilege the text! : a theological hermeneutic for preaching / Abraham Kuruvilla.
    pages cm
  Includes bibliographical references and index.
  ISBN 978-0-8024-0713-9
  1. Bible—Criticism, interpretation, etc. 2. Bible—Hermeneutics. 3. Preaching. I. Title.
  BS511.3.K87 2013
  220.601—dc23

                                            2012051288

We hope you enjoy this book from Moody Publishers. Our goal is to provide high-quality, thought-provoking books and products that connect truth to your real needs and challenges. For more information on other books and products written and produced from a biblical perspective, go to www.moodypublishers.com or write to:

Moody Publishers
820 N. LaSalle Boulevard
Chicago, IL 60610

5 7 9 10 8 6 4

Printed in the United States of America

CONTENTS

CHAPTER 4: *The* Aqedah *and Christiconic Interpretation* 211

To my students
past and present

הרבה למדתי מרבותי
ומחבירי יותר מרבותי
ומתלמידי יותר מכולן

I have learned much from my teachers,
more from my colleagues,
but from my students more than all.

R. Ḥanina, *b. Taʿanit* 7a

ABBREVIATIONS

ANCIENT TEXTS

1 Apol.	Justin Martyr, *First Apology*
1 Clem.	Clement of Rome, *First Clement*
2 Clem.	Clement of Rome, *Second Clement*
Adv. Jud.	Tertullian, *Adversus Judaeos*
Ag. Ap.	Josephus, *Against Apion*
Ant.	Josephus, *Antiquities*
Apol.	Tertullian, *Apologeticus*
Barn.	Barnabas
Comm. Rom	Origen, *Commentary on Romans*
Conf.	Augustine, *Confessions*
Congr.	Philo, *De congressu eruditionis gratia*
Corrept.	Augustine, *De correptione et gratia*
Deit.	Gregory of Nyssa, *De deitate Filii et Spiritus Sancti*
Dem. ev.	Eusebius, *Demonstratio evangelica*
Did.	Didache
Doctr. chr.	Augustine, *De doctrina christiana*
Ennarat. Ps.	Augustine, *Ennarationes in Psalmos*
Ep. 138 to Jerome	Augustine, *Epistle 138* to Jerome
Ep. ad Hedybiam	Jerome, *Epistula ad Hedybiam*
Ep. ad Pammachium	Jerome, *Epistula ad Pammachium*
Ep. ad Theodorum medicum	Gregory the Great, *Epistula ad Theodorum medicum*
Ep. mort. Ar.	Athanasius, *Epistula ad Serapionem de morte Arii*
Faust.	Augustine, *Contra Faustum Manichaeum*
Grat.	Augustine, *De gratia et libero arbitrio*
Haer.	Ireneaus, *Adversus haereses*
Hist. eccl.	Eusebius, *Historia ecclesiastica*
Hom. 1 Cor.	Chrysostom, *Homilies on 1 Corinthians*
Hom. Col.	Chrysostom, *Homilies on Colossians*

Hom. Gen.	Chrysostom, *Homilies on Genesis*
Hypoth.	Philo, *Hypothetica*
Inst.	Quintilian, *Institutio oratoria*
Institutes	Calvin, *Institutes of the Christian Religion*
J.W.	Josephus, *Jewish War*
L.A.B.	Pseudo-Philo, *Liber antiquitatum biblicarum*
Marc.	Tertullian, *Adversus Marcionem*
Opif.	Philo, *De opificio mundi*
Or. Brut.	Cicero, *Orator ad M. Brutum*
Paed.	Clement of Alexandria, *Paedagogus*
Pan.	Epiphanius, *Panarion*
Phaedr.	Plato, *Phaedrus*
Phil.	Polycarp, *Epistle to the Philippians*
PL	*Patrologia Latina*
Poet.	Aristotle, *Poetics*
Praescr.	Tertullian, *De praescriptione haereticorum*
Princ.	Origen, *De principiis*
Res.	Tertullian, *De resurrectione carnis*
Rhet. Alex.	Anaximenes, *Rhetorica ad Alexandrum*
Serm.	Augustine, *Sermon*
Spec. Laws	Philo, *On the Special Laws*
Spir. et litt.	Augustine, *De spiritu et littera*
Strom.	Clement of Alexandria, *Stromata*
Summa	Aquinas, *Summa theologica*
Test.	Cyprian, *Ad Quirinum testimonia adversus Judaeos*
Tract. Ev. Jo.	Augustine, *In Evangelium Johannis tractatus*
Ver. rel.	Augustine, *De vera religione*

RABBINIC AND TARGUMIC LITERATURE

ʾ*Abot R. Nat.*	ʾ*Abot de Rabbi Nathan*
B. Bat.	*Baba Batra*
Ber.	*Berakot*
CD	Cairo Genizah copy of the *Damascus Document*

Gen. Rab.	*Genesis Rabbah*
Giṭ.	*Giṭṭin*
Lev. Rab.	*Leviticus Rabbah*
Mak.	*Makkot*
Meg.	*Megillah*
Mek.	*Mekilta*
Menaḥ.	*Menaḥot*
Moʾed Qaṭ.	*Moʾed Qaṭan*
Ned.	*Nedarim*
Neg.	*Negaʿim*
Neof.	*Neofiti*
Pesaḥ.	*Pesaḥim*
Pesiq. Rab.	*Pesiqta Rabbati*
Pesiq. Rab Kah.	*Pesiqta de Rab Kahana*
Ps.-J.	*Pseudo-Jonathan*
Qidd.	*Qiddušin*
Sanh.	*Sanhedrin*
Šab.	*Šabbat*
Soṭ.	*Soṭah*
Taʿan.	*Taʿanit*
Tg.	*Targum*
Yebam.	*Yebamot*

OLD TESTAMENT APOCRYPHA AND PSEUDEPIGRAPHA

2, 4 Macc	2, 4 Maccabees
1 En.	*1 Enoch* (Ethiopic Apocalypse)
2 Bar.	*2 Baruch* (Syriac Apocalypse)
3 Bar.	*3 Baruch* (Greek Apocalypse)
As. Mos.	*Assumption of Moses*
Bar	Baruch
Jub.	*Jubilees*
Pss. Sol.	*Psalms of Solomon*
Sir	Sirach/Ecclesiasticus
Tob	Tobit

Dead Sea Scrolls

1QH^a	*Hodayot (Thanksgiving) Hymns* from Qumran Cave 1
1QM	*Milḥamah* or *War Scroll* from Qumran Cave 1
1QS	*Serek hayyahad (Rule of the Community)* from Qumran Cave 1
4Q225	psJub^a from Qumran Cave 4
4Q286	Ber^a from Qumran Cave 4
4Q385, 386, 388	psEzek from Qumran Cave 4
4Q387, 390	apocrJer from Qumran Cave 4
4QD^a	Damascus Document from Qumran Cave 4
11QMelch	Melchizedek from Qumran Cave 11
11QT^a	Temple Scroll from Qumran Cave 11

Other Abbreviations

ABC	Anchor Bible Commentary
ABR	*Australian Biblical Review*
AUSS	*Andrews University Seminary Studies*
BBR	*Bulletin for Biblical Research*
BECNT	Baker Exegetical Commentary on the New Testament
Bib	*Biblica*
BSac	*Bibliotheca Sacra*
BTB	*Biblical Theology Bulletin*
BZAW	Beihefte zur Zeitschrift für die alttestamentliche Wissenschaft
Cardozo L. Rev.	*Cardozo Law Review*
CBQ	*Catholic Bible Quarterly*
CI	*Critical Inquiry*
Columbia L. Rev.	*Columbia Law Review*
CTQ	*Concordia Theological Quarterly*
CTR	*Criswell Theological Review*
Ess. Crit	*Essays in Criticism*
EvJ	*Evangelical Journal*
ExAud	*Ex Auditu*

ExpTim	*Expository Times*
Fordham L. Rev.	*Fordham Law Review*
FOTL	Forms of the Old Testament Literature
GOTR	*Greek Orthodox Theological Review*
GTJ	*Grace Theological Journal*
HAR	*Hebrew Annual Review*
HorBT	*Horizons in Biblical Theology*
HTR	*Harvard Theological Review*
HUCA	*Hebrew Union College Annual*
IJST	*International Journal of Systematic Theology*
Int	*Interpretation*
Iowa Rev.	*Iowa Review*
J. Aes. Art Crit.	*Journal of Aesthetics and Art Criticism*
JAAR	*Journal of the American Academy of Religion*
JBL	*Journal of Biblical Literature*
JEHS	*Journal of the Evangelical Homiletics Society*
JETS	*Journal of the Evangelical Theological Society*
JR	*Journal of Religion*
JRE	*Journal of Religious Ethics*
JSNT	*Journal for the Study of the New Testament*
JSNTSup	Journal for the Study of the New Testament: Supplement Series
JSOT	*Journal for the Study of the Old Testament*
JSOTSup	Journal for the Study of the Old Testament: Supplement Series
JSSR	*Journal for the Scientific Study of Religion*
JTI	*Journal of Theological Interpretation*
LNTS	Library of New Testament Studies
LTQ	*Lexington Theological Quarterly*
NAC	New American Commentary
Neot	*Neotestamentica*
NICNT	New International Commentary on the New Testament
NICOT	New International Commentary on the Old Testament

NIGTC	New International Greek Testament Commentary
NLH	*New Literary History*
NPP	New Perspective on Paul
OBT	Overtures to Biblical Theology
PEQ	*Palestine Exploration Quarterly*
Phil. Rev.	*The Philosophical Review*
Phil. Sci.	*Philosophy of Science*
Pol. Sci. Q.	*Political Science Quarterly*
ResQ	*Restoration Quarterly*
RevQ	*Revue de Qumran*
RH	Redemptive-historical
RRR	*Reformation and Renaissance Review*
SBET	*Scottish Bulletin of Evangelical Theology*
SBJT	*Southern Baptist Journal of Theology*
SJT	*Scottish Journal of Theology*
Spec	*Speculum*
Texas L. Rev.	*Texas Law Review*
TJT	*Toronto Journal of Theology*
TrinJ	*Trinity Journal*
TS	*Theological Studies*
TSF Bull.	*Theological Students' Fellowship Bulletin*
TynBul	*Tyndale Bulletin*
USQR	*Union Seminary Quarterly Review*
VE	*Vox Evangelica*
VT	*Vetus Testamentum*
VTSup	Vetus Testamentum Supplement
WBC	Word Biblical Commentary
WTJ	*Westminster Theological Journal*
WUNT	Wissenschaftliche Untersuchungen zum Neuen Testament
WW	*Word and World*
ZAW	*Zeitschrift für die alttestamentliche Wissenschaft*
ZNW	*Zeitschrift für die neutestamentliche Wissenschaft*

INTRODUCTION

Tribu, ergo nobis verborum signficationem, intelligentiae lumen, dictorum honorem, veritatis fidem.

Bestow, therefore, on us the meaning of words, the light of understanding, nobility in diction, and faith in truth.

HILARY OF POITIERS, ca. 300–ca. 368[1]

Those who work pulpits on a weekly basis deal with "the astonishing supposition that texts which are between possibly 3,000 and almost 2,000 years old can offer orientation for the discovery of truth in the third millennium."[2] The lot of the homiletician is not easy: each week, this intrepid soul has to negotiate the formidable passage from ancient text to modern audience to expound, with authority and relevance, a specific biblical passage for the faithful.[3] The goal of this work is to create a bridge spanning those waters, by employing with profit concepts derived from hermeneutics and theology.[4]

The Bible affirms that "whatever was written in former times was written for our instruction" (Rom 15:4). How exactly "our instruction" is accomplished is a question that has not been satisfactorily resolved. The challenge of bridging

---

1. *De Trinitatis*, 1.38.13–14.

2. Christoph Schwöbel, "The Preacher's Art: Preaching Theologically," in Colin Gunton, *Theology through Preaching* (Edinburgh: T. & T. Clark, 2001), 7.

3. James D. Smart, *The Strange Silence of the Bible in the Church: A Study in Hermeneutics* (London: SCM, 1970), 33–34, called this "a perilous road."

4. While this work is placed in the context of the preaching endeavor, the question it seeks to answer is one that is pertinent for any context of biblical interpretation intended to culminate in application: Bible study groups, Sunday school classes, or even in one's own reading of Scripture.

the gap between an ancient text and a modern audience, both culturally con-
ditioned entities, is no doubt a burdensome one. On one side of this gap is the
historical entity of the text; on the other, the existential situation of the community of God addressed from the pulpit. Sandra Schneiders acknowledges that
it is indeed a "baffling question" how these two come together in the interpretation of the text.[5] Stanley Porter agrees: "[T]he move from the original text
of Scripture, with all of its time-bound character, to theological truths for life
today is one of the most demanding intellectual tasks imaginable"—a task that
confronts preachers each time the Bible is expounded.[6] Nonetheless, there can
be no gainsaying the crucial and essential nature of this enterprise; it is by the
instruction of Scripture, through its "perseverance and encouragement," that
Christians find hope (Rom 15:4). The crux of the hermeneutical problem is the
traversal from the *then* of the text to the *now* of the audience; words written in
an earlier age are to be transposed in some fashion across a divide into a later
era. Homileticians are at the forefront of this transaction to bridge that chasm,
and this work seeks to facilitate that solemn undertaking.

Preaching is not only the interpretation of an authoritative biblical text but
also the relevant communication of a God-given message to real people living
real lives with a real need for that message. The authoritative text is, thus, to be
extended to relevant praxis, "to enable God's revealed truth to flow out of the
Scriptures into the lives of the men and women of today."[7] William Tyndale pro-
nounced eloquently, in the sixteenth century, on the necessity of application—
this "flowing out" of Scripture into people's lives:

> Though a man had a precious jewel, and a rich, yet if he wist not the value there-
> of, nor whereof it served, he were neither the better nor richer of a straw. Even
> so though we read the Scripture, and babble of it never so much, yet if we know
> not the use of it, and wherefore it was given, and what is therein to be sought, it
> profits us nothing at all. It is not enough, therefore, to read and talk of it only,
> but we must also desire God, day and night, instantly to open our eyes, and to

---

5. Sandra M. Schneiders, "The Paschal Imagination: Objectivity and Subjectivity in New Testament Interpretation," *TS* 46 (1982): 65.

6. Stanley E. Porter, "Hermeneutics, Biblical Interpretation, and Theology: Hunch, Holy Spirit, or Hard
Work?" in I. Howard Marshall, *Beyond the Bible: Moving from Scripture to Theology* (Grand Rapids:
Baker, 2004), 121. "Anyone who proclaims how easy it is to do this is probably prevaricating, or is very
bad at the task, or is so very experienced at it as to have forgotten the intellectual and spiritual task that
it is" (ibid.).

7. John R. W. Stott, *Between Two Worlds: The Art of Preaching in the Twentieth Century* (Grand Rapids:
Eerdmans, 1982), 138.

make us understand and feel wherefore the Scripture was given, that we may apply the medicine of the Scripture, every man to his own sores; unless then we intend to be idle disputers, and brawlers about vain words, ever gnawing upon the bitter bark without, and never attaining unto the sweet pith within.[8]

If, then "[t]he capital art of a preacher is to bring his subject home to the bosoms of his hearers," how then should this art be undertaken?[9] Attempts by preachers to interpret Scripture for application essentially have fallen into two broad categories: systematization and atomization.[10]

Systematization and Atomization

There is systematization, by which all that is endeavored is an attempt to squeeze a given pericope[11] into the appropriate pigeonhole of systematic theology, by organizing facts and by systematizing detail. The healing of the blind man in Mark 8 must fit into the omnipotence of God/Jesus (theology proper). The story of Abraham's (non-)sacrifice of Isaac must accommodate substitutionary atonement (soteriology) and, perhaps, the love of God in that "he gave his only begotten Son." Second Samuel 11–12 (the account of David and Bathsheba) ought to remind us of the depravity of mankind (hamartiology) and the perfect messianic King (Christology). Revelation and the books of prophecy draw us into the end times, the Second Advent, and God's final judgment (eschatology). And so on. There is an element of *a priori* reception about all this, since systems of theology already inform us about how and what we must hear; so the task of interpretation becomes merely an exercise in discovering where in that neat system a given passage of Scripture fits. Such systematization is essentially generalization carried far beyond the terra firma of the text; the specificity of the texts is lost in favor of the generalities of systematized axioms.

This subsuming of all that a pericope says within the categories of systematic

---

8. William Tyndale, "A Prologue by William Tyndale Shewing the Use of the Scripture, which He Wrote before the Five Books of Moses," in *The Works of the English Reformers* (3 vols.; ed. Thomas Russell; London: Ebenezer Palmer, 1828–1831), 1: 6.

9. John Claude, *An Essay on the Composition of a Sermon* (3rd ed.; 2 vols.; trans. Robert Robinson; London: T. Scollick, 1782–1788), 2: 325 n. 1.

10. This broad-brush categorization is necessarily artificial, created for its illustrative power; the two poles are, undoubtedly, extreme. In actuality, it is doubtful if any preacher belongs in one or the other; there are, however, tendencies in either direction.

11. While acknowledging its more common connotation of a portion of the Gospels, "pericope" is employed here to demarcate a segment of Scripture, irrespective of genre or length, that forms the textual basis of an individual sermon.

theology reduces the particulars of the text to doctrinal maxims and truisms.[12] Whole genres and individual pericopes of Scripture simply become vehicles for the pronouncements of systematic theology. As far as preachers are concerned, if the specific thrust of a text is only an element of systematic theology, what will they do with a cluster of adjacent pericopes, each of which points to the same element of systematic theology? E.g., Jesus heals not one, but two blind men in Mark—in Mark 8:22–26 (albeit in two stages) and in Mark 10:46–52. Are both these healings reflecting the same systematic theology category, the omnipotence of God/Jesus over the entire optic apparatus and occipital cortex—nerves, vessels, tissues, cells, and all? Or is there something more being conveyed that is specific to the pericope in question? I am convinced there is: authors are *doing* something with what they are *saying!* In other words, yes, Mark is *doing* something different in Mark 10 than what he is *doing* in Mark 8.[13]

Then there is atomization. This is often the resort of those who have graduated beyond systematization, and have recognized that merely classifying a pericope into its proper slot in a tome of systematic theology leaves much to be desired when it comes to applying the specifics of that particular pericope into real life. Atomizers, therefore, react to the deficiencies of systematization, and attempt to make application out of every tidbit of textual material. A shotgun style of exegesis that chases every rabbit in every burrow is complemented by an equally shotgun mode of homiletics—atomization. No byte is unbitten. Every morsel has application, whether it be the escape of Paul in the dark of night ("we must be wise like Paul, avoiding our opponents"; Acts 9:25), or his picking up sticks on the island of Malta ("we must be humble like Paul, willing to engage in menial 'servant' tasks"—a convenient neglect of the snake that lay hidden in the cord; Acts 28:1–5), or the stones that David picked up for his battle with Goliath ("we must be like the stones, patiently being smoothened by God's waters of time, until he uses us"; 1 Sam 17:40), etc. A veritable free-for-all ensues, with a scouring of Scripture for what are ostensibly nuggets of practical wisdom. Thus,

---

12. Again, I speak from a preacher's perspective. While there is, of course, a proper role for systematic theology in the life of the church, I am simply claiming that the pulpit is not the place—at least not on a regular basis—for using biblical pericopes to launch weekly systematic theology lectures (this matter is addressed further in chapter 2).

13. For this approach applied to every pericope in Mark, including Mark 8 and 10, see Abraham Kuruvilla, *Mark: A Theological Commentary for Preachers* (Eugene, Oreg.: Cascade, 2012).

while textual details are respected in some sense, scant regard is given to the thrust of the text and of its author. What the author was *doing* with what he was saying (see chapter 1) is far from the mind of the interpreter; instead the quest is for some consumable textual tidbit that can be easily translated into the situation of the audience. Such inattention to the author's thrust on the part of both those who systematize and those who atomize is, at best, benign neglect, and at worst, culpable misinterpretation.

I agree with systematization in that some degree of generalizing is necessary so that the specifics of the pericope do not paralyze the effort to recontextualize its truths to an audience far away in space and time. For instance, ancient "wine" in "do not be drunk with wine" (Eph 5:18) must be generalized to "alcohol" to prevent intoxication with modern vodka or whiskey (for this see chapter 1). Equally important is the role of systematized theology in constituting a rule of faith for reading Scripture; this rule forms the interpretive boundaries that may not be encroached. For instance, the "angel of Yahweh" in certain passages of Scripture may not be construed as the *fourth* Person of the Godhead—systematized theology (the rule of faith) precludes such an inference (see the Rules of Reading in chapter 1 that take on this systematized role of guardian). I also agree with the burden of atomization, that application *must* be made in every sermon: lives *must* change in response to every pericope of Scripture, every week. However, neither systematization nor atomization attends to the trajectory of the particular text being considered (what the author is *doing* with what he is saying). On the one hand is the error of over-generalizing and thus neglecting the specifics of the text; on the other that of a willy-nilly ransacking of the Bible for usable scraps. Both transactions disregard what the author is *doing* with what he is saying, and both leave preachers—not to mention audiences—with a sense that something is lacking. Thomas Long described the symptoms of this malady precisely:

> [A]lert biblical preachers have been aware for some time that there is a bit of deception, a touch of legerdemain, built into that classical text-to-sermon process. The preacher takes the text and puts it through the paces of a good exegetical process. The grammar of the text is analyzed, word studies are conducted, the probable Sitz im Leben is established, and so on. The handle is turned, the wheels spin, the gears mesh, and in the end out pops a reasonably secure version of what the text meant in its historical context or, to put it more bluntly, what the text used to mean . . . Now, so what? The exegesis yielded

the information that Paul responded in such and such a way to a question in Corinth about meat offered to idols, a question that would never in a million years occur to anyone in Kingsport, Tennessee, or Fresno, California. So what?... The preacher is simply told that now the gap must be bridged from the history of the text to the urgency of the contemporary situation. It is presented as an obvious next step, a child's leap across a puddle, but the honest preacher knows that the distance between what the text used to mean and what the text may now mean yawns wide, and the leap seems difficult indeed.[14]

What is the cure? What can serve as a remedy for this plight of the preacher? This work proposes a *via media* between the two extremes of systematization and atomization—a theological hermeneutic for the operation of moving from text to application, that will, hopefully, make the preacherly "leap" considerably less difficult, and will prove to be a balm for the blight.

Theological Hermeneutic(s)

There is no question that "theological interpretation of Scripture" is at a resurgence. There is a *Dictionary for the Theological Interpretation of the Bible*, as well as a number of tomes with similar phrases in their titles, including a whole set of books from Baker under the series label "Studies in Theological Interpretation," not to mention a *Journal of Theological Interpretation*, and entire issues of *International Journal of Systematic Theology* and *Southern Baptist Journal of Theology* dedicated to the topic.[15]

---

14. Thomas G. Long, "The Use of Scripture in Contemporary Preaching," *Int* 44 (1990): 344.

15. Among the productions prolific are: Francis Watson, *Text, Church and World: Biblical Interpretation in Theological Perspective* (Grand Rapids: Eerdmans, 1994); Stephen E. Fowl, *Engaging Scripture: A Model for Theological Interpretation* (Oxford: Blackwell, 1998); A. K. M. Adam, Stephen E. Fowl, Kevin J. Vanhoozer, and Francis Watson, *Reading Scripture with the Church: Toward a Hermeneutic for Theological Interpretation* (Grand Rapids: Baker, 2006); D. Christopher Spinks, *The Bible and the Crisis of Meaning: Debates on the Theological Interpretation of Scripture* (London: T. & T. Clark, 2007); Daniel J. Treier, *Introducing Theological Interpretation of Scripture: Recovering a Christian Practice* (Grand Rapids: Baker, 2008); Stephen E. Fowl, *Theological Interpretation of Scripture* (Eugene, Oreg.: Cascade, 2009); J. Todd Billings, *The Word of God for the People of God: An Entryway to the Theological Interpretation of Scripture* (Grand Rapids: Eerdmans, 2010); etc. For the special issue journals, see *IJST* 12 (2010) and *SBJT* 14 (2010). In addition, there are those works that employ the label "theological hermeneutics": Werner Jeanrond, *Theological Hermeneutics: Development and Significance* (London: SCM, 1994); Jens Zimmermann, *Recovering Theological Hermeneutics: An Incarnational-Trinitarian Theory of Interpretation* (Grand Rapids: Baker, 2004); Mark Alan Bowald, *Rendering the Word in Theological Hermeneutics: Mapping Divine and Human Agency* (Aldershot, U.K.: Ashgate, 2007); Alexander S. Jensen, *Theological Hermeneutics* (London: SCM, 2007); etc. It is, as Fowl confesses, "a large and somewhat chaotic party" (*Theological Interpretation of Scripture*, x).

As a nascent field (or, at least, as a nascent *label*) "theological interpretation of Scripture" remains quite undefined with a number of variant approaches to this critical hermeneutical operation. This work, however, adopts a unique approach to theological hermeneutics. The vantage point of this entire offering is the pulpit, so to speak, not the desk of a Bible scholar or the lectern of a systematic theologian. In other words, the "theology" of this *theological* hermeneutic is not biblical or systematic theology. Rather, sustaining the focus on preaching, the theology employed is that of the pericope (see chapter 2): what the author is *doing* with what he is *saying* in the specific pericope chosen for the sermon. What in this unit text of preaching is intended to change the lives of listeners for the glory of God? It is unfortunate that such a focus on the pericope to generate a substantial hermeneutic of preaching has been sorely lacking. This is all the more poignant, for throughout the history of Christianity, the importance of sermonic proclamation has been widely acknowledged: "Preaching of the word of God," Aquinas declared, "is the noblest of all ecclesiastical functions."[16] Notwithstanding the Angelic Doctor's testimony, there has not been propounded, as far as I can tell, a theological hermeneutic for preaching. This work is a first attempt to fill that lacuna.

"There are two things on which every interpretation of Scripture depends: the way of discovering [*modus inveniendi*: hermeneutics] what should be understood and the way of presenting [*modus proferendi*: rhetoric] what has been understood" (Augustine, *Doctr. chr.* 1.1.1; 4.1.1). In fact, Augustine's work, *De doctrina christiana*, follows this scheme: books 1–3 concern themselves with *modus inveniendi*; and book 4, with *modus proferendi*.[17] This duality of hermeneutics and rhetoric will be foundational to the rest of this work: integral to any preaching endeavor is respect for the ancient text, as well as relevance for the modern audience. There needs to be privileging of the text, not for its own sake, but for the promotion of godliness among God's people. Borrowing from Augustine who solicited from Cicero who plumbed the depths of ancient rhetoric, Long suggests that the purposes of preaching—to teach, to delight, and to move—describe seasons of American preaching.[18] Until the 1970s, teaching took prominent place; then, with the advent of Craddock, Lowery, Buttrick,

16. *Liber contra impugnantes Dei cultum et religionem*, 2.6.

17.Translation from James Andrews, "Why Theological Hermeneutics Needs Rhetoric: Augustine's *De doctrina christiana*," *IJST* 12 (2010): 185.

18. Thomas G. Long, *Preaching from Memory to Hope* (Louisville: Westminster John Knox, 2009), 1–5.

et al., delighting was the main goal.[19] I would like to carry the saga onward and suggest that what we need to do now (and always)—not neglecting teaching and delighting—is to *move* people, to change their lives for the glory of God with the word of God. And so, I am very much in agreement with Moberly's definition of a theological hermeneutic—"reading the Bible . . . with a view to enabling the transformation of humanity into the likeness of God" (see chapter 4 for a discussion of this *imitatio Dei*).[20]

Additionally, this work will attend carefully to Webster's exhortation and plea: "[T]he most fruitful way of engaging in theological interpretation of Scripture is to do it. . . . We do not need much more by way of prolegomena to exegesis; we do need more exegesis."[21] Moberly, likewise, confesses to "a certain unease about the relative proportions of theory and practice in some of the literature. There tends to be more discussion about the nature of theological interpretation and theological hermeneutics than there is demonstration in persuasive and memorable readings of the biblical text." I will take Webster's critique to heart, and attempt not to further aggravate Moberly's disquiet, or help substantiate Frei's wry confession about his own work: "this essay falls into the almost legendary category of analysis of analyses of the Bible in which not a single text is examined, not a single exegesis undertaken."[22] Most of the chapters in this work will therefore contain rigorous exegesis of Scripture texts, to demonstrate the theological hermeneutic espoused herein, "rendering a rich and coherent interpretation of the text as sacred scripture of both church and synagogue."[23]

---

19. Preachers would do well to familiarize themselves—discriminatingly—with the "new homiletic" as espoused by Fred B. Craddock (*Preaching* [Nashville: Abingdon, 1985]; *As One Without Authority* [St. Louis, Mo.: Chalice, 2001]), Eugene L. Lowry (*The Homiletical Plot: The Sermon as Narrative Art Form* [rev. ed.; Louisville: Westminster John Knox, 2001]), and David G. Buttrick (*Homiletic: Moves and Structures* [Philadelphia: Fortress, 1987]).

20. R. W. L. Moberly, "What Is Theological Interpretation of Scripture?" *JTI* 3 (2009): 163. Or, as Miroslav Volf put it, "at the heart of every good theology lies not simply a plausible intellectual vision but more importantly a compelling account of a way of life" (*Captive to the Word of God: Engaging the Scriptures for Contemporary Theological Reflection* [Grand Rapids: Eerdmans, 2010], 43 [italics removed]).

21. John Webster, "Editorial," *IJST* 12 (2010): 116–17.

22. Moberly, "What Is Theological Interpretation of Scripture?" 169; and Hans W. Frei, in the preface to his *The Eclipse of Biblical Narrative: A Study in Eighteenth and Nineteenth Century Hermeneutics* (New Haven: Yale University Press, 1974), vii.

23. Brevard Childs, *Isaiah* (OTL; Louisville: Westminster John Knox, 2001), xi. For a more sustained exegetical exercise demonstrating how this theological hermeneutic is employed in the interpretation of sequential pericopes of a single book of the Bible for preaching, see Kuruvilla, *Mark: A Theological Commentary for Preachers*.

Précis of Chapters[24]

Chapter 1

Chapter 1 deals with a crucial facet of *general* hermeneutics that renders a text capable of exerting its influence into the future. The pragmatic operation of language—what authors *do* with what they *say*—is particularly important for this capacity of texts to impact future readers. What authors are doing is projecting a *world in front of the text* bearing an intention that is transhistorical, transcending the specific circumstances of the author and the writing; i.e., the text is given a future orientation, enabling valid application by readers at locations and times far removed from those of the event of inscription. Texts that function in this manner have been rightly recognized as "classics," with unique properties: they are perennial, having potential for future use; they are plural, rendering possible a wide variety of applications; and they are prescriptive, bearing a normative quality.

The Bible, too, is a classic—perennial, plural, and prescriptive—albeit of a unique kind, therefore calling for, in addition to a general hermeneutic, a *special* hermeneutic to be applied, when dealing with the interpretation of *this* unique text. The construal of the Bible as canonical and as divine discourse acknowledges that a special hermeneutic must prevail in the reading of this special book—a reading that respects it as "profitable for teaching, for reproof, for correction, for training in righteousness; so that the person of God may be adequate, equipped for every good work" (2 Tim 3:16–17). Chapter 1 concludes by offering six Rules of Reading unique for the special book that Scripture is, rules that have been widely employed by the church in the last two millennia. These rules serve as guardians of biblical interpretation, maintaining the outer frontiers beyond which readers may not go, if they are to remain faithful to the text. With these limits in place, the preacher may now interpret the particular preaching text in question, the pericope.

Chapter 2

The Bible is God's instrument for life change, so that mankind may conform to God's own character in Jesus Christ, by the power of the Spirit: "Be holy, for I am holy."[25] In the homiletical undertaking, the weekly portion of the biblical

---

24. Portions of chapters 1 and 2 are substantially reworked material from Abraham Kuruvilla, *Text to Praxis: Hermeneutics and Homiletics in Dialogue* (LNTS 393; London: T. & T. Clark, 2009).

25. Lev 11:44, 45; 19:2; 20:6; 21:8; 1 Pet 1:16.

text in focus is the pericope. This slice of text has, unfortunately, not been on the radar of biblical scholars; over the millennia, how a pericope functions theologically has scarcely been examined. Chapter 2 investigates this issue, pointing to the instrumentality of the pericope in accomplishing covenant renewal between divine Lord and human subjects, i.e., alignment of the latter to the divine demand of the former. The canon as a whole projects a plenary *world in front of the text*, outlining the precepts, priorities, and practices of God's ideal world, and each pericope projects a segment of this canonical world. This segment of the projected world—what I define as the *theology of the pericope*—is the crucial intermediary in the sermonic movement from ancient text to modern audience. An exegetical case study of 2 Sam 11–12 demonstrates how its pericopal theology is derived. Preaching is thus envisaged as a "two-step" enterprise: from text to theology, and from theology to application. Examples of how these steps are conducted, both in theological hermeneutics and in legal hermeneutics (the interpretation and application of a legal "classic," the U.S. Constitution), conclude chapter 2.

Chapter 3

The theology of the pericope intrinsically bears a divine demand—the call for God's people to live by the precepts, priorities, and practices governing God's ideal world. This brings up the question of how one is to interpret that particular genre of Scripture that explicitly makes divine demands—OT law. Are pericopes in this genre applicable to the Christian today? A broad survey shows that Reformed, Lutheran, and Dispensational approaches, as well as that of proponents of the New Perspective on Paul (NPP), agree that this ancient law is *not* applicable, excepting perhaps the "moral" facets thereof. This work, instead of creating categories within law, moral or otherwise, proposes that *all* of God's demands are applicable for everyone everywhere and in all time—applicable *theologically*. Chapter 3 utilizes pericopal theology to demonstrate how this works out in practice: integral to the theology of legal pericopes are the rationales of those laws, and it is these rationales that are binding upon God's people. Such obedience to divine demand is not for salvific purposes; rather it is a filial duty. In other words, the relationship between God and man precedes (and does not preclude) the responsibility of man to God—the "obedience of faith." Relationship first; responsibility second. Such a theological hermeneutic of biblical law (and of divine demand in every other genre) sees the role of pericopes as exhorting the children of God to fulfill their responsibility to be as holy as God himself is holy. If this is the case, if one is to respect the specific thrust of a particular pericope being preached, as is called for in this hermeneutic, how may one see Christ in OT texts? Would not that specific thrust of an OT pericope obviate a christological interpretation of the OT?

Chapter 4

Chapter 4 begins with the analysis of the *Aqedah* (Gen 22), a text tradition-ally utilized for christocentric interpretation and preaching. The examination of this pericope serves as a paradigm for how the theological hermeneutic pre-sented here may be put to work and how pericopal theology functions. In short, the hermeneutic of christocentric interpretation is found wanting; a more ro-bust hermeneutic is offered as an alternative, that respects the value of filial obe-dience to God, à la Abraham, and considers, as well, incentives for such obe-dience (rewards/divine blessing). This chapter, and this work, concludes with the proposal for a new model of christological reading of Scripture: *christiconic* interpretation that sees each pericope of Scripture portraying a facet of the ca-nonical image of Christ. God's goal for his children is that they be conformed to this image (εἰκών, *eikōn*) of his Son (Rom 8:29). As pericopes are sequentially preached, and the theology of each is applied, the people of God are gradually being molded into the image of Christ, a transformation that will, of course, be consummated only in the eschaton. This is, therefore, a *Trinitarian* theological hermeneutic for preaching: the text inspired by God the Spirit, that portrays God the Son, will then have become life in God's people, and thus the will of God the Father will have come to pass—God's kingdom established, and his name glorified.

Robert de Basevorn declared in the fourteenth century that "[p]reaching is the persuasion of the multitude . . . to worthy conduct."[26] This is indeed the goal of preaching: worthy conduct of the people of God—or, as this work pro-poses, their alignment to the divine demand in the pericope preached, i.e., their inhabitation of the *world in front of the text*, God's ideal world, by the adoption of its precepts, priorities, and practices. This world is, in a sense, the canonical image (εἰκών) of Christ, with each pericope in the canon illuminating part of

---

26. Robert de Basevorn, *Forma praedicandi*, in Th.-M. Charland, *Artes Praedicandi: Contribution a L'histoire de la Rhétorique au Moyen Age* (Paris: Libr. Philosophique J. Vrin, 1936), 238.

the "christicon." And so, to live in the *world in front of the text* and to abide by its precepts, priorities, and practices is to be more Christlike. Thus the theological hermeneutic proposed in this work (a christiconic mode of biblical interpretation) has as its goal the inculcation of Christlike conduct, by the power of the Spirit, and through the instrumentality of Scripture, pericope by pericope, week by week. From beginning to end this is God's work—the inspiring of the text, the inscripturation of demand, the image of perfection, the empowering of obedience, the endowment of rewards—all for the glory of God! "Theology is taught by God, teaches God, leads to God" ("*Theologia a Deo docetur, Deum docet, ad Deum ducit,*" Aquinas, *Summa* 1.1.7).

CHAPTER 1

GENERAL *and* SPECIAL HERMENEUTICS

[W]e are not to confine our view to the present period, but to look forward to remote futurity.
ALEXANDER HAMILTON, 1788[1]

How the preacher may move from Scripture to sermon, from an ancient text to modern praxis in the life of a Christian congregation, is the burden of this work. As with all literary productions intended to stand the test of time and the stretch of space, the Bible, in a very special way, was written to communicate, not only to an immediate audience, but also to God's people located far in place and period from those at the text's origin. And not just to communicate; God's goal is to conform his people into the image of his Son, the Lord Jesus Christ. This means that this ancient text must be preached to a modern audience in a manner that yields application to change lives for the glory of God. In reflecting on this whole process, where does the preacher begin?

It all starts with a text. Scripture, the predominant medium of divine communication to mankind, is textual. And so any approach to the interpretation of Scripture must begin with language, the essence of texts, the principle of all communication and, indeed, the universal medium of being—we are immersed

---

1. "The Federalist No. 34: Concerning the General Power of Taxation (continued)," *Independent Journal* (January 5, 1788), no pages.

in a sea of language from birth to death. Therefore, general hermeneutics, the science of interpretation of *any* text (hence *general* hermeneutics), comes into play in biblical interpretation. But the church has also construed Scripture as the word of God, divine discourse. In other words, Scripture is not simply any text; it is a *special* text. Therefore, special hermeneutics, the science of interpretation of this unique biblical text (hence *special* or *theological* hermeneutics), also has to operate in biblical interpretation. Chapter 1 addresses the essential features of general and special hermeneutics that enable the reading of Scripture by the preacher.[2]

PREVIEW: GENERAL AND SPECIAL HERMENEUTICS[3]

The peculiar features of the special text that the church calls "Scripture" include: its ultimate Author, the singular nature of its referent (what it is all about: God and his relationship to his creation), and its spiritually transforming power.[4] Therefore, seeking the intent of the text's author, comprehending its referent, and responding to it are critical features of biblical interpretation. In fact these are features transferrable to the interpretation of *any* text. One might even say that it is *because* the Bible is read that way—with attention to author, referent, and response—that other texts can be read that way, too, *mutatis mutandis*. George Steiner points out that "any coherent understanding of what language is and how language performs, . . . any coherent account of the capacity of human speech to communicate meaning and feeling [i.e., a general hermeneutic] is . . . underwritten by the assumption of God's presence [i.e., a special hermeneutic]."[5] For God is the ultimate Cause (or Author), enabling every other intermediate cause (or author); he is the ultimate Meaning, enabling every other meaningful discourse about referents; and he is the ultimate Authority, from whom is derived every other authority that beckons us to respond.

---

2. While the focus, here and throughout this work, will be squarely upon the function of the Bible in the pulpit, the paradigm of interpretation proposed in this work is critical for *any* reading of the Bible designed to culminate in application/life-change.

3. Portions of this chapter are reworked from Abraham Kuruvilla, *Text to Praxis: Hermeneutics and Homiletics in Dialogue* (LNTS 393; London: T. & T. Clark, 2009).

4. Paul Ricoeur, "Philosophical Hermeneutics and Theological Hermeneutics: Ideology, Utopia, and Faith," in *Protocol of the Seventeenth Colloquy, 4 November 1975* (ed. W. Wuellner; Berkeley: The Center for Hermeneutical Studies in Hellenistic and Modern Culture, 1976), 2–4.

5. George Steiner, *Real Presences* (Chicago: The University of Chicago Press, 1989), 3.

In effect, then, every book is to be read as the Bible is—seeking authorial intent, comprehending textual referent, and responding to its overtures. The reading of the Bible is the paradigm for every other kind of reading that respects author, privileges content, and applies truth. In other words, general hermeneutics exists because there exists a special hermeneutic—the construal of Scripture as the *viva vox Dei* ("living voice of God").[6] Special hermeneutics is, thus, one of a kind, not just a small plot in the larger terrain of general hermeneutics. Indeed, it is the other way around: "general hermeneutics is inescapably theological."[7]

However, this subjection of general hermeneutics to special hermeneutics does not mean that one can dispense with the former. After all, the Bible is a text, albeit a text like no other. But a text it remains, and the interpreter must resort to general hermeneutics in its interpretation. Therefore this chapter will first consider *general hermeneutics*; it will conclude with an examination of Rules of Reading that constitute the *special hermeneutic* of Scripture—the unique, special rules that govern the interpretation of this unique, special text. These reading guidelines serve as boundaries within which the interpreter must remain in order to be faithful to the text and to the intention of its Author and authors.[8] With the establishment of these markers the interpreter can now proceed to explore the particular preaching text, the pericope. This sermonic chunk of text will be the consideration of chapter 2.

GENERAL HERMENEUTICS

Discourse is the mediator between mind and world; what is thought in the mind becomes what is expressed in the world, "indefinitely extending the battlefront of the expressed at the expense of the unexpressed."[9] Both speech and writing expand the frontiers of expression as spoken and written utterances are made. While text inscription is distinct from vocal articulation in both performance

---

6. John Webster, *Word and Church* (Edinburgh: T. & T. Clark, 2001), 47, 58.

7. Kevin J. Vanhoozer, *First Theology: God, Scripture and Hermeneutics* (Downers Grove: InterVarsity, 2002), 213. Therefore, the "[u]nderstanding—of the Bible or of any other text—is a matter of ethics, indeed of spirituality" (ibid., 231).

8. For the purposes of this work, I do not make any particular distinction between the intentions of these two parties, divine and human. When referring to one, I will implicitly be referring to the other as well.

9. Paul Ricoeur, "Word, Polysemy, Metaphor: Creativity in Language," in *A Ricoeur Reader: Reflection and Imagination* (ed. Mario J. Valdés; Hertfordshire, U.K.: Harvester Wheatsheaf, 1991), 69. Or as T. S. Eliot put it, "a raid on the inarticulate" (*Four Quartets,* "East Coker," V).

and consequence, writing nevertheless shares with speech many of the properties of a communicative act; it is a particular kind of "saying."[10] But though textuality is kin to orality, the differences between the two are substantial. These differences have significant ramifications for textual interpretation, especially for the interpretation of the text that is the Bible, and most especially for the interpretation of that text for preaching—hermeneutics for homiletics.

Textuality and Its Consequences

Though the writing of Scripture was preceded by the utterances of the law-giver, the storyteller, the seer, the songwriter, the teacher, and the oral discourses of Jesus himself, it was the inscripturated word that was recognized by the Christian community as the canonical word of God, according the word preeminence in Christian faith and practice.[11] Such a lofty regard for the text is based on the assumption that "this kind of discourse is not senseless, that it is worthwhile to analyze it, because something is said that is not said by other kinds of discourse"—i.e., the overarching theme of God and his relationship to his creation.[12] Thus, biblical discourse, discourse of a special kind, calls for the employment of a special hermeneutic. Yet, there are some characteristics of texts in general, biblical and otherwise, that have to be considered (general hermeneutics) in the interpretation even of this special text.

The first and fundamental trait of any discourse, spoken or scripted, is that it is an *act* of communication whereby somebody "says" something to somebody else about something in some manner. In this, an inscribed discourse is no different from that which is spoken: both are communicative actions. However, in distinction from a speech-event, a text is a discourse that is fixed, preserved, archived, and disseminated by writing.[13] It is a stable locus of meaning, but—and this is key— one that has undergone significant upheavals in its passage from speech to script.

Something has happened when writing occurs, when compared to speaking.

---

10. This work sees texts, including biblical pericopes, as performing "speech" acts. See Mary Louise Pratt, *Toward a Speech Act Theory of Literary Discourse* (Bloomington, Ind.: Indiana University Press, 1977), 79–200; and Sandy Petrey, *Speech Acts and Literary Theory* (New York: Routledge, 1990), 71–85, for vigorous defenses of writing as a "speech" act.

11. Acknowledging the primacy of their written scriptures, the Qur'an refers to Christians and Jews as *ahl al-Kitāb* (أهل الكتاب, "people of the Book"; *Surah al-Ma'idah* 5:77, and elsewhere). Judaism, in like fashion, refers to Jews as עם הספר (*'m hspr*, "people of the book").

12. Paul Ricoeur, "Philosophy and Religious Language," *JR* 54 (1974): 71.

13. Paul Ricoeur, *Hermeneutics and the Human Sciences: Essays on Language, Action and Interpretation* (ed. and trans. John B. Thompson; Cambridge: Cambridge University Press, 1981), 145, 147.

In all discourse, there is an implicit dialectic between the *event* of the utterance (the act of saying) and the *content* thereof (what is said). In spoken discourse, there is an intimate association between these two poles with each getting adequate emphasis: the event of speaking is coincident with the conveyance of meaningful content. However, at the moment of writing, a radical breach is created between the event of communication and the content of communication, between the act of saying and what was said. The event is now potentially distanced from content, frozen as the latter is in its state of writtenness. What this change accomplishes is the fixation, not of the event of communication (the *saying*), but of the content of communication (the *said*). Ricoeur's observation is apt: "The human fact [and face!] disappears. Now material 'marks' convey the message"—no longer lung, larynx, and tongue, but ink, quill, and paper bear the fixed/frozen message. Writing has rendered the content of the saying autonomous, an orphan, dislodged from the event of saying.[14] In essence, texts have been estranged from their creators, their original audiences, and the circumstances of their composition.[15] This is the phenomenon technically called *distanciation*, the distancing between the event of saying and the content of saying. Distanciation is thus a constitutive element of the transaction of writing, and an integral property of all texts.[16] From an oral-aural world, where the utterance was spoken and heard, the message has been translocated into a textual-visual world where the discourse is written and seen. The resulting emancipation of the text from the oral situation has unique consequences for the affiliations between text and author, hearer, and referent of written discourse.

Text and Author
As was noted, the liberation of communication content from communication event, accomplished in the event of writing, proclaims the escape of the text's

---

14. Ibid., 134, 139–40.

15. Of course, this estrangement from author refers only to the alienation of the *human* agency involved in the creation of the text of Scripture. But, notwithstanding the constant presence of the Spirit of God (the divine Author of the Bible) with the believing interpreter and the inspired text, it is this remoteness of the *human* authors that ultimately necessitates the interpretive enterprise of the Bible—the engagement of languages, the exploration of historical contexts, the examination of literary and rhetorical aspects of the text, etc. Preaching itself is a consequence necessitated by the estrangement of Scripture's human authors. Were Paul and others available to congregations, the church would not need preachers.

16. Distanciation also occurs with audio and video recordings of speech that are disseminated far and wide, but to some extent, the event of communication is itself captured and frozen along with the content of communication. In any case, these technological advances came much later.

career from the finite horizons of its author. This, however, does not imply a total loss of tethering of text to authorial meaning, or that readers have to throw up their hands in despair. Though there is, in writing, some degree of freedom of text from the author, it is not a complete severance that would make authorial guidance totally unavailable for interpretation.[17] Distanciation does not render the text utterly autonomous, for the text bears with it, to some extent at least, artifacts of the event of writing and traces of the author in its script, medium, content, arrangement, etc.[18] For instance, even the determination by a reader of the language of a written composition is an acknowledgment of what its author intended. The phenomenon of "false friends" illustrates this eloquently: Should "g-i-f-t" be read in English or in German (= "poison")? The decision is always based upon an assumption of what language the author chose to write in, a choice manifest in the text.[19] Letters and wills are prime examples of texts always regarded as bearing the intentional presence of their authors or testators. Therefore the fallacy of baptizing the text as an authorless, absolute entity, detached and completely bereft of any authorial vestige, must be avoided.[20] In other words, despite distanciation, authorial fingerprints can be detected in the inscription; such residues of intent are essential for interpretation, and are sufficiently present in texts to establish the writer's purpose.

Text and Hearer

In the visual world of the text, receivers of the discourse are no longer hearers; they have been turned into readers, for the text has escaped not only the author, but also those within earshot, and it is now rendered accessible to reading audi-

---

17. Francis Watson stresses the human agency in writing: "Like speech, writing bears within it an essential reference to its origin in human action, and without this it cannot be understood" (*Text and Truth: Redefining Biblical Theology* [Grand Rapids: Eerdmans, 1997], 98). As Northrop Frye has noted, "[o]ne has to assume, as an essential heuristic axiom, that the work as produced constitutes the definitive record of the writer's intention" (*Anatomy of Criticism: Four Essays* [Princeton: Princeton University Press, 1957], 87).

18. In modern writing, these artifacts might include details of the edition, printing, and publication of the text, authorial bio data, acknowledgements, dedications, prefaces, etc.

19. Steven Knapp and Walter Benn Michaels, "Against Theory 2: Hermeneutics and Deconstruction," *CI* 14 (1987): 55–57.

20. One must also be careful to avoid the opposing fallacy of considering the text merely as a window through which one can see into the author's mind. The author's psyche, as well as events of the history recounted by the text, and speculative reconstructions of the text's forebears, are all elements that are *behind* the text (see chapter 2). For preaching purposes, it is the text itself that must be privileged, not anything behind it.

ences situated anywhere, anytime.[21] The unique nature of writing gives it the ability to reach receivers other than those originally intended by the author. As Lessig observed wryly, "Texts are transportable. They move. Because written, they are carried. Because carried, they are read—in different places and at different times. Nothing . . . can stop this semiotic peripateticism. If you write it, it will roam."[22] And these roaming pieces of communication, by virtue of their textuality and frozenness, can fall into the hands of a potential universe of readers.

Though writing may be addressed to a particular individual, this specification is less precise than in oral communication. The reader is, more often than not, beyond the physical vicinity of the author, and unknown to him or her. Anyone who can read and is willing to volunteer for the role of addressee may undertake the reading of that particular text. This potential universalization of the audience is one of the more radical effects of written communication. Yet, even when the identity of the reader is not stipulated and the possibility exists for an indiscriminate readership, the text may be directed towards an authorially intended consumer belonging to a particular community and perhaps even sharing the same authorial concerns that motivated the production of the text in the first place.[23] This is, of course, pertinent to the interpretation of the Bible within a congregation that recognizes that writing as its Scripture, within a community committed to the same God who inspired that text millennia ago. In short, textuality and the consequences of distanciation have made this special, divine discourse potentially accessible to all of God's people in every age.

Text and Referent
Thirdly—and this is perhaps one of the more notable consequences—distanciation affects ostensive referents, i.e., those items referred to in oral communication that can be shown, pointed out, labeled, or otherwise indicated by virtue of

21. The combination of authorial and readerly absence from the event of reading and the event of writing, respectively, Ricoeur calls a "double eclipse" (*Hermeneutics and the Human Sciences*, 146–47). The exclusion of an author-reader dialogue is what renders texts "inherently contumacious," for there is no way to directly refute an author—the text always says exactly the same thing as before. This asymmetry in written communication makes it almost an authorial monologue; there can be no arguing with the writer, perhaps "one reason why books have been burnt" (Walter J. Ong, *Orality and Literacy: The Technologizing of the Word* [London: Routledge, 1982], 79).

22. Lawrence Lessig, "The Limits of Lieber," *Cardozo L. Rev.* 16 (1995): 2249.

23. Watson, *Text and Truth*, 99, 102; Paul Ricoeur, *Interpretation Theory: Discourse and the Surplus of Meaning* (Fort Worth, Tex.: Texas Christian University Press, 1976), 31.

the collocation in time and space of speaker and hearer: this person, that house, these shoes, those trees, this day, and so on, elements that are integral to any vocal utterance between individuals sharing the same time and space. However, for those not directly addressed by the speaker, and not sharing time and space with the speaker, these referents are elusive. So also for the "orphaned" text, dislodged from its generating agent, event, and original addressees: ostensive referents of the text are no longer immediately and directly accessible to readers far away.[24] A bit of Jewish folklore, in the form of a letter, demonstrates this phenomenon well[25]:

> Dear Riwke,
>
> Be good enough to send me your slippers. Of course, I mean "my slippers" and not "your slippers." But, if you read "my slippers," you will think I mean your slippers. Whereas, if I write: "send me your slippers," you will read *your* slippers and will understand that I want *my* slippers. So: send me your slippers.

A "decontextualization" occurs with texts that the letter-writer to Riwke was acutely and painfully conscious of. Whose slippers are being demanded here? However, paradoxically, textuality is a *necessary* condition for the preservation of meaning across time and space, because textuality is designed to overcome the time and space restrictions imposed by orality. Those who could not be otherwise reached are now within reachable distance, for texts are transportable and movable, and they are carried and read. One need only imagine science, as we know it, occurring in a purely oral culture, to understand the immense value of texts and textuality. Notwithstanding this significant advantage, texts have undergone distanciation, and this distanciation of referents necessitates the enterprise of interpretation: What is the text all about—what is the author referring to, where and when, why and wherefore? In other words, if he is to respond to the writer in valid application, Riwke is going to have to figure out whose slippers are being referred to in that letter.

With regard to Scripture, these same consequences of distanciation operate by virtue of its textuality: the human author is unavailable; readers are located far from the origin of the text; and ostensive referents are not accessible in di-

---

24. Ricoeur, *Hermeneutics and the Human Sciences*, 134, 139–40, 145.

25. Marina Yaguello, *Language through the Looking Glass: Exploring Language and Linguistics* (New York: Oxford University Press, 1998), 8.

rect or immediate fashion. Yet, this unique discourse of the biblical text mandates its own application in times and spaces distant from the circumstances of its provenance.[26] If Scripture is to be employed in these new locales, this gap of distanciation must be bridged and, importantly, the referent of the text—what it is all about (its thrust)—must be discovered. All interpretation, especially that engaged in by the homiletician seeking valid sermonic application, is an attempt to understand this thrust of the text. How may this be faithfully and fittingly accomplished?

Here is where what is considered to be Paul Ricoeur's most important contribution to interpretation theory, the *world in front of the text*, achieves notability: this world is the text's referent (what the text is all about) that transcends the effects of distanciation. Ricoeur's notion provides the framework for the interpretation, by readers in ages and places far away, of a text that has undergone distanciation. For such texts, this concept is particularly useful, and even more so when their interpretation is intended to culminate in application, as with sermons on Scripture. What exactly is this *world in front of the text* and how does it help application?

The *World in Front of the Text*

The text is not an end in itself, but the means thereto, an instrument of the author's action of employing language to project a transcending vision—what Ricoeur called the *world in front of the text*. He explains:

> In oral discourse, face-to-face interlocutors can, in the final analysis, refer what they are talking about to the surrounding world common to them. Only writing can by addressing itself to anyone who knows how to read, refer to a world that is not there between the interlocutors. . . . It is neither behind the text as the presumed author, nor in the text as its structure, but unfolded *in front of* it.[27]

The role of this *world in front of the text* in theological hermeneutics, and its significance for the faith and practice of the Christian community—specifically, its importance for sermonic application—is the major consideration of this work.

Ricoeur's world is based on the understanding that literary texts are unique

---

26. See Deut 4:10; 6:6–7, 20–25; 29:14–15; Matt 28:19–20; Rom 15:4; 1 Cor 10:6, 11; 2 Tim 3:16–17; etc.

27. Paul Ricoeur, "Naming God," *USQR* 34 (1979): 217 (emphasis added).

referential phenomena. One does not attend, for instance, a performance of *Macbeth* to acquire knowledge of the history of Scotland; instead, one goes to the play to learn what it is to gain a kingdom and lose one's soul.[28] Aristotle would agree, for what *actually* happens in a narrative, even if representing historic reality (τὰ καθ᾽ ἕκαστον, *ta kath hekaston*, the specific), is portrayed as what *always* happens in the transactions of mankind (τὰ καθόλου, *ta katholou*, the universal/general)(*Poet.* 9.1–4, 9–10). Thus, in *Macbeth*, the actual story of the dastardly assassination of a king can be construed as what always happens in human dramas when people are driven by the lust for power. One may not descend to murder (the specific), but such craving and coveting without regard for morality or consequences leaves only tragedy in its wake and guilt in its maelstrom (the universal/general). The textual specifics (τὰ καθ᾽ ἕκαστον) thus portray a transcending generality (τὰ καθόλου). All manner of literary compositions, likewise, make these kinds of references, inviting their readers to occupy the place of those limned in the text, to partake of their experiences, and to feel as they did. Through the represented situations, the author is portraying experiences likely to be τὰ καθόλου common to humanity.[29] All of this is intended to elicit a response from the reader. The text is thus a tool the author employs for "manipulating language and structure to incorporate . . . a larger, more complex vision"—the *world in front of the text*.[30] It is to this projected world, the referent of the text, that the reader is called to respond.

Clifford Geertz's commentary on Balinese cockfights is an illuminating analogy of the use of texts as instruments to depict worlds, though in his account the discourse instrument is not a text, but a culture—which Geertz labels

---

28. Northrop Frye, *The Educated Imagination* (Bloomington, Ind.: Indiana University Press, 1964), 63–64. Philip Wheelwright asserted that religious and poetic discourses make such "a kind of trans-subjective reference" that points beyond the specifics of the text (*The Burning Fountain: A Study in the Language of Symbolism* [rev. ed.; Bloomington, Ind.: Indiana University Press, 1968], 4).

29. Literary works such as novels bear "links of possibility" between characters and reader that enable such identification; readers thereby recognize that story as their own (the general/universal), though the particular details of the novel (the specific) may differ greatly from those of their own lives. See Martha C. Nussbaum, *Poetic Justice: The Literary Imagination and Public Life* (Boston: Beacon, 1995), 5, 31.

30. Charles Altieri, "The Poem as Act: A Way to Reconcile Presentational and Mimetic Theories," *Iowa Rev.* 6.3–4 (1975): 107–8. Also see Paul Ricoeur, *Interpretation Theory*, 19–22. Ricoeur sees this movement operating with *every* textual utterance. See his *The Rule of Metaphor: Multi-disciplinary Studies on the Creation of Meaning in Language* (trans. Robert Czerny, with Kathleen McLaughlin and John Costello; London: Routledge & Kegan Paul, 1978), 256.

an "assemblage of texts."[31] The cockfight (the "culture-text" here) refers beyond itself to portray a greater reality, another world—a "meta-world." One does not participate in this wrangle of roosters merely to observe a fight between fowl, but rather to see "what a man, usually composed, aloof, almost obsessively self-absorbed . . . feels like when, attacked, tormented, challenged, insulted, and driven in result to the extremes of fury, he has totally triumphed or been brought totally low."[32] The Balinese cockfight points beyond the world *behind* the culture-text—the birds, the breeders, the bets, the battles—to project a world *in front of* the culture-text: the machismo of cockfight patrons. The cockfight thus beckons the Balinese man to live in this projected world of mannishness and dominance: "Be a virile specimen of masculinity!"

Thus a text may not only tell the reader about the world *behind* the text (what "actually" happened—the historical data: the cockfight, in our case), it also projects another ideal world *in front of* the text that bids the reader inhabit it (what it means to be macho, in the Balinese context). A view of life is portrayed, projecting for the reader a world beyond the confines of the text. Rather than being simply *presented* by a text, life is *represented* as something, inviting the reader to see the world in one way and not another, and to respond by complying with the demands of that world.[33] Allegories, parables, and moral fables are all examples of utterances supporting such projected worlds. By the telling of a tale, a point is made, a world is portrayed.

One sees this even in Aesop's fables. Take, for instance, the one about the dog that found a bone and was returning home with its booty. It happened to cross a bridge, and as it looked into the water it spotted another dog with a bone. You know the rest of the story: greed takes over, it barks at what was actually its own reflection in the stream, and loses the bone it had. While the story is about dogs, bones, streams, and reflections, it is *really* about not being greedy. It projects a world in which contentment is a key priority, a world in which a critical precept is that contentment will prevent loss, and a world in which one practices the prudence of contentment. In essence, this world is the referent of

31. Clifford Geertz, *The Interpretation of Cultures* (London: Fontana, 1993), 448 (see 412–53 for the entire account). "[C]ultural manifestations must be read as texts are read." Indeed culture has its own "grammar" (Morton W. Bloomfield, "Allegory as Interpretation," *NLH* 3 [1972]: 303).

32. Geertz, *The Interpretation of Cultures*, 450.

33. Martha C. Nussbaum, *Love's Knowledge: Essays on Philosophy and Literature* (New York: Oxford University Press, 1990), 5.

the text; this is the thrust of the text; this is what the text is about; and this is what Aesop would want readers to catch and respond to. Ricoeur's notion of the *world in front of the text* thus provides a conceptual category to commence the movement towards application.

That, however, is not a property of fiction alone. All literary texts function in this manner and project worlds in front of themselves; thus, a text serves as an instrument of that action.[34] In this way, such discourses have validity for the future, capable as they are of being applied, despite the effects of distanciation. Scripture, too, is intended to be employed far from its originating circumstances. It is to be applied to the faith and practice in the contemporary time, and all times, of those who accept the Bible as Scripture. Therefore, this unique and worthy discourse needs the gap of distanciation to be bridged and the referent of the text located. Then, and only then, can valid application be made by the reader. As will be developed, Ricoeur's idea of the *world in front of the text* plays a useful role in understanding how, by means of this projected world (the referent of the text), valid application may be derived. The *world in front of the text* is a world created by the author by means of the text; it is a world that is intended to be inhabited, by the reader's alignment with the precepts, priorities, and practices of that projected world (in the cockfight text, how "real men" ought to behave). Appropriate alignment with the implicit demands of the textual world constitutes valid application of that text. In other words, this world is the text's direction for application in the future.[35] The burden of the entire operation of hermeneutics, for Ricoeur, is the discernment of this world; the task of interpretation is the explication and subsequent application of that projected world.

For a text that has undergone distanciation and is intended to be applied in the future, as is Scripture, interpretation cannot cease with the elucidation of its linguistic and structural elements (what may be considered as the world *of* the text) or the history and events it represents (the world *behind* the text), but

---

34. Nicholas Wolterstorff, *Art in Action: Toward a Christian Aesthetic* (Grand Rapids: Eerdmans, 1980), 122, 124. Also see Raymond W. Gibbs, "Nonliteral Speech Acts in Text and Discourse," in *The Handbook of Discourse Processes* (eds. Arthur C. Graesser, Morton Ann Gernsbacher, and Susan R. Goldman; Mahwah, N.J.: Erlbaum, 2003), 358–61.

35. Such a world is specific to that text and derived from its particular and peculiar content: "[f]or every unique text there is such a world" proper to it (Ricoeur, "Philosophical Hermeneutics and Theological Hermeneutics," 11–12; idem, *Hermeneutics and the Human Sciences,* 140–42). Thus the text must be privileged in interpretation, for it alone forms the raw material for the discernment of the *world in front of the text*, its unique referent, what it is all about.

must proceed further to discern the world *in front of* the text—the referent of the author, the thrust of the text. This projected world which readers are invited to inhabit forms the intermediary between text and application, and enables one to respond validly to the text, for the world implicitly provides direction for future behavior.[36] In sum, by portraying such a world, the text becomes an advocate for that world, recommending adoption by the reader of the precepts, priorities, and practices of that world it projects. How exactly does the *world in front of the text* function in this way for its distant and future readers?

Futurity and Meaning of Texts

For any text, the content is consumed at an event of reading subsequent to the event of writing. Therefore, information conveyed by a text is not necessarily relevant to a readership far away in time and space; this is akin to reading a local newspaper from another city, a decade after its publication. In other words, the "literature of knowledge," that merely conveys information, usually becomes outdated as the distanciation of the text creates a breach between the event of communication and the content of communication. The relevance of the content for the reader is likely to diminish in proportion to the time-space distance of the content from the event. Pure information rarely transcends time and space to provide direction for future application; it merely tells us how things *were* in the past, not how things *could/should* be in the future. On the other hand, it is the "literature of power," projecting a world in front of itself, that never grows outdated. By its world projection, it retains the capacity to say something universally relevant across the passage of time.[37] Thus, its referentiality persists into an indefinite future, and the world projected gives readers direction for application.[38]

Authors of such literary compositions, conscious of the future-directedness of their work, typically intend meanings to go beyond what is attended to at that moment and locus of writing, so that the effects of such texts are boundlessly

36. How this may be conducted will be established in theory in this chapter and demonstrated in chapter 2, with regard to the pericope, the preaching unit of the biblical text.

37. Obviously, not all texts possess this futurity. Grocery lists, bank statements, inane blogs, emails, and a whole host of other published works that have only parochial concerns, provincial consequences, and personal value, will never interest anyone but the odd historian in a few decades' time. It will be shown below that those texts that do possess futurity are the ones rightly labeled "classics," specimens of the "literature of power."

38. E. D. Hirsch, "Past Intentions and Present Meanings," *Ess. Crit.* 33 (1983): 88.

extended in time and space. This future-direction of referents is an inherent property of textuality, particularly of those texts, such as the Bible, whose value has endured over time.[39] How are their future orientations carried by those texts? In brief, this section will demonstrate that it is by a text's projection of a world that bears a *transhistorical intention* that it achieves this futurity. The discernment of this projected world is therefore an essential task of the interpreter, for from this intermediary alone may valid application be derived.

In common usage, "meaning" is usually restricted to the *original textual sense*—the explicit utterance meaning of a text. Quite perspicaciously, E. D. Hirsch extended the idea of the "meaning" of a text beyond the original textual sense to encompass what might conceivably lie in the realm of that text's future use, for literature is typically an instrument designed for "broad and continuing future application." Meaning, in light of this future-directedness, includes a *transhistorical intention*—a conceptual entity projected by the text that carries its thrust beyond the immediate time-space circumstances of the writing—and also future *exemplifications*—i.e., valid applications arising from that transhistorical intention.[40] "Meaning," in the Hirschian model, thus comprises a triad: original textual sense, transhistorical intention, and exemplifications.

FACETS OF MEANING		
Original Textual Sense	*Transhistorical Intention*	Exemplifications

Here's an analogy: London's *Metropolitan Police Act* of 1839 makes it an offence to repair a "carriage" on a street in England: "Every person shall be liable to a penalty ... who, within the limits of the metropolitan police district, shall in any thoroughfare or public place ... to the annoyance of the inhabitants or passengers ... repair any part of any cart or carriage, except in cases of accident

---

39. Psalms 102:18 explicitly points to the future: "This will be written for a later generation."

40. E. D. Hirsch, "Meaning and Significance Reinterpreted," *CI* 11 (1984): 209; idem, *Validity in Interpretation* (New Haven: Yale University Press, 1967), 51, 65; idem, "Past Intentions and Present Meanings," 82; and idem, "Transhistorical Intentions and the Persistence of Allegory," *NLH* 25 (1994): 549–67. In the span of almost three decades, Hirsch managed to generate an array of labels for his notions. However, the concepts indicated by the diverse designations are remarkably consistent across time. Therefore, rather than demonstrate the chronological development of these various terms, for the sake of clarity this work will keep the nomenclature consistent, even if this involves occasionally attributing to that writer an anachronistic designation.

where repair on the spot is necessary."[41] Normally, "meaning" would be restricted to "carriage" (= original textual sense). But it is obvious, considering the genre of the text—legal literature—that what was being intended by "carriage" went beyond just a "horse-drawn buggy." In a future-directed sense, what the law meant by "carriage" was "vehicle using the road" (= transhistorical intention).

Though the *Act* was legislated at a time when automobiles were unknown, this transhistorical intention encompasses not only "carriage" (original textual sense), but also "truck," "car," etc. (exemplifications, i.e., potential future applications arising from the transhistorical intention). In this sense, all three—original textual sense, transhistorical intention, and future exemplifications—are, according to Hirsch, part of the "meaning" of the text, at least for interpretation leading to application. Exemplifications are valid applications of the original text simply because they fall within the boundaries of the text's transhistorical intention. Thus the law of 1839 prohibiting carriage repair was validly read in the future as prohibiting truck or car repair, as well, by virtue of its transhistorical intention ("no broken vehicles on road").

FACETS OF MEANING		
Original Textual Sense	*Transhistorical Intention*	**Exemplifications**
No carriage repair	*No broken vehicles on road*	No truck, car, . . . repair

In other words, the transhistorical intention of a text is not historically bounded (to "carriage," in this case), but can transcend the contemporaneous time of its inscription, thereby even including within its scope potential future exemplifications not explicit in the utterance or text, or even conceived of by its author.[42] Surely the creators of the 1839 law could not have had in mind motor vehicles of any kind. Rather, it is likely that what was sought to be imposed, in addition to the original textual sense ("carriage"), was a broader, more general, transhistorical intention that would encompass every possible future

---

41. *Metropolitan Police Act* 1839 [c. 47], s. 54 [1]. See Stephen Guest, *Ronald Dworkin* (Stanford, Calif.: Stanford University Press, 1991), 183–84.

42. Including future exemplification (he calls it "application" or "appropriation") within his concept of "meaning," Gadamer asserts that "[n]ot just occasionally, but always, the meaning of a text goes beyond its author" (Hans-Georg Gadamer, *Truth and Method* [2nd rev. ed.; trans. rev. Joel Weinsheimer and Donald G. Marshall; London: Continuum, 2004], 296).

exemplification of the text: *No broken vehicles of any kind on the road,* even those kinds of which the authors of the law were not consciously aware. The lawmakers may have been conscious of the transhistorical intention, but not necessarily of every one of the future exemplifications falling within it, whether truck, car, motorcycle, or rickshaw. Exemplifications in the future, though unconscious to the author, would nonetheless be valid (and part of the "meaning" of the text), provided they lay within the boundaries of the text's transhistorical intention.[43] Indeed, such a reading is reflected in the fact that more than a century later, in 1972, in an amendment to the original statute, the *Metropolitan Police Act* of 1839 was formally construed as including motor vehicles.[44]

Essentially, in the example of the *Act*, an ideal world was being projected in front of the text (à la Ricoeur) in which no one would be impeding London traffic by repairing broken vehicles on a public street. Hirsch's transhistorical intention is thus equivalent to Ricoeur's *world in front of the text.* This was the thrust of the *Act*: to keep London streets free of malfunctioning vehicles that would hinder traffic flow; this is the ideal *world in front of the text/*transhistorical intention. Exemplifications are valid if they are part of this projected world, i.e., if they fall within the boundaries of the transhistorical intention. Thus it is this projected world/transhistorical intention that gives texts their future-directedness. The value of such a concept for biblical interpretation is obvious: the validity of future applications is contingent upon whether such applications fall within the perimeter of the transhistorical intention/*world in front of the text.* What is fixed for the future in the past event of writing, then, is the transhistorical concept of deriving any number of future exemplifications for any number of future situations. The ancient text, whether it be legal statute or religious Scripture, fixes the transhistorical intention by means of its original textual intention ("carriage"). The transhistorical intention ("vehicle") in turn serves as the broad arena within which all valid applications ("car/truck") must be located. Thus a text projects a world with multiple possibilities for application.

The analogy posited by Ludwig Wittgenstein in this connection is illuminating[45]: He imagines a student being taught to continue a series of numbers

---

43. Hirsch, "Past Intentions and Present Meanings," 82–83; idem, *Validity in Interpretation,* 48–51.

44. For the amendment of the *Metropolitan Police Act* 1839, see *Road Traffic Act* 1972 [c. 20], s. 195.

45. *Philosophical Investigations* (2nd ed.; trans. G. E. M. Anscombe; London: Basil Blackwell, 1958), ¶185–87.

begun by the teacher by observing the rule "+2," the addition of 2 to each successive number in the series (= transhistorical intention). The pupil was guided in creating the sequence up to the number 1000 (0, 2, 4, 6, 8, 10, . . . , 1000 = original textual sense), and then asked to take over without help. Wittgenstein posits the situation where such a pupil then produces the set 1000, 1004, 1008, 1012, etc., imagining (wrongly!) that what the instructor meant by "+2" was that one was to add 2 only up to 1000, but 4 thence to 2000, and 6 thence to 3000, and so on. While it seems quite obvious that the teacher meant/intended for the student to arrive at 1002, 1004, 1006, . . . (= exemplifications), one could ask in what sense this was "meant/intended" by the teacher. Were "1002" and "1004" and "1006" actually thought of by that person? Surely, an infinite series of actual +2 numbers that followed 1000 could not have been conceived of or consciously "meant/intended." Wittgenstein responds that when the instructor "intended" the sequence of numbers that the student was supposed to come up with, all that was "intended" was that "if I [the instructor] had then been asked what number should be written after 1000, I should have replied '1002.'" This "intending" is not necessarily a matter of the teacher actually thinking of the specific numbers "1002, 1004, 1006, . . .," but of simply being able to generate the sequence of such exemplifications by means of the intended precept involved—the "+2" rule (= transhistorical intention). Thus it is the precept that is actually intended, not the specific and infinite outcomes (= exemplifications) of the employment of that rule.

FACETS OF MEANING		
Original Textual Sense	**_Transhistorical Intention_** (WORLD IN FRONT OF THE TEXT)	**Exemplifications**
0, 2, 4, 6, 8, . . . , 1000	*+2 rule*	1002, 1004, 1006, . . . , ∞

In other words, the instructor's intention was essentially a transhistorical intention, an ideal world of an infinite sequence of numbers following 1000 that increased in increments of 2. The recognition of this transhistorical intention makes possible the generation of unstated future iterations or exemplifications that are consonant with that rule. Because those exemplifications (1002, 1004, 1006, . . .) abide by the transhistorical intention (the +2 rule), and are part of the projected world of +2 numbers following 1000, those applications are valid. On the other hand, 1004, 1008, 1012, . . . (as a sequence), or 1005, 1007, 1009 (as individual numbers), do not abide by the transhistorical intention; and not being part of the *world in front of the text*, they are invalid applications.

In sum, the comprehension of the future-directed transhistorical intention of any text makes subsequent exemplifications (valid applications) of that text possible. In light of the fact that the communication intentions of texts such as the Bible or legal literature are future-directed, their "meaning" can, therefore, be said to extend beyond the original textual sense, to the level of transhistorical intention (the projected world), and also to future exemplifications. Exemplifications in the new readerly situation are true to the original textual sense and congruent to it, insofar as they remain within the bounds of the transhistorical intention (as part of the *world in front of the text*).[46] Thus, many different future exemplifications of a single transhistorical intention can be part of the same meaning. All this to say, for texts intended to be applied in the future, "meaning" must be seen as comprising original textual sense, transhistorical intention (*world in front of the text*), and exemplifications (valid applications).

While the analysis of the *world in front of the text* is tightly linked to the text in question and its particulars, there is a sense in which such a world has a non-semantic nature: it falls in the field of study that language philosophers have labeled "pragmatics." The next section will explore this critical facet of general hermeneutics that further elucidates the projected world and transhistorical intention. In short, we shall see that the *world in front of the text* (the transhistorical intention) is essentially what authors are *doing* with what they are saying.

Pragmatics: What Authors *Do* with What They *Say*

The interpretation of the *world in front of the text*, though constructed upon the semantics of the text (lexical, grammatical, and syntactical elements), is also, in part, a non-semantic operation, properly belonging to the domain of pragmatics—the analysis of what texts (or speakers/authors) *do* with what they say.[47] Quite frequently in communication, spoken or written, there is a disjunction between semantic meaning and pragmatic meaning. The prime example of this disjunction is irony. Suppose that upon seeing a patient in my dermatology

---

46. In a way, these exemplifications may be considered "identical" to the original textual sense. For this concept of "identity," see Kuruvilla, *Text to Praxis*, 50–51.

47. "The speaker is a *doer*" (Kevin J. Vanhoozer, *Is There a Meaning in This Text? The Bible, The Reader, and the Morality of Literary Knowledge* [Grand Rapids: Zondervan, 1998], 209).

clinic with a few warts on her hand, I remark, "Oh, dear, what shall we do—amputate?" No amount of lexical, grammatical, and syntactical analysis will enable comprehension of my odd utterance. It is only the pragmatics of the utterance, in the context of the entire event (our longstanding patient-physician relationship, the trivial nature of her affliction, the incongruity of dermatologists performing amputations, and my propensity for drama), that will enlighten the listener of my intent: irony.

That does not mean that the semantic elements are unimportant for the pragmatics of the text; on the contrary, they are essential. Semantic analysis may not be sufficient to arrive at the pragmatic meaning, but it is necessary for that move. If one cannot comprehend the semantic sense of "amputate," the listener will certainly not catch the pragmatic drift of my statement. Semantics is necessary for comprehension, but it is not sufficient, for there is a non-semantic part (i.e., the pragmatic element) to the interpretation of utterances and texts.[48] This is to emphasize that there is more to understanding what authors are *doing* than just dissecting out the linguistic, grammatical, and syntactical elements of what authors are saying. It is the non-literal nature of the *doing* that is the business of pragmatics.[49]

In the example provided earlier of the Balinese cockfight, the semantics dealt with the actual action; the pragmatics or the *world in front of the text* pointed to what the whole cockfight theater was about—establishing the machismo of its patrons. Likewise, the Hollywood genre of the western depicts a particular society in the western United States of the late nineteenth century by means of panoramic vistas, horses, outlaws, sheriffs, guns, and the narrative of their interactions (the semantic meaning: what the director was *showing*). These movies implicitly project a world with the themes of individual rights, responsibilities, and codes of honor in the face of evil (the pragmatic meaning: what the director

---

48. However, I will argue that the pragmatics of a sizable portion of a text (unlike my cryptic one-sentence utterance in clinic)—such as a biblical pericope—can, to a great extent, be determined from that text itself.

49. Stephen C. Levinson, *Pragmatics* (Cambridge: Cambridge University Press, 1983), 12, 17; Daniel Vanderveken, "Non-Literal Speech Acts and Conversational Maxims," in *John Searle and His Critics* (eds. Ernest Lepore and Robert Van Gulick; Cambridge: Basil Blackwell, 1991), 372. The debate as to what constitutes the line between pragmatics and semantics is ongoing; no doubt, there is a degree of overlap between the two fields. While the semantic and non-semantic/pragmatic transactions of a text are by no means separable, they are discriminable: what the author is *saying*, and what the author is *doing* with what he is saying, can be distinguished. See Stephen C. Levinson, *Presumptive Meanings: The Theory of Generalized Conversational Implicature* (Cambridge, Mass.: The MIT Press, 2000), 9, 168; and François Recanati, *Meaning and Force: The Pragmatics of Performative Utterances* (Cambridge: Cambridge University Press, 1987), 1–27.

was *doing* with what he/she was showing). Such pragmatic themes are always facets of implied ethical value, and so the determination of the pragmatics of an utterance is integral to the undertaking of hermeneutics, with the projection of the *world in front of the text* being the essential object of pragmatic analysis.[50] In terms of the Hirschian triad of meaning, the *world in front of the text* is what the author is *doing* with what he is *saying*. This is the product of pragmatic analysis, and it is this world that yields the transhistorical intention of the text.[51]

FACETS OF MEANING		
Original Textual Sense *or* **Author's Saying** (SEMANTICS OF UTTERANCE)	*Transhistorical Intention* (WORLD IN FRONT OF THE TEXT) *or* **Author's Doing** (PRAGMATICS OF UTTERANCE)	**Exemplification**

Without the pragmatic determination of this world (the transhistorical intention), I submit that valid application is impossible. For instance, when *A* tells *B*, "Hey, you are standing on my foot!" the *semantic* meaning (what the author is saying) asserts the spatial location of *B* upon the lower limb of *A*, while the *pragmatic* meaning (what the author is *doing* with what he is saying) is attempting to get *B* to relocate from that traumatic situation upon *A*'s anatomy, even though such a response was not explicitly called for. Rather, the discourse bears a surplus of meaning beyond the literal sense—a pragmatic meaning over and above a semantic meaning. While what *A* was saying simply pointed out the spatial location of *B* upon the lower limb of *A* (equivalent to original textual sense), what *A* was *doing* with what was said was to portray a world where no one would ever be stationed upon *A*'s lower extremities to produce distress. Or to put it differently, the transhistorical intention of the utterance/"text" is this: "I don't want anyone, anywhere, anytime standing on my foot causing me discomfort!" *A*'s desire was for *B* to be aligned with such an ideal "nobody-ever-standing-on-my-foot-to-cause-me-pain world" by lightening the burden upon *A*'s foot, thus alleviating the latter's agony (exemplification). Doing so, *B* would conform to the demands of that world, thus "inhabiting" it. In and with the pro-

---

50. Peter Seitel, "Theorizing Genres – Interpreting Works," *NLH* 34 (2003): 285–86.

51. For all practical purposes, I am treating these as synonymous: transhistorical intention, *world in front of the text,* author's *doing* with what he is *saying,* and pragmatics of the utterance.

jection of this world, *A* was actually expressing a transhistorical intention that went beyond merely a current application for *B*, the one directly addressed.

Via the projected ideal world, this intention would be applicable to anybody anywhere—*no one* ever ought to be standing on *A*'s foot causing *A* pain. While the specific application to *B* is, then, an integral element of this *world in front of the text*, and implicit in it, it is obvious that this ideal world governs everyone else (*X*, in the table below) who might potentially consider standing on *A*'s foot at any future time. In other words, as was seen earlier, this projected world/transhistorical intention is the text's (or utterance's) direction for application in the future. It is by the recognition of this referent, the text-projected world, that valid application may be discerned. The elucidation of this world by pragmatic analysis is, therefore, an essential aspect of the interpretation of texts for the purposes of application.

FACETS OF MEANING		
Original Textual Sense or **Author's Saying** (SEMANTICS OF UTTERANCE)	**Transhistorical Intention** (WORLD IN FRONT OF THE TEXT) or **Author's Doing** (PRAGMATICS OF UTTERANCE)	**Exemplification**
Location of *B*'s foot	No one on *A*'s foot to cause him pain	Relocation of *[X]*'s foot

Nicholas Wolterstorff notes that biblical narrative as a whole would fit in this category: "these stories were being told to make a point," not just to convey historical detail or cultural information.[52] As far as interpretation for preaching is concerned, the "point" or thrust of a text is what the author was *doing* with what he was *saying* (the pragmatics of the utterance, or as we have seen, the *world in front of the text*). In response, the people of God derive valid application from grasping that author's *doing*. Authors *do* things with what they say, and therefore interpreters of texts are obliged to discern what was being *done*

52. *Divine Discourse: Philosophical Reflections on the Claim that God Speaks* (Cambridge: Cambridge University Press, 1995), 212–15. I would claim that every act of communication, narrative or otherwise, biblical or otherwise, operates in this fashion. Speakers and authors *do* things with what they say. As another example, the prophet Nathan's narration of a parable in 2 Sam 12 (what he is saying) turns out to be a condemnation of King David (what he is *doing*). Of course, the fact that the author of 2 Sam is, himself, recounting this creates yet another layering: what *this* author is *doing* with what he is saying . . . about what Nathan is *doing* with what he is saying! For the reader, it is actually the *doing* of the author of the biblical text that is critical in the move to application, and that must be privileged.

with what was being said, if they are to generate valid application.

In sum, in any text, an author is always *doing* something with what he/she is saying. This concept is particularly critical for biblical interpretation for preaching, an endeavor geared to accomplish life-change. For such purposes, one must view the biblical text as saying something in order to accomplish some purpose. Without comprehending what the author is *doing* with what he is saying, there can be no valid application. If that earlier statement by A regarding the location of B's foot were an inspired utterance, the preacher expositing that "text" would conceivably expatiate on the derivation of the word "foot" from the Old English *fot* from the Latin *pes* from the Greek *pos*; he might discourse upon the foot's musculoskeletal structure (26 bones, 33 joints, over a hundred muscles, tendons, and ligaments), its vasculature, and its nerve supply; he would, no doubt, wax eloquent about the various abnormalities of that extremity (club foot, flat foot, athlete's foot, rheumatoid foot, etc.); and so on, all the while completely missing the intended valid application of that original utterance. In other words, unless one catches what A was *doing* with what he was saying (the pragmatics of the utterance and the *world in front of the text* with its transhistorical intention), valid application of A's utterance is impossible.

Reverting again to our favorite protagonists, if, on another occasion, A tells B, "The door is open," what A intends for B to do as a result is entirely dependent upon B catching the pragmatics of A's utterance. The discourse is an event, and a lexical-grammatical-syntactical apprehension of A's four-word utterance will get B nowhere. The event of discourse must be taken into account: if they have just had a quarrel in A's home, B is being told to leave. If they are leaving B's home together, B is being reminded to shut the door. If B is about to reveal a juicy bit of company gossip to A when the former drops into the latter's office, B is being asked to refrain from saying anything, at least until the open-door situation is rectified. And so on. What A was *doing* with what he was saying is critical to the proper response (valid application) of B to A's utterance.[53]

In other words, a communicative action with *semantic* meaning becomes the carrier for *pragmatic* meaning. The first-order semantic operation is seminal, the seed for the subsequent, second-order pragmatic meaning that is su-

---

53. The open-door "conversations" were modified from Thomas G. Long, "The Preacher and the Beast: From Apocalyptic Text to Sermon," in *Intersections: Post-Critical Studies in Preaching* (ed. Richard L. Eslinger; Grand Rapids: Eerdmans, 2004), 7.

pervenient upon the semantic meaning.[54] All this to say that a right response to an utterance/text (i.e., valid application) is possible *only* by discerning what the author is *doing* with what he is saying, the pragmatics of the utterance—i.e., the *world in front of the text*, the transhistorical intention. This phenomenon, I shall show in chapter 2, is valid for biblical interpretation as well, and especially for interpretation intended to subserve preaching. I shall also demonstrate that for larger chunks of the biblical text (pericopes, i.e., preaching texts of some size), the text itself provides adequate clues as to what the author is *doing* with what has been said.

Ricoeur's projection of a *world in front of the text*, Hirsch's transhistorical intention, and the concept borrowed from pragmatics of what authors *do* with what they *say* (for the purposes of this work, these are synonymous concepts) all attest to the fact that there is more to discourses than is apparent on the surface. There is more to a text than the semantics thereof.[55] As a function of their pragmatic capability, texts also project worlds with transhistorical intentions, guiding future appropriation and application. The elucidation of such worlds is, therefore, to be an essential transaction of hermeneutics, particularly hermeneutics for preaching, that seeks to culminate in application for life change. It is that pragmatic "surplus" of meaning that generates potential for application, and without this operation of projecting worlds, such application potential will remain unrealized. Therefore, a key task of biblical interpretation that intends

---

54. See Nicholas Wolterstorff, *Works and Worlds of Art* (Oxford: Clarendon, 1980), x, 107; idem, *Divine Discourse*, 212–13. Again, this means that such a *doing* by an author is closely linked to what he/she is saying in the text.

55. The indirect nature of such pragmatic communication may call for extra processing effort on the part of the readers, but this is offset by the advantages of procuring textual effects not otherwise achievable directly. Information theory, according to Levinson, has demonstrated the relative slowness of discourse encoding; he calls the process "a bottleneck" in the system, applicable to both phonetic articulation and alphabetic inscription. This communicational impediment is removed by letting not only the content but also the metalinguistic properties of the utterance (its form, genre, style, etc.) bear some of the speaker's meaning, creating "a way to piggyback meaning on top of meaning." For Levinson, making pragmatic inferences of this sort is more efficient than attempting, by an extended discourse, to encode *all* the "layers" of meaning exclusively in semantic fashion. Correspondingly, from the receiving end of the reader, decoding of such second-order meanings is more efficient if accomplished by pragmatic inference rather than by a meticulous and methodical unpacking of semantic codes (*Presumptive Meanings*, 6, 29). Not to mention the fact that pedantic and cumbersome encoding/decoding of all the nuances of a discourse would ruin the beauty and neuter the power of communication. "The process of interpretation is not a simple matter of decoding. . . . The gap between the encoded meaning of a lexical item and the meaning someone wishes to communicate in an utterance . . . is bridged by an inferential process" (Gene L. Green, "Lexical Pragmatics and Biblical Interpretation," *JETS* 50 [2007]: 806). While pragmatics deals with the contextual and inferential aspects of a discourse, it is entirely possible, as will be shown, to discern the pragmatic thrust of a sizeable portion of text from elements of and within that text itself.

to culminate in application is to unpack the manifold implications of this world and its transhistorical intention, the pragmatic *doing* of authors. How this may be accomplished by the preacher is the burden of this work.

Textuality was designed to overcome the restrictions imposed on orality by time and space. Implicit in the very nature of texts, then, is the splicing of two events—the writing event and the reading event. How is the past of the writing brought into the future of the reading? The bond between the event of inscription and the event of interpretation is consolidated in the transhistorical intention/*world in front of the text*. This entity gives direction for future exemplification. What is fixed for the future in the past event of writing is this intention that governs valid application. All applications that fall within the bounds of the transhistorical intention are considered valid and faithful to the text. Thus "meaning" is tripartite, comprising original textual sense, transhistorical intention, and exemplification (valid application). Such a concept and operation are particularly important for the biblical canon: valid application must fall within the limits of the transhistorical intention (the *world in front of the text*). Thus it is the transhistorical intention/projected world that enables the homiletician to navigate from Scripture to sermon with fidelity.

What sort of texts actually project such worlds and what characterizes such world-projecting texts? In the next section, we see that it is those texts that fall into the category of the "classic"—texts that have withstood the dispersion across time and space—that project worlds. Indeed, it might well be that it is by virtue of this very capacity to project worlds that they end up being classics.

The Classic and Its Characteristics

The overlapping concepts of the projected world and its time-transcending intention, as well as those of pragmatics and what authors do (those elements of the center column in the figure below), promote the futurity of the text.

FACETS OF MEANING		
Original Textual Sense	**Transhistorical Intention** (WORLD IN FRONT OF THE TEXT) *or* **Author's Doing** (PRAGMATICS OF UTTERANCE)	**Exemplifications**

Futurity is thereby built into texts, for texts are intended to be consumed at a time and space distant from the event of the original communication. And projected worlds with transhistorical intentions (the operation of pragmatics) facilitate this future consumption of texts. It is proposed here that it is primarily those texts that are considered "classics" that exemplify and exhibit this unique characteristic of future utility; the Bible, too, falls into that category and possesses the time-transcending properties of the classic.

Of course, one must choose between texts. Not all are worthy of being read in the future; not all project worlds worthy of habitation; not all have persuasive transhistorical intentions; not all that authors *do* with what they say is worth attending to. In fact, not all the books ever printed are still in print, a likely indication of their future readability and worth (or lack thereof). While it is impossible even to estimate, Google has tried to calculate the number of unique books ever published: 129,864,880 as of August 2010. And it claims that about 56 percent of the books it has online are out of print. Using that estimate as a rough guide, about 65 million of the total number of unique books ever printed are now out of print.[56] But even from among the survivors there are those that stand out—the classics.

Sandra Schneiders observes that classics have two essential general characteristics: perennial significance and the property of plurality—a surplus of application potential.[57] To this duo, I will add a third element peculiar to the Bible—prescriptivity, the characteristic stemming from its construal as a divine communiqué by Christians, that renders it authoritative to prescribe the faith and practice of the church. Gadamer declares that "the most important thing about the concept of the classical . . . is the normative sense."[58]

Perenniality
The abiding nature of the classic indicates the unlimited durability of the work as it imbues its receivers with "a consciousness of something enduring, of

56. Google took its raw data from the Library of Congress, WorldCat, etc. See Leonid Taycher, "Books of the World, Stand up and Be Counted! All 129,864,880 of You," n.p. [cited June 3, 2012]. Online: http://booksearch.blogspot.com/2010/08/books-of-world-stand-up-and-be-counted.html. Also see reports from the Electronic Frontier Foundation, especially Fred von Lohmann, "Google Book Search Settlement: Updating the Numbers, Part 2," n.p. [cited June 3, 2012]. Online: https://www.eff.org/deeplinks/2010/02/google-book-search-settlement-updating-numbers-0.

57. Sandra M. Schneiders, "The Paschal Imagination: Objectivity and Subjectivity in New Testament Interpretation," *TS* 46 (1982): 64. Tracy makes the same observation, that classic texts "bear a certain permanence and excess of meaning" (David Tracy, "Creativity in the Interpretation of Religion: The Question of Radical Pluralism," *NLH* 15 [1984]: 296). Also see Michael Levin, "What Makes a Classic in Political Theory?" *Pol. Sci. Q.* 88 (1973): 463, for his five criteria: philosophical quality, original content, influence on events, the foremost example of a certain category of thought, and extended relevancy beyond their own time of publication to the present, even to provide judgments of universal application.

58. Gadamer, *Truth and Method*, 288.

significance that cannot be lost and which is independent of all the circumstances of time—a kind of timeless present that is contemporaneous with every other present"; not that it is without the bounds of time, but that it is within the frontiers of *all* time.[59] The reason for the perenniality of Scripture is its unique penetrability: its transcendent referent, the *world in front of the text*, conquering distanciation, deals with matters of critical importance to mankind in every era. Thus this text remains vital and potent across the span of time. The classic demonstrates itself to be perennial, relevant, and material in each new generation, addressing the present as if it were its only audience or readership. And the canonical classic that the Bible is, has amply proven its perenniality over the millennia of its reading and application within the community of believers.

As has been detailed, the transhistorical intention/projected world is the pragmatic property of a discourse that gives it futurity. It clues the reader in on what is expected of him/her in the projected ideal world, and what sort of response is sought by the author. Particularly for preaching, this implies that potential for future application is conveyed by the biblical classic. For each specific audience in the future, it is the preacher's responsibility to translate the transhistorical intention of the sermonic text into specifics relevant for that audience. Or, in other words, it is the burden of the preacher to lead the flock into inhabiting the projected world, in accordance with that world's precepts, priorities, and practices.

In sum, the perennial characteristic of a classic acknowledges the permanence of the text, granted it by its transhistorical intention/*world in front of the text*. However, this intention/world may be actualized in a variety of ways in a variety of circumstances, generating a variety of applications. This brings us to the second characteristic of the classic, its plurality of application potential.

Plurality

Not only is a classic perennial in significance, the world it projects bears "the richness of the ideal meaning which allows for a theoretically unlimited number of actualizations, each being somewhat original and different from others."[60] That is to say, the transhistorical intention (what authors *do* with what they say) creates the potential for a plurality of exemplifications. The fact that classics are those texts that transport an excess of meaning (in their plurality) and yet retain

---

59. Ibid.
60. Schneiders, "The Paschal Imagination," 64.

a permanence of meaning across time (in their perenniality) is paradoxical on the surface. They appear to be stable in their textual fixity and timeless contemporaneity (perenniality), yet "unstable" in their plurality, as readers in an infinite variety of situations and settings apply those truths in an equally wide variety of ways.[61] Such a conception of simultaneous perenniality and plurality is an essential property of Scripture; its classic status reflects its possession of a surplus of meaning that crosses the bounds of time and goes beyond the needs of any one generation of its readers. And this ensures the Bible's utility into the future and its continued standing as a classic *sui generis*. As was discussed above, it is the broad compass of the transhistorical intention that makes possible a plurality of exemplifications for the future reader. Provided that these exemplifications are subsumed by the transhistorical intention (or are integral to the projected world), such exemplifications are faithful to the "meaning" of the text. The original textual sense ("carriage") of the *Metropolitan Police Act* of 1839 remains constant; so also does the transhistorical intention ("vehicle"). The latter, however, creates the potential for the generation of a plurality of possible applications ("car," "truck," "motorcycle," etc.).

Consider the example of Eph 5:18—"Do not be drunk with wine." While this text does not deal exclusively upon drunkenness, for the purpose of illustrating the plurality of meaning, focusing on the word "wine" in this verse will be profitable.[62] The imperative in that verse demands that one must not be drunk with "wine." Since only "wine" is expressly men-

---

61. David Tracy, *Plurality and Ambiguity: Hermeneutics, Religion, Hope* (San Francisco: Harper and Row, 1987), 12, 14.

62. Community governance is in view in the latter half of Eph, with guidelines for living embedded in a cascade of contrasts between the dynamics of the "new self" and the "old self" (4:17–5:14). The pericope of 5:15–20 itself contains three contrasts (μὴ . . . ἀλλὰ, *mē . . . alla*, "not . . . but"): between those who are wise and those who are not (5:15–16), between being foolish and being cognizant of the will of the Lord (5:17), and between being drunk with wine and being filled by the Holy Spirit (5:18–20). Drunkenness is thus paralleled with walking unwisely and being foolish, and is explicitly labeled ἀσωτία (*asōtia*, "dissipation"), used elsewhere in the NT only in Titus 1:6 (1:7 mentions addiction to wine) and 1 Pet 4:4 (4:3 has drunkenness). Wine, while its use is not condemned in the NT (see 1 Tim 5:23), is clearly not to be abused (3:3, 8; Titus 1:7; 2:3): inebriation is folly, and a characteristic of those who operate in the lifestyle of the old self. Filling by the Spirit, on the other hand, is a characteristic of the wise, those displaying the lifestyle of the new self. In exhorting the Ephesians to be filled by the Spirit rather than be drunk with wine, the biblical writer is essentially commanding them to become, corporately, the unique temple of God, the dwelling place of God in Christ, by the Spirit. Corresponding to the πλήρωμα (*plērōma*, "fullness") language of the OT that depicted the glory of God in the temple (LXX of Isa 6:1–4; Ezek 10:4; 43:5; 44:5; Hag 2:7; etc.), in Eph the church is the new temple of God serving his presence, where the fullness of Christ dwells (1:23)—the new body comprising both Jews and Gentiles, "a holy temple in the Lord," "a dwelling of God in the Spirit" (2:19–22; also 3:16–19). See Kuruvilla, *Text to Praxis*, 184–87.

tioned in the text, would it be acceptable to be drunk with an alcoholic beverage other than wine, say vodka? Distanciation of the text from the circumstances and culture of the first century C.E., where the only known alcoholic beverage was οἶνος (*oinos,* "wine"), calls for the imperative of Eph 5:18 to be recontextualized in the new circumstances of readers and listeners in order to generate valid application. The transhistorical intention of the text is clearly "all manner of alcoholic drinks," thus prohibiting drunkenness with vodka, beer, Scotch, or one's libation *du jour*—the plurality of application. This plurality will include future alcoholic concoctions that are yet to be conceived, compounded, and consumed. The consequences for application are evident: drunkenness with any ethanol-containing brew is proscribed. This transhistorical intention forms the basis for the derivation of plural exemplifications; what the author of Ephesians is *doing* is projecting a world in which the people of God refrain from intoxication with alcoholic beverages of any kind.[63]

FACETS OF MEANING		
Original Textual Sense	**Transhistorical Intention** (WORLD IN FRONT OF THE TEXT) *or* **Author's Doing** (PRAGMATICS OF UTTERANCE)	**Exemplification**
wine	*all manner of alcoholic drinks*	vodka, beer, Scotch, . . .

In other words, valid application (exemplification) by way of the transhistorical intention/projected world is an integral feature of classics. This is especially so for the greatest classic of them all—the Bible. And its plurality, by virtue of the scope of its transhistorical intentions, enables application in a variety

---

63. One could hypothetically broaden this transhistorical intention to "all *drugs* capable of rendering one intoxicated," thereby including as its exemplifications other addictive substances that are ingested, inhaled, or injected. However, in light of the focus of the text on "filling" (a fluid-related phenomenon), and emphasis upon the contrast between the results of Spirit-filling ("speaking . . . , singing . . . , making melody . . .") and the implied manifestations of wine-filling (Eph 5:19)—likely corresponding vocal expressions that are usually common with the abuse of alcohol—it seems judicious to restrict the transhistorical intention to "alcohol." There is, no doubt, a degree of interpretive freedom here.

of ways, in a variety of situations, notwithstanding the distanciation in time and space between the writing of the text and the reading of the text.[64]

Prescriptivity

"No serious writer, composer, painter has ever doubted, even in moments of strategic aestheticism, that his work bears on good and evil, on the enhancement or diminution of the sum of humanity in man and the city. . . . A message is being sent; to a purpose"—such works deemed ethically valuable by their creators are intended to be prescriptive.[65] Whether that prescription is authoritative enough to demand compliance is another matter. However, for Scripture, the community of God's people holds that this divine discourse that is the Christian canon is prescriptive in a manner that no other classic can ever be.[66] This prescriptive corpus, the Bible, makes itself binding upon the faith and practice of the community that recognizes it as Scripture and reads it as such. That is precisely why the preaching of the Scriptures with a view to expounding its application is essential for the life of the church.

This is not to assert that the Bible gives Christians individually specific guidance on every potential issue that might confront them in any location and in any age. U.S. Supreme Court Chief Justice Marshall observed about another classic, the U.S. Constitution:

> A constitution, to contain an accurate detail of all the subdivisions of which its great powers will admit, and of all the means by which they may be carried into execution, would partake of the prolixity of a legal code, and could scarcely be embraced by the human mind. It would probably never be understood by the public. Its nature, therefore, requires that only its great outlines should be marked, its important objects designated, and the minor ingredients which compose those objects be deduced from the nature of the objects themselves.[67]

---

64. Though plural, the various exemplifications are related to each other and to the original textual sense, bounded as they all are by the transhistorical intention. One can conceive of other analogies that demonstrate this kind of identity. In my own medical vocation as a dermatologist, a case of psoriasis in one patient differs from cases of the same affliction in others—i.e., there is no explicit identity shared between them; individual manifestations of the disease are variegated and nuanced for each patient, as regards intensity of illness, distribution of lesions, concern to patient, and response to treatment. Yet there is clearly an identity of some sort between all cases of psoriasis, linked as they are by the same "transhistorical" pathophysiology, natural history, complex of symptoms, and therapeutics of the disease that remain constant and subsume every instance of the condition.

65. Steiner, *Real Presences*, 145.

66. The next section, in a description of Rules of Reading for Scripture, outlines the special hermeneutics of this text and considers its unique properties, including its character as divine discourse.

67. *McCulloch v. Maryland*, U.S. 17 (4 Wheat.) (1819): 316, 407.

Likewise, for the Bible to direct every possible twist and turn in the life of every individual Christian and of every community of God in every millennium would be absolutely impossible. Instead a canonical *world in front of the text* is projected, with each pericope of the text portraying a slice of this plenary world, each with its own transhistorical intention.[68] Such intentions are therefore necessarily generic, capable of being applied in a variety of situations (the plurality discussed above). That the process of interpretation of the text will therefore involve some reduction of its specifics into more general transhistorical intentions is thus inevitable (see chapter 2); these broad intentions may then be appropriately applied to the particular contexts of auditors. With regard to the Bible, this specification of application is the task of the preacher; with regard to the U.S. Constitution, it is the task of the judge. Both preacher and judge bring the transhistorical intention of their respective texts to bear upon the specificities of the lives they deal with, one in the pews and the other before the bar. The prescriptivity of the text is thereby maintained, as original textual sense generates a transhistorical intention which, in turn, generates valid application (exemplification).

In sum, the prescriptive nature of the Bible renders it profitable for application in the life of its readers; its perennial standing projects its relevance across the span of time; its plurality enables a wide variety of valid applications in any number of specific circumstances for a spectrum of discrete audiences in the future. These critical attributes of a classic suggest that for the biblical canon, future-directedness is an intrinsic property of its textuality and its referent (the world it projects/transhistorical intention/what authors *do*). Indeed, it is by means of this futurity that the canon is endowed with a reach that extends beyond the immediate time-space realms of its composition. Such an orientation to the future enables readers to deploy the biblical text for application in circumstances distant from, and dissimilar to, the original contexts of its composition.

"When we read any classic . . . we find that our present horizon is always provoked, sometimes confronted, always transformed by the power exerted by that classic's claim."[69] Perennial and plural in character, the canonical classic of Scripture demands to be read—it is prescriptive. And in the lives of those readers

---

68. This role of pericopes is discussed in chapter 2.

69. David Tracy, *The Analogical Imagination: Christian Theology and the Culture of Pluralism* (New York: Crossroad, 1981), 134.

volunteering to be challenged by the claims of this text, the Bible brings to bear its transformative properties. The primary task of interpreters of this text, therefore, is to apprehend its truth-claims and illuminate the possibilities for its application in the present, in contexts quite different from that of the author, the writing-event, and that of all prior readers and their reading-events.[70] In short, the characteristics of the biblical canon with potent repercussions for homiletics and thus, for the life of the Christian community, are its prescriptive nature, its perennial standing, and its plurality of significance.

Excursus: On Significance

In the case of the *Metropolitan Police Act* of 1839, the world projected is one wherein traffic on English streets remains unimpeded by disabled vehicles of any kind whatsoever. The law implicitly projected the kind of ideal world it was intending to mandate—a world in which no broken vehicles on London roads would block traffic. The determination of the projected world/transhistorical intention is thus critical in the navigation from text to praxis. Thus my Honda Civic, with its broken radiator, if stranded on a London road, should be immediately removed therefrom without my attempting its extended repair on the roadside (exemplification), lest I be in violation of the aforementioned *Act*—a failure to inhabit the world projected by the text of the law. Proper inhabitation of that ideal world of "no-broken-vehicles-on-London-roads" (transhistorical intention/*world in front of the text*) involves the removal of my broken Honda from such roads.[71]

Now, if the *Metropolitan Police Act* of 1839 were an inspired text and I were preaching the "carriage" pericope, it would be perfectly valid for me to suggest, as a homiletical imperative, that my congregation, in response to the text, should they be stuck on London roads in an incapacitated vehicle, would do well to

---

70. In this act of transformative reading and hearing, the role of the Holy Spirit must not be underestimated. A proper and fitting reading of this classic emphasizes "both the overruling and redirecting activity of the Spirit in the reader . . . and also the reader's own invocation of the Spirit." The reader is to approach this "demanding" text with an appropriate attitude: a faithful hearing exhibits a "self-forgetful reference to the prevenient action and presence of God. . . . the Christian reading is a kind of surrender," in effect, a prayerful submission to the authority of God's word, in the power of God's Spirit (Webster, *Word and Church*, 43, 82–83). Regretfully, the role of the Spirit in interpretation will not be considered in any detail in this work.

71. As was noted earlier, other applications in the future ("truck/motorcycle/etc.") that fall within the scope of the transhistorical intention of that text ("vehicle") are also part of the future-directed meaning of the text ("carriage") and may therefore be deemed *valid* applications. See Hirsch, "Meaning and Significance Reinterpreted," 207, 210. Also see idem, *The Aims of Interpretation* (Chicago: The University of Chicago Press, 1976), 80.

remove forthwith their disabled Toyotas, Fords, Saabs, and Peugeots from the streets. Being the good shepherd of my flock, farsighted and perceptive, I might go further and advise my audience to join The Automobile Association ("The AA," the U.K. version of American Automobile Association [AAA] in the U.S.), in order to preclude undue delays in getting their stuck vehicles off the road. It is obvious that "Join The AA," as an application, does not fall within the bounds of the transhistorical intention which simply called for the removal of broken-down vehicles. But in my infinite pastoral wisdom, I called my flock to take the shrewd and sagacious step of subscribing to The AA, so that, should their automobiles be stranded, they would be in a good position to arrange for rapid removal of the offending vehicle from London's thoroughfares. In other words, the application "Join The AA" is not a *valid* one in response to the *Act* of 1839. Nonetheless, "Join The AA" serves to move one *towards* a valid application: the tow truck dispatched by The AA would help one achieve the goal promulgated by the law.

Applications such as these, which are *not* bounded by the transhistorical intentions, Hirsch labeled "significance"; these latter applications are not part of textual meaning. In our case, "Join The AA" is not mandated by the *Metropolitan Police Act*, but is a means of helping the motorist abide by that law should his or her vehicle break down. This action of subscribing to The AA falls into the category of significance, and is not an exemplification; rather it is a *means of accomplishing* the exemplification of the law—the removal of a crippled car from London's traffic. Though not directly commanded by the *Act,* this preemptive enrollment enables alignment to that "no-broken-vehicles-on-London-roads" world. The goal, in obedience to the *Act,* would be to inhabit that world of no-broken-vehicles-on-London-roads as quickly as possible and to the best of one's ability—in this case, by the expeditious removal of one's distressed automobile from Her Majesty's asphalt, a task aided by one's membership in The AA.

FACETS OF MEANING			
Original Textual Sense	Transhistorical Intention (WORLD IN FRONT OF THE TEXT)	Exemplification	Significance
No carriage repair	No broken vehicles on road	No Honda Civic repair	Join The AA
		FACETS OF APPLICATION	

Application is thereby split between exemplification (within "meaning") and significance (outside "meaning"). The utility of significance in preaching is that the preacher need not be restricted to the precise exemplifications of the textual demand, but may also suggest significances for application that move one toward accomplishment of the exemplification demanded by the text. Significances enable one to abide in the *world in front of the text*, aligned to its precepts, priorities, and practices.

Here is another example: The transhistorical intention of Eph 5:18, discussed earlier, prohibits drunkenness with alcohol—an ideal world in which God's people are never intoxicated with the substance. If the congregation I am preaching to is, for some strange reason, prone to getting drunk on vodka, the immediate application would be to remind them that the biblical text prohibits such inebriation. This application to refrain from vodka-fueled intoxication falls within the transhistorical intention (since vodka is an alcoholic product). But if I am aware that many in the audience are also avid consumers of *Wine Spectator* magazine, and if I suspect that perusing that publication is a prime temptation that leads to their drunkenness on vodka, I could, with my preacherly and pastoral authority, suggest that they cancel their subscriptions to the aforementioned publication. The application "Cancel subscription to *Wine Spectator*" is, of course, not a mandate of the transhistorical intention/*world in front of the text*. However, it is certainly prudent counsel which, if heeded, may help one accomplish the valid application/exemplification not to get drunk with vodka. Such applications that help one move towards achieving the exemplification are significances. They are not "valid" in the strict sense of their being part of the triadic meaning of the text, but they are, nevertheless, applications, and appropriate ones at that, for they help one to arrive at the state (in this case, a state of sobriety) demanded by the text.[72]

---

72. Significances might not be "valid" applications, but they are certainly *appropriate* applications, provided they help one accomplish what the text calls for. Significances, therefore, rightly belong in the preacher's quiver of homiletical arrows. Of course, in practice, the interpreter must first determine valid application before deciding on significances. In the heuristic process, valid application comes first. So for the rest of this work, I will focus on valid applications, but the reader should bear in mind the utility of significances in preaching. It is also obvious from this discussion how important it is for the preacher to know the flock to whom the sermon is directed. In my opinion, preaching can therefore never be separated from shepherding.

FACETS OF MEANING			
Original Textual Sense	**Transhistorical Intention** (WORLD IN FRONT OF THE TEXT)	**Exemplification**	**Significance**
No drunkenness with wine	*No drunkenness with alcohol*	No drunkenness with vodka	Cancel subscription to *Wine Spectator*
		FACETS OF APPLICATION	

Thus, the validity of an application in a future reading of the text is contingent upon its falling within the boundaries of the transhistorical intention (i.e., within the demands of the text-projected world). This intention/world is an unchanging conceptual component of the text that creates a virtually infinite potential of exemplifications that may be realized in a myriad of future reading contexts. It is this transhistorical entity, the projected world, which gives texts their future-directedness. This work proposes that for biblical pericopes as well, the transhistorical intention/*world in front of the text* is the conceptual entity that enables the generation of future exemplifications, and thereby it mediates a valid move from Scripture to sermon. How this is accomplished for biblical pericopes will be explored in chapter 2.

Section Summary: General Hermeneutics

Texts are instruments of discourse that transcend the boundaries of time and space. In other words, they undergo distanciation. That does not necessarily impact the future potency of a text, for the *world in front of the text*, the transcendent referent of the discourse, bears a transhistorical intention that guides readers situated afar into application. The past of a text is thereby linked to the future of its readers. Such an operation is critical for the canon of Scripture: it is this transhistorical intention of the projected world (the pragmatic consideration of what authors *do* with what they say) that enables preachers to develop valid application for the people of God. Such future directedness is characteristic of "classics," characterized by their perennial relevance, their plural possibilities of diverse application, and their prescriptivity or normative sense. Indeed, Scripture, by these characteristics, also falls into the category of the classic; this canonical classic has been construed as perennial, plural, and prescriptive by the church for over two millennia.

While the projection of a *world in front of the text* is applicable to all classic texts (a feature of *general* hermeneutics), what gives this concept momentum for biblical interpretation are the unique features of Scripture (*special* hermeneutics, applicable to this unique text alone): its ultimate Author, the singular nature of its divine referent, and its spiritually transforming power. It is the special nature of this hermeneutic, by which the church has recognized the biblical text to be its Scripture, that lends this opus gravity and declares it (and every pericope it contains) worthy of being preached and applied everywhere, to everyone, in every era. The implications of special hermeneutics for the interpretation of Scripture for preaching will be dealt with next.

SPECIAL HERMENEUTICS

The church's construal of the Bible as Scripture and as divine discourse (a special text, indeed) dictates how this classic is to be read for preaching purposes. It is as "Scripture" and all that that designation implies that the canon is rendered applicable, with perennial, plural, and prescriptive standing. Not only the collection as a whole, but individual texts and pericopes as well, bear those characteristics. The canonical classic is thus a text of great consequence, and the world in front of it is a critical referential construct. Scripture is therefore not to be neglected, but read, and its projected world appropriated. It calls for a surrender to the substantiality of the text and to the will of God—a willingness to inhabit the *world in front of the text*. This charge will be spelled out below as a collection of rules for reading, which reflect the perennial, plural, and prescriptive characteristics of this classic *non pareil*: thus, *special* hermeneutics.

Role of Rules

This section will address the employment of special hermeneutics in biblical interpretation by taking an inventory of the rules that have governed the reading and interpretation of Scripture in the age of the church. The rules proposed here, it must be noted, are more like rules of thumb, than like inviolate and unassailable rules of nature. That is, they are more descriptive than prescriptive.[73] Rule-creation for the interpretation of the Bible is not a new enterprise: the Jewish rabbis had several sets of these—the seven rules (מִדּוֹת, *middot*) of Hillel

---

73. See Frederick Schauer, *Playing by the Rules: A Philosophical Examination of Rule-Based Decision-Making in Law and Life* (Oxford: Clarendon, 1991), 1–3, for a description of the types of rules mankind lives by.

(*t. Sanh.* 7.11; *'Abot. R. Nat.* 37), the thirteen of Ishmael (*Baraita de Rabbi Ishmael* 1), etc. Christians were not remiss in this activity, either: note the seven rules of Tyconius that Augustine revised (*Doctr. chr.* 3.30–37), and Matthias Flaccius Illyricus's "The Rule for Becoming Acquainted with the Sacred Scriptures" (in his *Clavis Scripturæ Sacræ* [late seventeenth century]). Kelsey observes that "to call a set of writings 'scripture' is to say that they ought to be used in certain normative and *rulish* ways in the common life of the church."[74] I will attempt to register the special ways of reading this special text as rules.

What are these rules of reading (playing?) the language game of the biblical corpus and how do they help preaching?[75] The rules are essentially statements of the reading habits that govern the interpretation of this special text—they reflect the employment of a *special* hermeneutic. In terms of the function of these rules, their broad scope necessarily limits them to the role of guardians: the interpreter must not cross the boundaries laid down by these rules; rather he or she must operate within them. In other words, these rules oversee and superintend the hermeneutical operation without defining how precisely a specific text may be interpreted. The particularities of a text are not elucidated by the application of these rules.

For instance, the utilization of the six rules listed below will not lead one to the original textual sense, transhistorical intention borne by the projected world, or the valid applications of Eph 5:18. The rules will only affirm the validity of using the book of Eph (Rule of Exclusivity), encourage the interpretation to be consistent with the rest of Scripture (Rule of Singularity), approve the use of the textual form of Eph 5:18 as we have it (Rule of Finality), permit the discovery of application from this text (Rule of Applicability), warn against interpretation that is incongruent with what the church has consistently taught (Rule of Ecclesiality), and remind us that the demand of the text is a facet of

---

74. David H. Kelsey, *The Uses of Scripture in Recent Theology* (Philadelphia: Fortress, 1975), 164 (emphasis added).

75. The use of rules to describe the playing practices of any text is appropriate, for texts are a category of Wittgensteinian "language games." Wittgenstein postulated that language games are discourses that *do* something, for they comprise not only the words, phrases, and sentences of the utterance, but also the action that is accomplished by them. "We call something a language game if it plays a particular role in our human life" (Ludwig Wittgenstein, "Notes for Lectures on 'Private Experience' and 'Sense Data,'" ed. R. Rhees, *Phil. Rev.* 77 [1968]: 300; and idem, *Philosophical Investigations*, ¶7). Also notice his other remarks underscoring this theme: "language is an instrument"; "words are also deeds" (ibid., ¶¶432, 546); etc. For further details see Kuruvilla, *Text to Praxis*, 15–19.

what it means to be Christlike (Rule of Centrality).[76] In other words, the rules merely delimit the process and determine what would, in broad and general terms, be valid or invalid; they do not specify what particular texts mean or how exactly they might be applied. The rules, instead, further respect for the canonical corpus as a special text, and champion a special hermeneutic, for no other text is read or interpreted in this fashion.

While not universally applied, these rules have had wide custom and have played a crucial role through the history of the church in chaperoning the interpretation of the foundational text of the believing community. However, it must be remembered that broad employment of the rules within Christendom does not equate to exceptionless, universal application thereof. Neither should the set of rules be considered a monolithic code that is applied in all-or-none fashion. This collection, in all likelihood, has never functioned as a single, unified, global statute-book rigidly applied *in toto*. Local variations certainly abound amongst communities that use some or all of these rules to varying degrees, exploiting their nuances to varying extents, and applying them variably to discrete texts within the canon. And examples surely exist that demonstrate a disregard for, or negation of, individual rules.[77] Nonetheless, most of these rules have been widely employed, as the historical citations demonstrate.

A descriptive bias, reflecting a Protestant and evangelical tradition, will, no doubt, be discernible in the enumeration of these rules of canon interpretation: obviously these rules reflect my own reading practices with regard to Scripture. That, however, does not invalidate them *tout court*. A perspectival description is not necessarily for that reason alone rendered unviable; the fact that a description is motivated does not disqualify it "since an unmotivated description independent of any interpretative frame or purpose is impossible to imagine."[78]

---

76. See below for further details on these rules.

77. Footnotes to each rule will direct the reader's attention to such contrasting material. While this work acknowledges the breadth of acceptance of these rules across the span of Christian traditions and over much of Christian history, the qualifications noted provide a necessary counterpoint in order to generate a realistic view of these guidelines and the limited scope of many of them. It must be reiterated that all such rules are of the nature of counsel and caution rather than imperative and injunction: rules of thumb.

78. Francis B. Watson, *Text, Church and World: Biblical Interpretation in Theological Perspective* (Grand Rapids: Eerdmans, 1994), 37. Full disclosure: I come to Scripture as a conservative Protestant Christian, an Indian-American with no formal political affiliation, schooled in Asia, N. America, and Europe, who is heterosexual in orientation but celibate for the cause of Christ, and who is a professor, a preacher, and a physician.

Indeed, an explicitly confessed frame of reference enables one "to see the events considered from one's own . . . perspective as capable of a different, but not necessarily inaccurate and usually complementary portrayal."[79] No single frame of reference can capture every aspect of the phenomenon being observed; the contribution of this work is therefore made from a vantage point that is unique, and, hopefully, the description of rules provided here will complement those made by other observers from a variety of traditions.

Rules of Reading

The six rules of reading that have found widespread acceptance amongst Christians throughout the church age are: the Rules of Exclusivity, Singularity, Finality, Applicability, Ecclesiality, and Centrality.

> **RULE OF EXCLUSIVITY**
>
> *The Rule of Exclusivity demarcates those canonical books that alone may be utilized for applicational purposes.*

This Rule discriminates between what is acceptable for inclusion in the canon and what is not. In effect, the canon is an ancient form of "copyright" protecting the corpus as a whole from distortion and deformation.[80] For the purposes of interpretation, then, the Rule of Exclusivity demarcates what textual discourses may (or may not) function in the edification of the community. It restricts authority to particular texts, and only these selected writings may be preached from and applied.[81] The canon commissions such texts to be repeatedly utilized in the community to bring its corporate life and the lives of the individuals it comprises into alignment with the will of God.

Through a reflective evaluation of its literary heritage, the early church in the second century construed as canonical a set of authoritative writings. It

---

79. Sidney Ratner, "Presupposition and Objectivity in History," *Phil. Sci.* 7 (1940): 504.

80. George Aichele, *The Control of Biblical Meaning: Canon as Semiotic Mechanism* (Harrisburg, Penn.: Trinity, 2001), 20.

81. This Rule of Exclusivity does not regulate the specific composition of the canon. No one list of the books of the canon is preferred by this rule over others. The rule as stated implies that applicational practices of a community will be dependent upon the boundaries of the canon that it submits to. The belief in purgatory, for instance, may depend on whether the tradition includes within its canon the deutero-canonical books of Maccabees; the doctrine of purgatory is partly based upon 2 Macc 12:45 (see *The Catechism of the Catholic Church* [2nd ed.; New York: Doubleday, 2003], ¶1032).

realized that without a written norm, its station in time was too distant from the apostolic age for it to be able to guard the purity of what had been handed down. This principle of canon was an acknowledgement by the community of believers that thenceforth, every subsequent tradition would be submitted to the control of the authoritative apostolic tradition that was fixed in, and bounded by, the canon. Such a settled and stable body of literature was deemed an adequate norm, sufficient for regulating the teaching office of the church, and upon which norm such office would be dependent.[82]

The primary yardsticks that served in the assessment of texts for inclusion in the canon were traditional usage (including catholicity) and orthodoxy of the candidate volumes.[83] The criteria of authorship and inspiration played a more indirect role for the recognition of books as canonical.[84] However, in the face of attacks on the canon by Marcion and others, when forced to justify its acceptance of some books and not others, the church employed apostolic authorship of those texts as a condition for their inclusion within the canon. Tertullian declared as of primary importance "that the evangelical Testament has apostles for its authors, to whom was assigned by the Lord himself this office of publishing the gospel" (*Marc.* 4.2).[85] In addition, Clement of Rome acknowledged that Paul wrote "with true inspiration" (*1 Clem.* 47.3).[86] The Bible's own claim to being inspired (2 Tim 3:16) must be respected. To make sense of the Bible on its own terms and upon its own claims, one, of course, need not believe in inspiration or, indeed, even the rules of grammar, but one *must* postulate both.[87] Thus the concept of inspiration must be taken seriously by the interpreter of this special

82. Oscar Cullman, *The Early Church* (London: SCM, 1956), 90–91.

83. Bruce M. Metzger, *The Canon of the New Testament: Its Origin, Development, and Significance* (Oxford: Clarendon, 1987), 254; Harry Y. Gamble, *The New Testament Canon: Its Making and Meaning* (Philadelphia: Fortress, 1985), 67–68.

84. F. F. Bruce noted that "inspiration is no longer a criterion of canonicity: it is a corollary of canonicity" (*The Canon of Scripture* [Downers Grove: InterVarsity, 1988], 268).

85. Likewise, the Muratorian canon also adduced the personal qualifications of the authors, either as eyewitnesses or as apostles, as grounds for the canonicity of several of the NT books (translated in Metzger, *The Canon of the New Testament*, 305–7).

86. Some of the writers of the canonical texts understood the inspired nature of their own writings: the author of the Apocalypse, for instance, denoted his writing as "the words of this prophecy" (Rev 22:19). The readers of the seven letters in Rev 2–3 were adjured, in each of those epistles, to "hear what the Spirit says to the churches," again implying that those texts had a divine imprimatur (also see 2 Tim 3:16 and 2 Pet 1:21).

87. Meir Sternberg, *The Poetics of Biblical Narrative: Ideological Literature and the Drama of Reading* (Bloomington, Ind.: Indiana University Press, 1987), 81.

text, along with attribution of authorship to those held as founders and leaders of the community of God's people through the ages.

Traditional usage of a document was, perhaps, one of the most important elements for deciding upon the canonicity of a text. The texts included in the canon were, for the most part, those that consistently enjoyed pre-eminence in the church as useful for the nurture, sustenance, and promotion of the faith of the first Christian communities.[88] Formal acceptance of such recognized books were quite early events in the life of the church; Paul credits the Thessalonians, for instance, with having received his word as the word of God (1 Thess 2:13). The designation of Luke's Gospel as "Scripture" also acknowledges its canonical reception by the church from early days (1 Tim 5:18 expressly labels it as such, citing Luke 10:7; also see 2 Pet 3:15–16). Traditional usage was also closely linked to the catholicity of the documents: to be deemed authoritative, a document had to be relevant to the community of God's people as a whole. For instance, despite the particularity of the Epistles, addressed as they were to specific individuals and congregations, the early church recognized their broader appeal and utility.[89] Tertullian could therefore ask rhetorically: "But of what consequence are the titles [of the letters], since in writing to a certain church the apostle did in fact write to all?" (*Marc.* 5.17). The goal of the criterion of traditional usage and catholicity was to preclude idiosyncratic, esoteric, and sequestered documents of limited relevance and utility from entering the canon. Passing muster, on the other hand, were texts that were widely accessible and generally approved of as bearing perennial significance for edification (Heb 4:12; 2 Tim 3:17). Augustine asserted that the Christian interpreter of the Scriptures should prefer those texts "accepted by all catholic churches, to those which some do not accept" (*Doctr. chr.* 2.8.12). Traditional usage (and catholicity) thus marked those documents that finally found inclusion within the canon.

---

88. Gamble, *The New Testament Canon*, 70–71. He observes that some writings that met the criterion of traditional usage were excluded (*The Shepherd of Hermas, 1 Clement, Didache*). On the other hand, others that were perhaps not as widely utilized were included (Jas, 2 Pet, 2 and 3 John). This ambiguity of the status of certain books is a countervailing force upon the applicability of the Rule of Exclusivity that adduces traditional usage as evidence for its employment.

89. For instance, the Colossians are asked to have their letter passed on to other Christian assemblies (Col 4:16). Revelation 1:3 also assumes a wider readership than the seven churches to which John wrote; the Muratorian canon says of Rev that "John also in the Apocalypse, though he writes to seven churches, nevertheless speaks for all" (see its translation in Metzger, *The Canon of the New Testament*, 305–7). The case for the OT is made more easily, since Jesus and the apostles accepted the already formulated Jewish canon (Matt 23:35; Luke 24:44; etc.).

One remembers that usage came first, before the formal acknowledgement of those writings as canonical. In other words, while critics determine *what ought to be* appreciated, it is readers who determine *what actually is* appreciated.[90] The construal of certain books as canonical is thus only a recognition of an already established fact, after the fact, for the verdict of readers preceded that of critics.

Another fundamental gauge of canonicity was the text's consistency and congruence with apostolic teaching—the *orthodoxy* (and, perhaps, orthopraxy) of the church. If the canon was ultimately the product of divine authorship, then what was asserted in the candidate document, were it truly canonical, would be in concord with the instruction of the apostles. The "apostolic deposit," over the decades and centuries of the church, became the core of the authoritative litera-ture of the NT, by which standard the doctrine of the books vying for canonical inclusion was judged. Regarding disputed books, Eusebius wrote: "[T]he char-acter of [their] style is at variance with apostolic usage, and both the thoughts and the purpose of the things that are related in them are so completely out of accord with true orthodoxy that they clearly show themselves to be the fictions of heretics" (*Hist. eccl.* 3.25.7).[91] Orthodoxy, along with traditional usage/catho-licity, thus demarcated those texts deemed worthy of being accorded canonical status.

In applying the Rule of Exclusivity, the church was, in effect, asserting that the world projected by the canon should be constituted by the contributions of a selected coterie of texts; such texts alone, making up the canon, were to be au-thoritative for the depiction of the canonical world and, therefore, for preach-ing and application.

RULE OF SINGULARITY

The Rule of Singularity calls the interpreter to consider the canonical text as a single unit for applicational purposes—an integral whole, intrinsically related in all its parts.

---

90. George Steiner declared that "[t]he critic prescribes a syllabus; the reader is answerable to and internal-izes a canon" ("'Critic'/'Reader,'" *NLH* 10 [1979]: 445).

91. The very existence of contradictory claims regarding certain books indicates that the Rule of Exclusiv-ity was not an absolute mandate universally applied. Eusebius's distinctions between texts that were *homologoumena* (recognized), *antilegomena* (disputed), *notha* (spurious), and heretical suggests that all was not being smoothly administered by this Rule (see *Hist. eccl.* 3.5.5–7; 3.25.1–7). However, one must admit that contested books form only a fraction of the total canonical content; there is substantial agreement as to what constitutes the remainder.

The Bible has traditionally been perceived and comprehended as a unity, despite its variegated authorship and despite the fact that its constituent parts were written over a period of at least two millennia. It is as a unity that this classic has fired literary imaginations and stoked artistic dreams, and it is as a unity that the church has utilized the Scriptures as the norm for its faith and practice.[92] This singularity is also evidenced in the common practice of prefacing a biblical quote with, "The Bible says . . . ," evincing a widespread conception of the Scriptures as *one* book, a unified corpus.[93] At the same time, the singularity attested here affirms that the canon is a *singularity*, not a simplicity in the sense of being unanalyzable, indivisible, or uncompounded. Rather the Bible is analyzable (and necessitates rigorous analysis), divisible (attesting to the diversity of its human authorship), and compound (its constituent parts are interdependent, contributing to an integral whole). Singularity is also reflected in NT references to OT writings; these citations construe the latter as a single book as, for instance, in the formulas introducing the citations in Matt 26:24; Mark 9:13; and 14:21 (καθὼς γέγραπται, *kathōs gegraptai*, "just as it is written"), or in Luke 18:31; 21:22; and 24:44 (τὰ γεγραμμένα, *ta gegrammena*, "the things that are written"). To assert that the Bible is "God's book" is not to say that it is a collection of books authored by God; instead, it is to declare that the Bible is "the *one* book of God"—the Rule of Singularity in operation. "The entire Scripture is one book and was revealed by the one Holy Spirit" (Cyril of Alexandria, *Commentary on Isaiah*, on Isa 29:11–12). That this singularity reflects a divine intentional act justifies the ascription "divine discourse" to the canonical text.[94]

The singularity of the canon results in a singularity of its function as well: the unified goal of these writings is to proclaim God and his relationship with his people, uniformly and with one voice. Thus there is one canonical world that the text *in toto* projects in a unified and coherent fashion, the habitation

---

92. Northrop Frye, *The Great Code: The Bible and Literature* (New York: Harcourt Brace & Company, 1982), xiii.

93. The seismic move from scroll to codex in the compilation of the Christian canon also enabled a "singular" reading technology; now a reader could go back and forth within and between books with great ease—"a crude form of hypertext" that recognizes and employs the corpus as a single unit. See Aichele, *The Control of Biblical Meaning*, 48–49.

94. Wolterstorff, *Divine Discourse*, 53; also see idem, "The Importance of Hermeneutics for a Christian Worldview," in *Disciplining Hermeneutics: Interpretation in Christian Perspective* (ed. Roger Lundin; Grand Rapids: Eerdmans, 1997), 25–47. John 10:35 uses "word of God" in parallel with "Scripture"; also see Mark 7:9–13, where "commandment of God," what "Moses said," and "word of God" are interchangeably employed, all attesting to the singularity of the corpus as divine discourse.

of which world is the means by which believers are conformed to the image of Christ (Rom 8:29; see chapter 4). All of Scripture is geared to this end, and this in turn abounds to the glory of God. This unity of the biblical canon, a wholeness comprising discrete parts, is manifested in the harmony of its doctrine and its depiction of this single doxological purpose. While one must acknowledge that the Bible does not have the kind of unity and coherence one might expect of the literary product of a single human author, there is, nevertheless, a unity between the various parts of the canon that bespeaks a singularity.[95]

Individual texts and sections of the canon recognize the history of preceding parts and portions, and cumulatively add to what has gone on before. Genesis through 2 Kgs constitutes the story from creation to the exile; 1 and 2 Chron cover the same ground, utilizing an extended nine-chapter genealogy to represent the period from Adam to David. The replication of the last two verses of 2 Chron (36:22–23) at the beginning of Ezra (1:1–3a) also signifies the continuation of the historical narrative. In the NT, the account of Jesus and the apostles is considered the sequel to the OT story of Israel. The genealogy of Matt 1 retells, in structural and formulaic fashion, the biblical story thus far, indicating the providential design of the terrain of Israelite history between the major landmarks—Abraham, David, and the exile. The periodic summaries in both Testaments attest to the unity and integrity of the biblical narrative as found in the entirety of the canon.[96]

Moreover, in the demarcation of history "from Abel to Zechariah" (Matt 23:35), Jesus encompasses all the OT martyrs, from the one in the first book to the one in the last (Gen to 2 Chron, in the Jewish ordering of the canon). Indeed, Gen to Rev outlines a singular trajectory of human history that begins in a verdant garden containing the tree of life (Gen 2:8–17) and ends in a glorious city

---

95. Confounding factors seemingly militating against this rule include potential contradictions within the canonical corpus: Is the OT God of war (Ex 15:3) the same as the NT God of peace (Rom 15:33)? Is one justified by faith (Rom 3:28) or by works (Jas 2:24)? The 400-year gap in the narrative history of Israel, the intertestamental period between the Old and New Testaments, also points to a less than completely cohesive and tight story. Nonetheless, Christian tradition has generally chosen to privilege unity and singularity over potential contradictions and seeming diversities.

96. These summaries are located in Deut 6:20–24 (exodus to occupation of the promised land); 26:5–9 (settlement in Egypt to occupation of the land); Josh 24:2–13 (Abraham to occupation of the land); Neh 9:6–37 (creation; Abraham to the return from exile); Ps 78 (exodus to David); Ps 105 (Abraham to occupation of the land); Ps 106 (exodus to exile); Ps 135:8–12 (exodus to occupation of the land); Ps 136 (creation; exodus to occupation of the land); Acts 7:2–50 (Abraham to Solomon); and Acts 13:17–41 (patriarchs in Egypt to the resurrection of Christ). See Richard Bauckham, "Reading Scripture as a Coherent Story," in *The Art of Reading Scripture* (eds. Ellen F. Davis and Richard B. Hays; Grand Rapids: Eerdmans, 2003), 40–42.

that also contains a tree of life (Rev 22:1–2). The garden at the commencement of the story served as the place where man engaged in עָבַד (*'abad*, "cultivation," Gen 2:5, 15). This word later acquired strong liturgical connotations and came to be used regularly for the service of worship (as in Num 3:7–8; 8:25–26; 18:5–6; etc.), hinting at the kind of activity Adam may have (at least symbolically) been engaged in, in that primeval agricultural paradise. It is no coincidence, then, that the δοῦλοι (*douloi*, "bond-servants") of the Lamb, in the restored garden that is the heavenly city, will also be "serving" (Rev 22:3; from λατρεύω, *latreuō*, also used frequently of worship as, for example, in Heb 10:2; 13:10; Rev 7:15; etc.). Eden was the garden of God, with God's presence its central and dominating feature (see Isa 51:3 and Ezek 28:13); quite appropriately, the canon concludes with another divine sanctuary, the New Jerusalem wherein is stationed "the throne of God and of the Lamb" (Rev 22:3).[97] These recurring motifs acknowledge the Bible's overall unity and authority, *in tota scriptura*, and legitimize it as a single metanarrative. In other words, a single canonical world is projected in front of the biblical text; it is at the canonical level that the *world in front of the text* assumes its plenary shape.[98] Thus the Rule of Singularity, asserting the unity and univocity of the canon, helps portray a singular and plenary world in front of the canonical text, facets of which are projected by the individual pericopes comprising Scripture (more about the role of pericopes in chapter 2).

This rule also calls for an assumption of broad coherence and consistency among the various texts within the canon. In other words, individual parts of the corpus are complementary to one another in what they affirm. The construal of the canon as a single unified discourse forms the basis for attributing congruence between the discrete texts of the corpus. Not only is such a rule the reflection of the Bible's canonical unity, it is also a fundamental precept of charitable reading of *any* text, the first reflex of the reader that accords the text the benefit of such an assumption of congruence.[99] The church throughout the

---

97. William J. Dumbrell, "Genesis 2:1–17: A Foreshadowing of the New Creation," in *Biblical Theology: Retrospect and Prospect* (ed. Scott J. Hafemann; Downers Grove: InterVarsity, 2002), 53–65.

98. See Vanhoozer, *First Theology*, 292.

99. John Barton, *The Spirit and the Letter: Studies in the Biblical Canon* (London: SPCK, 1997), 139; Vanhoozer, *Is There a Meaning in This Text?* 32. Understanding involves a starting assumption, an "initiative trust, an investment of belief," which is an act of charity towards author and text. To begin with doubt, Booth warned, "is to destroy the datum"—the material and subject of interpretation (Wayne C. Booth, *The Company We Keep: An Ethics of Fiction* [Berkeley, Calif.: University of California Press, 1988], 32). In other words, a primary act of assent and surrender is the essential first step in approaching a text—any text.

ages has deemed Scripture to be internally coherent and consistent. Thus no one place in this unique discourse may be so expounded "that it be repugnant to another" (Art. 20, *The Thirty-Nine Articles,* 1563).[100] Therefore the canon not only bestows upon the Bible organization, cohesion, and unity, but also promotes the reading of each text in the complementary light of all the others.[101] The concord between the texts of the canon is exemplified in Daniel's acceptance of Jeremiah's prophecy (Dan 9:2 citing Jer 25:11–12 on the seventy-year length of the Babylonian captivity) and the grounding of the former's own revelatory vision in the שָׁבֻעִים שִׁבְעִים (*shabu'im shib'im,* "seventy sevens/weeks," Dan 9:24). Another example is the identity of the serpent of Gen 3:1–5 that has traditionally been understood as being disclosed in Rev 12:9 as "the devil and Satan" (also see Rev 20:2). Irenaeus wisely noted (*Haer.* 2.28.3):

> [A]ll Scripture, which has been given to us by God, shall be found by us perfectly consistent; and the parables shall harmonize with those passages which are perfectly plain; and those statements the meaning of which is clear, shall serve to explain the parables; and through the many diversified utterances [of Scripture] there shall be heard one harmonious melody in us, praising in hymns that God who created all things.

In Justin's *Dialogue with Trypho* (65.2), he rebukes Trypho for having attempted to cast doubt on the consistency of the Scriptures: "I am entirely convinced that no Scripture contradicts another." The Rule of Singularity is thus reflected in the complementarity of the constituent parts of the canon, a congruence that is the consequence of the Bible being divine discourse.[102]

---

100. In W. H. Griffith Thomas, *The Principles of Theology: An Introduction to the Thirty-Nine Articles* (London: Longmans, 1930).

101. Gamble, *The New Testament Canon,* 79. The existence of multiple editions of "Study Bibles" besprinkled with cross-references testifies to the importance of the Rule of Singularity for the Christian community. Frances Young finds that in patristic exegesis, cross-references were frequently made in order to discern the sense intended by the authors, the whole approach to the text being shaped by "well-rehearsed assumptions that Scripture was a unity" ("The 'Mind' of Scripture: Theological Readings of the Bible in the Fathers," *IJST* 7 [2005]: 133–34).

102. One danger of carrying the concept of this complementarity and congruence too far is the inevitable synoptic readings, especially of the Gospels; for instance, the valiant attempts to harmonize seemingly contradictory texts: the multiple cock crowings at the time of Simon Peter's denial of Christ, the Matthean and Lucan genealogies of Jesus Christ, the Sermon on the Mount (in Matt 5–7) and the Sermon on the Plain (in Luke 6), the accounts of the "Temple Cleansings," the number of trips to Jerusalem undertaken by Jesus, etc. However, the very existence of the fourfold Gospel indicates that the church as a whole does not hold that the Gospels be harmonized at all costs, ablating the discrete agendas of their individual authors. See the discussion on the Gospel of Mark in chapter 2.

This rule enables the diverse texts of the Bible to project a world in front of the canon in a united and coordinated fashion. The contribution of each pericope complements that of every other to yield a fully orbed depiction of the canonical world. Together, the particular elements or facets of the world that are projected by individual texts compose the singular and plenary world in front of the canonical text.

RULE OF FINALITY

The Rule of Finality affirms that the final form of the canonical text should be considered the object of interpretation for applicational purposes.

The Rule of Finality designates the final form of the text of Scripture as the basis and context for the undertaking of interpretation that leads to application. The synchronic view that the Rule of Finality espouses is opposed to the diachronic bias of the historical-critical tradition.[103] The synchronic approach affirms the importance of working with the final form of the canon as we now have it. The diachronic approach is criticized by Francis Watson for "dissipating its energies on speculative reconstructions [of textual forebears] that serve only to distract attention from the texts themselves." It is the integrated function of the text in its relatively stable final shape, rather than discrete functions in hypothetical precursors, that is to be accorded precedence.[104] Preachers, in particular, should focus on the text as it stands, rather than seeking to go *behind* it, in a search for its antecedents or to identify the natural history of textual development. It behooves interpreters to align themselves to the text after the fashion of the community that calls the canonical Scriptures its own, a community that has continued to use the final form of the canonical text, considering that form of the text alone as having utility for applicational—thus, preaching—purposes.

The structuring of individual psalms within the canonical Psalter gives evidence of the significance of the final form of that larger corpus in which they appear. For instance, the close connection between Pss 1 and 2 enables them to serve jointly as the introduction to the compilation. On the one hand, in these

---

103. Brevard S. Childs, *Introduction to the Old Testament as Scripture* (London: SCM, 1979), 75.
104. *Text, Church and World*, 16–17, 35.

chapters, are the "just"—those whose lives are molded by the Torah, whose ways are known to Yahweh, and whose allegiance is to Yahweh's anointed; their happy lot is announced in 1:1 and 2:12 (they are "blessed," אַשְׁרֵי, 'ashre). On the other hand are the "wicked," the "sinners," the "scoffers," and others of the same rebellious ilk; their doom is proclaimed in 1:6 and 2:11–12 (they will "perish," אָבַד, 'abad).[105] Indeed, the joint nature of the prologue, linking Pss 1 and 2, is echoed in the variant reading (*Codex Bezae,* D [fifth century]) for Acts 13:33, where Ps 2 is cited with the words ἐν τῷ πρώτῳ ψαλμῷ γέγραπται (*en tō prōtō psalmō gegraptai,* "in the first psalm it is written"). This notable inauguration of the Psalter is renewed and revived in Ps 149, where ultimate victory over the unrighteous is achieved. The "nations," "peoples," "kings," and "nobles"—the insurrectionists in 2:1–2—now become the objects of Yahweh's retribution in 149:7–9. The locus of the king's anointing, Yahweh's holy mountain, Zion (2:6), evolves into the parent whose children rejoice in their king (149:2). The subjugation of the riotous ones with a "rod of iron" (2:9) also reappears in 149:8, where apparently the same horde is bound with "fetters of iron." All of this signals a careful and systematic effort to organize the entire collection of Psalms, evidence of which is visible in both its opening and closing sections. The final canonical form of the book thus appears to have been deliberately collated to perform its integral role within Scripture, the projection of a canonical world; one does not need to work with textual precursors for interpretation, at least for applicational purposes.[106]

In Judaism, the estimation of the final form of the text as sacred is evident in the system of *kethib* ("[what is] written") and *qere* ("[what is] read"). Readings in the margins of the Masoretic text of the OT distinguish a small number of those instances where the traditional recited version of the Hebrew text (*qere*) differs from the traditional written version (*kethib*).[107] James Barr has suggested that the person reciting the text usually did so from memory and therefore did not need the *qere* instructions for reading purposes. What the system was

---

105. Joseph P. Brennan, "Psalms 1–8: Some Hidden Harmonies," *BTB* 10 (1980): 25–26.

106. This is not to decry the efforts of scholars seeking to arrive at the final form of the text—the goal of textual criticism. Rather, the rule simply discourages, particularly in the preaching enterprise, excessive speculation about textual precursors at the expense of attending to the present form of the text.

107. For instance, Ruth 3:5 has אֵלַי (*'elay,* "to me") in the *qere* (i.e., that word was traditionally recited), but not in the *kethib* (i.e., it was not recorded in the text). However, many English translations choose to include the phrase.

designed to preclude, rather, was the error of a scribe who, misled by the strongly remembered recitation tradition, might record the wrong graphic signs: he might mistakenly put down the recited tradition in his transcript, not the traditionally written version. The *qere* notations, therefore, may have served as a rendition of the reading tradition intended to prevent scribes from erroneously lettering the text that way—a clear case of respect for the final form, the *kethib*, of the text, even at the risk of diverging from the read, recited, and familiarly heard version.[108] It is the text itself, in its final form, that is to be privileged.

The Rule of Finality takes the judgment of the process of canonization as authoritative and perpetuates this authority in the final disposition of the text. In this decisive role in the interpretation of the canon, the rule establishes and fixes the profile of each individual text of the Bible. This is, of course, not to deny the imprecision of what exactly constitutes the completed form. As stated, the Rule of Finality simply sees a fixity of text-form as bearing the most utility for the community that recognizes the text as Scripture; the rule itself does not recommend what that final form should look like for any given tradition. Text critical issues notwithstanding, the Rule of Finality asserts its importance, despite the blurring of the borders of its object—the final canonical form. Fuzziness does not render a given text unrecognizable or unusable. Or as Lawrence Lessig declared, "Fray at the border does not of necessity undo the cloth."[109] As the plethora of modern translations of the Bible and their widespread utilization amply attest, the final form, as far as it is attainable, is adequate for the faith and practice of the church, as it has indeed been for over two millennia. Both Eusebius (*Quaestiones ad Marinum* 1) and Jerome (*Ep. ad Hedybiam*), for instance, discuss the variant endings of Mark, entertaining more than one option without questioning the Gospel's utility on the basis of that uncertainty.[110] Imprecision at the edges is no bar to application. A certain degree of inexactness is acceptable, and does not render application of biblical texts to daily life impossible. For

---

108. James Barr, "A New Look at *Kethibh-Qere*," in *Remembering all the Way...* (Oudtestamentische Studiën 21; ed. B. Albrektson; Leiden: Brill, 1981), 36–37; and Barton, *The Spirit and the Letter*, 123–24.

109. "Fidelity and Constraint," *Fordham L. Rev.* 65 (1996–1997): 1417.

110. See James A. Kelhoffer, "The Witness of Eusebius' *ad Marinum* and Other Christian Writings to Text-Critical Debates concerning the Original Conclusion to Mark's Gospel," *ZNW* 92 (2001): 78–112. Even today, the same issue of where Mark 16 concludes generates practices that are unique; the example, admittedly extreme, of serpent-handling prevalent amongst certain sects of Pentecostalism in the southeastern U.S. is to a significant extent dependent upon Mark 16:18. See W. Paul Williamson and Howard R. Pollio, "The Phenomenology of Religious Serpent Handling: A Rationale and Thematic Study of Extemporaneous Sermons," *JSSR* 38 (1999): 203–8.

homiletical purposes, the final form of the text effectively projects a canonical world that is sufficient to enable a valid movement to application.

RULE OF APPLICABILITY

The Rule of Applicability asserts that every text in the canonical Scriptures may be utilized for applicational purposes by the church universal.

All the biblical writings are to be utilized in the life of the Christian community for the determination of its faith and the coordination of its practices "because the power of God's kingly rule graciously shapes human identity and empowers new forms of life in persons through Scripture." The divine discourse that the canon is, renders it efficacious for the transformation of the individual and community into the will of God.[111] The canon asserts the right of every one of its constituent parts to be heard: *all* Scripture is profitable for application, to render the child of God ἄρτιος (*artios*, "complete/competent/capable") for every good work (2 Tim 3:16–17). Neither did Paul hesitate to confirm, in Rom 15:4, that "whatever was written" in earlier times was written for the instruction of the contemporary reader. The canon mandates application of all Scripture because all Scripture is efficacious, and all Scripture is efficacious because all Scripture is divinely empowered; thus is begotten the Rule of Applicability that announces the potential of all Scripture for application. This rule expects that no text included in the canon will be disregarded for the purposes of application. No part of the canon is without worth; for instance, in 1 Cor 9:9, Paul considers Deut 25:4, a relatively unimportant text in the OT, as significant for the practice of the community of believers. If the canon projects a world in front of itself, and individual texts portray facets thereof, then for the discernment and appropriation of the plenary world, all texts must be utilized. It is the totality of the canonical package—the diverse forms of its communicative action—that governs the activities of the people of God.[112]

However, Gamble's assertion that "the creation of the canon had a leveling effect upon its contents" may not be historically sustainable. Not all texts were treated equally. It seems, instead, from the early days of the church, that ecclesial

---

111. David H. Kelsey, "The Bible and Christian Theology," *JAAR* 48 (1980): 395.

112. Kevin J. Vanhoozer, *The Drama of Doctrine: A Canonical-Linguistic Approach to Christian Theology* (Louisville: Westminster John Knox, 2005), 149–50.

practice utilized some books of the corpus more than others: Genesis, Psalms, and the prophecies of Isaiah appear to have had more currency than other canonical texts. A complete literary work presumes the thematic and formal relevance of all its constituent details, but that is not to say that *all* those details are equally relevant at any given time. Rather, "to identify the structure of a work is to construct a *hierarchy* of relevance that makes some of its details central and others peripheral. No detail, however, can be completely irrelevant," or, at least, permanently irrelevant.[113] Despite the potential variation in degree of relevance between texts, every individual portion of the canon must be construed as contributing, in its own fashion, to the projection of the canonical *world in front of the text*.

Canonicity of the corpus assigns each of its constituent pericopes equal weight, potency, and normativity for life transformation. Every pericope is thus profitable in moving readers towards Christlikeness (see chapter 4). The Rule of Applicability thereby renders the canon potentially relevant in every part for every believer in every era. Chrysostom declared that what was written in the Bible was "written for us" and, therefore, worthy of diligent attention.[114] The Talmud, citing Ex 13:8, also asserted the relevance of the Scriptures for all: "It is therefore incumbent on every person, in all ages, that he should consider it as though he had personally gone forth from Egypt" (*m. Pesaḥ.* 10). Such an acceptance of the universal relevance of the biblical text emphasizes the significance of the Rule of Applicability.[115]

---

113. Gary Saul Morson, *The Boundaries of Genre: Dostoevsky's* Diary of a Writer *and the Tradition of Literary Utopia* (Austin, Tex.: University of Texas Press, 1981), 42; Gamble, *The New Testament Canon,* 75. This hierarchy of relevance may, in practical terms, be a contravention of this Rule of Applicability for, over a period of time, when certain books are preached from more often than others, those less-preached texts are being effectively relegated to some degree of insignificance and neglect.

114. Chrysostom, *Hom. Gen.* 2:2. The Bible itself consistently affirms the relevance of its message for future generations. The words of the Mosaic law, for instance, were expressly intended to transcend the immediate audience: in Deut 29:14–15, Yahweh explicitly establishes his covenant not only with those Israelites present, but also with "those who are not with us here today." Also see Deut 6:6–25; 31:9–13; 2 Kgs 22–23; Neh 7:73b–8:18; Ps 78:5–6; Matt 28:19; Rom 15:4; 1 Cor 9:10; 10:6, 11; 2 Tim 3:16–17; etc.

115. While the emphasis on universality of relevance in the Rule of Applicability may be widely accepted in principle, large tracts of Christendom do not necessarily agree that every portion of the canon can be applied to everyone, everywhere. The fact that the NT seemingly declares that the Mosaic law is no longer in force upon those of the new covenant (Rom 6:14; 10:4; Eph 2:15) raises the question of whether this rule is too broadly stated (see chapter 3 for a discussion of this very issue, and a suggested resolution). Should some texts be eliminated from consideration for preaching and application? Christian Reconstructionists (theonomists) would demur: biblical law, for them, ought still to be applicable as such today. See William S. Barker and W. Robert Godfrey, eds., *Theonomy: A Reformed Critique* (Grand Rapids: Zondervan, 1990). In any case, the Mosaic code remains firmly entrenched in the Christian Bible, and lectionaries continue to draw from it, assuming that the Pentateuch can be treated like other biblical material.

The concern for recontextualization and application of the canonical Scriptures dominated both Jewish and Christian communities from very early days. Expositional application was a fixture of synagogue worship. Philo observed that on the Sabbath, a day of learning for all, Scripture is read and "some of those who are very learned explain . . . what is of great importance and use, lessons by which . . . lives may be improved."[116] This Jewish orientation of reading for application was retained in the hermeneutics of the church. Justin Martyr's description of a second-century worship service in Rome noted that after the reading of the Gospels, "the presider verbally instructs, and exhorts to the imitation of these good things" (*1 Apol.* 67). Of an expositor of the Scriptures, Augustine wrote that the aim to be pursued by such a one was "to be listened to with understanding, with pleasure, and *with obedience.*" This church father also borrowed from Cicero, on the goal of the orator: "instructing is a matter of necessity, delighting a matter of charm, and *moving them* a matter of conquest."[117] Application of Scripture was to be the culmination of interpretation.

The reverence and respect that God's people have accorded Scripture, and the responsibility with which its exposition has been undertaken over the centuries, amply testify to the applicability of the canon. The exuberant production of commentaries, homilies, and tracts that have been developed register this pre-eminent quality of the Bible. The early church was instrumental in encouraging a proliferation of such interpretive tomes on Scripture. By Epiphanius's account (*Pan.* 64.63.8), the prodigious output of Origen included about 6,000 writings, falling into three categories—commentaries, homilies (on almost the entire Bible; over 200 preserved), and *scholia* (brief summaries of difficult biblical texts).[118] Equally productive was Chrysostom, who bequeathed over 900 sermons (i.e., those that survive), a large proportion of them being homilies on scriptural texts: 55 on Acts, 34 on Heb, 15 on Phil, 16 on 1–2 Thess, etc.[119] Ironically, even the myriad controversies that have dogged the church throughout its

116. *Spec. Laws* 2.15.62. Also see *Hypoth.* 7.13.

117. *Doctr. chr.* 4.15.32; and 4.12.27 (from Cicero, *Or. Brut.* 21) (italics added). Augustine decried the futility of persuading hearers of the truth, or delighting them with style, if the learning process did not result in action (*Doctr. chr.* 4.13.29).

118. For an ordered list of the works of Origen mentioned in Jerome's *Ep. ad Paula*, see Henri Crouzel, *Origen* (trans. A. S. Worrall; Edinburgh: T. & T. Clark, 1989), 37–39.

119. See Wendy Mayer and Pauline Allen, *John Chrysostom* (London: Routledge, 2000), 7; and J. N. D. Kelly, *Golden Mouth: The Story of John Chrysostom—Ascetic, Preacher, Bishop* (London: Duckworth, 1995), 132–33.

existence testify to the applicability of the corpus. Scripture matters, therefore interpretations matter and are material enough to be vigorously defended, as indeed they were, sometimes even violently.[120]

The Rule of Applicability testifies to the prescriptive, perennial, and plural significance of the biblical canon for the faith and practice of the church, asserting the universal relevance of this canonically recontextualized colligation of documents. This is a text that must be applied by those who acknowledge this corpus as their Scripture. In such application, readers inhabit the *world in front of the text* with its precepts, priorities, and practices, thus aligning the community of God of all time and in all places into the will of God.

RULE OF ECCLESIALITY

The Rule of Ecclesiality obligates the reading of Scripture for applicational purposes to be conducted under the auspices of the community that recognizes its canonicity.

The Bible is, without doubt, the church's book and, therefore, attributing to that book the qualities and properties of Scripture is to acknowledge the preeminence of the canon in shaping the life of the church and the individual when it is employed in the context of the Christian community.[121] Thus, for its reading and application, the arena of action is the congregation of God's people of all time. This normative, fixed corpus of religious literature is to be interpreted within the community of faith that acknowledges it as Scripture and affirms its applicability to its life.[122] The hermeneutical significance of the Rule of Ecclesiality is that it calls upon its readers to maintain interpretive solidarity with the Christian community. This rule contends that Christians and local congregations, as part of the one, holy, catholic, and apostolic church, must not seek to interpret Scripture as if they were the only ones ever to undertake such an

---

120. It may also be argued that these bellicose polemics and the often irreconcilable dissensions only prove that while agreement may be widespread on the Rule of Applicability of the canonical text, how exactly the text is to be applied is up for debate. Iconography, creedal clauses, glossolalia, timing of future events, baptism, indulgences, etc., have all been bones of contention, generating considerable disunity within the church.

121. Aichele, *The Control of Biblical Meaning*, 20.

122. Brevard S. Childs, *Biblical Theology in Crisis* (Philadelphia: Westminster, 1970), 99; Kelsey, *The Uses of Scripture*, 91–93.

endeavor; the task of biblical hermeneutics is to be conducted in concert with the universal community of God, past and present.[123] Indeed, the same Holy Spirit who invigorates and empowers the body of Christ, and who inspired the text of Scripture, continues to illuminate readers of the biblical text (1 Cor 2:12–15). At least two millennia of evidence of this enlightenment is available to the reader today. It is the presence of the Holy Spirit in the church throughout the ages that makes possible the assertion that the right reading of the canon is the reading of the church which, after all, is the *creatura verbi divini* ("creature of the divine word") and subject to it.

Origen asserted that "the teaching of the church . . . is to be accepted as truth which differs in no respect from ecclesiastical and apostolical tradition" (*Princ.*, preface), echoing the claim of Scripture itself that the church of the living God is "the pillar and support of the truth" (1 Tim 3:15). It is the responsibility of the church universal, charged with the custody of the Scriptures, to serve as the conduit and channel for the truth therein. Irenaeus declared that it was the church that "receiving the truth from the apostles, and throughout all the world alone preserving them in their integrity, has transmitted them to her sons" (*Haer.*, preface). Such a Rule of Ecclesiality clearly had ramifications for the practices of the early church, especially with regard to guarding orthodoxy. One of the bases of the rejection of Arianism by Athanasius in the third and fourth centuries was that the heresy was "unworthy of communion with the church," and "although it receive[d] the support of the Emperor and of all mankind, yet it was condemned by the church herself" (*Ep. mort. Ar.* 4). The Rule of Ecclesiality, thus, operated implicitly from the emerging days of the church.[124] This rule governs interpretation by keeping it within the constraints of what has generally been considered orthodoxy by the church universal. With regard to

---

123. Stephen E. Fowl, *Engaging Scripture: A Model for Theological Interpretation* (Malden, Mass.: Blackwell, 1998), 205; Webster, *Word and Church*, 64. This is, of course, not to deny the interpreter independence or to deprecate pioneering scholarship; it is but the sounding of a caution against idiosyncratic readings of Scripture. Neither does this rule generate an artificial polarity between tradition and Scripture; the Rule of Ecclesiality does not require the interpreter to opt for a stance that pits one against the other.

124. However, one must inject here a note of caution. What is "ecclesial" is often a matter that is decided in the eye of the beholder and adjudicated by those in power. While wide acceptance of the Rule of Ecclesiality laid down the path of what is generally considered orthodoxy, the numerous schisms and secessions that have occurred in the last two millennia—not least of which was the Protestant Reformation of the sixteenth century when Luther broke away from the established order of the church— suggest that this rule may not command universal subscription.

texts that appear to support multiple interpretations, Christian communities can at least agree that not *all* interpretations are contextually legitimate.[125]

To acknowledge the canon is to lobby for the use of this body of texts in particular ways approved by the body of Christ for ecclesial faith and praxis. The primary locus for such a mode of reading and preaching is the church, both local and universal, a setting that provides the direction and thrust for its interpretation, as well as the criteria by which the validity of such readings may be judged. In short, there can be no dichotomy between the canon and the community that treasured it. Vanhoozer perceptively comments that "the church is less the cradle of Christian theology than its *crucible*: the place where the community's understanding of faith is lived, tested, and reformed."[126] The church is rightly the divinely authorized arena for the reading and interpretation of Scripture. The depiction of the world projected by the canonical text is therefore governed by the hermeneutic of the church, the primary agent of its interpretation and application. Thus the Rule of Ecclesiality functions as a guardian of biblical hermeneutics, providing a communal constraint upon the shape and scope of the *world in front of the text*.[127]

RULE OF CENTRALITY

The Rule of Centrality focuses the interpretation of canonical texts for applicational purposes upon the pre-eminent person of Christ and his redemptive work that fulfills the will of the Father in the power of the Spirit.

The Rule of Centrality points the interpreter to what God has done, is doing, and will do, in and through Christ, underscoring the pivotal nature Christology plays in the orientation of the canon. Indeed, Christology plays a key role in the overall purpose of God with regard to humanity. It is in the image of Christ, the Son of God, that God intends to conform those who have placed

---

125. Umberto Eco argues that "any community of interpreters . . . can frequently reach (even though non-definitively and in a fallible way) an agreement" about the text under consideration, ruling out readings that are clearly groundless (*The Limits of Interpretation* [Bloomington, Ind.: Indiana University Press, 1990], 41).

126. Vanhoozer, *The Drama of Doctrine*, 25; also see Childs, *Biblical Theology in Crisis*, 99.

127. At the same time, this rule also reminds the preacher stationed within a local ecclesial context to attend to the specificity of the circumstances of that particular body of believers, for application is to be tailored to the unique situation of a given assembly of auditors.

their trust in this Second Person of the Trinity as their only God and Savior (Rom 8:29). This rule therefore subsumes under its aegis all the discourses in the canon, for the communicative action of Scripture is geared towards achieving this goal of restoring the *imago Dei* in man. In fact, what the canon is doing is offering a theological description of Jesus Christ and Christlikeness; this is the content of the world in front of the canonical text, a picture of the perfect Man. Scripture's focal point is the key figure of *Heilsgeschichte*, the Lord Jesus Christ, the paramount *imago Dei* himself (Col 1:15; 2 Cor 4:4; Heb 1:3). All interpretation of the Bible must be in concord with this bedrock—the image of Christ portrayed by the canon.[128]

The Rule of Centrality, of all the rules, is perhaps the one that has had the widest acceptance among Christians. Nevertheless, the mode of application of this rule has not won universal endorsement. What sort of transaction is the interpreter to perform on OT texts, for instance, to see Christ therein? Variations in approaches to this issue (allegorical, typological, redemptive-historical, promise-fulfillment, etc.) render the application of this Rule of Centrality a somewhat delicate operation. The strategy recommended by this work for preaching purposes is unique—a *christiconic* mode of interpretation (see chapter 4).

The incarnated Word portrayed in the inscripturated word is the ultimate goal of revelation, the *summum bonum* to which mankind is called to be aligned, and in whose image it is to be conformed. Preaching Christ is rightly the goal of the homiletical endeavor, i.e., proclaiming Christ as the *imago Dei* portrayed in every portion of the grand narrative of Scripture. This Second Person of the Trinity, the Lord Jesus Christ, is the only one who fulfilled all the demands of God, perfectly and without residue, for he is the power of God and the wisdom of God, in whom is the fullness of deity.[129] The plenary depiction of the Christ, the image of God, is the *telos* of the entire canon and the world it projects, and it is the will of God to conform his people to this image of his son (Rom 8:29). Thus, the Rule of Centrality superintends the interpretation of Scripture geared

---

128. In the divine act of communication, Jesus Christ takes center stage: as God, Christ is the sender; as the incarnate Word, he is the message; as the one who fulfilled God's word, he is the perfect receiver. Christ's person and work, therefore, form the focus of all hermeneutical operations upon Scripture. See Graeme Goldsworthy, *Gospel-Centred Hermeneutics: Biblical-Theological Foundations and Principles* (Nottingham, U.K.: Apollos, 2006), 56. The concept of every biblical pericope portraying a facet of the canonical image of Christ is central to the preaching endeavor, and will be dealt with in detail in chapter 4.

129. Matt 5:17; 1 Cor 1:30; Col 2:9.

to application, and plays a critical role as guardian of the hermeneutical process in homiletics, maintaining the focus of each pericope upon the *imago Christi*.

Section Summary: Special Hermeneutics

The Rules of Reading were proposed as guidelines for interpretation, with the caveat that these rules, while widely accepted, are not necessarily universal in ratification or application. Such rules are not creations *de novo;* rather, they are fairly self-evident and reflect the established practices of the church in reading Scripture in the two millennia of her existence. They function as the foundation for all subsequent interpretive activities that are intended to lead to application. Exercising their "rule" over the interpretive process, these rules lay the groundwork for the interpretation of specific biblical pericopes for application purposes.

SUMMARY: GENERAL AND SPECIAL HERMENEUTICS

Textuality has major consequences for the interpretation of any text (thus, *general* hermeneutics). As frozen and fixed discourse, texts move and this distanciation affects the relationships between text and author and hearer. Especially germane to the thesis of this work, distanciation also affects the referential function of the discourse—what the text is all about. This work, borrowing from Ricoeur, suggests that a world is projected in front of the text: what authors are *doing* with what they are saying, a function of the pragmatics of discourse. It is this projected world and its transhistorical intention that enables a text to speak to the future, to elicit valid responses from readers far removed from the original circumstances of the writing. Texts that have maintained this potency to influence readers across the boundaries of time and space are "classics." Such texts are perennial, they enable a plurality of future applications, and they are prescriptive, bidding the reader to inhabit the worlds they project.

The Bible, bearing those same characteristics, is, therefore, also a "classic," though of a special kind and mandating a special approach (thus, *special* hermeneutics). Its construal as Scripture by the church calls for special Rules of Reading that must be employed in the interpretation of this special text. Such rules are the virtual guardians of interpretation, and to abide by these widely recognized mandates is the responsibility of the interpreter. This is not to say that the employment of these rules will provide the interpreter with specific answers to what particular pericopes mean for the church today or how exactly they must be applied. Rather, these rules govern the overall process, serving as boundaries that must not be crossed. Interpretation of specific pericopes for preaching, within those boundaries, will be addressed in the next chapter. The next chapter will, therefore, move from the overviews in chapter 1 of general and special hermeneutics, to a narrower focus upon the preaching text employed in the homiletical undertaking. In this chapter, the world projected by the pericope will be defined and described as the theology of that pericope.

CHAPTER 2

PERICOPES, THEOLOGY, and APPLICATION

Πῶς ἀναγινώσκεις;
(Pōs anaginōskeis?)
How do you read?
LUKE 10:26

hapter 1 considered an essential facet of general hermeneutics pertinent to biblical interpretation for preaching: the pragmatics of the text—what authors *do* with what they *say.* Employing a concept from Paul Ricoeur, it was shown that what authors do is project a *world in front of the text*, with a transhistorical intention. World-projection thus endows texts with a future orientation and makes them "classics," rendering them perennial, plural, and prescriptive. The Bible, too, is a classic, but one that is *sui generis* by virtue of its being divine discourse. This characteristic demands a special hermeneutic, abridged in chapter 1 as a set of Rules of Reading. Such rules superintend the interpretation of Scripture, as boundaries that must be respected. With these rules in place and subscribed to, the interpreter can now proceed to the preaching text in focus, the pericope.

PREVIEW: PERICOPES, THEOLOGY, AND APPLICATION[1]

This chapter deals with the textual object of sermonic focus, the biblical pericope. While the theology of larger tracts of the biblical text have often been

---

1. Portions of this chapter are reworked from Abraham Kuruvilla, *Text to Praxis: Hermeneutics and Homiletics in Dialogue* (LNTS 393; London: T. & T. Clark, 2009).

the subject of scholarly focus, the theology of these smaller plots has received hardly any attention. The utilization of pericopes in an ecclesial setting will be considered first, drawing upon the concept of covenant renewal as a paradigm for the homiletical enterprise. Such a program, it will be proposed, is mediated by the segment of the canonical world that is projected by the pericope, to which world readers are bidden to align their lives. This segment of the plenary world in front of the canonical text that portrays God and his relationship to his people is the theology specific to a particular pericope (*pericopal theology*), and this theology, bearing a transhistorical intention, functions as the crucial intermediary in the homiletical move from text to praxis that respects both the authority of the text and the circumstances of the hearer. A case study of 2 Sam 11–12 demonstrates the discovery of the theology of that pericope, a hermeneutical transaction that privileges the text and discerns the world in front of it. Thus the pragmatic referent of the pericope is discerned, making possible valid application despite the distanciation of the text.

A two-step transaction is thereby envisaged in the preaching process: the task of the preacher consists in moving from pericope to theology, and subsequently from theology to application.

> The odd idea that preachers can move from text to sermon without recourse to theology by some exegetical magic or a leap of homiletic imagination is obvious nonsense. Theo-*logic* is required to understand the "whys" of episodic juxtaposition in plot, is required for a reading of deep structures, and is surely required if we wish to grasp the depth of implication in a field of concern. Moreover, if exegesis involves some translation of biblical imagery into theological meaning, homiletics involves a reverse procedure, namely the retranslation of theological understandings. . . .[2]

It is proposed here that pericopal theology enables the preacher to arrive at valid application that retains the authority of Scripture and remains relevant to the audience. This chapter will conclude by discussing the move from theology to valid application (exemplification), showing how this works not only in theological hermeneutics, but also in legal hermeneutics.

In short, chapter 2 will consider pericopes, their theology, and how application is derived from the theology of the pericope.

---

2. David G. Buttrick, "Interpretation and Preaching," *Int* 35 (1981): 57.

PERICOPES

As noted in the introduction, "pericope" (περικοπή, *pericopē*= section, passage) refers to a portion of the biblical text that is of manageable size for homiletical and liturgical use in an ecclesial setting. Though traditionally applied to segments of the Gospels, the term in this work will indicate a slice of text in any genre, as it is customarily utilized in Christian worship for preaching—in other words, a preaching text. It is through pericopes, read and exposited in congregations as fundamental units of the scriptural text, that the community of God corporately encounters the Bible. Indeed, it is impossible to conceive of a gathering of the faithful that does not implement such a reading and interpretation of biblical pericopes.

At first glance, the reason for the serviceability of pericopes might appear simple: the impossibility of grasping the entirety of the magnificent breadth of canonical thought on any single occasion, within the constraints of time spent in the corporate assemblies, dictates the employment of a smaller quantum of text that may be conveniently read and adequately exposited. In the second century, Justin Martyr reported on a Sunday gathering of Christians where the Gospels and the Prophets were read "as long as time permits" (μέχρις ἐγχωρεῖ, *mechris enchōrei*; *1 Apol.* 66), suggesting that a relatively fixed period of time had been allocated for the weekly event. Pericopes are eminently usable, given this temporal restraint.

Incontrovertible is the fact that no single sermon can capture and do justice to all the specific thrusts of all the pericopes in the canon, or even of all those smaller units within a single book. Instead, it is as individual pericopes that these portions of Scripture lend themselves to ecclesial use. The substantial and momentous nature of the content of the corpus promotes this use of pericopes in the ecclesial setting; the density of this divine discourse, packed as it is with significance and meaning, makes it possible, even advisable, to engage the Scriptures in smaller segments. Considered one at a time, pericopes allow a more intensive exploration of the depth and force of the text, enabling the particularity and potency of each pericope to impact the congregation. Thus, sermon by sermon, pericope by pericope, the various aspects of Christian life, individual and corporate, are effectively brought into alignment with the will of God (i.e., to God's ideal world and its precepts, priorities, and practices; see below). The goal of a homiletical endeavor, after all, is not merely to explicate the content of the chosen pericope, but to expound it in such a way that its implications for current hearers are brought home with conviction, to transform lives for God's glory.[3] Life change is not a one-time phenomenon, and neither is it accomplished instantaneously; it involves a lifetime of progressive, gradual, incremental reorientation and re-alignment to the demands of the *world in front of the text*. Such an approach to the edification of God's people necessitates the use, in any given sermon, of a unit-sized pericopal block of Scripture, incorporating a single thrust capable of being applied.

However, it is not only the constraint of time or the density of canonical content that imposes a limit upon the length of the biblical text utilized in the liturgical setting. The function of a pericope as a coherent "sense-unit" must also be taken into account. While Scripture is considered as a singularity, ex-hibiting univocity and congruence in the main, it obviously does not comprise one unbroken, run-on thought. And, while its substantial content is ultimately grounded upon God and his relationship to his creation, neither is Scripture a serialized and exclusive display of this abstract subject replicated in variegated fashion in multiple genres and in a multitude of pericopes. Instead, a number of specific matters pertaining to the Christian's life in relationship to God are addressed pericope by pericope. Several distinct topics germane to the faith and practice of the community in its orientation to God are registered within the canon. This makes the assimilation of the canon, pericope by pericope, es-sential. In other words, the canonical text projects a single world that comprises discrete segments featured by individual pericopes concerning particular is-sues. Any given pericope therefore is essentially a self-intact sense-unit bearing a relatively complete and integral idea that contributes to the whole, a defined portion of Scripture that reflects a unified span of thought and content, and that can be exposited within the constraints of time in the corporate gathering.[4] For the edification of believers, then, the employment of pericopal portions of the biblical text for preaching is of considerable significance.

---

3. Tertullian stated: "We assemble to read our sacred writings, . . . with the sacred words we nourish our faith, we animate our hope, we make our confidence more steadfast; and no less by inculcations of God's precepts we confirm good habits" (*Apol.* 39). Such practices of reading for application were prevalent in the Jewish context as well. Philo observed that on the Sabbath people were taught lessons of virtues "by which the whole of their lives may be improved" (*Spec. Laws* 2.15.62; also see *Creation* 128; and Josephus, *Ag. Ap.* 2.18).

4. For the purposes of this work, a theoretical acceptance of "pericope" as a preaching unit/text that carries a preachable idea will suffice, whatever its length, and however it is delimited; length and delimitation are, of course, the responsibility of the preacher.

Liturgical Use of Pericopes

Scripture has always been integral to the corporate activities of the community of God. For instance, Timothy is enjoined in 1 Tim 4:13 to give attention to the public reading of the Scriptures. The corpus attended to there was, of course, the OT. With time, these communal transactions came to utilize every major portion of the Christian canon. That the Law and the Prophets were in use in the early church is evident from Acts 13:15; Paul's sermon at Antioch is said to have commenced after the readings from these two sections of the OT. By the time of Justin Martyr, a weekly worship service in Rome also included readings of "the memoirs [ἀπομνημονεύματα, *apomnēmoneumata*] of the apostles" along with the writings of the Prophets (*1 Apol.* 67).[5] Thus it appears that by the mid-second century, at least some of the Gospels had also achieved authoritative liturgical status. In addition, even towards the close of the NT canon, the letters of Paul were beginning to be considered alongside the "rest of the Scriptures" (2 Pet 3:15–16).[6] Polycarp, late in the second century, asserted the pedagogical value of the Pauline Epistles, which "if you carefully study, you will find to be the means of building you up in that faith which has been given you" (*Phil.* 3.2). Later, these missives came to be included in the essential readings at corporate assemblies. The *Constitutions of the Holy Apostles* (ca. fourth century) includes information about the lections of Scripture; the Clementine Liturgy therein (8.5) appears to call for several biblical readings in ecclesial gatherings—from the Law and the Prophets, the Epistles, and the Gospels.[7]

While most of the evidence about the liturgical practice of the synagogue comes from the second century onwards, it is clear that quite early on, this pattern of communal utilization of Scripture in measured doses came to be directed by a lectionary. Appropriately divided sections of the text (pericopes) were read in continuous fashion (*lectio continua*), each subsequent reading taking up from where the previous reading had left off. This was the oldest approach to readings of the canonical text, and it was the standard practice on non-festival

---

5. In *1 Apol.* 66, Justin asserts that these memoirs were called "gospels" (εὐαγγέλια, *euangelia*).

6. Paul, himself, appears to have anticipated the authority of his writings; see 2 Thess 2:15; 3:14.

7. *Constitutions of the Holy Apostles* has another description of the liturgy that prescribes readings from the OT, Acts, Epistles, and Gospels, in that order (2.57). For the use of a fixed pericope by Jesus for preaching (Luke 4:16–30), see Kuruvilla, *Text to Praxis*, 145–50.

Sabbaths in Jewish synagogues.[8] In all likelihood, this protocol of continuous reading (*lectio continua*) was bequeathed to the church; this mode of contact with Scripture appears to have been the norm for most of early church history.[9]

In weekly expositions of pericopes of Scripture for the community, especially with a hiatus of several days between these corporate encounters with the Bible, there is always the danger of dislodging a narrow sliver of text from its broader context. This threat is attenuated, no doubt, by the necessary explanatory glosses within the sermon that clarify and explain the textual locus and logical environs of the pericope. However, particularly effective for maintaining the continuity of the subject matter of the text from week to week, and for respecting its trajectory, is *lectio continua*. A tacit assumption operates under the practice of continuous reading: individual pericopes find their proper position in the context of the rest of the book and the canon, for there is an integrity to the whole that must not be fragmented. Preaching passages of Scripture that he suspected would be considered offensive to his listeners, Chrysostom pleaded, "I have no wish to violate decency by discoursing upon such subjects, but I am compelled to it"; he was led perforce by providence to preach through all of the text, including those parts he did not particularly care for.[10]

By the time of the fifth century, however, the proliferation of feasts in the calendar and the allotment of specific biblical texts for each of those days rendered readings almost entirely *lectio selecta* ("reading selectively"), the textual assignment for an occasion being based upon the significance of a saint or that special feast. The complexity of the festal calendar required that texts allocated for particular occasions be listed formally, and lectionaries configured for this purpose came into existence.[11] Unlike for most of church history, the Middle Ages, therefore, suffered from a dearth of *lectio continua* sermons. It was not until the Reformers that this practice returned to popularity in churches. Martin

---

8. See the tractate *b. Meg.* 4; skipping passages of the Torah was looked upon with disfavour. Also see Harry Y. Gamble, *Books and Readers in the Early Church: A History of Early Christian Texts* (New Haven: Yale University Press, 1995), 208–11, 217.

9. Among others, Origen, the Cappadocian Fathers, Cyril of Alexandria, John Chrysostom, Ambrose of Milan, and Augustine abided by *lectio continua*, as evidenced in their methodical production of sermons from biblical books. See Hughes Oliphant Old, *The Reading and Preaching of the Scriptures in the Worship of the Christian Church* (7 vols.; Grand Rapids: Eerdmans, 1998–2010), 1:344; 2:36, 51–52, 83, 105–6, 173–74, 327, 345–68.

10. *Hom. Col.* 8 (on Col 3:5–7).

11. See Old, *The Reading and Preaching of the Scriptures*, 3:85, 289; and John Reumann, "A History of Lectionaries: From the Synagogue at Nazareth to Post-Vatican II," *Int* 31 (1977): 124.

Luther advised: "[O]ne of the books should be selected and one or two chapters, or half a chapter, be read, until the book is finished. After that another book should be selected, and so on, until the entire Bible has been read through." Huldrych Zwingli explained to the bishop of Constance in 1522 that he followed *lectio continua:* Matthew for a whole year, then Acts, then the letters to Timothy, the letters of Peter, and Hebrews.[12] Martin Bucer, too, was an avid proponent of *lectio continua,* calling for such a practice among all pastors, a reversion to the custom of the ancient church.[13] In sum, continuous reading and exposition emphasizes the relationship of the part to the whole: while the pericope is the smallest unit of text attended to in a given gathering, the community affirms its indissoluble unity with its textual neighborhood. Such an approach to Scripture also propagates the conviction that every part of the canon is worthy of exposition. *Lectio continua* requires the interpreter to seek application in every portion of the canon, pericope by pericope, week by week. As will be discussed later, a pericope portrays a segment of the larger world projected by the canon, offering this segment for appropriation by the people of God. The sequential employment of contiguous pericopes to discern the segments of the canonical world they project thus enables the full breadth of that plenary world to be appropriated over time.

Actualization or realization of Scripture in the "here and now"—the application of the text to the circumstances and contexts of the current auditors of the word—is the ultimate end of all exposition of biblical pericopes in the ecclesial setting. It comes as no surprise, therefore, that the Bible itself consistently asserts the relevance of its message for subsequent generations.[14] In achieving this goal of application, the formal utilization of a pericope in the context of the church gathering plays a crucial theological role. Pericopes are not merely conveniently packaged textual units suitable for weekly uptake. Their self-

---

12. Martin Luther, "Concerning the Order of Public Worship (1523)," in *Liturgy and Hymns* (vol. 53 of *Luther's Works;* trans. Paul Zeller Strodach; rev. Ulrich S. Leupold; Philadelphia: Fortress, 1965), 12; Gottfried Locher, *Zwingli's Thought: New Perspectives* (Leiden: Brill, 1981), 27.

13. *Martin Bucers Deutsches Schriften* (ed. R. Stupperich; Gütersloh, Germany: Mohn, 1960–1975), 7: 281. The Strasbourg Church Service (1525) promoted *lectio continua* rather than the preaching of "chopped-up fragments" (*stuckwerk*) (Friedrich Hubert, *Die Strassburger Liturgische Ordnungen im Zeitalter der Reformation* [Göttingen, Germany: Vandenhoeck and Ruprecht, 1900], 79). Calvin, also, preached slowly and surely through most of the books of the Bible, meticulously abiding by *lectio continua.* See T. H. L. Parker, *Calvin's Preaching* (Edinburgh: T. & T. Clark, 1992), 80.

14. See Deut 4:10; 6:6–25; 29:14–15; 2 Kgs 22–23; Neh 7:73b–8:18; Matt 28:19–20; Rom 15:4; 1 Cor 10:6, 11; 2 Tim 3:16–17; etc.

contained and defined nature, their potential use in *lectio continua* fashion, and their regular and periodic employment in church assemblies for application, all render them as agents of a unique and momentous phenomenon that serves to align the faithful with their God: this is the theological function of pericopes.

Theological Function of Pericopes

The theological role played by pericopes and their exposition in the worship of the church has not been a matter that has attracted much academic interest. While attention has been lavished upon the theology of individual books, broader themes, and that of the canon as a whole, consideration of the theology of these liturgically and homiletically critical tracts of Scripture, the functional units of the canon that confront the people of God weekly in formal fashion, has languished. Such a neglect is all the more regrettable since it is by these regular encounters with the demarcated entities of the biblical text that life change is addressed, so that individual and community may be aligned to the will of God. This work proposes that the theological function of pericopes is the facilitation of covenant renewal, the restoration of God's people to a right relationship with him.[15] As pericopes are sequentially preached from, the resultant transformation of lives reflects a gradual and increasing alignment to the values of God's kingdom (his "world"). Such an understanding of the role of pericopes is illustrated by the account of the prototypical transaction of covenant renewal in Neh 7–8.

Covenant Renewal in Nehemiah 7:73b–8:12

The paradigmatic notion of God's people as "purchased and delivered" by him reflects not only the primeval event of the exodus from Egypt, but also all acts of deliverance God performs for his people, especially the redemption wrought in Jesus Christ, the Passover Lamb.[16] The redeemed of God of all time thus become citizens of God's kingdom, for liberation by God involves a change of master— "a passage from a distressing, foreign and arbitrary yoke to contentment and

---

15. I do not intend any particular biblical covenant when using the term "covenant renewal." It simply serves as a convenient template for the description of the alignment of God's people to their sovereign in a formal and corporate context, in response to the preaching of God's word.

16. Moses' and Miriam's Song of the Sea (Ex 15:1–21) clearly marked out the Israelites as having been bought and redeemed by Yahweh (Ex 15:16). This theme is also reflected in the NT in 1 Cor 6:20; 7:23; Titus 2:14; 1 Pet 1:18–19; 2:9; Rev 5:9; etc.

security under rightful authority."[17] This extraordinary relationship between Redeemer and redeemed stipulates that the maintenance of such a filiation be given significant and constant attention in the corporate life of the people of God. The transaction of covenant renewal provides the perfect occasion for the community to focus jointly and formally upon its unique status and particular responsibilities under God. Reminding itself of the status and responsibilities of their privileged position, the community, in covenant renewal, commits itself to aligning to the will of its divine sovereign. Just as clauses of contemporaneous ancient Near Eastern treaties, repeatedly and publicly spelled out at recurrent intervals, helped preserve relationships between clients and overlords, regular and frequent readings of their foundational text played a critical role in the Israelites' covenant relationship with Yahweh, the one to whom they owed ultimate allegiance.[18] However, distinct from every other secular enterprise of this sort, Israel's covenant renewal was Torah-centered, as she pledged loyalty and swore fealty to her Lord. In doing so, the nation placed itself under obligation to abide by the revealed will of God. Historically, therefore, the reading of Scripture was always intertwined with this principle of covenant renewal; it is particularly exemplified in Ezra's proclamation of the law in ca. 444 B.C.E.[19]

The reading of the law in Neh 7:73b–8:12 is considered one of the oldest descriptions of a "liturgy of the Word."[20] This event was the watershed phenomenon in the life of the postexilic community of Israel: it formed the climax of the Ezra-Nehemiah joint corpus. The missions of the two protagonists, Ezra and Nehemiah, converge precisely within this enterprise, and for the first time they are mentioned together in this section (8:9). Within the larger body of the account (6:1–12:47), the renewal of covenant forms the center of a chiasm.

---

17. David Daube, *The New Testament and Rabbinic Judaism* (London: Athlone, 1956), 273. For this concept of servanthood under God, see Lev 25:55; Isa 43:1; and, in the NT, Rom 6:17–23; 1 Cor 7:22; Col 4:7; etc.

18. Ancient Near Eastern documents attest to the readings of treaties and the transactions of covenant renewal on a periodic basis to remind subjects of their responsibilities to their sovereign. It is conceivable that such practices as classically flourished in the environs of Israel influenced that nation's concept of her relationship with God and her dealings with him. See Robert H. Pfeiffer, *One Hundred New Selected Nuzi Texts* (trans. E. A. Speiser; New Haven: American Schools of Oriental Research, 1936), 103. Gary Beckman, *Hittite Diplomatic Texts* (Atlanta: Scholars, 1996), 42, 47, 76, 86, details treaties that mandated repeated reading. See also Moshe Weinfeld, *Deuteronomy and the Deuteronomic School* (Winona Lake, Ind.: Eisenbrauns, 1992), 64–65.

19. Deuteronomy 31:10–13 reports on a similar transaction under Moses.

20. Old, *The Reading and Preaching of the Scriptures,* 1:95–96.

6:1–7:4	**A**	Completion of the city walls
7:5–73a	**B**	List of ancestral inhabitants
7:73b–10:39	**C**	Covenant renewal
11:1–12:26	**B'**	Repopulation of Jerusalem
12:27–47	**A'**	Dedication of the city walls

The location of the chiastic convergence (C) is significant. The interpolation of covenant renewal within the broader undertaking that restored the Holy City signified the importance of this transaction as the singular event that definitively reconstituted the children of Israel. It provided both the pivot for the account of rebuilding, and the prerequisite for the successful re-emergence and re-founding of the nation after years of having been wrenched into exile. With this milestone, the identity of the nation was rediscovered, and its standing before God re-established.[21]

In the accounting of this drama, the book of the law, rightly, occupied center stage; indeed, covenant renewal is always Scripture-centered and forms the basis of any realignment to God's will. Noteworthy in this regard is that of the twenty-one references to תּוֹרָה (*Torah*) in Nehemiah, all but two are found in the section containing the covenant renewal account (7:73b–10:39). One might go so far as to assert that Scripture-centering always leads to covenant renewal, whereby the precepts, priorities, and practices of God's world are established and realized in the life of the community. Bounded as it is between the detailed accounts of the rebuilding of the fortifications of Jerusalem—the formal restoration, if you will, of God's people—the act of covenant renewal under Nehemiah has wider theological ramifications for the community of God of all time. Covenant renewal, at the core of communal restructuring and reorientation to the will of God, may be considered the paradigm for the reading and exposition of Scripture undertaken in corporate contexts for the people of God.

Especially pertinent to this work is the activity of the Levites in Neh 8:7–8. Their task was to facilitate the community's comprehension of what God required of them. It had to be ensured that with any reading of Scripture, its content was understood and its application apprehended by auditors; this was the responsi-

---

21. Michael W. Duggan, *The Covenant Renewal in Ezra-Nehemiah (Neh 7:72b–10:40): An Exegetical, Literary, and Theological Study* (Atlanta: SBL, 1996), 73. For further details, see Kuruvilla, *Text to Praxis*, 151–55.

bility of the Levites (and it continues to be that of preachers today). The Levites' giving the sense of the reading involved an "explanation" (מְפֹרָשׁ, *mporash*), the outcome of which was "understanding."[22] The root בין (*byn*, "to understand") occurs six times in the account (8:2, 3, 7, 8, 9, 12), emphasizing the importance of the comprehension of the Scriptures for the spiritual formation of the community. Psalm 119:34 ("Give me understanding [בין], that I may observe your law, and keep it wholeheartedly") indicates that the end-point of such understanding is obedience.[23] The exertions of the Levitical mediators of Scripture in Neh 8 also bore fruit in the Israelites' subsequent response. Comprehension by the congregation included application of Scripture to their lives: an epistemological movement from worship, to hearing, to provisional understanding, to full cognition, to prompt and precise application—the celebration of the Feast of Tabernacles (Neh 8:9–12, 16–18). The fundamental thrust of Neh 8 is that Scripture reading with explanation leads to understanding, which in turn issues in joyful obedience (8:10–12, 17).[24] This is at the core of covenant renewal; the reading and exposition of the biblical text in a corporate, ecclesial context, an event mediated by the preacher, culminates in application that readjusts the congregation to their God and his demands, and restores them in proper relation to him, thus reaffirming their status as those purchased and delivered by God.

Pericopes as Literary Instruments of Covenant Renewal

The account in Neh 7–8 may be considered a prototype for all future communities that desire to orient themselves towards God and align themselves to the demands of his word. Such a conception of the role of pericopes of the biblical text as instruments of periodic covenant renewal must necessarily result in a response to the demands of God in the text (application), without which response, (re)alignment to God's will remains unrealized.[25]

Thus covenant renewal may be considered the conceptual model for all

---

22. The Aramaic term מפרש used in a document of ca. 428 B.C.E. denotes "plainly, exactly, or separately set forth" (see A. E. Cowley, *Aramaic Papyri of the Fifth Century B.C.* [Oxford: Clarendon, 1923], 51–52). The root of the word (פרש, *prsh*) in Lev 24:12 and Num 15:34 refers to legal judgments awaiting clarification.

23. The use of בין in the Hiphil in Neh 8 corresponds to its utilization in that stem in Prov 28:7—"He who keeps the law is an understanding son": obedience is intrinsic to comprehension.

24. See H. G. M. Williamson, *Ezra, Nehemiah* (WBC 16; Dallas: Word, 1985), 286, 299.

25. Such periodic call to renewal, and the contemporary weekly nature of preaching, is an acknowledgement of the humanity of God's people and their tendency to drift away from the will of God, calling for frequent reminders of their standing with their Creator and a fresh alignment to divine demand.

sermonic exposition of the Bible: it is a summons to God's people to return to and renew a Scripture-centered relationship with the one who is truly their sovereign. In other words, what is being sought in the weekly homiletical undertakings of the church is corporate alignment with divine demand. Pericopes of the biblical text, handled weekly in sermons, are best construed as literary instruments of covenant renewal and (re)alignment to divine demand. A pericope performs this crucial function by portraying a segment of the canonical world projected by the text of Scripture. It is to the divine demand in this segment (its transhistorical intention) that individuals are bidden, in each homiletical event, to orient themselves. In so doing they align themselves to the particular aspects of the will of God prescribed by that pericope. Covenant renewal thus forms the backdrop to all homiletical utilization of Scripture in the church setting.

The goal of regular reading and exposition of pericopes of Scripture in the gathering of the church, then, is application; at each such event a particular aspect of the life of the individual and community is addressed, as the pericope of that day dictates. Listeners are called to respond to the text by "inhabiting" the pericopal segment of the world projected in front of the canonical text. In that each pericope considers a specific facet of life lived in relationship with God—the divine demand of that pericope—covenant renewal is the cumulative outcome of expositions of pericopes conducted over time. As sermons are preached pericope by pericope, more and more facets of life are aligned to divine demand. The culmination of these ecclesial transactions is the reorientation of the church to the plenary world projected by the canon. This canonical world projected by Scripture depicts a mode of existence in which God's precepts operate, his priorities are supreme, and his practices are enacted: "precepts"—why things happen in the *world in front of the text*; "priorities"—what things matter in the *world in front of the text*; and "practices"—how things run in the *world in front of the text*. This, God's ideal world, is where his precepts are acted upon, his priorities are upheld, and his practices are conformed to. Such a divine world is a potential way of life open to those who, in obedience to Scripture, choose to live in the will of God by aligning their lives to demands of that world. As biblical pericopes are applied in the lives of readers and hearers, the projected world is appropriated by God's people, and covenant relationship is renewed, week by week. The facilitation of this realignment to divine demand is the responsibility of the preacher, the one in the community of God entrusted with the task of interpretation and application of the text, the chaperone of the move from text to praxis. This mediation of covenant renewal between God and his people, between sovereign and subjects, is a duty of immense gravity for the preacher, as emphasized in the mandate to Timothy: "I solemnly charge you before God and Christ Jesus . . . preach the word" (2 Tim 4:1–2).[26]

Section Summary: Pericopes

The pericope is an oft-neglected quantum of text, at least for the study of how it functions theologically within the body of God's people. As the fundamental unit of text encountered by Christians on a weekly basis, this omission is, to say the least, surprising. The liturgical function of the pericope was considered in this section, as well as their sequential reading and assimilation—*lectio continua*. It was proposed that pericopes function as agents of covenant renewal—the alignment of people with their divine sovereign and his demands. A pericope projects a segment of the canonical *world in front of the text* and it is to this segment that children of God are weekly called to be aligned. What each pericope propounds for consideration—the precepts, priorities, and practices of the world it projects—is, this work claims, the theology of the pericope.

THEOLOGY OF PERICOPES

The biblical pericope is not only a literary object, but also an instrument of action that projects a segment of the canonical world that, when inhabited, renews God's people in a right relationship with their sovereign. As the *object* of a creative literary enterprise, the text must be investigated for what is "behind" and "within" the text (i.e., its historical basis, rhetorical situation, and linguistic particulars). Interpretation, however, must not cease with the elucidation of these essential entities, but, considering the text as an *instrument* of action, must proceed further, to the discernment of the projected world "in front of" the text in order to derive valid application of the text and accomplish covenant renewal. This section will explore the operation of pericopes: authors are *doing* something with what they are *saying*; and pericopes project segments of the canonical *world in front of the text*. Furthermore, it will be submitted that this segment of the world projected by the pericope is the theology of that unit of text—*pericopal theology*. This section will conclude with a discussion of this

---

26. Similarly, Ezra's reading and proclamation of the law was an undertaking of great moment, executed by one "skilled in the law of Moses" (Ezra 7:6, 10), and one commissioned by Artaxerxes to teach the "law of your God" (7:25–26).

species of theology and a case study of the narrative of 2 Sam 11–12 demonstrating how pericopal theology is discerned.

Authors Are *Doing* Something

That the writers of Scripture were *doing* something with what they were saying was considered in chapter 1. Authors' literary products are agenda-driven and discoursed for a purpose, not merely created to convey information. For instance, Ladd asserted that the Gospels were "not pure, 'objective' history, if 'objective' means the work of detached, disinterested authors. Each evangelist *selected* his material and to some degree *shaped* his material to suit his particular theological and ecclesiastical interests."[27] And what each was trying to do was convey the theological thrust of the text, pericope by pericope: "the way in which the stories have been told has been more surely controlled by questions of a theological and religious nature than by purely historical concerns."[28] Dealing with narratives—and we shall focus on Mark's Gospel here as an example—authors have considerable freedom to deal with time and history as they wish, creating a discourse geared to further their theological goals.[29]

Authors' Freedom and Their Agendas

Consider the literary elements available to authors with regard to just one narrative facet—time: flash forward (e.g., the proleptic foretelling of Jesus' passion, Mark 8:31–32; 9:31–32; 10:33–34); flash back (e.g., the analeptic recounting of the death of John the Baptist, 6:14–29); summary (e.g., the condensation of Jesus' forty days in the wilderness, 1:13); ellipsis (e.g., the unmentioned departure of Judas from the gathering of Jesus with his disciples, 14:17–26; the silence with regard to the day following the crucifixion, 16:1); pause (e.g., Mark's stopping of the story clock to interpolate glossing remarks of his own, 7:3–4); stretch (or slow motion; not a feature of this Gospel at all—Mark's favorite word is "immediately," εὐθύς, occurring about forty times in the Gospel); repetition (iteration or an implication thereof, by means of the Greek imperfect tenses; e.g., 1:22; 3:21, 22); etc. The shackles of tyrannical time are shed by means of the literary

27. George Eldon Ladd, *I Believe in the Resurrection of Jesus* (Grand Rapids: Eerdmans, 1975), 74. Also see Daniel I. Block, "Tell Me the Old, Old Story: Preaching the Message of Old Testament Narrative," in *Giving the Sense: Understanding and Using Old Testament Historical Texts* (eds. David M. Howard and Michael A. Grisanti; Grand Rapids: Kregel, 2003), 411.

28. Ronald E. Clements, "History and Theology in Biblical Narrative," *HorBT* 4–5 (1982–1983): 56.

29. For an exploration of an entire Gospel in this fashion, discovering what the author was *doing* with what he was saying pericope by pericope, see Abraham Kuruvilla, *Mark: A Theological Commentary for Preachers* (Eugene, Oreg.: Cascade, 2012).

liberty possessed by the narrator—all done to accomplish his agenda.

Philip Scott puts it well: "The quarryman delivers the heaps of stone; the architect needs the stones cut and dressed. Mark was not a quarryman; he was an architect," and, as one, he was working with an intentional blueprint, cutting and dressing events into a textual edifice of his planning.[30] Thus, events of history—the actual sequence of events *behind* the text—are frequently molded, rearranged, and shaped, with some facts emphasized, others ignored, some summarized, others detailed. A possible analogy might be the difference between a portrait and a caricature: both represent the same person, but the portrait attempts to translate everything on the visage of the sitter to the image on the canvas, whereas the caricature "samples" a hooked nose, a beady eye, a cauliflower ear, or a bushy eyebrow. Not every physiognomic element is equally worthy of representation in a caricature; some elements are, and they are often emphasized and amplified.[31] Likewise a text—in particular for this discussion, a narrative—is more like a caricature than a portrait; not everything need be told, not everything need be minutely detailed, not everything needs to adhere precisely and meticulously to the original. An agenda-driven storytelling focuses upon certain aspects, aspects that further that agenda.

Mark, for instance, has his Gospel structured as one long journey with Jesus from Galilee to Jerusalem, while John, on the other hand, mentions at least three trips to Jerusalem that Jesus made during his years of ministry. And then, of course, Mark concludes his account abruptly in 16:8.[32] However, in 16:7 there is a clear indication that this is not *finis*; in fact, the journey is beginning again, with the exhortation to the disciples to return to Galilee where their Master would be waiting for them to commence the next iteration of the "trip of discipleship." For Mark, this structure furthers his goal of depicting discipleship as a journey. The writer's use of characters also reflects his intentional shaping of history: minor characters are largely positive in depiction, and the disciples

---

30. M. Philip Scott, "Chiastic Structure: A Key to the Interpretation of Mark's Gospel," *BTB* 15 (1985): 18.

31. See Ben Austen, "What Caricatures Can Teach Us About Facial Recognition," WIRED Magazine, July 2011. Cited June 3, 2012. Online: http://www.wired.com/magazine/2011/07/ff_caricature/all/1/.

32. I accept the Gospel as ending at Mark 16:8 (the "shorter" ending); the majority of scholars appears to hold this view. For comprehensive summaries on Markan endings, see, in addition to standard commentaries, Daniel B. Wallace, "Mark 16:8 as the Conclusion to the Second Gospel," in *Perspectives on the Ending of Mark: 4 Views*, by David Alan Black, Darrell Bock, Keith Elliott, Maurice Robinson, and Daniel B. Wallace (Nashville: Broadman & Holman, 2008), 1–39; Aída Besançon Spencer, "The Denial of the Good News and the Ending of Mark," *BBR* 17 (2007): 269–83; and Robert H. Stein, "The Ending of Mark," *BBR* 18 (2008): 79–98.

and religious authorities, largely negative. Obviously that cannot be true to life: surely the disciples and religious leaders must have performed more commendably than they are given credit for (see 12:34 for Jesus' approval of at least one scribe). It is equally likely there were minor characters in the Jesus story who were not necessarily always conducting themselves in the best light (the women in Mark 16, for example). In other words, Mark is purposefully *doing* something with what he is saying in each pericope.[33] He seeks "to do something to the hearer or reader" and "the Gospel is designed to seduce us permanently."[34] His goal, as well as the goal of all the other authors of Scripture, is a particular response of life-change from readers and listeners to their inspired words.

As Tzvetan Todorov declared: "No narrative is natural; a choice and a construction will always preside over its appearance; narrative is a discourse, not a series of events."[35] This is not to cast doubt upon the veracity of the narrator, but to assert that any narrator of any text has the freedom to prioritize, schematize, synthesize, and organize his raw material for his express purpose. "[T]he historian and the agent of history choose, sever and carve them [their raw materials] up, for a truly total history would confront them with chaos. . . . History is therefore never history, but *history-for*." Not everything that happened is recounted in exhaustive, encyclopedic fashion; thus every narrative "inevitably remains partial—that is, incomplete—and this is itself a form of partiality."[36] This is also true for the Bible: "In the Scriptures historiographic compositions are primarily ideological in purpose. The authoritative meaning of the author is not found in the event described but in the author's interpretation of the event, that is, his understanding of their [*sic*] causes, nature, and consequences. But that interpretation must be deduced from the telling." Block therefore calls for a "careful attention to the words employed and the syntax exploited to tell the story. But they also require a cautious and disciplined reading between the lines, for what is left unstated also reflects an ideological perspective."[37]

---

33. For an extended example of a particular incident, the cameo of Mark 14:51–52, being employed to *do* something, see Abraham Kuruvilla, "The Naked Runaway and the Enrobed Reporter of Mark 14 and 16: What Is the Author *Doing* with What He Is *Saying*?," *JETS* 54 (2011): 527–45.

34. Robert M. Fowler, *Let the Reader Understand: Reader-Response Criticism and the Gospel of Mark* (Minneapolis: Fortress, 1991), 10.

35. Tzvetan Todorov, "Primitive Narrative," in *The Poetics of Prose* (trans. R. Howard; Oxford: Basil Blackwell, 1977), 55.

36. Claude Lévi-Strauss, *The Savage Mind* (Chicago: University of Chicago Press, 1966), 257–58 (emphasis added).

37. Daniel I. Block, *Judges, Ruth* (NAC 6; Nashville: Broadman & Holman, 1999), 604–5.

In other words, for preaching purposes, to discover what the author is *doing* with what he is saying, the crucial undertaking is the consideration of the text itself. It is the text which must be privileged, for it alone is inspired. While some events *behind* the text may be revelatory, they are not inspired and thus not expressly "profitable for teaching, for reproof, for correction, for training in righteousness; so that the person of God may be adequate, equipped for every good work" (2 Tim 3:16–17). Again, this is not to claim that the events so described in the biblical text did not happen, but simply that it is the Holy Spirit's *biblical accounts* of those events that are to be attended to for life transformation, not the restoring and deciphering of those behind-the-text events themselves. It is the text that must be privileged. All this to say that the text is not merely a *plain glass* window that the reader can look *through* (to discern some event behind it). Rather, the narrative is a *stained glass* window that the reader must look *at*.[38] A stained glass window is carefully designed by the craftsman in accordance with a particular theme, style, location in the building, size and structure of window, nature and availability of glass, demands of patron, expertise of artist, etc. The glass, the stains, the lead, the copper, and everything else that goes into its production are meticulously planned for the appropriate effect, to tell a particular story. So too with narratives, textual or otherwise. The interpreter must, therefore, pay close attention to the text, not just to what is being said, but also how it is being said and why, in order that the agenda of the author may be discerned—what the author was *doing* with what he was saying. Instead, for the most part, much energy in biblical studies has been expended upon dissecting out the intricacies of the actual events that lie *behind* the text. For sure, the events behind the text are important: Christian faith is built upon certain constitutional events that happened as they were reported, and there is a place for the chronological organization and harmonization of these events. The focus for preaching, however, is not to be upon events *behind* the text (or anything else behind the text, including authorial methodology, writing material, etc.; see chapter 4 for more on this); rather, it is the inspired text, itself, that must be privileged—the theological agenda of the authors must be respected: the *world in front of the text*.

---

38. This metaphor is borrowed from Sidney Greidanus, *The Modern Preacher and the Ancient Text: Interpreting and Preaching Biblical Literature* (Grand Rapids: Eerdmans, 1989), 196: "[N]o historical narrative is a transparent windowpane for viewing the facts beyond; historical narratives are more like stained-glass windows which artistically reveal the significance of certain facts from a specific faith perspective. One must do justice to the text." Privilege the text!

Categories of Interpretive Approaches

How is this approach, that focuses on authors' *doings*, distinguished from other operations of biblical studies?[39] For purposes of illustration, some broad brushstrokes will be employed to discriminate between critical, traditional, and pragmatic views of approaching the textual narrative (the last of the three is the one proposed in this work).

If $A \to B \to C$ denotes the actual sequence of events A, B, and C behind the text in real life, the *critical* view of biblical narrative sees the text as likely mutating or transforming the historical sequence of events, a biased operation of the author, altering those events into a sequence of other happenings ($X \to Y \to Z$ in the text). The text is therefore like a ground glass window that is only a distorted version of reality: parts of the text are outright fabrications. The task of the interpreter, therefore, is to delve *behind* the text of this unreliable author to recover the interpretive goal, i.e., what actually happened ($A \to B \to C$).

The *traditional* view of biblical narrative admits that the author may have changed some of the historical events to some extent, but that those changes are not intended to deceive; rather, they serve to smoothen the telling of the story, and involve minor shifts in emphases or changes in chronology, etc., incidental variations from actual history that reflect authorial and literary idiosyncrasies ($A \to B \to C$, the set of actual events behind the text, becomes $a \to B \to c$ in the text: insignificant changes that do not amount to much). Such an approach, in general, does not take into account those "idiosyncrasies" as reflecting a particular authorial agenda—what the author is *doing*—and so the interpretive goal remains, as with the critical view, the ascertainment of the events *behind* the text, after straightening out those altered elements to re-create the real-life sequence: $A \to B \to C$. The text here is, therefore, like a plain glass window through which one sees events behind the text largely undistorted. An example of this endeavor is the tendency to harmonize the Gospel accounts. While admitting incidental variations in the four narratives, the traditional interpreter puts all four together to reconstruct a reasonable recital of historical events, and then proceeds to preach that reconstruction, with the result that the particular agenda of each of the writers

---

39. The discussion below borrows from John H. Sailhamer, *Introduction to Old Testament Theology: A Canonical Approach* (Grand Rapids: Zondervan, 1995), 75–83, but with significant modifications.

is obscured.[40] Needless to say, as was detailed in chapter 1, without arriving at the agenda of the author in a given pericope, there can be no valid application.

As against these views, the *pragmatic* approach espoused in this work seeks to privilege the text for the purposes of homiletics.[41] The agenda of the author determines how he narrates the events, what is said, how, and why. Thus some "alteration," if one is to call it that, is to be expected in *any* narrative, inspired or otherwise ($a \rightarrow B \rightarrow c$ becomes the agenda-driven account of the actual events $A \rightarrow B \rightarrow C$). The changes, emphases, structures, and styles, are intentional and point to what the author is *doing* with what he is saying. The distinctive of the pragmatic approach is that its interpretive goal is *not* the historical events and what actually happened; rather, its goal is the agenda of the author projected in front of the text, discerned by privileging the text. The text is, therefore, a stained glass window that tells a "story" in itself, *at* which one must look, rather than a ground glass or plain glass window *through* which one may gaze. That thrust (the *world in front of the text*, described below as the theology of the pericope) is what is to be preached ($a \rightarrow B \rightarrow c$).

APPROACH	EVENTS	TEXT	INTERPRETIVE GOAL	MODEL
CRITICAL	$A \rightarrow B \rightarrow C$	$X \rightarrow Y \rightarrow Z$	$A \rightarrow B \rightarrow C$	ground glass window
TRADITIONAL	$A \rightarrow B \rightarrow C$	$a \rightarrow B \rightarrow c$	$A \rightarrow B \rightarrow C$	plain glass window
PRAGMATIC	$A \rightarrow B \rightarrow C$	$a \rightarrow B \rightarrow c$	$a \rightarrow B \rightarrow c$	stained glass window

Every historical narrative, Hayden White declared, "has as its latent or manifest purpose the desire to *moralize* the events of which it treats," thus creating a "*moral* drama"—the agenda of the author, what he is *doing* with what he

---

40. Dynamic translators are particularly prone to engaging in this mode of interpretation focusing on the events *behind* the text. For instance, to my knowledge, שְׁמַע לְקוֹל דִּבְרֵי יְהוָה (*shma' lqol dibre yhwh*) in 1 Sam 15:1 is translated literally as "Listen to *the voice of* the words of Yahweh" only in the KJV and the NKJV. That redundancy is swept under the rug in all other major English translations. What the author really meant, translations assert, was: "Listen to the words of Yahweh" (or something close). Whereas, "voice" (קוֹל, *qol*) forms a critical element of the whole story and is the key to determining what the author was *doing* in that pericope. See, likewise, in 15:4 where קוֹל becomes "bleating" and "lowing" (also see 15:19, 20, 22, 24, for the significance of "voice" in the narrative). The author's *doing* with what he is saying is completely attenuated by a misguided enthusiasm for what actually happened *behind* the text (and, perhaps, for a smooth written rendition of those events in English). Instead, for preaching purposes at least, the interpreter *must* privilege the text, for only in so doing can one discover what is projected *in front of* the text.

41. Again, my perspective is from the pulpit: what preachers ought to do, what sermons ought to be.

is *saying*.[42] This is in no way a misrepresentation of facts. Rather, it is, pure and simple, "narrative"; such narratival and agenda-driven recounting of events is a characteristic of *all* storytelling, inspired or otherwise, that deals with historical events.[43] The story gets told in a particular fashion in narrative, in just one of the innumerable other ways the selected events and interpersonal encounters could potentially have been represented. The path actually chosen by the narrator was one that would effectively project the *world in front of the text* (what he was *doing* with what he was *saying*) and culminate in valid application for the reader. Scripture thus represents a "comprehensive 'curriculum of persuasion,'" designed to change lives for the glory of God.[44] Buttrick is surely right: "True 'biblical preaching' will want to be faithful not only to a message, but to an *intention*. The question, 'What is the passage [or author] trying to do?' may well mark the beginning of homiletical obedience."[45] How may one demonstrate this kind of submission to the particular text preached, the pericope?

Pericopes and Their Projected Worlds

Given that a pericope is both an object and instrument of action, it has a twofold thrust—and the mark of a classic text is its ability to function with this dual focus: it portrays the particular and specific, while it simultaneously yields a snapshot of what is universal and general: the *world in front of the text* bearing a future-directed transhistorical intention.[46] The classic text is thus rendered

---

42. "The Value of Narrativity in the Representation of Reality," in *On Narrative* (ed. W. J. T. Mitchell; Chicago: The University of Chicago Press, 1981), 11, 14, 19–20. He asks rhetorically, "Could we ever narrativize *without* moralizing?" (ibid., 23). Indeed, "narrative has the power to teach what it means to be *moral* beings" (idem, "The Narrativization of Real Events," in *On Narrative*, 253).

43. John A. Beck, *God as Storyteller: Seeking Meaning in Biblical Narrative* (St. Louis.: Chalice, 2008), 4–5.

44. Peter M. Candler, Jr., *Theology, Rhetoric, Manuduction, or Reading Scripture Together on the Path to God* (London: SCM, 2006), 60. Or as Meir Sternberg described, "[T]he biblical storyteller is a persuader in that he wields discourse to shape response and manipulate attitude" (*The Poetics of Biblical Narrative: Ideological Literature and the Drama of Reading* [Bloomington, Ind.: Indiana University Press, 1985], 482).

45. Buttrick, "Interpretation and Preaching," 58.

46. Shakespeare, Coleridge declared, could effect a "union and interpenetration of the universal and the particular," characteristic of "all works of decided genius and true science" ("The Friend: Section the Second, Essay IV," in *The Collected Works of Samuel Taylor Coleridge* [ed. Barbara E. Rooke; London: Routledge & Kegan Paul, 1969], 457). Goethe asserted that the poet "should seize the Particular and . . . thus represent the Universal" (*Conversations with Eckermann (1823–1832)* [trans. John Oxenford; San Francisco: North Point, 1984], 95). A philosopher, Philip Sidney claimed, provides only the abstract and general precept; the historian, on the other hand, gives only the concrete and particular. Neither is sufficient as it is to "make men good." Only "doth the peerless poet perform both," supplying the general precept *and* the particular example, i.e., the general and universal projected by the specific and particular ("An Apology for Poetry," in *Criticism: The Major Statements* [2nd ed.; ed. Charles Kaplan; New York: St. Martin's, 1986], 118–19).

perennially significant and prescriptive: it now has potential for a plurality of applications across the temporal and spatial gulf created by distanciation.

The projected textual world is the pragmatic referent, unique to the text and derived from the particulars of its inscription. Such referents of Scripture display to readers a world of divine values and demands, and offer to them the possibility of appropriating that world by subscription to those values and obedience to those demands. A new way of living—God's way—is depicted by the world projected by Scripture, and it is in the habitation of this world by the people of God that the text effects covenant renewal. The *world in front of the text*, located between ancient inscription and contemporary application, forms the hermeneutic intermediary by which application is facilitated. The textual corpus *in toto* projects a canonical *world in front of the text*, a world into which God's people are beckoned to enter. Scripture, in this reckoning, displays to readers how God relates to his creation, by portraying a world governed by divine precepts, priorities, and practices, and offers to believers the possibility of inhabiting that projected world by endorsement of those criteria.

However, in the weekly homiletical transaction that moves the church towards application, it is the pericope that remains the most basic textual component of covenant renewal. As the fundamental scriptural entity in ecclesial and homiletical use, and as the relatively irreducible textual element composing a single sense unit, each pericope projects a segment of that broader world projected by the canon. It is in, with, and through an individual pericope, that this specific segment of the canonical world is revealed. The cumulative world-projections of all the individual pericopes of Scripture constitute the plenary, singular, and integrated world in front of the canonical text. Weekly, however, God's people are called to respond to the preached text by inhabiting the pericopal segment of the larger canonical world, the details of which segment are unique to that portion of Scripture, and are derived from its particulars.

The task of the preacher, therefore, in interpreting a pericope for applicational purposes, is to move from the biblical text via the intermediary of the *world in front of the text* to arrive at relevant application in the modern day for specific listeners. Therein lies the genius of the projected world, for it is this pragmatic referent, with its transhistorical, future-directed intention, that makes possible valid application in contexts far removed from those of the original utterance or discourse (see chapter 1). Insofar as this move from text to praxis is accurately accomplished, and to the degree that the community, in obedient response, inhabits the world so projected, it participates in the ongoing and dynamic relationship between God and his creation—covenant renewal in operation.

Pericopal Theology

What is proposed in this work is that the world projected in front of the text is the *theology of the pericope* inasmuch as it portrays God and the relationship he intends to have with his people. It is a world wherein his precepts operate, his priorities are supreme, and his practices are enacted. This world bears a transhistorical intention that guides God's people to a correct response to the text. Therefore it can rightly be called "theology"—"that skein of thought and language in which Christians understand themselves, the Bible, God, and their everyday world."[47] Speaking as it does of God and his relationship with his creation, and bearing as it does direction for life change, this projected world is the concern and focus of theology as a discipline. Dale Ralph Davis is on the right track: "I'm using the term here to refer to the theology of a biblical text, that is, what the text means to say about God, his ways and his works. Or to put it a bit differently, I use the term to refer to the *intended message* of a biblical text."[48] This theological "intention" is the joint work of the human authors and the divine Author of Scripture. "The Spirit's goal is to bring us to view all reality in accordance with God's program of molding creation into conformity with the divine eternal purpose through Jesus Christ, the Son, so that as the community of Christ we might inhabit a world that truly reflects God's purposes for creation. Because this program is in part linguistic, participating in it is theological work."[49] The theology projected by a pericope is a specific segment of the larger canonical world, and all such segments together compose a holistic understanding of God and his relationship to his people. This composite

---

47. Paul L. Holmer, *The Grammar of Faith* (New York: Harper and Row, 1978), 9. As Kaufman noted, "[T]heology is, and always has been, an activity of what I call the 'imaginative construction' of a comprehensive and coherent picture of humanity in the world under God" (Gordon D. Kaufman, *An Essay on Theological Method* [3rd ed.; Atlanta: American Academy of Religion, 1995], ix).

48. Dale Ralph Davis, *The Word Became Fresh: How to Preach from Old Testament Narrative Texts* (Ross-Shire, U.K.: Mentor, 2006), 32.

49. Stanley J. Grenz and John R. Franke, *Beyond Foundationalism: Shaping Theology in a Postmodern Context* (Louisville: Westminster John Knox, 2001), 53–54.

and integrated canonical world is the basis of biblical faith and the foundation of covenant renewal.[50]

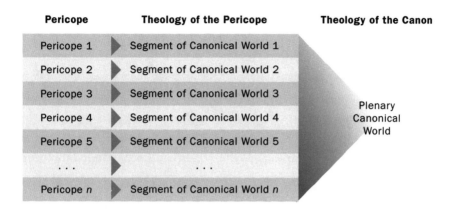

Pericopal Theology Defined

Thus *pericopal theology* by definition is *the theology specific to a particular pericope, representing a segment of the plenary world in front of the canonical text that portrays God and his relationship to his people, and which, bearing a transhistorical intention, functions as the crucial intermediary in the homiletical move from text to praxis that respects both the authority of the text and the circumstances of the hearer.* It is such a world, projected by the pericope and unique to that text, that the congregation is invited to inhabit; by so doing, the ecclesial community renews its covenant relationship with God as it (re)aligns itself with his demands. Each individual quantum of pericopal theology forms the ground of progressive life transformation by calling for alignment to the demands of God as propounded in the projected world.

The goal of these ecclesial and homiletical transactions is the gradual alignment of the church to the precepts, priorities, and practices of the plenary canonical world. This is to adopt God's new way of life that is open to all those who, in obedience to Scripture, choose to live in the will of God by orienting

---

50. Mudge likens the *world in front of the text* to a model in the natural sciences which functions as a heuristic device. In similar fashion, the projected world re-describes reality enabling readers to discover how that new world, a world according to God, may be actualized in their lives (Lewis S. Mudge, "Paul Ricoeur on Biblical Interpretation," in *Essays on Biblical Interpretation*, by Paul Ricoeur [ed. Lewis S. Mudge; Philadelphia: Fortress, 1980], 25).

their lives to that world. "Once more we stand before this 'other' new world which begins in the Bible. In it the chief consideration is not the doings of man but the doings of God . . . the establishment and growth of a new world, the world in which God and *his* morality reign."[51] A biblical pericope is thus a literary instrument projecting a specific segment of the canonical world for God's people, inviting them to organize their lives in accordance with the precepts, priorities, and practices characteristic of this world-segment as revealed in that pericope. One pericope at a time, the various aspects of Christian life, individual and corporate, are progressively and gradually brought into alignment with the will of God for the glory of God: this is the goal of preaching.

The interpretation of a pericope at the weekly gathering of the community of God must therefore discern the particular portion of the canonical vision featured by that pericope. In other words, each homiletical undertaking must delineate the theology of the pericope under consideration, elucidating what that specific text affirms about God and his ongoing and dynamic relationship to mankind (an example is worked out below).[52] What the pericope so affirms in its theology forms the basis of the subsequent homiletical move to derive application; pericopal theology is the station from which the interpreter may move on to the destination of praxis.[53]

Pericopal theology is, therefore, neither the imposition of a systematic or confessional grid on the raw material of the text, nor the result of an exclusively historical, sociological, or anthropological focus on the subject matter. Rather, the textually mediated theological truth of the pericope is elucidated, attending to the contribution of that particular textual unit to the plenary canonical world that displays God and humanity rightly related to him. The cumulative

---

51. Karl Barth, "The Strange New World within the Bible," in *The Word of God and the Word of Man* (trans. Douglas Horton; London: Hodder and Stoughton, 1928), 39–40.

52. This "theological interpretation" is essentially exegesis done with theological lenses—of *pericopal* theology, that is. Such an approach earmarks those elements of the text that serve as "clues" to the theology of the pericope, and synthesizes these "clues" into a theological focus of the pericope. See the example on 2 Sam 11–12 below (and Gen 22 in chapter 4). Also see Kuruvilla, *Mark*, where each pericope of the Gospel is analyzed in this theological fashion.

53. Theology stands "midway between the Bible and actual church preaching" (Heinrich Ott, *Theology and Preaching* [Philadelphia: Westminster, 1963], 17). The concept of theology as a bridge between text and sermon has oft been proposed in the past, although what "species" of theology it is, how exactly it performs this role, or how it may be discerned has not been explicated. See John Goldingay, *Approaches to Old Testament Interpretation* (Leicester, U.K.: InterVarsity, 1981), 43; John R. W. Stott, *Between Two Worlds* (Grand Rapids: Eerdmans, 1982), 137; and Timothy S. Warren, "A Paradigm for Preaching," *BSac* 148 (1991): 463–86.

integration of the theology of all the pericopes of Scripture thus constitutes the theology of the canon—the plenary canonical world in front of the biblical text. However, in any gathering of the faithful, it is by the mediation of the theology of an individual pericope that the Scriptures may be brought to bear upon the situation of the hearers, thereby aligning the congregation to the *world in front of the text*. Week by week, pericope by pericope, sermon by sermon, the community of God is progressively and increasingly (re)oriented to the will of God, gradually implementing covenant renewal. The vector of such an interpretive transaction leads the preacher from the text, via the posited world (pericopal theology) bearing a transhistorical intention, to arrive ultimately at application—the inhabitation of that projected world. Therefore in each expository undertaking geared for application, the preacher sets the interpretive focus upon the theology of the particular text utilized. It is the pericopal theology of the particular pericope preached that must be applied. As far as producing valid application is concerned, then, biblical interpretation that does not elucidate this crucial intermediary of pericopal theology is *de facto* incomplete.[54]

Pericopal Theology Distinguished

In the operation proposed here, pericopal theology differs from systematic or biblical theology (at least as they are commonly defined). Systematic theology, attending to the entailments of what is written, draws conclusions deductively from one text and integrates those with deductions from other texts (for instance, the ascertainment of the divinity of the persons of the Trinity from a number of discrete biblical passages).[55] By virtue of its systematizing and correlating activity, it operates at a level that is more general than does perico-

---

54. John Bright, *The Authority of the Old Testament* (Nashville: Abingdon, 1967), 147–48, 173.

55. "By *systematic theology* I refer to the branch of theology that seeks to elaborate the whole and the parts of Scripture, demonstrating their logical (rather than their merely historical) connections" (D. A. Carson, "Unity and Diversity in the New Testament: The Possibility of Systematic Theology," in *Hermeneutics, Authority and Canon* [eds. D. A. Carson and John D. Woodbridge; Grand Rapids: Baker, 1995], 69–70). According to Wayne Grudem, "systematic theology involves collecting and understanding all the relevant passages in the Bible on various topics and then summarizing their teachings clearly so that we know what to believe about each topic" (*Systematic Theology: An Introduction to Biblical Doctrine* [Grand Rapids: Zondervan, 1994], 21, 23). Ryrie asserts that "[s]ystematic theology correlates the data of biblical revelation as a whole in order to exhibit systematically the total picture of God's self-revelation" (Charles C. Ryrie, *Basic Theology: A Popular Systematic Guide to Understanding Biblical Truth* [Chicago: Moody, 1999], 15). For Erickson, to say that theology is "systematic" indicates that "it attempts to relate the various portions [of the Bible] to one another, to coalesce the varied teachings into some type of harmonious or coherent whole" (Millard J. Erickson, *Christian Theology* [Grand Rapids: Baker, 1985], 21).

pal theology. The latter, on the other hand, is more inductively derived, and is constrained by the trajectory of a specific pericope.[56] It deals with matters pertaining to the relationship of God to his creation as proposed in *that* pericope, addressing the divine demand, in that text, that the people of God must abide by, if they are to inhabit God's canonical world.

The operation of biblical theology, too, tends to be more general than that of pericopal theology, identifying as it does the development of broader biblical themes across the canon, with a strong emphasis on temporality and timelines.[57] Goldsworthy asserts that when pericopes are being dealt with weekly, biblical theology is "the major way of addressing the question of the gap between the text and the reader."[58] However, seeing a text in the wider historical context of the canon, for which biblical theology is certainly helpful, is not the same as seeing how a particular pericope makes a specific transhistorical demand of its reader. "From the evangelical preacher's point of view, biblical theology involves the quest for the big picture, or the overview, of biblical revelation."[59] But big canonical pictures tend to miss the small pericopal miniatures. And it is these miniatures (i.e., the theology of the individual pericopes) that are essential for the week by week life-changing transactions of homiletics.

For the preacher, there is a singular advantage in the employment of pericopal theology in the homiletical undertaking: by way of its greater degree of

---

56. This, of course, is not to deny the development of themes in contiguous pericopes, or that adjacent pericopes, together making up an entire book, influence the theology of the specific pericope being exposited.

57. So Geerhardus Vos, who asserted that biblical theology was characterized by "historical progressiveness of the revelation-process." While in biblical theology the principle is one of historical construction, in systematic theology, according to him, it is one of logical construction (*Biblical Theology: Old and New Testament* [Grand Rapids: Eerdmans, 1948; repr. 1975], 5–9, 16). So also Clowney: "Biblical theology formulates the character and content of the progress of revelation" (Edmund P. Clowney, *Preaching and Biblical Theology* [Nutley, N.J.: Presbyterian and Reformed, 1977], 15–16). According to Sidney Greidanus, "it is especially the discipline of biblical theology that helps us trace longitudinal themes from the Old Testament to the New" (*Preaching Christ from the Old Testament: A Contemporary Hermeneutical Method* [Grand Rapids: Eerdmans, 1999], 267). "By *biblical theology* I refer to that branch of theology whose concern it is to study each corpus of the Scripture in its own right, especially with respect to its place in the history of God's unfolding revelation. The emphasis is on history and on the individual corpus" (Carson, "Unity and Diversity in the New Testament," 69). "Biblical theology . . . focuses on the biblical storyline" (Thomas R. Schreiner, "Preaching and Biblical Theology," *SBJT* 10 [2006]: 22).

58. Graeme Goldsworthy, *Gospel-Centred Hermeneutics: Biblical-Theological Foundations and Principles* (Nottingham: Apollos, 2006), 263.

59. Idem, *Preaching the Whole Bible as Christian Scripture: The Application of Biblical Theology to Expository Preaching* (Grand Rapids: Eerdmans, 2000), 22.

specificity for the chosen text, it makes possible the weekly movement from pericope to pericope, for those who seek to preach in that fashion. The theological thrust of a given book is thereby elucidated pericope by pericope, with the preacher generating specific and discrete application in each sermon. On the other hand, with systematic and biblical theology as the basis of individual sermons, distinctions between the theological thrusts of successive pericopes are harder to maintain. Operating as these species of theology do, at a level of generality somewhat removed from the immediacy of the text and its details (at least at a level further removed than the locus of pericopal theology), sermons on contiguous pericopes will often tend to have similar thrusts and applications, making *lectio continua* difficult to sustain. On the other hand, given the degree of specificity prescribed by pericopal theology, the sequential preaching of pericopes would not be impeded by this handicap; the specific theological thrust of each pericope would be heard clearly.[60]

Nonetheless, while this work concentrates on one particular kind of Christian proclamation—the preaching of a sermon from sequential pericopes—even for this specific endeavor, systematic and biblical theology are valuable: what is discerned in the theology of the pericope must be consistent with the organized datum of theological information obtained from the remainder of the canon (systematic and biblical theology). The construal by the church of the biblical corpus as a singular work (Rule of Singularity; see chapter 1)—a whole, comprising discrete parts—mandates a reading that assumes coherence between its various components. Moreover, such a coordinated reading attenuates the threat of dislodging a narrow sliver of text (the pericope) from its broader context in the canon. Systematic and biblical theology provide a schematized version of biblical information, outlining the gradual revelation thereof along the timeline of biblical history. A comprehensive grasp of both these facets of theology is essential, for they provide the guardrails for interpretation; one must never cross the systematic and biblical theology lines that are canonically drawn.

For instance, as was noted, if, coming upon the "angel of Yahweh" in Gen 22:11, 15, one concludes from that pericope that there are now *four* persons in the godhead (the Father, Son, Holy Spirit, *and* the Angel of Yahweh), one must be constrained by the fences of systematic theology and admit to an error in interpretation. In other words, what is specifically discovered in any pericope of

---

60. This issue is dealt with further in chapter 4.

Scripture must not violate what is accepted as the general premises of systematic and biblical theology. Thus, while the specificity of the interpretations of each pericope is not directly dictated, they are guarded and bounded by systematic and biblical theology. This is a reflection of the general nature of systematic and biblical theology; they serve as guardians of interpretation, delineating boundaries that may not be transgressed. In contrast, the more specific and text-related nature of pericopal theology identifies the specific demand of the text in question and enables the preacher to derive valid application in the sermon that is unique for the pericope under consideration. All this to say, pericopal theology is not an orphan, dislodged from systematic and biblical theology; it remains consistent with these, yet its terms are more specific, its textual object more precise (the pericope), its operation granular (divine demand at a finer level of discrimination; see chapter 4), and its goal singular—application via a sermon on that pericope, to change lives for the glory of God.

Such an approach does not devalue sermons based upon systematic or biblical theology. The goal of this proposal is simply to complement other preaching modalities with one that will conceivably aid the preaching of Scripture pericope by pericope on a weekly basis, gradually unveiling the world projected by the canon. Pericopal theology, as defined here, will help bring that specific portion of the biblical text to bear upon the situation of the hearers, thereby aligning congregation to canon, God's people to God's word. Pericope by pericope, the community of God is thus increasingly oriented to the will of God as it progressively inhabits the canonical world. By means of this intermediary, pericopal theology, a specific pericope can be validly applied to the gathered Christian community. In such application, readers (or listeners of sermons) inhabit the *world in front of the text*, thus molding the community of God—of all time and in all places—to the will of God. "If Scripture is ever again to be a living source for theology, those who practice theology must become less preoccupied with the world that produced Scripture and learn again how to live in a world Scripture produces."[61]

Summary: Pericopal Theology

The theology of the pericope thus functions as the bridge between text and praxis, between the circumstances of the textual inscription and the lives of

---

61. Luke Timothy Johnson, "Imagining the World Scripture Imagines," *Modern Theology* 14 (1998): 165.

the reading community. Pericopal theology thereby facilitates the interpretive move from canonical inscription to valid sermonic application. What was there-and-then in the ancient text is thereby permitted to speak validly in the here-and-now to modern readers. Divine discourse is thus forward looking, for the *world in front of the text* is the world that God is graciously inviting his people to inhabit. This world is not necessarily the way the world actually *is*. Rather, it depicts God and his covenant relationship to his creation—a world that *should be* and *would be*, were God's people to align their lives to it: in a sense, an *eschatological* world. This world guides believers to future action, directing them to fresh appropriation of God's truth into their own particular contexts. This appropriation (or application) is the remaking of the reader's world after the fashion of the *world in front of the text*, as "the strange new eschatological world being created by the Spirit" is rendered real.[62] To this possibility, this potentiality, God's people are bidden to make their lives congruent, for application involves discovering the world projected in front of the text and aligning oneself to that world. Such an alignment restores the relationship between God and his community. A pericope, by way of its theology, thus contributes to the corporate mission of covenant renewal. I submit that what God would have is that his people be captivated by the world projected in front of the text, and that they seek to be its inhabitants, aligning themselves to its precepts, priorities, and practices. This is God's gracious divine demand. Therefore, for preaching, it is the *world in front of the text* (pericopal theology) that should be the focus of attention, not the entities *behind* the text. In other words, one must privilege the text!

For practical purposes, to aid the preacher in sermon preparation, a convenient statement of the theology of the pericope may be useful, as long as the interpreter remembers that such a verbal summary (in this work, "Comprehensive Theological Focus"; see below) simply serves as a workable précis of the pragmatics of the text for the preacher during sermon preparation. It does not mean that that statement is all that needs to be preached, and that the text may now be

---

62. See Richard Briggs, *Reading the Bible Wisely* (London: SPCK, 2003), 111; and Kevin J. Vanhoozer, *The Drama of Doctrine: A Canonical-Linguistic Approach to Christian Theology* (Louisville: Westminster John Knox, 2005), 111, 318, 420. Ricoeur, too, acknowledges this eschatological nature of religious language—"a capacity to create a new way of life and to open my eyes to new aspects of reality, new possibilities. You may call that eschatology in the sense that it's the horizon of another world, the promise of a new life" (Paul Ricoeur, "Poetry and Possibility," in *A Ricoeur Reader: Reflection and Imagination* [ed. Mario J. Valdés; Hertfordshire, U.K.: Harvester Wheatsheaf, 1991], 455).

conveniently dispensed with. The theology of the pericope cannot be reduced to a statement or expression thereof. "[W]hile ideas are surely uncovered in biblical interpretation, there are also moods, movements, conflicts, epiphanies, and other experiences that cannot be pressed into a strictly ideational mold. Sermons should be faithful to the full range of a text's power, and those who carry away only main ideas, . . . are travelling too light."[63] Pericopal theology embraces *all* of what the author is *doing*, and thus forms the legitimate locus from which to launch application. The statement of that theology ("Comprehensive Theological Focus"), on the other hand, is a concise and convenient expression thereof, for pedagogical purposes. Such a distinction between the more exhaustive *pericopal theology* and its functional statement emphasizes that the latter serves only as a succinct paraphrase of its more expansive and multifaceted kin.

This process of discovery of pericopal theology, then, is an endeavor focused on a specific text and all the properties of its textuality. The *world in front of the text* is peculiar to that text and derived from the particular features inherent to it and proposed by it: "[f]or every unique text there is such a world" proper to it.[64] The derivation of the theology of a specific pericope, 2 Sam 11–12, will form the case study in the next section to illustrate this critical movement.

Text to Theology—A Case Study: 2 Samuel 11–12[65]

This accounting of the theology of 2 Sam 11–12 will be conducted in the context of the theology of 1–2 Sam as a whole. While acknowledging the importance of the pericope as a fundamental textual unit of preaching and its singular role as the instrument of covenant renewal, the preacher may not deny the unity of the wider text of which the pericope is part. Indeed, the theology of the pericope can be grasped only in light of the theology of the broader context; the segment of the world projected by the pericope is a coherent and integral element of the world projected by the larger body of text. In considering the entire corpus of 1–2 Sam, the theme of faithfulness to Yahweh is found to be dominant. For instance, the two hymns that bracket 1–2 Sam (1 Sam 2:1–10, Hannah's song; and

---

63. Thomas G. Long, *The Witness of Preaching* (2nd ed.; Louisville: Westminster John Knox, 2005), 101.

64. Paul Ricoeur, "Philosophical Hermeneutics and Theological Hermeneutics: Ideology, Utopia, and Faith," in *Protocol of the Seventeenth Colloquy, 4 November 1975* (ed. W. Wuellner; Berkeley: The Center for Hermeneutical Studies in Hellenistic and Modern Culture, 1976), 11–12.

65. Portions of this section were published in Abraham Kuruvilla, "Pericopal Theology: An Intermediary between Text and Application," *TrinJ* 31ns (2010): 265–83.

2 Sam 22:1–23:7, the concluding hymn of David) emphasize this key principle of the *world in front of the text*: in both, Yahweh is exalted for his exploits and his excellence; the blissful lot of the faithful is extolled, while dire consequences are predicted for unfaithfulness. This characterization of God implicitly affirms that the one who rewards faithfulness with blessing must be trusted; the one who repays unfaithfulness with retribution must be feared. As 2 Sam 11–12 is exposited, these foundational assertions of who God is and what he expects from his people (faithfulness) will also undergird the sermon.

Second Samuel 10–12 is structured by the framework of the Ammonite War that forms an *inclusio* for this section (see below); it is within this plot enclosure that the shocking story of David is planted. The phrase וַיְהִי אַחֲרֵי כֵן (*wayhi ahare ken,* "now it happened afterwards") begins both 2 Sam 10 and the next section in 2 Sam 13, isolating chapters 10–12 as a unit. The curtain falls on the narrative of 2 Sam 10–12 with an obvious closure at 12:31—"then David and all the people returned to Jerusalem"—marking an end to the hostilities, as victor and army return to the capital in triumph. Though 2 Sam 10–12 forms an integral narrative unit and part of a larger whole that spans chapters 9–20, for the purposes of this analysis the focus will be upon the specific pericope dealing with David's adultery and murder and his subsequent indictment (2 Sam 11–12). Considering this pericope, that narrates King David's misdemeanors, one discovers four specific aspects of the discourse ("clues") that point to the distinctive theology of this pericope—the world projected in front of the text.

The Send *Motif*

A striking feature of the opening episode of the narrative (11:1–5) is the recurrence of the verb שׁלח (*shlh,* "to send"). Altogether in 2 Sam 10–12, this term appears twenty-three times. In the larger unit of 2 Sam 9–20, it is utilized forty-four times; only thirteen instances occur in the rest of 2 Sam. For the most part, it is the king who does all the sending here: he *sends* to inquire about Bathsheba, he *sends* for Bathsheba, he *sends* for Uriah, he *sends* Uriah back to the battle-front bearing his own death warrant, and so on (11:1, 3, 4, 6 [×3], 12, 14, 27).[66]

---

66. The *leitmotif* of שׁלח resurfaces in 2 Sam 13 as well. It is David who *sends* Tamar to Amnon (13:7; she is the victim in an illicit sexual encounter); and it is he who *sends* Amnon with Absalom (13:27; Amnon is killed). In distinction to 2 Sam 11, where David sends for the victims of his predatory actions, in 2 Sam 13 he unwittingly sends his own children as victims, to have visited upon them the evils he had perpetrated upon Bathsheba and Uriah (James S. Ackerman, "Knowing Good and Evil: A Literary Analysis of the Court History in 2 Samuel 9–20 and 1 Kings 1–2," *JBL* 109 [1990]: 48–49).

This repeated element, "send," then, is a motif indicating regal power and imperial authority, as David, supreme in his kingdom, sends people hither and thither; they all jump to do his bidding.[67] This "sending" emphasizes David's selfish transactions with Uriah (and with Bathsheba who belonged to Uriah), callously undertaken and with an utter disregard for consequences, even if it meant denigrating God's name in the process (12:9–14). It is clearly not what God expects from his chosen; neither is the *world in front of the text* one that condones such odious behavior—the shameless flaunting of power and the total contempt for the victims of abuse. Here was a potentate abusing his power in the service of his immoral desires; indeed, this was power that was not inherently his, but that had been granted him in the first place. Yahweh, exercising his sovereignty, had chosen David from being a "nobody," to replace a predecessor who had himself been warped by his own fantasies of omnipotence. David, exercising *his* "sovereignty," had chosen to have his own way, not God's. The *send* motif thus points to a significant facet of the theology of the pericope (the world it projects).

THEOLOGICAL FOCUS[68]

Faithful allegiance to God, the true sovereign, is the priority to which believers are called to be aligned, manifest in the reined exercise of power.

---

67. John I. Lawlor, "Theology and Art in the Narrative of the Ammonite War (2 Samuel 10–12)," *GTJ* 3 (1982): 195–96; Uriel Simon, "The Poor Man's Ewe-Lamb: An Example of a Juridical Parable," *Bib* 48 (1967): 209. Bailey considers the ascription of the verb שלח to Bathsheba (2 Sam 11:5) significant; apparently she had some authority as well. He notes that the only other women within Deuteronomic history who are subjects of this verb all wield influence of some sort (Rahab helps the Israelite spies escape, Josh 2:21; Deborah summons Barak to battle, Jdg 4:6; Delilah invites the Philistines to capture Samson, Jdg 16:18; and Jezebel plots against Elijah and Naboth, 1 Kgs 19:2; 21:8). In addition, the threefold verb patterns of David's actions in 2 Sam 11:2 and 11:3 are mirrored by a parallel array of three verbs with Bathsheba as subject in 11:5b (after her conception is announced in 11:5a). Similarly, both David and Bathsheba are allotted three verbs each in 11:4, and two verbs each in 11:27. Some complicity on Bathsheba's part is perhaps being implied by the depiction of her actions in congruence with those of David (Randall C. Bailey, *David in Love and War: The Pursuit of Power in 2 Samuel 10–12* [Sheffield: JSOT, 1990], 85–88, 99).

68. The "Theological Focus" serves to summarize the preceding analysis. At the end of the analysis of the entire pericope, 2 Sam 11–12, all these discrete elements will be gathered into a single "Comprehensive Theological Focus," a succinct statement of the theology of the pericope. These foci will, in general, be positive restatements of the negative examples of David's life.

The Hittite Model

Significant contrasts emerge between the Jewish king and the Hittite warrior, Uriah, as the narrative negotiates its nuanced turns. Uriah, at the battlefront with the army, was engaged in war; David, at home, was engaged in illicit pleasure, lying with another man's wife (שכב, *shkb*, 11:4). When summoned from war, Uriah refused to succumb to the joys of rest and relaxation at home while his compatriots (and the ark) were encamping on open ground. This loyal soldier, instead, chose to lie at the door of the king's house (שכב, 11:9) rather than go home to lie with his wife (שכב, 11:11), as David was manipulating him to do. Later, even while inebriated, Uriah opted to "lie" with the servants of the king (שכב, 11:13). In desperation, Uriah is sent (again, שלח, 11:14) to his death. David's fornication, begun under cover of darkness ("evening," 11:2), had now become cold-blooded murder in daylight ("morning," 11:14). The very loyalty of Uriah that had frustrated the king's machinations was itself the instrument of this dedicated soldier's murder: Uriah faithfully bears the letter carrying his own death sentence, and his faithfulness to his king, army, and nation gets him killed on the battlefront.[69] Even after he is disposed of, the storyteller does not allow Uriah to vanish from the narrative: in 11:26, the awkward recurrence of that soldier's name in "the wife of Uriah" and "Uriah her husband," and the repeated assertion in the same verse of Bathsheba's marital status (אִישָׁהּ and בַּעְלָהּ, *'ishah* and *ba'lah*, "her husband"), keep the focus unwaveringly upon the innocent victim of David's egregious actions.[70] He who ought to have been, as Yahweh's earthly representative, the guardian of the people's rights and the upholder of their justice, murders his loyal servant and causes the death of several other faithful soldiers. The condemnation of David's deeds is almost palpable; unfaithfulness to Yahweh could not be more starkly depicted, and the attendant theology of the pericope could hardly be more explicit.

So, on the one hand was the king of Israel, unfaithful and disloyal; deliberately and willfully he had engaged in adultery with the spouse of one of his warriors. On the other hand was that very warrior, besotted Uriah, emerging

---

69. J. P. Fokkelman, *King David (II Sam. 9–20 & I Kings 1–2)* (vol. 1 of *Narrative Art and Poetry in the Books of Samuel*; Assen, Netherlands: Van Gorcum, 1981), 60.

70. The child that is born to this illicit union is also referred to as the one that "Uriah's widow" bore (12:15). Uriah also makes an appearance again at the very end of the book (23:39). The narrator does not intend that the reader forget this ignominious incident, and, to the very end, this brazen malfeasance blacklists David.

more faithful to Yahweh, liege, and comrades, than was the sober and scheming David. The loyal, abstinent, and self-sacrificing soldier is requisitioned as a foil for the disloyal, indulgent, and selfish king: the theology of the pericope thus depicts a practice desirable in the projected world.

> **THEOLOGICAL FOCUS**
> *Faithfulness to Yahweh is manifested in the restriction of one's self-indulgent passions.*

The Ophthalmic Malady

In light of the overarching theology of 1–2 Sam, one would expect this evil perpetrated by David to incur the wrath of Yahweh. However, quite strikingly, the narrative of 2 Sam 11 fails to make any mention of Yahweh, until one gets to 2 Sam 11:27. There, the main character in the *dramatis personæ*, Yahweh, finally makes his appearance.

Wanton sexual morals, rooted in base self-indulgence, had culminated in a tyrannical unconcern for the wounded "third party." Uriah was heartlessly slaughtered, the zenith of an unbroken sequence of escalating malignity. Indeed, this last act succeeds in getting not just one man killed, but many, some of them the nation's best warriors ("valiant men," 11:16). David's reaction is a cavalier comment to Joab through a messenger: "Don't let this thing be evil in your eyes" (בְּעֵינֶיךָ, *b'eneka*, 11:25). But immediately afterwards, divine disapprobation is registered in no uncertain terms (in fact, it employs the same metaphor of sight): "But the thing that David had done was evil in the eyes of Yahweh" (בְּעֵינֵי יְהוָה, *b'ene yhwh*, 11:27b). There appears to have been an ophthalmic incompatibility between David and Yahweh: king and God were not seeing eye to eye.[71] What David saw as not evil was expressly seen and condemned as evil by Yahweh, and the conflict between David and God becomes most intense at this juncture: Who gets to decide what is evil and what good—David or Yahweh?

Perhaps David imagined that God was nowhere present; in that case, he was only deluding himself—God is one character that cannot be written out of the

---

71. Already the larger plot had presented the symptoms of David's ophthalmic deficits: in contrast to the Ammonites who *saw* firsthand the (mis)fortunes of war (10:6, 14, 15, 19), David did not see; he only *heard*, secondhand, the news from the front (10:5, 7, 17). See Uriel Simon, *Reading Prophetic Narratives* (trans. Lenn J. Schramm; Bloomington, Ind.: Indiana University Press, 1997), 95.

narrative script. Not only was Yahweh implicitly present as David went about his nefarious activities, but Yahweh had also seen! There is no deed so shrouded in darkness that it will be invisible to an all-seeing, omnipresent God. As if to rectify any misconception about the presence of deity on stage, from this point onwards, Yahweh, "absent" in the previous scenes, becomes almost tangible: the Tetragrammaton occurs thirteen times in 2 Sam 12, in the section that details the judgment, sentence, and punishment of the king (another example of the author's literary *doings*). God had seen, and now would take action to bring justice and closure to this sinister episode; punishment was now inevitable. The verse that points to God's seeing, 11:27, turns out to be the focal point of the chiastic structure of 2 Sam 10–12, emphasizing the crux of the narrative—what God considered "evil in his eyes".

10:1–19	**A** War—partial victory over the Ammonites	
11:1–5	**B** Sin; Bathsheba conceives	
11:6–13	**C** Concealment of David's sin	
11:14–27a	**D** Murder of the innocent Uriah	
11:27b	**E** Evil in the eyes of Yahweh	
12:1–6	**D'** Murder of the lamb	
12:7–15a	**C'** Exposure of David's sin	
12:15b–25	**B'** Death; Bathsheba conceives	
12:26–31	**A'** War—complete victory over the Ammonites	

Interestingly, an addendum in 1 Kgs 15:5 points out again this malady with David's eyesight, as it asserts that David did what was right (בְּעֵינֵי יְהוָה) all the days of his life, "except in the case of Uriah the Hittite." For the development of the theology of the pericope, the recognition of evil for what it is in the eyes of God is an integral practice of the projected world. David, instead, had despised God's word and denigrated God's name (2 Sam 12:9, 14).

THEOLOGICAL FOCUS

Faithfulness to God involves recognizing evil for what it is in God's eyes.

The Punishment Merited

That the climax of the narrative has been reached in 2 Sam 11:27b (the crux of the chiasm; see above) is also indicated in the very next verse as the prophet Nathan is commissioned to play the prosecuting attorney. For a change, Yahweh is the one now doing the sending (שלח, 12:1—"Then Yahweh *sent* Nathan..."). The tables had been turned! Resolution was forthcoming. The punishment would now fit the crime: Yahweh would take David's wives (לקח, *lqh*, 12:11)—a grim reminder to David of how he had taken Bathsheba (לקח, 11:4; 12:9, 10), just as the rich man had taken the poor man's ewe lamb in Nathan's parable (לקח, 12:4).[72] This taking by Yahweh would be "in his [David's] sight"—his wives would be lain with "in the sight" of the sun (12:11; see 16:22 for Absalom's fulfillment of this curse, upon the same roof whence David had commenced his contemptible conspiracy). The scorning of Yahweh and his word (12:9, 10) was heinous indeed, and that not by a private individual but by Yahweh's anointed himself, the king of God's chosen people (Israel/Judah is mentioned five times in 12:7–15). The fact that these nefarious affairs had given occasion for the enemies of Yahweh to blaspheme him (12:14) would also not be forgotten. Indeed, the fourfold punishment (12:6), when exacted, would take the life of four of David's children: Bathsheba's newborn, Amnon, Absalom, and Adonijah. In the theology of the pericope, there is an important corollary to the precept that faithfulness to God yields blessing.[73]

THEOLOGICAL FOCUS

Unfaithfulness to God, manifest in the disrespecting of his word and the public dishonoring of his name, will often get its just deserts.

---

72. In Nathan's denunciatory fiction, the poor man's lamb would eat (אכל, *'kl*) of his bread, and drink (שתה, *shth*) of his cup, and lie (שכב, *shkb*) in his bosom (12:3). Earlier, in response to David's urging that Uriah go home—an attempt by the king to hide his own paternity of Bathsheba's illegitimate child—that soldier had indignantly replied, "Shall I then go to my house to eat [אכל] and to drink [שתה] and to lie [שכב] with my wife?" (11:11). David, the prophet implies, was as callous as the parabolic rich man who slew the poor man's favorite pet.

73. A remedial thrust is also part of the narrative, portraying the grace of God to the repentant sinner (2 Sam 12:13). David's sins take their tragic and traumatic toll, but the accusatory unit ends positively. Once again Yahweh "sends" (שלח), and once again it is Nathan who is sent by him, but this time with a message of tenderness: the second child of David and Bathsheba would be "beloved of Yahweh" (12:24). Though the consequences of sin would remain, forgiveness had been achieved.

A similar theme of fidelity is constantly in the background of the larger context of 1–2 Sam: God's commission of his human agents entails, on their part, the responsibility to be faithful in their respective offices to the divine sovereign who appointed them. This principle was concretely (mis)represented in the lives of the two kings, Saul and David, whose stories are narrated in 1 Sam 13–2 Sam 24. The first turned out to be unfaithful, and as a result, the Holy Spirit departed from him to come upon faithful David who then became Israel's anointed king (1 Sam 16:13–14). The ark was subsequently returned to the nation, and blessing upon the land ensued (2 Sam 6–8)—the projected world's principle of reward for faithfulness. But those halcyon days were not to last; Saul's flawed performance would not serve as a warning to David. And the catastrophic consequences of David's own subsequent transgressions would prove the precept of divine recompense for unfaithfulness. Whereas 1 Sam 16–2 Sam 8 lauds David's character and rule, 2 Sam 9–20 laments its corruption and collapse—the regrettable, but not unexpected, conclusion to the earthly king's infidelity towards the one who was truly King.[74]

A world is projected which endorses God's right to reign over his people through his chosen representatives, underscoring, in turn, the priority for his subjects to remain faithful to their divine ruler. In its depiction of God as one who sees and labels evil for what it is, the pericope also virtually guarantees that punishment for unfaithfulness will follow. Specifically, the plot points to one sovereignly chosen by God, who develops a crack in the foundation of his character—unrestrained sexual desire that became a runaway disaster accumulating evil upon evil, and that resulted in his disparaging God's word and dishonoring God's name (as Nathan's accusation specified in 2 Sam 12:9–14). God's reputation was no longer the pre-eminent priority; instead it was unbridled passion and abusive power that reigned supreme. The subsequent drive to protect self-honor without an iota of repentance demonstrated a descent to the depths of depravity, culminating in murder. Instead of demonstrating loyalty to God, subordinates, and nation, here was a leader disloyal to all. The consequences would be severe; unfaithfulness would not remain unpunished; its ramifications would echo across generational divides: a period of blessing

---

74. The result of David's unfaithfulness was the dissipation of his authority, both over family and over nation, and attendant discord at home and disorder in the land. David's adultery and murder consumes significant textual space (2 Sam 10–12), denoting its essential status as the *fons et origo* of the subsequent complications: incest, fratricide, rebellion, and civil war (2 Sam 13–20).

ends therewith, and an inexorable decline begins.[75] In summary, considering the story in its broader context, the theology of the pericope (the segment of the *world in front of this text*) may be summarized positively, attending to the four aspects of the discourse pointed out:

COMPREHENSIVE THEOLOGICAL FOCUS

Reverence for God and deference to his word (priorities of the world in front of the text) *is manifested in the reined exercise of power, the restriction of self-indulgent passions, and the recognition of evil as reprehensible in the sight of God* (practices of the world in front of the text); *this respect for the authority and rulership of the true sovereign brings blessing* (precepts of the world in front of the text).

It must be remembered that in the broad context of 1–2 Sam, it was not only the nation's kings who were unfaithful. Even before the regents registered their infidelity, the people, in calling for a monarchy, had themselves dismissed Yahweh: "They have rejected me," God declared, "from being king over them" (1 Sam 8:7), a unilateral abrogation of the Mosaic covenant whereby God was to be the nation's ruler (Ex 15:18; 19:5–6). Therefore, the theology of this pericope is a lesson for both ruler and ruled, both crown and commoner.

As is evident in the analysis and summary of 2 Sam 11–12, pericopal theology imparts to the particulars of the text a significance that transcends the historical circumstances of the text's origin. The semantic potency of a work of literary art, especially of one that is a classic, causes it to go through a "reversal," a movement from "*individual to universal* which constitutes the text's relevance" for its readers, rendering its significance perennial.[76] Ultimately, this pericope (and, indeed, the entire Davidic saga in 1–2 Sam) is more than a narrative about a historical personage, "but about the highest values in the narrated David (as shown or as violated by him) which are the same as those of our own human existence."

---

75. Forgiveness, though available, advanced by God and accepted by sinner, does not completely erase the consequences and the sentence of justice. Yet to the penitent and contrite, God offers restoration (as the events in 2 Sam 12 prove).

76. Fokkelman, *King David*, 421. This is, of course, the movement from the specifics of the text (original textual sense) to the *world in front of the text*/pericopal theology (transhistorical intention) described in chapter 1.

The analysis here suggests that the proposed *world in front of the text*—the theology of the pericope—portrays these "highest values": the precepts, priorities, and practices operating in the projected world, propounded for appropriation by readers (and, via the preacher, by listeners of sermons).[77] This was not merely history that was being written; the author was adapting his material in such a way that universal human values in the text would be emphasized, allowing the past to flow over into the present, overcoming distanciation. It is, therefore, pericopal theology that mediates the ancient text's contemporary application, and it is in such appropriation that that text becomes life in the one who reads.[78]

Principlization, Generalization, and Levels of Theology

From the case study of 2 Sam 11–12, it is evident that in the discovery of pericopal theology, the interpreter moves from the specifics of the text to the level of pericopal theology; this movement is, in some sense at least, a generalization from particulars. How does this operate?

Problems of Principlization

While pericopal theology is concerned with the divine precepts, priorities, and practices of God's world, these elements must be distinguished from "principles" as are commonly encountered in homiletical literature—"universally available and more or less self-interpreting truths."[79] Frequently, such principles are discovered quite arbitrarily, without sustained exegesis to substantiate those principles as intentional on the part of the author, or as the product of the author's *doing* with what he is saying. There is also the tacit assumption in principlizing that, once one distinguishes those elements in the text that are not time- or culture-

---

77. The particularly local significance subsides, but without being lost, as it makes room for its "universal human significance." Fokkelman believes that the writers of such texts were aware of the transtemporal values embedded in their work—the transhistorical intentions/theology of texts awaiting application by future readers (Fokkelman, *King David*, 423–25).

78. Suggestions for application of this pericope will be discussed in chapter 4.

79. Waldemar Janzen, *Old Testament Ethics: A Paradigmatic Approach* (Louisville: Westminster John Knox, 1994), 29, 55. The procedure for discovering these principles is often called "principlization." See Walter C. Kaiser, "A Principlizing Model," in *Four Views on Moving Beyond the Bible to Theology* (ed. Gary T. Meadors; Grand Rapids: Zondervan, 2009), 22: "To 'principlize' is to (re)state the author's propositions, arguments, narrations, and illustrations in timeless abiding truths with special focus on the application of those truths to the current needs of the Church." So also Bernard L. Ramm, *Protestant Biblical Interpretation* (rev. ed.; Grand Rapids: Baker, 1970), 199–200: Principlizing is a "process of deduction that brings [principles] to the surface." Charles H. Cosgrove, *Appealing to Scripture in Moral Debate: Five Hermeneutical Rules* (Grand Rapids: Eerdmans, 2002), 61–62, calls the process "principiation."

bound, these unconstrained transcultural principles are more valuable than the text itself. Kaiser, for instance, thinks that cultural issues "intrude" on the text, seemingly a distraction from the principle of the text: "Principles . . . must be given priority over accompanying cultural elements."[80] All of this can imply that genres were essentially a mistake on God's part. One would then wonder at God's wisdom in giving the bulk of his Scripture in non-propositional form. Perhaps God would have served himself and his people better had he just stuck to a list of timeless propositions (the "kernel") rather than messy stories and arcane prophecies and sentimental poetry, all of which turn out to be merely illustrations (the "husk") for underlying principles. Vanhoozer is right in his assessment: "Kaiser may not go beyond the sacred page, but he certainly goes *behind* it."[81]

Invariably, the one seeking to discover principles is searching *behind* the text for whatever it was that prompted the writing of that text. This is particularly a problem with the interpretation of biblical narrative: the biblical writer, so it would seem, began with a principle (*behind* the text) and then hunted in his illustration database for an appropriate story in which to couch his principle. Such principles end up having a self-contained existence denuded of all that is textually specific. Craddock put it well: "Much preaching that aims at propositions and themes and outlines does just that: the minister boils off all the water and then preaches the stain in the bottom of the cup."[82] The Bible, however, is not a compendium of principles, but "a rather untidy and incredibly complex assortment" of the products of a variety of people, in a variety of times, in a variety of places. "Treating all this great collection of texts merely as the expendable container for independent universal principles we can express more simply and tidily denies the character of the Bible as God has given it to us, and might even seem to render Bible reading a waste of time."[83] Rather than pursuing an imagi-

---

80. Kaiser, "A Principlizing Model," 21.

81. Kevin J. Vanhoozer, "A Response to Walter C. Kaiser Jr.," in *Four Views on Moving Beyond the Bible to Theology*, 59 (italics added). Vanhoozer accuses the "kernel/husk" (or is it "candy/wrapper"?) camp of being almost docetic in their dichotomizing tendency to divide Scripture into text and principle (ibid., 60–61).

82. Fred B. Craddock, *Preaching* (Nashville: Abingdon, 1985), 123.

83. Christopher J. H. Wright, *Old Testament Ethics for the People of God* (Downers Grove: InterVarsity, 2004), 71. However, I will suggest in chapter 3 that in the interpretation of biblical law for application, the investigation of "rationale" ("principle"?) is productive. The Bible itself appears to "principlize" OT laws: Ezra 9:1–2 condemns Jewish alliances with non-Canaanite Gentiles, citing Deut 7:1–5 that was used to proscribe marriage between Israelites and Canaanites. Other examples include 1 Cor 9:9–14 and 1 Tim 5:18 (using Deut 25:4); 2 Cor 13:1 (using Deut 17:6–7; 19:15); 2 Cor 6:14 (using Deut 22:10); 1 Cor 5:1–3 (using Lev 18:8, 29); 1 Cor 5:13 (using Deut 17:7); Heb 9:22 (using Lev 17:11); etc.

nary principle-like entity *behind* the text, interpreters should seek the theology of the pericope—what the author is *doing* with what he is saying, the world projected *in front of* the text. In, with, and through the "untidy" details of narrative pericopes, the author is *doing* something with what he is saying. The particular portrayal of characters and situations and the particular structures and styles employed in exactly this way, and not another, is accomplishing something quite specific, discoverable to the interpreter who privileges the text, paying attention not only to the story, but also to the way the story is told.

The difference between the two approaches may be summarized thus: in the "principlizing" hermeneutic, the *principle* is antecedent to the text (and the text is often considered reducible to that principle *behind* it); by the theological hermeneutic espoused in this work, the *text* gives rise to the world/theology (and the text is irreducible to that world *in front of* it/pericopal theology). (The arrows in the figure below indicate the movement of the hermeneutic, beginning with text and ending at application.)

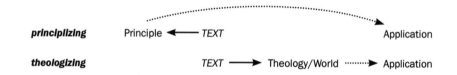

Necessity of Generalization

That some sort of generalization is essential in this process is obvious. In fact, the process of generalization might actually be physiological: "To generalize is to engage in a process that is part of life itself. Our confrontations are commonly with particulars—this person, that building, these rocks, those words—but we hold on to the world by organizing those particulars within larger groupings. The particulars we perceive are as a result not only particulars, but are particular x's, being instances or tokens of more encompassing categories."[84] Pragmatic efficiency calls for generalization, as neuroscientists and cognitive psychologists have increasingly come to recognize. "With respect to general cognitive economy, the basic level is the level of abstraction at which the organ-

---

84. Frederick Schauer, *Playing by the Rules: A Philosophical Examination of Rule-Based Decision-Making in Law and in Life* (Oxford: Clarendon, 1991), 18.

ism can obtain the most information with the least cognitive effort."[85] Lakoff and Johnson cite the example of a human eye: it has 100 million light-sensing cells, but only one million neural fibers lead from the eye to the optic cortex of the brain. Thus each incoming image on those 100 million light sensors must be reduced by a factor of 100. "That is, information in each fiber constitutes a 'categorization' of the information from about 100 cells. Neural categorization of this sort exists throughout the brain, up through the highest levels of categories that we can be aware of." Therefore, Lakoff and Johnson assert that categorization (which in essence is generalization or reduction) is "a consequence of how we are embodied." In other words, living systems generalize.[86]

However, generalization is not only a physiological response, but a pragmatic one, too: "life is short and mental space is finite," and so humankind generalizes.[87] Thus, even in textual interpretation, a certain amount of reduction is valid, for without it, the concrete specifics of the ancient text would never be transferable to a modern audience. "[T]he preacher must move beyond the opacity of the particular [in the text] to the clarity of the universal."[88] Thus for every particular, there exists a general or universal. Apparently it was the particularity of a falling apple that gave rise to Newton's law of gravity. Of this and other laws of motion proposed by Newton, Alasdair MacIntyre notes: "Being universal they extend beyond what has actually been observed in the present or the past to what has escaped observation and to what has not yet been observed."[89] By these generalizations, potential future exemplifications may be accurately predicted or proposed. All that is to say, without the generalization that is accomplished by the transhistorical intention borne by the *world in front of the text* (i.e., pericopal theology), there can be no futurity for a classic text, and no valid application at times and in places beyond those of the text's own circumstances of writing. Any move from text to praxis involves the unfolding of a notion of transcendence, inherent

---

85. Eleanor Rosch, "Human Categorization," in *Studies in Cross-cultural Psychology* (vol. 1; ed. Neil Warren; New York: Academic, 1977), 29.

86. George Lakoff and Mark Johnson, *Philosophy in the Flesh: The Embodied Mind and Its Challenge to Western Thought* (New York: Basic Books, 1999), 18.

87. Schauer, *Playing by the Rules*, 18–19. See his chapter, "Rules as Generalizations" (ibid., 17–37).

88. David M. Greenhaw, "As One *with* Authority: Rehabilitating Concepts for Preaching," in *Intersections: Post-Critical Studies in Preaching* (ed. Richard L. Eslinger; Grand Rapids: Eerdmans, 2004), 105. Of course, it is not enough to arrive at some generalization; the burden of the preacher is to bring it back to real life—to the lives of the ones in the audience. This is a move back to particulars, the second step of the "two-step" hermeneutic for preaching (text → theology → application; see below).

89. Alasdair MacIntyre, *After Virtue*, 2nd ed. (Notre Dame: University of Notre Dame Press, 1984), 82–83.

in the world projected. Moral judgments, especially, presuppose such a transcendence or implicit universality. By their very nature, these ethical axioms point beyond the particularities of the concrete as they are "generalized, abstracted and enlarged, and extended to an ideal communication community."[90] For instance, the specific statement "The Honda Civic stopped because it ran out of gas" implies the truth that "All cars that run out of gas will stop." Likewise, "Bill should be punished for his theft" signifies that "All who steal deserve punishment." This, in the field of ethics, is the rule of generalization. "[A]n ethic without universals would be no ethic, a series of disconnected, arbitrary imperatives."[91] An example where Jesus himself sought to generalize a transhistorical intention from a narrative text is found in Mark 2:25–26 (employing 1 Sam 21:1–7).[92]

Without generalization, most forms of teaching are rendered impossible, for what is conveyed for pedagogical purposes is, in most cases, some sort of generality, whether it be in a driving school on how to shift gears (in any car), in a cooking school on how to bake pies (of any kind), or in a medical school on how to treat melanomas (in any patient). Generalizations enable the one taught to act correctly in other future circumstances distant from the learning event, by the application of those generalities to specific situations; otherwise "every generation would have to start from scratch and teach itself."[93] Zechariah Chafee, the American judicial philosopher of the early part of the last century noted wryly that

> it is one thing to say that abstractions must be used cautiously, and another to urge, that, unless they can be verified by the methods of the natural sciences, they must not be used at all. The higher ranges of the hierarchy of words are indeed dangerous, but so are high buildings and high voltages. Modern life would be hampered without these; and every department of intellectual activity

---

90. Jürgen Habermas, *Justification and Application: Remarks on Discourse Ethics* (trans. Ciaran Cronin; Cambridge: Polity, 1993), 50, 52.

91. Oliver M. T. O'Donovan, "The Possibility of a Biblical Ethic," *TSF Bull.* 67 (1973): 18. Also see Marcus George Singer, *Generalization in Ethics* (London: Eyre & Spottiswoode, 1963), 13–33, 34–46; and R. M. Hare, *Freedom and Reason* (Oxford: Clarendon, 1963), 4–5, 10–13. "The value of a generalization is that while it leaves out the specific features that are of the individual or of the moment, it expresses features that are general to a class"—the loss of specificity is a gain in applicability (Richard M. Weaver, *Language Is Sermonic: Richard M. Weaver on the Nature of Rhetoric* [eds. Richard L. Johannesen, Rennard Strickland, and Ralph T. Eubanks; Baton Rouge, La.: Louisiana State University Press, 1970], 125–26).

92. And, as is essential, he applied it back again to particulars: what his disciples, in the first century, were justified in doing—picking heads of grain from the fields through which they were passing.

93. See R. M. Hare, *The Language of Morals* (Oxford: Clarendon, 1961), 60–61.

including law would be slowed down almost to a standstill if we did not employ shorthand expressions to denote great masses of fact.[94]

Thus there is a place for generalization, but with a caveat: *any generalization must be shown to have been validly drawn from the text and its particulars.*[95] Thorough exegesis—i.e., privileging the text—is invaluable for this substantiation.

And such an approach as is envisaged in this work asserts that those general theological truths in the text could have been expressed in no better way than they have been in those texts. Whatever the theology from whichever the pericope, the biblical form of the text was the best way to express that truth. Yes, there is a pragmatic operation of inference required of the interpreter to discern those theological values—the pericopal theology. But language theorists have discovered that language ordinarily functions in a way that maximizes such inferential communication.[96] More can be done with a metaphor, a proverb, irony, or narrative, than can be achieved with several pages of text paraphrasing those utterances and spelling out every nuance and connotation thereof. In other words, the balance in communication is significantly tilted towards pragmatics; the most efficient way to convey much, if not all, of the theology of a biblical pericope, is exactly the way it was originally inscribed in the text, whether in song or story, letter or law. God was certainly not negligent or mistaken in manifesting divine demand in a variety of genres. Since nothing can substitute for the text or its genre to communicate its precise thrust (theology) with precisely the same force and import, it is the text that must be privileged, and it is the text (with its pericopal theology) that must be preached, with all its cognitive and emotional potency, and not a boiled-down ersatz version of divine discourse. Let me reiterate: The text itself is to be privileged; the text (with its theology) is to be preached.

Level of Theology
At what degree of generalization from the specifics of the text is its theology located? Of course, the "highest" level of God's demands in Scripture is that of the two greatest commandments—love of God and love of neighbor. Every divine demand falls within the purview of those two. The "lowest" level would be the

---

94. Zechariah Chafee, "The Disorderly Conduct of Words," *Columbia L. Rev.* 41 (1941): 391.

95. Again, for application purposes, such generalizing moves must return to particulars that relate relevantly to the specifics of the listening audience.

96. "[I]nference is cheap, articulation expensive, and thus the design requirements are for a system that maximizes inference." See Stephen C. Levinson, *Presumptive Meanings: The Theory of Generalized Conversational Implicature* (Cambridge, Mass.: The MIT Press, 2000), 29.

literal command, which is exquisitely specific for the situation of the audience directly being addressed. To see divine demand as theologically applicable to all of God's people everywhere (Rule of Applicability; see chapter 1), one must opt for a "middle" level of theology between "high" and "low." In other words: *Go as high as you need to, stay as low as you can.*[97] For instance, consider Prov 11:1: "Dishonest scales are an abomination to the LORD, but a just weight is his delight." On one hand one could opt for a theologically "high" level of operation and deal with a non-specific thrust for this text such as "honesty/integrity" as the character trait that pleases God. This broadens the set of future applications to include almost anything that has to do with honesty or integrity: don't cheat on one's spouse; don't cook the books for tax purposes; don't falsify your self-reporting reading assignment for class; pay employees on time; etc. Moreover, at so "high" a level, the theological idea is likely to be shared by any number of other biblical texts, leading one to suspect that the specificity of *this* particular text has not been adequately attended to. While the concept and theology of "honesty" is perfectly biblical, the specificity of Prov 11:1 becomes attenuated at this high altitude.

FACETS OF MEANING		
Original Textual Sense	*Pericopal Theology* (WORLD IN FRONT OF THE TEXT)	**Exemplification**
HIGH just weights and scales	*honesty*	integrity in marriage, tax filings, academics, wages, ...

On the other hand, because the specifics of the text deal with "just weights and balances," one could opt for the theologically "lowest" level—literally, the use of just weights and measures in commerce. But if that were the level of the working theology of the text, there might not be much application that could be offered that would be relevant for people in most contemporary western societies, where merchants usually do not deal with weights and scales as in the ancient Near East.[98]

---

97. I call this the "Plimsoll premise," after Samuel Plimsoll who, in the late 1800s, invented the Plimsoll Line drawn on ships to designate the legal limit to which they may be loaded with cargo, to ensure adequate buoyancy, without which capsizing becomes imminent.

98. In a society that does deal with such weights and balances, it is perfectly legitimate to remain at the "lowest" level that can be carried across the gap of distanciation.

FACETS OF MEANING			
	Original Textual Sense	*Pericopal Theology* (WORLD IN FRONT OF THE TEXT)	Exemplification
LOW	just weights and scales	*just weights and balances*	?

A better approach is to locate the theology and transhistorical intention at a "middle" level: "honesty in business practices/commerce." That would narrow the possible exemplifications (from those listed above in the "high" category) to specifically commercial ones: paying employees on time, and perhaps even the honest filing of taxes.[99]

FACETS OF MEANING			
	Original Textual Sense	*Pericopal Theology* (WORLD IN FRONT OF THE TEXT)	Exemplification
MIDDLE	just weights and scales	*honesty in business practices*	integrity in paying wages,...

And there is the added responsibility of the preacher: to specify this "middle" ground (the theology of the pericope) into the lives of the listening congregation, i.e., how that theology may be validly applied in relevant fashion for this particular audience.[100]

Section Summary: Theology of Pericopes

The manner in which the preaching movement from Scripture to sermon may be undertaken, in order to arrive at the destination of valid application and

---

99. Clearly there is some flexibility and freedom in the choice of level. This is where pastoral sensibility, spiritual maturity, and godly wisdom on the part of the preacher come into play—the one with "senses trained to discern good and evil" (Heb 5:14). Needless to say, these character traits are indispensable for good preaching.

100. The operation proposed in this work is uniquely "granular" and text-specific, in that the pericopal theology elicited by interpretation is specific to the particular preaching text (this, as opposed to the more general nature of biblical and systematic theology, as was observed earlier). I suspect that scholars and theologians, who are usually not preachers, are more comfortable grappling with the canon, with testaments, and with broad generic categories—i.e., their approach is far less focused on a specific text than that advocated here from a preacher's point of view.

accomplish covenant renewal, is at the heart of this work. Pericopal theology (the *world in front of the text* bearing a transhistorical intention), standing between ancient inscription and contemporary application, forms the intermediary by which the reader is enabled to respond to the text. This theology, depicting God and his relationship with his people, directs one to valid application. In following this projected trajectory of application, covenant renewal is affected through the instrumentality of the pericope. A case study of 2 Sam 11–12 demonstrated how this theology is discerned.

In sum, pericopal theology implies a certain level of generalization, without which the futurity of the biblical text—the potential of its future application—would be negated. Yet this operation must be conducted with care, privileging the text, substantiating conclusions with scrupulous exegesis, and *going as high as one needs to, and staying as low as one can.* All of these transactions are in aid of one ultimate goal: to arrive at application that is valid. This, in a sense, is a return to concrete specificity: from the specificity of the text, through theology, back to specificity of application for a specific audience.

APPLICATION

From the early days of the church, Scripture was envisaged as a single, universal, but unfinished, story, the continuing relevance of which was to be explicated by the preacher. A proper reading of Scripture countenances such an understanding of the contemporaneity of the ancient text (the Rule of Applicability; see chapter 1). The concern of interpreters, both ancient and modern, has never simply been the reconstruction of the *Sitz im Leben* of the text, but also the elucidation of its *Sitz in unserem Leben,* its situation in *our* life, in the situation of current readers of the text and hearers of the sermon.[101] Application is thus an indispensable component of preaching; indeed, it is its endpoint: preaching cannot be reckoned complete without application. Without application, the field of homiletics lies fallow, preaching unproductive, and the sermon stillborn. Application is "the life and soul of a Sermon; whereby these Sacred Truths are brought home to a man's particular conscience and occasions, and the affections engaged unto any truth or duty."[102] In other words, application is the alignment of God's people to God's demand,

---

101. Brian E. Daley, "Is Patristic Exegis Still Usable?" *Communio* 29 (2002): 200.

102. John Wilkins, *Ecclesiastes or A Discourse concerning the Gift of Preaching, as it falls under the Rules of Art* (7th ed.; London: A. J. Churchill, 1693), 29.

the inhabitation of the *world in front of the text* by the adoption of that world's precepts, priorities, and practices.

Two-Step Preaching

That theology involves praxis is undeniable. James 1:22–25 emphasizes the importance of application—"become doers of the word, and not merely hearers who delude themselves"; the one who applies the text is "a doer of works . . . blessed in what he does." It is not enough to *know;* one must also *be.* Only in personal application does the text accomplish its meaning; therefore, Gadamer could assert that application was an integral part of the hermeneutical process.[103] A response to the text from readers is thus essential, for the segment of the world projected by the pericope beckons and awaits an answer. Indeed, the text *demands* to be appropriated in this fashion, for the projected world of Scripture is "destined for autocracy" and, unlike other worlds spun to enchant or flatter, this world seeks readers' subjection.[104] A text, thus projecting the possibility of application, is more than informing; it is potentially transforming, for application of pericopal theology aligns lives with God's will, effecting covenant renewal within the community of saints.

Therefore, it is not enough to elucidate the theology of a text; it is also incumbent upon the preacher to delineate, in each sermon, the intersection of that theology with the faith and practice of God's people—how exactly pericopal theology shapes and changes the lives of hearers, how exactly it ought to be applied. The crucial nature of this transaction charges the preacher to generate, from theology, application that is valid, the specific response to be undertaken by hearers to the expounded pericope. There is, thus, a twofold aspect to the overall homiletical undertaking: the exposition of the theology of the unit text (the *theological* move: biblical pericope → pericopal theology), and the delineation of how theology may be applied in real life (the *homiletical* move: pericopal theology → valid application).

---

103. Hans-Georg Gadamer, *Truth and Method* (2nd rev. ed.; trans. Joel Weinsheimer and Donald G. Marshall; London: Continuum, 2004), 307. So also Ricoeur: The goal of overcoming distanciation "is attained only insofar as interpretation actualizes the meaning of the text for the present reader" (Paul Ricoeur, *Hermeneutics and the Human Sciences: Essays on Language, Action and Interpretation* [ed. and trans. John B. Thompson; Cambridge: Cambridge University Press, 1981)], 85, 159).

104. Erich Auerbach, *Mimesis: The Representation of Reality in Western Literature* (trans. Willard R. Trask; Princeton: Princeton University Press, 1953), 14–15.

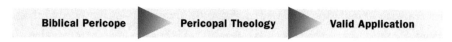

The first move, from pericope to theology, draws meaning *from* the biblical text (its authority); the second, from theology to application, directs meaning *to* the situations of listeners (its relevance). "The honest rhetorician therefore has two things in mind: a vision of how matters should go ideally and ethically and a consideration of the special circumstances of his auditors. Toward both of these he has a responsibility."[105] One might apply the same sentiment toward homileticians: they have a responsibility both to the text of Scripture ("how matters should go ideally and ethically") and to the world of their listeners ("the special circumstances of auditors"). In fact, this is the crux of the preaching endeavor—to bring to bear divine guidelines for life from the biblical text upon the situations of the congregation, to align the community of God to the will of God, for the glory of God. In other words, the ancient text is to be applied to the modern audience via theology. This bifid nature of communication is fundamental to the process, if the ancient text is to be brought to bear in a relevant way upon the lives of contemporary listeners.

In the two-step operation, the theology of the pericope thus functions as the bridge between text and praxis, between the circumstances of the text and those of the reading community, enabling the move from the "then" to the "now," from inspired canonical inscription to valid sermonic application. In applying theology in the second move into the discrete and specific circumstances of believers, the values of the cosmos are gradually subverted and undermined, and those of God's world are progressively established in the life of the community: covenant renewal is achieved. This is part of what it means to acknowledge, "Thy kingdom come."

The Second Step: Pericopal Theology to Application

The caveat that "universalizability is a necessary condition of morality, not a sufficient condition" is valid.[106] Leaving matters at the level of generalities, abstractions, and universals fails to provide the specificity required for concrete responses on the part of God's people to God's word. This is the rationale for the

---

105. Weaver, *Language Is Sermonic*, 211.

106. Stanley Hauerwas, "The Self as Story: Religion and Morality from the Agent's Perspective," *JRE* 1 (1973): 81.

second step, theology to application. Not only does the preacher need to move from the specifics of the text to the theology of the pericope, he must also go from theology to the specifics of life, applying pericopal theology into the real lives of real people. If week after week he has nothing to offer his congregation but the imperative to love or be honest (or other such "high-level" abstractions), in reality, the pastor offers his flock nothing but anodynes. As the seventeenth-century bishop of Chester, John Wilkins, asserted: "The chief end of an Orator, is to persuade (say the Philosophers): And therefore that Preacher who in his discourses does only flourish in general notions, and does not drive at some particular argument, endeavouring to press upon his Auditory [i.e., audience] the *belief* or *practice* of some *truth* or *duty,* is like an unwise fisher, who spreads his net to the empty air, where he cannot expect any success of his labors."[107]

On the other hand, Emil Brunner asserts that God only requires love from his people: "We are never bidden to do anything else."[108] That assertion is debatable; even in Deut 6 where the abstract commandment to love is prominent (6:4–5), when the inquisitive son enquires about the meaning of God's commandments (6:20), he is not referred to the *Shema,* but to "*all* these statutes," and "*all* these commandments" (6:24–25, emphasis added)—no abstractions here.[109] Likewise, in Luke 10:25–37, Jesus answered the question of who one's neighbor was with the parable of the Good Samaritan, portraying specific deeds of love. Specificity, in other words, is the essence of application. Bigger, broader, and grander truths must be brought down the ladder of abstraction, and specific application must be provided by the preacher to the congregation if life change is being sought. "If our faith is real, it must encroach upon our life. . . . There must be *translation,* for example, into the language of the newspaper," into the vernacular and idiom of listeners, into the routines of their life and being.[110] A sermon is intended to be a persuasive discourse—"it urges audiences not just to *think* in particular ways, but

---

107. Wilkins, *Ecclesiastes,* 36–37. "[T]o make a general principle worth anything, you must give it a body; you must show in what way and how far it would be applied actually in an actual system" (Oliver Wendell Holmes, "The Use of Law Schools," in *Speeches by Oliver Wendell Holmes* [Boston: Little, Brown, and Company, 1934], 34–35; this oration is dated Nov 5, 1886). Or, as popular business writers Chip and Dan Heath observe: "Any successful change requires a translation of ambiguous goals into concrete behaviors. In short, to make a switch, you need to *script the critical moves*" (Chip Heath and Dan Heath, *Switch: How to Change Things When Change Is Hard* [New York: Broadway, 2010], 53–54 [italics original]).

108. Emil Brunner, *The Divine Imperative: A Study in Christian Ethics,* (trans. Olive Wyon; Philadelphia: Westminster, 1947), 133.

109. Janzen, *Old Testament Ethics,* 70.

110. Karl Barth, *Dogmatics in Outline* (London: SCM, 1966), 32–33.

also to *act* in particular ways."[111] If such translation does not occur in a sermon, as the preacher offers guidelines for valid and specific application, the goal of realigning God's people with God's demand will not be achieved either. Thus this second half of the interpretive move—from theology to application—is a critical move in homiletics and, indeed, for the faith and practice of the church nourished on the preaching of God's word. How is the validity of this second step maintained?

Fidelity to what has gone on before is essential, for the church remains under the authority of the text of Scripture and seeks to be faithful to it in its application. Faithfulness is maintained by pericopal theology that is derived from, and grounded firmly upon, the text (the first move from pericope to theology). On the other hand, novelty is also called for in the fresh context of current auditors, as the church applies an ancient text to its own modern setting. Application, while beholden to the text, is not an attempt to repeat what is in the text or to reiterate the historical event that stands behind it. "Rather, creativity must be involved as we seek to mediate, translate, interpret its meaning—the meaning in front of the text—into our own horizon."[112] This is a call for novelty—application of the ancient text for a new setting, for a new audience.

As the end of the Gospels and the beginning of Acts make clear (Matt 28:18–20; Acts 1:8), God desires to involve his people in the ongoing drama of creation and redemption with new members entering the stage in each generation.[113] Believers are to undertake their own "improvisations" that demonstrate faithfulness to the past (i.e., derived from pericopal theology) and newness towards the future (i.e., relevant for a fresh audience). Such improvised applications are not the aping of deeds once done, nor the repetition of words once uttered, but a re-articulation and re-presentation of the ongoing saga in new circumstances. Verbatim and unimaginative imitation of what transpired in the previous acts of the drama is inadequate and inappropriate in the new context of the present troupe of performers. Instead, a novel reading of the unchanged

---

111. David S. Cunningham, *Faithful Persuasion: In Aid of a Rhetoric of Christian Theology* (South Bend, Ind., University of Notre Dame Press, 1991), 76.

112. David Tracy, "Creativity in the Interpretation of Religion: The Question of Radical Pluralism," *NLH* 15 (1984): 298.

113. In Vanhoozer's concept of the theo-dramatic rendition of the script (Scripture), the Father is the playwright and producer of the play, the Son the principal actor, and the Holy Spirit the director. Pastors are homileticians, and elders and church leaders are assistant directors, with the theologian taking the role of the dramaturge, a technical adviser to the dramatic company that is the church, the *troupe of actors* (Vanhoozer, *The Drama of Doctrine*, 106, 244, 247).

(and unchangeable) text has to occur in a changed context in order to maintain fidelity to the normative text—"a kind of relativism, to be sure, but one that *establishes* rather than undermines biblical authority."[114]

For instance, to disregard the change in the context of the text "2/12/1991" written in the U.K., but read in the U.S.A., would thoroughly mislead the reader: that sequence of digits, depending on one's location, could either stand for December 2, 1991, or February 12, 1991. In America, the British text "2/12/1991" must be read as "12/2/1991" in order for the reading to remain faithful to the original transhistorical intention ("the second day of the twelfth month of the year 1991 C.E."). Obviously, classic and normative texts cannot themselves be altered, but readings can and should be changed, to maintain fidelity to the thrust of the original utterance. Such a reading is not an option; it is necessary *in order that* the interpretation maintain fidelity to the original, and be thoroughly relevant to those in a fresh reading context.[115] Here is the seeming paradox: novelty is necessary for fidelity!

FACETS OF MEANING		
Original Textual Sense	*"Pericopal Theology"* (WORLD IN FRONT OF THE TEXT / TRANSHISTORICAL INTENTION)	Exemplification
2/12/1991 (U.K.)	*second day of the twelfth month of the year 1991 C.E.*	12/2/1991 (U.S.)

Fidelity in this transaction involves sustaining the identity of exemplification with the original textual sense. One could maintain identity by slavish imitation (2/12/1991 [U.K.] → 2/12/1991 [U.S.], completely violating authorial intent. Or one could maintain identity by skillful improvisation (2/12/1991 [U.K.] → 12/2/1991 [U.S.]), remaining faithful to authorial intent. This latter approach demands training and a developed sensibility for what is fitting in a given situation. In biblical exposition, these interpretive moves are best undertaken by those who "speak what is fitting for sound doctrine" (Titus 2:1). It requires of the preacher attentiveness to new contexts of interpretation, sensitivity to the unfolding continuities of the work, and responsibility for, and accountability to,

---

114. Ibid., 260–61.

115. See Lawrence Lessig, "The Limits of Lieber," *Cardozo L. Rev.* 16 (1995): 2258, 2260, 2262; idem, "Fidelity in Translation," *Texas L. Rev.* 71 (1992–1993): 1170; and idem, "Fidelity and Constraint," *Fordham L. Rev.* 65 (1996–1997): 1370.

the particular community of co-performers, fellow improvisers, and auditors.

Thus the task of the preacher is to improvise, delving into the past and suggesting in the present how the past may be creatively exemplified/applied in the future. Keith Johnstone's analogy is apt: "The improviser has to be like a man walking backwards."[116] This is one who, with eyes on the past, must be guided by it—by the canonical Scriptures. Yet the improviser is also headed "forward," away from the past, transposing it into the future of hearers. Thus the situation of the auditors must also be an important parameter that governs the activities of the interpreter. When the same text is "performed" in different contexts to produce discrete improvisations on the same theme, the same pericopal theology is brought to bear upon those different reading situations in order to generate faithful applications. Such applications, though administered by the same theology, may—and, indeed, should—look different, for each reader, hearer, congregation, and context is different: "[O]ne and the same exhortation does not suit all, inasmuch as neither are all bound together by similarity of character. . . . Therefore according to the quality of hearers ought the discourse of teachers be fashioned, so as to suit all and each in their several needs, and yet never deviate from the art of common edification."[117] Application must be tailored for relevance to each individual context. However, insofar as these varied applications fall within the bounds of the same pericopal theology, they are but exemplifications of a single transhistorical intention, and therefore all such improvisations remain faithful to the text.[118] To arrive at praxis

---

116. *Impro: Improvisation and the Theatre* (London: Methuen, 1981), 116.

117. Gregory the Great, *Pastoral Rule,* "Part Three: How the Ruler, While Living Well, Ought to Teach and Admonish Those That Are Put Under Him: Prologue." This reflects the property of the "classic" to carry the potential for a plurality of applications (see chapter 1).

118. In a different way, this point was made with the Hirschian triad in chapter 1. For an insightful analysis of improvisation in jazz, with clear parallels for the present discussion, see James O. Young and Carl Matheson, "The Metaphysics of Jazz," *J. Aes. Art Crit.* 58 (2000): 125–33. Musicians performing this genre recognize "jazz standards" as providing instructions for improvising. Such operations are not *totally* spontaneous, for to be an instance of a jazz standard, the performance has to be in accord with a given set of guidelines embodied by the standard. Young and Matheson discuss what they call the "canonical model" of such tacit rules that constitute a standard: introduction, head (statement of the melody), improvisations, recapitulation of the head, and ending. According to the model, two jazz performances are instances of the same standard if their heads utilize the same melody and their improvisations are grounded on the chord patterns of the head ("theology" and the "transhistorical intention" it bears?), while yet being obviously very different from each other. Indeed, many of these performances are based on *The Real Book,* a set of unauthorized, but ubiquitous, volumes (there are recent legal versions as well [3 vols.; Milwaukee.: Hal Leonard, 2006]), scoring the melody and chord changes of an exhaustive listing of jazz standards. All paginated identically (chapter and verse?) and coming in editions to suit B♭, E♭, and C instruments (multiple translations/versions?), these tomes, in a sense, form the "canon" of jazz (Young and Matheson, "The Metaphysics of Jazz," 126, 128–29).

that is faithful to text and relevant to the listeners is the goal of the homiletical undertaking. The burden of the preacher is, therefore, to move validly and relevantly from Scripture to sermon, enabling the community of God to align itself to the *world in front of the text* (pericopal theology) to accomplish covenant renewal. Application of Scripture is thus the culmination of the move from text to praxis.

In sum, the entire two-step operation of preaching, from text to theology and from theology to application, is the task of the church in every age, and pericopal theology is the authoritative guide for this faithful-yet-new performance of the text in unprecedented situations. The application so generated is not an act of creation *ex nihilo*, but rather a *re*-creation—an improvisation of an ancient textual sense in a new setting for a new audience. Scripture remains the plenary source, the authoritative playbook of action, with each pericope contributing specific instructions for the "performance" of the segment of the canonical world it projects. Valid application is generated from the text by a reading characterized by fidelity and novelty. For the maintenance of fidelity and novelty, pericopal theology is critical. Insofar as the congregation applies the theology into their lives, they will have aligned themselves to the divine demand in that pericope, and theology will have become less a matter of *in*doctrination than of *ex*doctrination—pericopal theology lived out in practice.[119]

Such a notion of application pertains not only to religious literature but to legal literature as well, ancient texts that homiletician and jurist, respectively, seek to apply to their contemporary eras. There is much that may be learned by comparing theological and legal hermeneutics: the tasks of practitioners in both fields are conceptually parallel.

Exemplification in Legal Hermeneutics

It has been observed that the interpretation of legal texts, such as the U.S. Constitution, is "bringing into the present a text of the past," a straddling of two worlds simultaneously.[120] The continuing life of a binding legal or religious classic depends on ongoing recontextualization in new circumstances. Like the Scriptures, a civic constitution, too, is "intended to endure for ages to come, and, consequently, to be adapted to the various crises of human

---

119. Vanhoozer, *The Drama of Doctrine*, 400. Also see N. T. Wright, "How Can the Bible Be Authoritative?" *VE* 21 (1991): 26–28.

120. James Boyd White, "Judicial Criticism," in *Interpreting Law and Literature: A Hermeneutic Reader* (eds. Sanford Levinson and Steven Mailloux; Evanston: Northwestern University Press, 1988), 403.

affairs."[121] The similarity between the hermeneutics of law and Scripture are considerable: both judge and preacher are hermeneuts handling classic texts; both mediate those texts for their hearers and readers; and the literature of both fields exists to be applied to specific situations in subsequent time, one to serve the execution of justice through pronouncing verdicts, the other to serve the exercise of faith through preaching sermons. Upon the jurist falls the burden of finding application from an ancient text like the eighteenth-century U.S. Constitution, for petitioners in the modern era. Likewise, upon the preacher is the onus of deriving application from the ancient text of Scripture for contemporary auditors of the sermon who have to struggle with real-life issues of their day. Generating applications is the task of the judge who moves from the text of law to judicial philosophy and thence to the adjudication of the case currently at the bar. And the homiletician, this work proposes, generates applications by moving from the pericope of Scripture to theology and thence to the congregation currently in the pews. Of particular interest, then, is the similarity between application in legal and scriptural interpretation.

Legal literature is replete with examples of such a movement from original textual sense, through transhistorical intention, to future exemplification. Valid application must be made of the text of law in situations and circumstances distant from, and unforeseen at, the event of the original inscription. For instance, the U.S. Constitution empowers Congress "[t]o raise and support armies," "[t]o provide and maintain a navy," and "[t]o make rules for the government and regulation of the land and naval forces" (Article I, ¶8, clauses 12 and 13). As written, this edict is silent about any support for an air force. However, despite the absence of any explicit reference in the Constitution to this branch of the armed forces, the U.S. government continues to raise and support, provide and maintain, govern and regulate an air force. Presumably, the concrete terms "army" and "navy" in that late eighteenth-century document projected a broader category, namely, "all manner of national defense undertakings." The transhistorical and pragmatic thrust of the declaration was, clearly, to designate any conceivable

---

121. U.S. Supreme Court Chief Justice John Marshall, *McCulloch v. Maryland,* U.S. Reports 17 (4 Wheat.) (1819): 415 (emphasis removed). "They are not ephemeral enactments, designed to meet passing occasions. They are, to use the words of Chief Justice Marshall, 'designed to approach immortality as nearly as human institutions can approach it.' . . . In the application of a constitution, therefore, our contemplation cannot be only of what has been but of what may be" (U.S. Supreme Court Justice Joseph McKenna, *Weems v. United States,* U.S. Reports 217 [1910]: 373; the citation of Chief Justice Marshall is from *Cohens v. Virginia,* U.S. Reports 19 [1821]: 387).

military force as worthy of establishment and maintenance by Congress; such an intention would necessarily include an air force and, potentially, even a space force, or a robot force, as future exemplifications (see the table below).[122]

To take another example, the Fourth Amendment (1791) of the U.S. Constitution proclaims "[t]he right of the people to be secure in their persons, houses, papers, and effects, against unreasonable searches and seizures." Certainly "papers" (the original textual sense) should, in the twenty-first century, include all manner of information storage media (the transhistorical intention), including DVDs, CDs, flash drives, hard drives, and, perhaps, even cloud storage, among others (exemplifications).

FACETS OF MEANING		
Original Textual Sense	**Transhistorical Intention** (WORLD IN FRONT OF THE TEXT) or **Author's Doing** (PRAGMATICS OF UTTERANCE)	**Exemplification**
army, navy	all manner of national military undertakings	air/space/ robot force, . . .
papers	all manner of information storage media	DVDs, CDs, flash drives, . . .

Of course, no canonical corpus can be expected to bear the burden of explicitly expressing all possible exemplifications for all possible people in all possible future times. In biblical interpretation, it is the pericopal theology (transhistorical intention) that in its generalization encompasses every conceivable option of exemplification *mutatis mutandis,* and governs what may be considered valid and what may not, what is faithful to the original and what is not. U.S. Supreme Court Justice Antonin Scalia recommends that in changed eras, the court must follow the "trajectory" of the original law; he admits that "that enterprise is not entirely cut-and-dried but requires the exercise of judgment"— there is clearly room for jurisprudential discernment.[123]

Judicial discrimination is called for in legal hermeneutics; similarly, pastoral discrimination is to be exercised in theological hermeneutics for preaching. The original words of such texts as the U.S. Constitution or the Bible establish

---

122. See Lessig, "Fidelity and Constraint," 1376–77.

123. Antonin Scalia, *A Matter of Interpretation: Federal Courts and the Law* (Princeton: Princeton University Press, 1997), 38, 45.

the breadth of meaning of what is written therein (i.e., the transhistorical inten-
tion/pericopal theology), and this intermediary entity functions as the standard
by which the validity of all subsequent interpretive endeavors must be gauged.
For biblical hermeneutics the transhistorical thrust of the pericope is captured
in the theology of the pericope which thereby becomes the arbiter of the legiti-
macy of the application that is proclaimed.

Exemplification in Theological Hermeneutics

The final homiletical move, the second step, from theology to application, is the
culmination of the preacher's undertaking that began as an encounter with a
pericope of Scripture in an ecclesial context. In this latter stage, the particular
cares of the day are to be diligently considered by the preacher, as the transhistorical is now couched in the timely context of the hearers, "[f]or what else is good
preaching but vernacular theology?"—theology in the *lingua franca*, applied to
the real lives of real people. Without such relevant and specific application, the
"antiquarian interest" in an ancient document is simply a futile endeavor "to
massage the dead."[124] Without it, the thrust of the text of God is negated, the goal
of God aborted, and the people of God left without guidance. The preacher must
grapple, therefore, with both the canon of God and the concerns of mankind,
and employ pericopal theology as a mediator between the two, arriving at application with both fidelity and novelty. In that applications are subsumed by the
theology of the pericope, these applications are faithful to the text, and therefore
authoritative. In that applications are appropriate for the specific circumstances
of the community being preached to, these applications are relevant, tailored
to the congregation to whom the message is delivered.[125] The "embodiment" of

---

124. Holmer, *The Grammar of Faith*, 14, 16. Only historical ignorance or cultural chauvinism, notes Hays,
would lead one to presume that no such hermeneutical operation—"metaphor-making"—is required for
the meaning of the ancient text of Scripture to be carried into the contemporary context of the church
(Richard B. Hays, *The Moral Vision of the New Testament* [San Francisco: HarperSanFrancisco, 1996], 6).

125. Applications may operate with different aims. Classical rhetoric knows of three directions of audience
responses sought by a rhetor: a *judicial* assessment of past events (for instance, the goal of Paul's apologetic for his early ministry in Corinth, in 2 Cor), a *deliberative* resolve with regard to future actions
of the audience (e.g., parabolic teachings that call for explicit responses), or an *epideictic* appreciation
of particular beliefs or values in the present (as put forward by Jesus in his farewell discourse in John
14–16). See Quintilian, *Inst.* 3.7–9; Anaximenes, *Rhet. Alex.* 1421b; also see C. Clifton Black, "Rhetorical Criticism," in *Hearing the New Testament: Strategies for Interpretation* (ed. Joel B. Green; Grand
Rapids: Eerdmans, 1995), 261. Application, in parallel to this three-fold shape of rhetorical purpose,
may also have one or more of these broad aims: a change of mind (a response of cognition), a change
of action (a response of volition), or a change of feeling (a response of emotion).

pericopal theology in specific application for specific audiences is the ultimate goal of the homiletical undertaking, rendering possible covenant renewal between God and his people, as lives are transformed according to the will of God.

In all such transactions, however, it must be borne in mind that it is the scriptural text that ultimately remains normative for the community of God's people. Therefore the authority behind applications depends upon the cogency of the interpretive process by which they have been generated—primarily upon the careful derivation of pericopal theology. To the degree that these hermeneutical operations upon the text have been performed with due diligence, the triadic components of textual meaning (textual sense, pericopal theology, and valid applications) bear the vigor of the text itself in its prescriptivity, perenniality, and plurality.[126]

Exemplification for 2 Samuel 11–12

The elucidation of theology from the particulars of the pericope was demonstrated earlier in this chapter with 2 Sam 11–12: *Reverence for God and deference to his word is manifested in the reined exercise of power, the restriction of self-indulgent passions, and the recognition of evil as reprehensible in the sight of God; this respect for the authority and rulership of the true sovereign brings blessing.* The theology of this unit of text warns against unfaithfulness to God manifesting in uncontrolled desire and sexual incontinence, combined with an outrageous abuse of power. Unchecked, such a disregard for God's reputation and the demands of his word only lead one deeper into a maelstrom of misdeeds. Even human life becomes of dubious value in the eyes of one who is more interested in preserving his or her own reputation, rather than God's. Faithfulness to God clearly involves a vigilant, tenacious, and unyielding commitment to the values of God for the sake of his reputation.

The specific exemplification of this theology in the lives of hearers will, of course, be determined to a great extent by characteristics of the particular

---

126. It may be noted here that the concept of inspiration implies that the entirety of the canonical speech act—including all three components of meaning—is attributed to divine authorship and is therefore authoritative (see Gregg R. Allison, "Speech Act Theory and Its Implications for the Doctrine of the Inerrancy/Infallibility of Scripture," *Phil. Christi* 8 [1995]: 1–23). Poythress also agrees that authority attaches to valid applications generated from the text (Vern S. Poythress, "Divine Meaning of Scripture," *WTJ* 48 [1986]: 251). Yet, the hermeneut must grasp all these interpretive results with a degree of humility, for they are derivations from the normative text and no interpreter is infallible. "Our metaphorical readings must be tested prayerfully within the community of faith by others who seek God's will along with us through close reading of the text" (Hays, *The Moral Vision of the New Testament*, 304). This is also the demand of the Rule of Ecclesiality (see chapter 1).

congregation for the sermon. Nonetheless, the case study of King David is a dramatic example of how discontent and concupiscence, abetted by power run amok, and unrestrained by a respect for God's word or name, can plunge one deeper into the abyss of transgression (the brunt of Nathan's accusation, 2 Sam 12:9, 14). This drama of David (and its dire consequences) serves, by its theology, as an unmistakable deterrent for the one tempted to slide in that downward direction of unfaithfulness to God. Considering the position of the king as one wielding considerable authority, the thrust of this narrative may also be brought home effectively to those who are in positions of leadership and authority. If one would live faithfully under the hand of God in such situations, one must be resolute about exercising power with utmost responsibility, with great care and concern for one's subordinates, especially when tempted by lusts of the flesh to fall into dissolution and debauchery.

Obviously, not all in a congregation are heads of state or those who administer the kind of power that was wantonly abused by David. Nevertheless, whether in the workplace or at home, amongst classmates or co-workers, in the field or in the marketplace, most individuals exercise some degree of authority by virtue of official capacity, social standing, or organizational membership. Even for one who might not be part of any such hierarchy, the lesson of turpitude degenerating into further baseness, when uncurbed by the moral demands of God to honor his name and his word, is one to be taken to heart, for many a Christian has fallen—and, sadly, many continue to fall—prey to such licentiousness. While 1–2 Sam appears to deal primarily with the iniquities of two Israelite kings, the lessons therein for the people of the nation (and for subsequent readers and hearers of the text) must not be neglected. In opting for monarchy, the people had themselves rejected God (1 Sam 8:7). The wrongdoings of their rulers reflected the people's own unfaithfulness to God; this endows the text with potential for universal applicability—for both crown and commoner. Thus, 2 Sam 11–12 bears potential for general application by all readers, the specificities of exemplification being governed by the situation of address and the station of the addressees.[127]

---

127. With those who claim that the failure of King David in this pericope only points to the perfections of the ultimate Davidic King, Jesus the Messiah, I would heartily agree. However, I would argue that the thrust of the text is not merely to have us hope for the day of the heavenly King. Rather the text demarcates those failures of the earthly king as *un*Christlikeness, and readers are pointed to the perfect regent to encourage them, the people of God, to be like him in his perfect humanity, conformed to his image. It is a facet of that image that is powerfully expressed and manifested in the pericopal theology of 2 Sam 11–12. But I get ahead of myself; see chapter 4 for more on the concept of bearing the image of Christ.

A controlled exercise of passion and power as demanded by the theology of this pericope necessitates accountability to God (and to his agents), as one strives to "see" things the way God does, to live humbly and contentedly under him who alone holds supreme power, and to recognize immoral behavior as evil in the eyes of God. The preacher might consider proposing, as significance (application outside the proper realm of meaning; see chapter 1), the setting up of an accountability group of godly, responsible people who, corporately personifying the prophet Nathan's office, would be granted the freedom and authority by individual Christians to provide them counsel, as well as correction, when necessary. Such an application, when put into practice, would be a means of realizing the pericope's theological imperative of living faithfully unto God, under God. It must be noted again that the particular characteristics of a given congregation will determine the specific nature of the application proposed by the homiletician—the element of its relevance. At the same time, such application is to be governed by the theology of the pericope—the element of its authority. The text is thus endowed with potential for universal applicability.

Section Summary: Application

In sum, the move from original textual sense to exemplification is made possible by the transhistorical intention of pericopal theology; improvisation is undertaken with fidelity and novelty to generate valid application. Such applications subsumed by pericopal theology demonstrate fidelity to the text of Scripture under consideration; the novelty of improvisation is reflected in the relevant adaptation of application to the specificities of listeners' contexts. The preacher thus serves as the conscience of application for the community of God, with the dual responsibility to understand what God has said, and to generate valid application in order that God's people may be aligned to the *world in front of the text*—the theology of the pericope. Covenant renewal is thus accomplished in the church as she submits to divine demand. The task of the preacher is therefore one of great consequence for the community of God's people.

Thus the preacher is a mediator between the text and church, script and actors. It is this one's task to interpret the text for the community and to propose how it may be applied in valid praxis. Combining canonical script analysis and contextual situation analysis, the sermon bridges text and application via theology. Application is thus both authoritative and relevant. "[T]ruth and timeliness together make the full preacher"—fidelity to the text ("truth") and novelty towards audience ("timeliness").[128] By such valid application, the church renews its covenant with its God. The pericope has, thus, performed its role as an instrument of covenant renewal in the ecclesial context, and the preacher has fulfilled the mandate to mediate this crucial undertaking to the people of God.

Summary: Pericopes, Theology, and Application

This chapter has focused upon the move made by the preacher from text to praxis—the passage from pericope, through theology, to application. The function of biblical pericopes in ecclesial settings was established as promoting covenant renewal, the restoration of a right relationship between God and his people. Pericopes, these assimilable portions of the canon, project segments of the canonical world projected by Scripture. Each such segment constitutes the theology of that particular pericope. It is pericopal theology that serves as the intermediary in the movement from text to application, bidding readers inhabit the world so portrayed. In other words, God's people are beckoned to inhabit his world and abide by its precepts, priorities, and practices.

This work has sought to further that understanding of the role of theology in the homiletical undertaking. A definition of the theological entity—pericopal theology—has been accomplished and a delineation of the potential of pericopal theology for discovering application has been described. Interpretation, to be sure, is not complete with the discovery of pericopal theology, the move from text to theology. The preacher must also consummate the homiletical undertaking by proceeding further, from theology to application. The first step (text to theology) sustains the authority of the text in the sermon; the second (theology to application) endows the sermon with relevance. Under the auspices of pericopal theology, authority and relevance are thus maintained in balance, as valid application is generated. The people of God are now enabled to obey Scripture, implementing covenant renewal and aligning individual and community to the will of God for the glory of God.

From the discussion in this chapter, it is implied that every pericope in Scripture, projecting a segment of the plenary canonical world, generates a divine demand for the people of God. Does this then mean that even the pericopes within the genre of OT law are also applicable for the Christian today? If

---

128. Phillips Brooks, *Lectures on Preaching, Delivered before the Divinity School of Yale College in January and February, 1877* (New York: E. P. Dutton, 1877), 220–21.

so, how? Chapter 3 will explore answers to these questions, and in answering them, we will discover what God, in every age, requires of his children in response to every part of Scripture, and every one of its pericopes.

CHAPTER 3

DIVINE DEMAND *and* FAITHFUL OBEDIENCE

*[O]ne should first accept upon himself the yoke of the kingdom of heaven
and then take upon himself the yoke of the commandments.*
R. JOSHUA B. KARHA[1]

Chapters 1 and 2 dealt with general and special hermeneutics, and the theology and application of pericopes, respectively. In chapter 1 the concept of the *world in front of the text*—what authors *do* with what they *say* (the pragmatics of the text)—was introduced. Texts, particularly classics, project worlds with transhistorical intentions to overcome the distanciation they have undergone; thus they render themselves perennial in influence, plural in application potential, and prescriptive in advancing a way of life. Scripture, too, is a classic, howbeit of a "special" kind, the reading of which is governed by a set of implicit Rules of Reading that God's people have generally abided by over the millennia. In chapter 2, the theological role of pericopes was considered. These fundamental textual units of preaching are literary instruments for aligning the faith and practice of the people of God with their sovereign. Each pericope projects a segment of the canonical, plenary *world in front of the text*. Such a segment, it was proposed, was the *theology of the pericope*, from which is derived application, the culmination of the sermon resulting in changed lives for the glory of God. Thus preaching is best undertaken as a bipartite (two-step)

---

1. See *m. Ber.* 2:2.

endeavor: from text to the theology of the pericope, and from theology to application. This is to say that every pericope makes a divine demand, a claim, upon the people of God; the exposition of that demand and how, in response, specific application may be made, is the task of the preacher.

> What we bring across the bridge from text to sermon is . . . this claim upon the hearers. A text's claim involves both a message and intention bound up in the text's own manner of embodying that message, both what the text wishes to say and what the text wishes to do through its saying. . . . This is what the preacher should bring from text to sermon: the claim of the text, the intention of the text to say and do something to and with the hearers.[2]

Broadly conceived, divine demand includes anything God desires and expects of mankind, in terms of relationship, behavior, responsibilities, and so on. Indeed, divine demand is the gracious call of a loving Father to his children to align their lives with the precepts, priorities, and practices of his ideal world. But if every pericope makes such a claim, a divine demand, does that imply that even the pericopes in the genre of OT law are applicable to the Christian today? This work proposes that it does; biblical law *is* applicable today. This chapter will deal with how exactly this is the case and how the interpreter might discern the divine demand in biblical law. Thus a theology of obedience for the people of God will be established.

PREVIEW: DIVINE DEMAND AND FAITHFUL OBEDIENCE

While divine demand is discernible in any biblical genre, here I shall address that of OT law that comprises the *explicit* imperatives of Scripture.[3] In this category, the Mosaic law occupies the largest slot, consuming as it does a sizeable chunk of the Pentateuch. The question of whether ancient Israelite law is applicable to the Christian today has always been perplexing. A brief survey of traditional approaches (Reformed, Lutheran, and Dispensational) to this issue will be followed by an examination of the take of adherents of the New Perspective on Paul (NPP).[4] While the differences between the traditional approaches

---

2. Thomas G. Long, *The Witness of Preaching* (2nd ed.; Louisville: Westminster John Knox, 2005), 107–8.

3. Even narratives, as was shown in chapter 2 with 2 Sam 11–12 (also see chapter 4 for the same operation with Gen 22), implicitly project the divine demand by means of the *world in front of the text*.

4. The choice of these representatives is to enable a comparison and establish a contrast for the purposes of my argument. There is no doubt that there have been, and are, other viewpoints and nuanced variations thereof in Christendom.

and NPP are significant, in this they seem to agree: ancient biblical law (i.e., the Mosaic law) is *not* applicable to the Christian today, except perhaps for the category of that law that is termed "moral" (as opposed to "civil" and "ceremonial"). In contrast, this work holds that *all* of God's demands are always applicable for everyone everywhere. However, the drastic contextual changes between the circumstances of the giving of the law and its reading today have rendered this universal application of biblical law not a straightforward transaction.

I shall show that pericopes of biblical law are to be applied today by employing a *theological* hermeneutic that considers the rationale of the law (the transhistorical intention implicit in the theology of the pericope) as binding upon God's people. These OT laws, it must be noted, are not criteria for salvation, but are guidelines for sanctification. In other words, the keeping of divine demand (in the genre of biblical law and elsewhere) assumes a prior relationship between divine sovereign and human subjects. The children of God are to fulfill their filial responsibility to obey, because they already are children of God by faith in Christ.[5]

This chapter goes on to demonstrate that this filial responsibility to keep divine demand is an "obedience of faith" (Rom 1:5; 16:26). Unlike legalism—merit-seeking works, attempted with one's own resources, for one's own glory—obedience of faith is dependent upon God's grace, for it recognizes that only through the power of the Spirit can obedience to divine demand be possible or be pleasing to God: "Grace was given that the law may be kept" (Augustine, *De Spir. et litt.* 19.34). Such obedience also acknowledges that failures do occur, and joyfully accepts the forgiveness offered through Jesus Christ. In sum, this theological hermeneutic of biblical law (and indeed of divine demand everywhere in Scripture) rests upon God's gracious provision through the Son and an equally gracious operation through the Spirit, while yet exhorting believers to fulfill their Christian responsibility to meet divine demand and thereby be as holy as God himself is holy.

DIVINE DEMAND

Lying at the core of Israel's defining story, law is placed at the commencement of the nation's overarching narrative. Enfolded in the texture of narrative, law is

---

5. As will be evident as the chapter progresses, although "divine demand" bespeaks the authority of a God over his people, such a "demand" is by no means peremptory, capricious, or tyrannical. "Demand," here, is being used broadly to indicate God's expectation of his people to respond to his will: relationship precedes, but does not preclude, responsibility.

dependent upon the surrounding text for the marking of time; the embedding of the Mosaic law in the Pentateuch sustains the organic connection of the founding events of the nation of Israel with their law.[6] But are those ancient demands made to the covenanted people of God meant to be applied in the life of the believer today? Paul seemingly declared the law to be no longer binding (Rom 6:14), it having come to bring about wrath, increase transgression, and arouse sinful passions (4:15; 5:20; 7:5). Moreover, Christ abolished the law in his flesh (Eph 2:15), and the first covenant was rendered "obsolete" (Heb 8:13). Also, Deut 4:8 and Ps 147:19–20 explicitly noted, in connection with God's giving his statutes and ordinances to Israel, that he had not dealt thus with any nation, suggesting the uniqueness of the Mosaic law and, perhaps, its inapplicability for other peoples.[7] Yet, paradoxically, the law is said to have been written for all believers (1 Cor 9:8–10) and, frequently, demands of the Christian made in the NT are grounded upon those same OT laws (Rom 13:9; Gal 5:14; Eph 6:2; 1 Tim 5:18; Jas 2:8–11; 1 Pet 1:15–16; etc.).[8] After all, *all* Scripture is profitable (2 Tim 3:16). Indeed, the laws of the OT are God's laws (Rom 7:22, 25; 8:7; 1 Cor 7:19), and they are declared to be good, holy, righteous, and spiritual (Rom 7:12–14, 16; 1 Tim 1:8). So much so, Paul can "joyfully concur" with this law of God (Rom 7:22) and "establish" it (3:31).

How is the interpreter to reconcile these seeming inconsistencies? In his 1750 sermon, "The Original, Nature, Property, and Use of the Law," John Wesley acknowledged that "there are few subjects within the whole compass of religion so little understood as this."[9] Particularly for homiletics, how does the preacher approach the legal literature of the Bible with a view to proposing application in sermons today? The fundamental question is this: Is the Mosaic law still applicable to the contemporary Christian?

Approaches to the Law

For the purposes of this work, the various approaches to the Mosaic law in the church today may be broadly divided into two: the traditional approach

---

6. Paul Ricoeur, "Toward a Hermeneutic of the Idea of Revelation," in *Essays on Biblical Interpretation,* by Paul Ricoeur (ed. Lewis S. Mudge; Philadelphia: Fortress, 1980), 82.

7. Also see Pss 89:34; 119:160; Eccl 12:13; Mal 3:6. New Testament texts that seem to convey the same sentiments include: Mark 7:19; Acts 11:8–9; Rom 6:14; 10:4; 14:14; 1 Cor 7:19; Gal 5:18; Heb 7:11–19, 28; 9:23–25; 10:1–9; etc.

8. Also see Matt 5:17–20; John 7:19; Rom 3:31; 1 Cor 14:34; 2 Tim 3:16–17.

9. "Sermon 34," in *The Works of John Wesley: Vol. 2: Sermons II* (ed. Albert C. Outler; Nashville: Abingdon, 1985), 4.

(including Lutheran, Reformed, and Dispensational—this is not to deny the numerous variations on these main themes within each camp), and the New Perspective on Paul (NPP). Needless to say, this division employs a brush of broad dimensions; the purpose of such a capacious categorization is simply to show the continuity or discontinuity that each camp understands as operating between law and grace, and between works and faith, in the two major economies of the Bible—that of the old covenant and that of the new.[10]

TRADITIONAL APPROACHES	NEW PERSPECTIVE ON PAUL
More discontinuity: law vs. grace/works vs. faith	More continuity: law-grace/works-faith
Focus on vertical axis: man-God relationship	Focus on horizontal axis: Jew-Gentile relationship
Mosaic law not applicable to the Christian	Mosaic law not applicable to the Christian

The problem with the traditional approaches, which see significant discontinuity between law and grace, and between works and faith, is the difficulty of answering why God gave the law to the Jews in the first place, and in so much exquisite detail, consuming so much space in Scripture, only to "change" it all into a different scheme (grace/faith) later.[11] On the other hand, in the NPP approach, where the focus is primarily on the Gentile-Jew relationship without soteriological distinction between law/works and grace/faith, one encounters the difficulty of answering what actually changed with Christ's atoning work and the subsequent relationship between God and man, beyond just the expansion of the socio-anthropological boundaries to include Gentiles in the community of God's people.[12]

With regard to these two polarities, traditional and NPP, the approach of my work falls somewhere in between. Unlike the traditional camp, I see law working

---

10. There are differences—and some of them significant—between the three groups included in the traditional camp. These differences, when pertinent to my argument, will be described. In the main, however, for the discussion of (dis)continuity between law/works and grace/faith for the purposes of sanctification, Lutheran, Reformed, and Dispensational modes of thought are not entirely strange bedfellows. No doubt, there are also shades and nuances that are passed over in my description of the NPP camp. For the most part, I will restrict the discussion of NPP to what is commonly considered the "Sanders-Dunn-Wright" line of thought, with these individuals as the major interlocutors.

11. Or one could ask why Christians should attend to OT law if it has been superseded.

12. The NPP generally looks upon the difference between law and grace as more sociological and anthropological, than soteriological or theological; see below.

with grace and works *with* faith; in that sense, I do see more continuity between law and grace and between works and faith. But unlike the NPP camp, I do not see the core issue as being a horizontal one—concerning interethnic relationships—but rather a vertical one—bearing upon the relationship between God and his people.[13]

Traditional: Lutheran Approach

For Luther, the Mosaic law was binding on Gentiles only if it reflected natural law—law that is self-evident to human nature. "I keep the commandments which Moses has given, not because Moses gave the commandment, but because they have been implanted in me by nature, and Moses agrees exactly with nature, etc. But the other commandments of Moses, which are not by nature, the Gentiles do not hold."[14] Thus the OT law is "abrogated in the sense that we are free to keep it or not to keep it."[15] As to how, in the OT, one might distinguish between law that is "natural" from law that is not, Luther is silent. So, as far as the specifics of the Mosaic law itself is concerned, Luther's approach is that the Christian today should obey them only if their stipulations are "natural."[16]

Moo, calling his a "modified Lutheran" approach, takes a similar stance: the Mosaic law "no longer functions as the ultimate and immediate standard of conduct for God's people," rather being refracted through Jesus' teachings.[17] Nonetheless, he does see an *indirect* utility of the law for Christian praxis: several of the commandments of the Mosaic law are reapplied in the NT (Gal 5:14; Eph 6:2; Jas 2:8–12; etc.); the Mosaic law also has some role in "filling out" some of the demands of God (e.g., Ex 21 helps one conclude that the killing of a fetus

---

13. As far as justification is concerned, I park myself in the traditional camp. My differences are almost entirely with what constitutes sanctification—and this from a homiletical/pastoral vantage point.

14. Martin Luther, "How Christians Should Regard Moses," in *Luther's Works*, vol. 35 (ed. E. Theodore Bachmann; Philadelphia: Muhlenberg, 1960), 168. And "[w]e will regard Moses as a teacher, but we will not regard him as our lawgiver—unless he agrees with both the New Testament and the natural law" (ibid., 165). Also see Martin Luther, "Against the Heavenly Prophets in the Matter of Images and Sacraments, Part I," in *Luther's Works*, vol. 40 (trans. Bernhard Erling; Philadelphia: Muhlenberg, 1958), 97.

15. Martin Luther, "Temporal Authority: to What Extent it Should Be Obeyed," in *Luther's Works*, vol. 45 (trans. J. J. Schindel; rev. Walther I. Brandt; Philadelphia: Muhlenberg, 1963), 97.

16. In general, Luther was quite negative about the Mosaic law. For example: "For Christ, to whom this law applied, has annulled it completely, killed it, and buried it forever through his passion and resurrection. He rent the veil of the temple and subsequently broke up and destroyed Jerusalem with its priesthood, principality, law, and everything" ("On the Councils and the Church," in *Luther's Works*, vol. 41 [trans. Charles M. Jacobs; rev. and ed. Eric W. Gritsch; Philadelphia: Fortress, 1966], 63–64).

17. Douglas J. Moo, "The Law of Christ as the Fulfillment of the Law of Moses: A Modified Lutheran View," in *Five Views on Law and Gospel*, by Greg L. Bahnsen, Walter C. Kaiser, Douglas J. Moo, Wayne G. Strickland, and Willem A. VanGemeren (ed. Stanley N. Gundry; Grand Rapids: Zondervan, 1996), 343, 357.

is the taking of human life); and, in addition, the Mosaic law serves as a witness to the fulfillment of God's plan in Christ. Thus, in Moo's "modified Lutheran" approach, the authority of the Mosaic law persists in some sense, though what exactly would be lost if this code were absent from the Bible is not very clear: the requirements binding upon the Christian are, in this approach, only those that are (re)asserted in the NT. At best, the OT law serves as a source of some information that "fills out" the rationale of divine demands in the NT.[18]

At any rate, "modified" or otherwise, the Lutheran approach to the Mosaic law tends to minimize, if not nullify, its *direct* application to believers today.

Traditional: Reformed Approach

Calvin was clear about the value of Mosaic law: the divine demand of God reflects the perfection of the Lawgiver, thus these laws contain "a perfect pattern of righteousness," and all of mankind needs this daily instruction of God's law so that they may "advance to a purer knowledge of the Divine will" (*Institutes* 2.7.6–13). Disregarding it, he accused, was a "profane notion" that ranked of impiety. Yet it appears that Calvin, here, was most concerned with the "moral" aspects of the Mosaic law, for he then proceeded to comment at length on the Decalogue (*Institutes* 2.8.12–15).[19] Calvin's is a common understanding in the Reformed approach to the Mosaic law that sees it consist in three varieties: moral, ceremonial, and civil law. The Decalogue expresses the moral law (or is the prime example of such); the other legalities in the Pentateuch govern ceremonial and civil matters that are not applicable to the Christian today.[20] Essentially, in the Reformed approach, only the moral law is applicable to Christians, primarily to lead both believers and unbelievers away from sin (Westminster Confession

---

18. Ibid., 375–76.

19. Likewise, Calvin's 1541 "Catechism of the Church of Geneva" asks in Question 131: "What rule has he given us by which we may direct our life?" The answer follows: "His Law," and then Calvin goes on to describe the Decalogue.

20. In this view, the *ceremonial* law deals with the rituals, sacrifices, festivals, and cultic obligations: these have typological significance as foreshadowing the Redeemer and, as such, have now been set aside with the coming of Christ ("[a]ll . . . ceremonial laws are now abrogated, under the New Testament," Westminster Confession 19.3). The *civil* law, governing the unique theocracy of Israel, is, therefore, also not pertinent to the believer today (Westminster Confession 19.4). See Willem A. VanGemeren, "The Law is the Perfection of Righteousness in Jesus Christ: A Reformed Perspective," in *Five Views on Law and Gospel*, by Bahnsen et al., 30. So also Walter C. Kaiser, *Toward an Old Testament Theology* (Grand Rapids: Zondervan, 1978), 114–18. Such a trifold division actually goes back to Aquinas who so classified the "old [Mosaic] law" (*Summa* 2.99.4; also see Calvin, *Commentary on Galatians and Ephesians*, Gal 4:1).

19.5–6). The ceremonial and civil laws are not directly applicable to believers today, though they may have pedagogical significance, especially the former, because they foreshadow and point to Christ.[21]

Clearly the Bible itself appears to demonstrate a hierarchy of laws: Matt 23:23; 1 Sam 15:22–23; Isa 1:11–15; Amos 5:21–24; Hos 6:6; etc. Nevertheless, there is far too much overlap between categories to distinguish with any clarity between moral, civil, and ceremonial law—moral aspects are found in all these categories. For instance, Lev 20:22–26 undergirds *all* God's statutes and *all* his ordinances with a declaration of God's holiness and his desire that his people be like him. Even the Decalogue is more than simply moral law: there is ceremonial, familial, and civil law within that list; and there are cultural idiosyncrasies therein (idols, aliens within gates, land, particular species of oxen and donkeys, etc.).[22] Therefore, not only is it impractical to make such distinctions between moral, civil, and ceremonial laws, it is also difficult to sustain the argument that only the moral law is repeated in the NT; rather, the NT sees the Mosaic law as a monolithic unit (Matt 5:19; Gal 5:3; Jas 2:10; etc.).[23]

Traditional: Dispensational Approach

Dispensationalists have oft noted "The End of the Law" in the current dispensation of the church.[24] Ryrie observes that the Mosaic law, as a "code," has been

---

21. See Calvin, *Institutes* 2.7.16. Augustine, too, appears to have distinguished between the "moral" and "symbolic" aspects of the law (*Faust.* 6.2, 7, 9), the latter being equivalent to the ceremonial law and which is not incumbent upon Christians to obey "because their fulfillment is in Christ" (*Faust.* 19.18). Nonetheless, even these laws are "valid for faith and remain susceptible for allegorical interpretation" (*Ver. rel.* 17.33), and are not to be "immediately shunned with abhorrence, like the diabolical impieties of heathenism" (*Ep. 138* [to Jerome], 20).

22. Joe M. Sprinkle, *Biblical Law and Its Relevance: A Christian Understanding and Ethical Application for Today of the Mosaic Regulations* (Lanham, Md.: University Press of America, 2006), 4–5, notes that even the civil law dealing with the goring ox (Ex 21:28) apparently had a ceremonial facet to it, in that the flesh of the stoned offending animal could not be eaten, likely due to its ceremonial uncleanness. A single law, the Sabbath law, for instance, appears to have multiple facets: moral (Ex 20:8–11; Lev 26:2); civil (23:12; Deut 5:13–15); and ceremonial (Ex 31:13–16; 34:21; 35:2–3; Lev 23:3). Paul's employment of a "civil" law (Deut 25:4) in 1 Cor 9:9 and 1 Tim 5:18 for what appears to be a "moral" issue—the compensation of the Christian worker—also substantiates this point.

23. See David A. Dorsey, "The Law of Moses and the Christian: A Compromise," *JETS* 34 (1991): 322, 330–31; Christopher J. H. Wright, *Living as the People of God: The Relevance of Old Testament Ethics* (Leicester, U.K.: InterVarsity, 1983), 158; and Gordon J. Wenham, *The Book of Leviticus* (NICOT; Grand Rapids: Eerdmans, 1979), 32. Among the Jews, the unity of the law seems to have been an accepted concept, as R. Hillel's statement indicates: "What is hateful to you, do not to your neighbor: that is the whole Torah, while the rest is the commentary thereof; go and learn it" (*m. Šabb.* 31a). One remembers Jesus' similar words to this effect (Matt 7:12; also see 22:37–40). Besides, תּוֹרָה (*Torah*) is invariably used in the singular in the Pentateuch—a unified, undivided view of the law.

24. See Charles C. Ryrie's article by that title, *BSac* 124 (1967): 239–47.

"done away in its entirety." The dispensation of the church is now said to be governed by a new "code"—the law of Christ (1 Cor 9:21; Gal 6:2). This new code, however, also contains a reworking of some of the laws from the older code. But as an integral unit, the Mosaic law code—the older law qua *older* law—has no bearing on the Christian; only individual laws from the old code reiterated in the new law-of-Christ code are applicable today.[25] While this "code" explanation does make sense, the verbatim quotation by NT authors of OT law to promulgate ecclesial praxis seems to undermine such an understanding (for instance the strong dependence upon Lev 19 by James: Lev 19:12 and Jas 5:12; Lev 19:13 and Jas 5:4; Lev 19:15 and Jas 2:1, 9; Lev 19:16 and Jas 4:11; Lev 19:17b and Jas 5:20; Lev 19:18a and Jas 5:9; and Lev 19:18b and Jas 2:8).[26] These and other examples appear to suggest an *en masse* transfer of the old code to the church age, rather than a selection from the old to include within a new code. Needless to say, the "code" concept also reduces the value of the OT and its law for preaching purposes today, for if the code has been rewritten, one might as well focus exclusively upon the refashioned product expressed in the NT.

Dispensationalists, as a rule, have attended carefully to changes in context in the Scriptures. There is no doubt that the laws given to the theocracy of Israel were intensely contextual and inapplicable, as such, to current circumstances (see below). And, most certainly, the coming of Christ and his atoning work for mankind created a sharp differential between the days of the old covenant and those of the new. Nonetheless, such an interpretive framework tends to lay undue stress on the dichotomy between law and grace, particularly for homiletics.[27] If the older Mosaic dispensation is no more, how should one preach OT law in the contemporary era?

---

25. Ryrie, "The End of the Law," 246–47. Erich Sauer noted in the 1950s that in a "new period" of God's dealings there is a continuance of certain ordinances, an annulment of others, and an introduction of new ones (*The Dawn of Word Redemption* [Grand Rapids: Eerdmans, 1951], 194).

26. Sprinkle, *Biblical Law and Its Relevance*, 9.

27. A more recent subset of dispensationalism, labeled "progressive dispensationalism," seeks a more nuanced view of God's workings along the timeline of history. Progressive dispensationalists have not made significant pronouncements on their view(s) of the law and its validity for the Christian. However, its proponents seem to agree with the earlier versions of dispensationalism that the "Mosaic covenant law has ended dispensationally," being "replaced by new covenant law" (Craig A. Blaising and Darrell L. Bock, *Progressive Dispensationalism: An Up-to-Date Handbook of Contemporary Dispensational Thought* [Wheaton: Victor, 1993], 199). Likewise, Lowery, in a volume of essays by progressive dispensationalists, sees the Mosaic law as "no longer applicable," for "the leading of the Spirit renders the law obsolete." See David K. Lowery, "Christ, the End of the Law in Romans 10:4," in *Dispensationalism, Israel and the Church: The Search for Definition* (eds. Craig A. Blaising and Darrell L. Bock; Grand Rapids: Zondervan, 1992), 246.

I agree with Sprinkle, who notes that the "law was in fact a gracious gift of God to his people to guide them and show them whether or not they were in compliance with the covenant"—i.e., these were principles of sanctification, rather than the means of justification.[28] God's relationships with Abraham and with Israel (Gen 12:1–3; Ex 20:2; Deut 7:7–9) were established *before* the giving of the Mosaic law. Salvation (covenant entry and the commencement of a special divine-human relationship), whether of Abraham or of the Israelites or of the Christian, is always by grace through faith and not by obedience to law—a fact that dispensationalists are not slow to affirm: "The basis of salvation in every age is the death of Christ; the *requirement* for salvation in every age is faith . . . ."[29] The Mosaic law governed the sanctification of a chosen people, already saved (as all of God's law always does)— not simply by virtue of genetics or geography, but by faith, à la Abraham (Gen 15:6; Rom 4:3–16).[30] Thus, if these commandments, by divine intention, dealt with the sanctification of a chosen people, rather than their salvation, surely those divine requirements have some role to play in the sanctification of God's people of all time. This is the crux of the issue addressed in this chapter.

New Perspective on Paul

E. P. Sanders in 1977 accused the traditional description of Second Temple Judaism as being faulty. Analyzing Jewish texts from 200 B.C.E. to 200 C.E., he claimed that rather than being legalistic in the sense of seeking salvation by works (as has been recognized by standard Protestant reckoning as the religious philosophy of that period), Jewish thinking focused upon how covenant members may *stay in* the covenant, not upon how to *get in*. Torah-keeping, in his view, was not a means of entry into the covenant but rather a means of remaining within it; Sanders called this schema "covenantal nomism." Paul's only gripe with this system was, according to Sanders, that it was not Christian; post-Christ, the Torah-system is simply not the way to salvation as ordained by God, and Judaism is just *not* Christianity.[31]

---

28. Sprinkle, *Biblical Law and Its Relevance*, 7.

29. Charles C. Ryrie, *Dispensationalism* (rev. ed.; Chicago: Moody, 1995), 115.

30. No doubt there were people without faith amongst genetic and geographic Israel, just as there are in churches today.

31. E. P. Sanders, *Paul and Palestinian Judaism: A Comparison of Patterns of Religion* (London: SCM, 1977), 180. Needless to say, like most movements, the NPP too is multifaceted; writings that highlight the nuances of its different facets have consumed reams of paper. Only a brief summary is attempted here, with a view to focusing broadly upon the movement's understanding of the Mosaic law and its application to the Christian today.

Accepting Sanders' critique of the traditional Protestant approach to Paul, James D. G. Dunn went on to postulate that what separated Judaism from Christianity was the "works of the law" (Gal 2:16) which, according to him, consisted of the requirements of the law that separated Israel, God's covenant people, from Gentiles, those outside the covenant. While these "works of the law" would include all of the Torah, Dunn stressed that, in particular, the separation between the two peoples was based on such distinctively Jewish observances as circumcision, dietary restrictions, and the Sabbath. By decrying these "works of the law," Paul was not attacking salvation by works; rather, in Dunn's reading (and in keeping with the ideas promoted by the NPP), Paul was merely dismantling the wall of separation between Jews and Gentiles; he was reacting to "Jewish exclusivism"—"their misplaced emphasis on the outward and physical, their claim to an exclusively Jewish righteousness." Paul, according to Dunn, objected specifically to this "stunted and distorted understanding" of the requirements of the Mosaic law as an instrument of separation.[32] With the advent of Christ, the fundamental opposition was therefore not law/works vs. grace/faith (a focus on the vertical divine-human axis), but Jewish exclusivism vs. Christian inclusivism (a focus on the horizontal human-human axis).

In other words, the ceremonial and ritualistic aspects of the law ("works of the law") are, in this day of Christ, no longer valid and binding. Those separatist commandments which marked out Israel "could be regarded with indifference," whereas the remainder of God's commandments were "still expressive of God's will for humankind."[33] Thus, one can see that the distinction being made in the NPP between types of laws, at least between ceremonial laws and the rest, is the same as that made by the traditional approaches to law. In general terms, then, for proponents of the NPP, the non-ceremonial portions of the Mosaic law are still valid and have "a positive function in the direction of life" of the Christian, but in a different way: the law is not fulfilled by works, but by the divine commandment to love, i.e., the law of Christ.[34] How exactly one may separate "ceremonial" law

---

32. James D. G. Dunn, *The New Perspective on Paul* (rev. ed.; Grand Rapids: Eerdmans, 2005), 114, 139–40, 384, 417. N. T. Wright, too, inclines in this direction, holding that what Paul was objecting to was not Judaism's legalism or works-righteousness but the post-Christ, and now-defunct, idea that "fleshly Jewish descent guarantees membership of God's true covenant people" ("The Paul of History and the Apostle of Faith," *TynBul* 29 [1978]: 65).

33. Dunn, *The New Perspective on Paul*, 457.

34. "'[T]whole law' is not fulfilled by 'works of the law,' as in the time before Christ, but in the one word, the well-known, 'You shall love your neighbor as yourself'" (ibid., 275).

from other kinds is unclear. Neither is any help given as to how this rather general and vague imperative to love is to be drawn and applied from the fine-grained specificity of the laws of the OT that deals with everything from agriculture and homebuilding to sexual practices and clothing. Is every legal pericope (within the non-ceremonial category) merely exhorting love of some kind? How would such an understanding help a preacher struggling with, say, Ex 23:19 (or 34:26 or Deut 14:21), the prohibition of boiling kid goats in their mothers' milk?

All things considered, it seems clear that some factions of first-century Judaism did hold the position that law-keeping could provide salvation; assertions of period literature refer to the Mosaic law as "law of life" (Sir 17:11; 45:5), "commandments of life" (Bar 3:9), etc. And "all who hold her fast will live, and those who forsake her will die" (Bar 4:1; see also *4 Ezra* 14:30; 7:129; *Pss Sol.* 14:2).[35] "If, for some Jews at least, law-observance was indeed a condition of divine saving action, then there is no longer any reason to deny that Paul might have contrasted this emphasis on human action with his gospel's emphasis on the radical priority of divine action."[36] It is quite likely that with time, what God had intended to be guidelines for sanctification became misconstrued as means for salvation: a self-glorifying, merit-gaining, faith-minimizing obedience to OT law—the legalism Paul excoriated. So although the NPP has kindled serious exploration and discussion on what exactly Paul was opposing and why, the apostle's traditional identity remains intact: he was, indeed, responding to the legalistic aspects of Judaism and early Christianity.[37]

In any case, the NPP view of the Mosaic law is not far from that of the traditional approaches in this aspect: both assert that, for whatever reason, the Mosaic law (except its "moral" parts, though it is doubtful if such a distinction can be sustained) is not valid for the Christian.[38] In the following sections, I will

---

35. See Simon J. Gathercole, *Where is Boasting? Early Jewish Soteriology and Paul's Response in Romans 1–5* (Grand Rapids: Eerdmans, 2002), 37–160, for other examples from first century Jewish literature that appear to require works as essential for justification. For other sustained defenses of the traditional Paul, see the various essays in *Justification and Variegated Nomism* (2 vols.; eds. D. A. Carson, Peter T. O'Brien, and Mark A. Seifrid; Tübingen: Mohr Siebeck, 2001). Also helpful is Andrew A. Das, *Paul, the Law, and the Covenant* (Peabody, Mass.: Hendrickson, 2001).

36. Francis B. Watson, "Not the New Perspective" (unpublished paper delivered at the British New Testament Conference, Manchester, U.K., September 2001), n.p. [cited June 3, 2012]. Online: http://www.abdn.ac.uk/divinity/staff/watsonart.shtml.

37. See Stephen Westerholm, *Perspectives Old and New on Paul: The "Lutheran" Paul and His Critics* (Grand Rapids: Eerdmans, 2004), 351.

38. Once again, it needs to be pointed out that here I am specifically comparing the ramifications of the views of these camps upon the preaching and application of OT law. In that regard, the similarities between the traditional and NPP approaches outweigh the differences.

claim that in a different sense—a *theological* sense—all of the law continues to operate for the believer today.

Law Continues to Operate

Several of the verses commonly adduced to indicate the "end" of the law are discussed below; it will be argued that these texts are open to, and consistent with, an interpretation that sees the law as operative in this age.

> **ROMANS 9:30–32a**
>
> *What shall we say then? That Gentiles, who did not pursue righteousness, attained righteousness, that is, the righteousness by faith; but Israel, pursuing a law of righteousness, did not arrive at that law [of righteousness]. Why? Because [they pursued the law of righteousness] not by faith, but as though [it were] by works.*

All throughout Rom 9–11, there is a positive picture being painted of νόμος (*nomos*, "law") beginning with 9:4–5, where νομοθεσία (*nomothesia*, "legislation"/"giving of the law") is one of the advantages of being part of Israel, to whom also belong "adoption as sons and the glory and the covenant" and "the temple service and the promises," and "whose are the fathers, and from whom is the Christ." Yet Israel appears to have failed in relation to the law. The parallels between the Gentiles' attaining to righteousness and the Jews failing to do so are illuminating.

ROMANS 9:30	ROMANS 9:31–32a
. . . Gentiles,	. . . Israel,
who did not pursue righteousness,	pursuing a law of righteousness,
attained righteousness,	did not arrive at that law [of righteousness].
that is, the righteousness	Why? Because [they pursued the law of righteousness]
by faith.	not by faith, but as though [it were] by works.

Paul's use of φθάνω (*phthanō*, "arrive," 9:31), to indicate Israel's failure, portrays their defeat in a race; the metaphor is apropos, for the Gentiles, latecomers and *nouveau arrivé*, had overtaken the Jews to the goal. The reason for the latter's failure was that they pursued the law of righteousness not by faith, "but as though [it were] by works" (ἀλλ᾽ ὡς ἐξ ἔργων, *all hōs ex ergōn*—a wrong turn in the race). On the other hand, the Gentiles reached the finish line of righteousness (κατέλαβεν δικαιοσύνην, *katelaben dikaiosunēn*, "attained righteousness"; καταλαμβάνω, *katalambanō*, also has the sense of "overtake"), because they took the right course, the way of faith (ἐκ πίστεως, *ek pisteōs*).[39] What is significant here is the placement in parallel of the right pursuit of righteousness—by faith (and the resulting attainment)—with the wrong pursuit of a law of righteousness—without faith (and the resulting failure of attainment). The reason Paul employed the phrase "law of righteousness" (9:31) for the Israelites' object of pursuit, instead of simply "righteousness," as he did for the Gentiles' in 9:30, was to emphasize that Israel had been given an actual law to aid its movement towards righteousness. By this law, Israel could be righteous before God, *if it were obeyed in faith*, that is,

> by accepting, without evasion or resentment, the law's criticism of one's life, recognizing that one can never so adequately fulfill its righteous requirements as to put God in one's debt, accepting God's proffered mercy and forgiveness and in return giving oneself to Him in love and gratitude and so beginning to be released from one's self-centredness and turned in the direction of a humble obedience that is free from self-righteousness.[40]

Apparently righteousness could have been arrived at had the Jews pursued the νόμον δικαιοσύνης (*nomon dikaiosunēs*, "law of righteousness")—righteousness "promised, witnessed, made known or aimed at by the law" (Rom 10:4)—correctly: by faith.[41] Indeed, Paul's complaint was not at all about the *goal* being pursued, but about the *course* that that pursuit took (or the *means* of that pursuit)—ἐξ ἔργων (rather than ἐκ πίστεως): "working it out as it were by themselves, not believing that it is God who works within them" (Augustine,

---

39. Robert Badenas, *Christ The End of the Law: Romans 10.4 in Pauline Perspective* (JSNTSup 10; Sheffield: JSOT Press, 1985), 104.

40. C. E. B. Cranfield, *The Epistle to the Romans* (International Critical Commentary, 2 vols.; Edinburgh: T. & T. Clark, 1979), 2: 508, 510.

41. Badenas, *Christ The End of the Law*, 104.

Spir. et litt. 50.29). In other words, law is not being disparaged in Rom 9 (also see 3:21–22, 27; 3:31–4:25; 10:2–10); rather, law had always been intended to be "pursued" by faith so that righteous standing would be attained not by works in which one may boast, but by the grace of God enabling obedience (as well as offering forgiveness for failure to obey) in which God alone gets the glory.

ROMANS 10:4

For Christ is the goal [τέλος, telos] *of the law for righteousness to everyone who believes.*

The meaning of τέλος could be temporal (i.e., "Christ has abolished/ended the law": attesting to the discontinuity between the law and Christ, between OT Judaism and NT Christianity), teleological (i.e., "the law pointed to Christ and had Christ as its goal/outcome": attesting to the continuity between the law and Christ, between OT Judaism and NT Christianity), or completive (i.e., "Christ has fulfilled/accomplished the law" in a prophetic fashion without making a statement about the continuing validity, or lack thereof, of the law).[42] In the NT, there are five occurrences, including Romans 10:4, of the predicate τέλος + genitive, followed by a subject:

Rom 10:4	τέλος . . . νόμου Χριστός (telos . . . nomou Christos)
Rom 6:21	τέλος ἐκείνων θάνατος (telos ekeinōn thanatos) = the outcome of those things is death
Rom 6:22	τέλος [ἐκείνων] ζωὴν αἰώνιον (telos [ekeinōn] zōēn aiōnion) = the outcome [of those things] is eternal life
1 Tim 1:5	τέλος τῆς παραγγελίας ἐστιν ἀγάπη (telos tēs parangelias estin agapē) = the goal/outcome of instruction is love
1 Pet 1:9	τέλος τῆς πίστεως σωτηρίαν (telos tēs pisteōs sōtērian) = the outcome of faith is salvation

The four uses, besides Rom 10:4, are generally considered to have a teleological sense of "goal/outcome." It is reasonable, then, that the same sense

---

42. There is clearly a sense in which the teleological ("goal/outcome") and completive ("fulfillment") senses of τέλος coincide. For the purposes of this work, no particular distinction will be made between the teleological and completive senses. The point, here, is simply that the sense of τέλος is *not* temporal (i.e., the law has *not* been abolished).

of the construction should be applied to 10:4 also. After having suggested, in 9:30–32, that the goal of pursuit (the law of righteousness) was legitimate when approached by faith, it does not appear likely that Paul intends to assert the "termination" of that same law in 10:4 (the temporal sense of τέλος).[43]

Badenas has demonstrated convincingly that throughout the history of the church, τέλος (or its Latin equivalent *finis*) was not considered to be temporal in the sense of a time-limited abrogation of the Mosaic law by the Christ-event.[44] The vast majority of early interpreters held to a more continuous view of pre-Christ and post-Christ eras, whether teleological or, more likely, completive, thus precluding an absolute nullification of the Mosaic law by Christ. Origen, Eusebius, and Clement of Alexandria, among others, held to a prophetic fulfillment (completive) view of Rom 10:4.[45] Augustine explains that the "end" is not "consumption," as in the "end" of food that is eaten, but rather "consummation" or "perfection," as in a garment at the end of weaving (Augustine, *Enarrat. Ps.* 55.1).[46] So also Aquinas: "And note that 'the end' does not always mean destruction, but sometimes perfection, as in that, 'Christ is the end of the Law'" (*Catena Aurea, Matthew* 10); and Calvin: "For as he is the *end of the law* (Rom 10:4), so he is the head, the sum—in fine, the consummation—of all spiritual doctrine" (*Commentary on Corinthians*, on 2 Cor 5:19).[47] Badenas concludes that from the days of the early church through the Middle Ages, the sense of "termination" for τέλος (the temporal view) was rarely found.[48] In modern times, Barth also did not believe that law was "antiquated, superseded, set aside and abrogated."

> Where in all these chapters [Rom 9–10] (but also in all the rest of Pauline theology) do we find the slightest indication that the apostle of the Church regarded the Law of Israel as a gift of God cancelled and invalidated by Christ? It was not to the Law but to an ignorant adoption and application of the Law, to its desecration and misuse through unbelief, that . . . Paul opposed the righteousness

---

43. Badenas, *Christ The End of the Law*, 78, 113–14.

44. Ibid., 4 (and all of 7–37).

45. Origen, *Comm. Rom.* 8.2; Eusebius, *Dem. ev.* 8.2.387; Clement of Alexandria, *Strom.* 2.9; 4.21.

46. Also see Augustine, *Tract. Ev. Jo.* 55.13.2; *Enarrat. Ps.* 46.1; 57.2; 68.1; etc.

47. After all, Christ, as the perfect Man, is the one who met all of God's demands.

48. Badenas, *Christ The End of the Law*, 18. "Thus the term *finis* is consistently interpreted with prophetic, completive, perfective, final, or teleological connotations, but never in the sense of 'abrogation' and very seldom in the sense of 'supersession.' The theological problem of the so-called antithesis between the law and Christ is so completely absent from these writers" (ibid., 14).

of faith. According to the unambiguous statement of Rom 3:31 (in harmony with Matt 5:17) he was not seeking to abrogate the Law by his preaching but to establish it.[49]

How exactly Christ is the "goal"/ "fulfillment" of law (not its nullification) will be considered later in this chapter; its implications for sanctification (and preaching) will be dealt with in chapter 4. However, in brief, it might be stated here that as the τέλος of the law, Jesus Christ is its perfect embodiment, the one "who committed no sin" (1 Pet 2:22; also 2 Cor 5:21; Heb 4:15); in his absolute obedience, he was also the only one who could pay the price for mankind's transgression of the law (Heb 9:28; 1 Pet 2:24; etc.). Having done so, he made possible the indwelling of the Holy Spirit that now empowers the child of God to keep the law (Rom 8:1–17).[50]

ROMANS 10:5–8

For Moses writes about the righteousness by the law: the man who does these things will live by them [Lev 18:5]. *And the righteousness by faith speaks as follows: "Do not say in your heart, 'Who will ascend into heaven?' (that is, to bring Christ down), or 'Who will descend into the abyss?' (that is, to bring Christ up from the dead)." But what does it say? "The word is near you, in your mouth and in your heart"—that is, the word of faith which we preach* [Deut 30:12–14].

Most translations consider the post-positive δέ (*de*) in Rom 10:6a as an adversative: "*but* the righteousness by faith . . ." That is to assume that Lev 18:5 cited in Rom 10:5 indicates salvation by works, and that in 10:6 Paul is countering such an approach with salvation by faith: "righteousness by the law [followed by a citation of Lev 18:5] . . . , *but* the righteousness by faith [followed by Deut 30:12–14] . . ." (Rom 10:5–6a, emphasis added). There is, however, no need to pit these OT citations against each another, for the connective particle δέ could as easily be read as "and," with the following clause in 10:6 complementing and

---

49. Karl Barth, *Church Dogmatics*, II/2: *The Doctrine of God* (trans. G. W. Bromiley; eds. Thomas F. Torrance and G. W. Bromiley; Edinburgh: T. & T. Clark, 2004), 244–45.

50. The "goal" of the law was Christ, for the law depicted what the perfect Man would look like. The "fulfillment" of the law was Christ, for the law was perfectly obeyed by this Man. Such a reading integrates the teleological ("goal") and completive ("fulfillment") senses of τέλος in Rom 10:4.

expanding on what was asserted in 10:5.[51]

The context of Lev 18, the source of Paul's first OT quote in this passage, must be considered. That chapter dealt with the lifestyle that God's people ought to have been adopting, in contrast to the mores of the Egyptians and Canaanites who surrounded the Israelites. God's concern was with distinguishing the life-style of his people from that of the heathens around them, by their obedience to his statutes and judgments (18:3–5). While the abominable practices of the Gentiles (18:22, 26, 27, 29, 30), if adopted, would lead to defilement (18:20, 23, 24, 25, 27, 28, 30) and punishment by expulsion from the land (18:25, 28–30), abiding by the demands of Yahweh would lead to life (18:5), ostensibly within the land (as in 20:22; 25:18–19; 26:5; etc.). The parallel structure of Lev 18:4 and 18:5 points to the thrust of these verses—how God wanted his people to live, meeting divine demand:

18:4	**A** You must perform my judgments and keep my statutes	
18:4		**B** to live according to them;
18:4		**C** I am the LORD your God.
18:5	**A'** So you must keep my statutes and my judgments	
18:5		**B'** which a man must do and live by them;
18:5		**C'** I am the LORD.

The parallelism demonstrates that *B* and *B'* are equivalent, supporting a locative understanding—the sphere in which God's people are to live, namely, within the horizon of God's commands (divine demand). The life lived in this sphere is one of blessing under the hand of God, in intimate relationship with him (Deut 8:1; 30:15–18; etc.). Thus Lev 18:5 is not referring to eternal life, but to life in submission to the demands of God, that results in divine blessing; Lev 18:5 is not dealing with salvation by works, but with an "abundant life" (a life of sanctification and resulting blessedness, John 10:10).[52] With this understanding of Lev 18:5—as an exhortation of God's people to a lifestyle of obedience—its citation in Rom 10:5 is unlikely to be setting up an antithesis between works and faith.

---

51. The syntax of a γὰρ (*gar*)-clause followed by the connective δὲ *not* being used adversatively is found elsewhere in Paul, for example, Rom 10:10; 11:15–16; 13:1; 1 Cor 4:7; 10:4.

52. Anne Lawton, "Christ: The End of the Law—A Study of Romans 10:4–8," *TrinJ* 3 (1974): 18–20.

Badenas makes the intriguing suggestion that the utilization of two OT witnesses in Rom 10:5–8 (Lev 18:5 and Deut 30:12–14) may be the vestige of a Jewish practice of employing double witnesses that are complementary to one another (also see Rom 9:25–26, 27–28, 30; 10:11–13, 20–21; 11:8–9, 26–27; etc.).[53] Substantiating this is the fact that Deut 30:15–16, the passage following the OT text cited in Rom 10:6–8, is parallel to Lev 18:5—חֻקָּה (*huqqah*, "statute") and מִשְׁפָּט (*mishpat*, "judgment") occur in both, and both promise life. The two OT quotes in Rom 10:5–8 thus complement, not contradict, each another. It is also striking that the hunt for the commandment in heaven and beyond the sea in Deut 30:12–13 becomes, in Rom 10:6–7, the search for Christ in heaven and in the abyss; and the ῥῆμα (*rhēma*) of the commandment in one's heart, Deut 30:14 (LXX), becomes the ῥῆμα of faith in Rom 10:8.

DEUTERONOMY 30:12–14	ROMANS 10:6–8
Commandment sought in heaven and beyond the sea	Christ sought in heaven and in the abyss
ῥῆμα of commandment in mouth and heart	ῥῆμα of faith in mouth and heart

It appears that Paul is deliberately conjoining concepts of faith (in Christ) and obedience (to commandment). Indeed, to obey divine demand in any age is to obey *with/in/by faith* in God. The necessity of this element of faith for sanctification was quite clear in the OT. For instance, "doing" the law included the recognition that one's law-keeping was imperfect; the law itself prescribed sacrifices to make atonement for those failures (see Lev 17 that precedes the chapter from which Paul quotes). Thus the concept of righteousness by faith was not new to Paul or to the NT. While there was significant expansion and consummation of an OT concept (especially as regards the object of faith—Christ and his work), the concept itself, at its core, was not novel in the NT—the "faith-full" modus operandi of obedience had always been God's demand of his people. By citing the Pentateuch in Rom 10:5–8, Paul demonstrates it to have been God's intention all along. And such an obedience of faith, Paul avers, is not an impossible task as one might surmise (Rom 10:6–8 citing Deut 30:12–14: "Who will

53. Badenas, *Christ The End of the Law*, 123.

ascend . . . ? Who will descend . . . ?"). Rather, Deut 30:11 indicates, "this commandment . . . is not too difficult for you, nor is it remote for you"; a righteous status *can* be achieved, by an obedience that functions by faith. God has made obedience by faith possible and proximal (the announcement of the nearness of the "word" is emphatic in Rom 10:8 [ἐγγύς, *engus*])—his gracious invitation to his people to abide by divine demand, in order that they may be blessed.

Of interest also is that Deut 30:6 (in proximity to 30:12–14 cited by Paul here in Rom 10) exhorts readers to "love" Yahweh with all their "heart and soul," and to turn to Yahweh with all their "heart and soul" (Deut 30:2, 10). Surely one could not love God and turn to him in this fashion without faith! In fact, 30:6 makes this *loving of Yahweh with heart and soul* a condition for "living," i.e., being blessed ("to love the LORD your God with all your heart and with all your soul, so that you may live"), while 30:16 makes love and *obedience* a condition for "living" ("to love the LORD your God, to walk in his ways and to keep his commandments and his statutes and his judgments, that you may live"). What is called for, then, in such a complementary juxtaposition of faith and obedience, is simply the "obedience of faith"!

The transactions of law in the earlier dispensation were divinely intended to operate by faith, with God's gracious forgiveness being incorporated into the law for any failure to comply with that law. As opposed to this operation of man's faith and God's grace, humankind sinfully, and in vain, attempted to comply with the demand of God, on its own merit, with its own resources, neglecting the OT requirements for faith, repudiating God's mercy. By construing the Torah as a code of human performance and duty for the gaining of some sort of justificatory merit with God, Israel missed its thrust as a divine guide to sanctification, intended to be obeyed in faith.[54]

---

54. On the other hand, Westerholm asserts that "to say that the Mosaic code is based on faith, not works, is simply incompatible with what Paul says elsewhere" (Stephen Westerholm, *Israel's Law and the Church's Faith: Paul and His Recent Interpreters* [Grand Rapids: Eerdmans, 1988], 127). Indeed, it was not *based on* faith; rather, it *functioned by* faith. To abide by divine demand that is impossible for sinful humanity to keep, requires faith in God's enablement, and the acceptance of God's mercy and forgiveness for the failure that is inevitable. Faithfulness is the *only* possible approach to the law, as Rom 9:30–32 makes clear; all else is illegitimate, indeed sinful. "[T]he Law itself can be kept and fulfilled . . . only in faith. But this was precisely what this Israel lacked. . . . [I]t did lack the work of all works, the one work which is fundamentally and decisively required in and with all works required in the Law. . . . The omission of the one work of faith required of it is Israel's transgression of the Law" (Barth, *Church Dogmatics*, II/2: 241).

2 CORINTHIANS 3:6

[God] also made us adequate as servants of a new covenant—not of the letter but of the Spirit; for the letter kills, but the Spirit gives life.

2 CORINTHIANS 3:11

For if that which is rendered ineffective [was] with glory, much more that which remains [is] in glory.

Second Corinthians 3 appears to draw a dramatic contrast between the killing "letter" and the enlivening Spirit. The old and new covenants are contrasted in 3:3—"tablets of stone" (from Ex 24:12) vs. "tablets of human hearts" (from Jer 31:33; Ezek 11:19–20; 36:26). The arrival of a new covenant does not, however, indicate the introduction of a new law to replace the Mosaic code; in fact, "my law" in Jeremiah 31:33 implies the *same* law of God operating in the new covenant.[55] In Ezek, the wording is more explicit: God's people are promised a new heart and spirit "that they may walk in my statutes and keep my judgments, and do them" (Ezek 11:19–20; so also 36:26–27; and 37:14, 23–24). What is anticipated in those prophetic passages is not the abrogation of law but "its true and effective establishment" with the agency and aid of the Holy Spirit, as opposed to a legalistic enterprise that relied on the feeble and faulty resources of one's self (the "flesh") to abide by divine demand.[56] The fundamental change between the old and new covenants, then, is not a change in law or divine demand: that remains the same always. Rather, the newness is in the Spirit-aided means of keeping divine demand, an empowerment available to every believer in this dispensation as a consequence of the work of Christ. Acquiescence and abiding by divine demand is always to be accomplished not on one's own strength, but by the grace of God and the enablement of the Spirit, through the instrumentality

---

55. In this connection, Col 2:14 describes the cancellation of "the certificate of debt consisting of ordinances" (τὸ ... χειρόγραφον τοῖς δόγμασιν, *to ... cheirographon tois dogmasin*). This is hardly likely to be the entire law, but rather the law's condemnation of sinners (the debt they owe) that is cancelled. Ephesians 2:15 states that Christ in his flesh nullified the enmity, "the law of commandments in ordinances" (τὸν νόμον τῶν ἐντολῶν ἐν δόγμασιν, *tōn nomon tōn entolōn en dogmasin*). This, too, does not indicate the nullification of the law, but rather of the *enmity* between the community of God (2:12) and those outside it, arising from the divine demand (law) that called for the "set apartness" of God's people. That it does not mean an abrogation of law as such is evident from the subsequent citation of the Decalogue in 6:2.

56. Cranfield, *The Epistle to the Romans*, 2:855.

of faith. Therefore the contrast between "letter" and "Spirit" in 2 Cor 3:6 is not one between an old law and a new one, but rather between a legalistic attempt at compliance with God's demands and a spiritual one with faith as the instrument and the Holy Spirit as the empowering agent. "In the absence of the Spirit the law is misused and comes to be for those who misuse it simply 'letter'. . . , and this law without the Spirit 'killeth,'" offering only condemnation for its violation.[57]

> [Letter vs. Spirit is] a contrast between the life of those who, though possessing the law, have not yet been enabled by the Holy Spirit rightly to understand it in the light of Christ, and the life of those whom the Holy Spirit has both enabled to understand the law aright in the light of Jesus Christ and also set free to make a beginning of trying to obey it with humble joy.[58]

Therefore, Moses' ministry, "which is rendered ineffective" (2 Cor 3:11), can be labeled the "ministry of [i.e., "that brought"] death" (3:7), since the result of the giving of the law was ultimately condemnation upon those who vainly tried to obey it without faith ("ministry of [i.e., "that brought"] condemnation," 3:9). On the other hand, Paul's ministry—and the point of 2 Cor 3:11 is, in fact, the contrast between two *ministries,* not between two covenants—is an abiding ministry ("which remains," 3:11), as he serves the new covenant characterized by the enablement of the Holy Spirit for meeting divine demand in faith.

GALATIANS 3:10
For all who are of the works of the law are under a curse.

GALATIANS 3:25
But now that faith has come, we are no longer under a guardian.

GALATIANS 5:18
But if you are led by the Spirit, you are not under the law.

It has been observed from the time of Calvin, that Paul, in Gal 3:25, is confining himself to one particular role of the Mosaic law—as a "guardian"

---

57. Ibid., 2:854. So also Rom 7:6: the "oldness of the letter" is the condemnatory stance of the law. And such a consideration of law, apart from the Spirit, makes it a "denatured" law, for God's law by nature is "spiritual," affirming its divine origin, ongoing authority, and the Spirit-empowerment of its obedience (7:14) (ibid., 2:851; also see ibid., 1:339–40).

58. C. E. B. Cranfield, "Has the Old Testament Law a Place in the Christian Life? A Response to Professor Westerholm," in *On Romans and Other New Testament Essays* by C. E. B. Cranfield (London: T. & T. Clark, 1998), 122.

(παιδαγωγός, *paidagōgos*). In that narrow and specific use, it is evident that now, in the time of Christ, the law's "tutorial" or "guardianship" function—to point one to the Savior—has been rendered redundant for believers. This verse is, therefore, not referring to the inutility of the law *in toto*.[59] Neither is Gal 5:18; here the contrast (continued from 5:17) is between the deeds of the flesh and those of the Spirit: the deeds of the flesh indicate the *legalistic* endeavor of law-keeping, "seeking to be justified by law" (5:1)—i.e., to be "under the law" (5:18). Such legalism is the utilization of one's own depraved and impotent resources to obey God, and that for one's own glory. Paul has already declared that what was important was the obedience of faith—"faith working through love" (5:6). The legalists are those who are "of the works of the law" (3:10), who are self-righteously trying to obey divine demand, attempting, in vain, to gain their own justification and sanctification. These are "under a curse," for obedience to divine demand is impossible, without divine empowerment through the agency of faith.[60] The resulting transgression only invites the law's condemnation (curse) upon the faithless. Such a faithless approach to righteousness, attempted on one's own strength, is to cast aside God's mercy and grace. Not only is that an erroneous assumption of one's own capacity for law-keeping, it is also a diminution of God's righteousness, considering his perfect standard easily attainable by sinful man employing his own devices and stratagems. Thus legalism is not only futile, it is also "positively *sinful*," because it reflects the rebellious rejection of one's need for and dependence upon God and his grace for a sanctified life (righteousness).[61] "R. Zadok said: 'Make them [the commands of the Torah] not a crown wherewith to magnify thyself'" (*m. ʾAbot* 4:5). Instead, in humility, the child of God is to meet divine demand by faith: it is not law *or* faith, one or the other; it is both one and the other, law *and* faith—the obedience of faith (see later in this chapter).[62]

---

59. See Calvin, *Commentary on Galatians and Ephesians*, on Gal 3:19; and Cranfield, *The Epistle to the Romans*, 2:859.

60. See C. F. D. Moule, "Obligation in the Ethic of Paul," in *Christian History and Interpretation: Studies Presented to John Knox* (eds. W. R. Farmer, C. F. D. Moule, and R. R. Niebuhr; Cambridge: Cambridge University Press, 1967), 393.

61. Ibid., 394.

62. Cranfield describes the more common understanding of the law as being abrogated as a "modern version of Marcionism" that regards the biblical history as "an unsuccessful first attempt on God's part at dealing with man's unhappy state, which had to be followed later by a second (more successful) attempt (a view which is theologically grotesque, for the God of the unsuccessful first attempt is hardly a God to be taken seriously)" (*The Epistle to the Romans*, 2:862).

Summary: Law Continues to Operate

The Mosaic law is the law of God: Rom 3:2; 7:22, 25; 8:7; and because it is the law of God, it is holy, righteous, good, and spiritual (7:12, 14, 16), providing the knowledge of sin (3:20; 5:20; 7:8, 11), and condemning all that is antithetical to God and his character (7:10; also see Gal 3:10; 2 Cor 3:9). It also creates the possibility—indeed, the temptation—of self-righteous legalism: a faith*less* obedience, a form of bondage (Gal 2:4; 5:1). Fallen man can never fully obey divine demand or attain to God's standard of righteousness (Rom 3:21), but the self-exalting tendency to attempt such compliance is ever-present and strong. God's gift of righteous standing, however, cannot be earned meritoriously; to assume it can be is legalism, doomed to failure without a "faith-full" acceptance both of God's gracious forgiveness for failure to obey and his gracious empowerment for the ability to obey. The key distinction here is "between two different attitudes to and uses of law—on the one hand, the recognition of law as a revelation of God's will and purpose [that must be obeyed in faith], and, on the other hand, the attempt to use it 'legalistically,' to establish one's rightness"—"uncreaturely attempts at boasting and autonomy." What must be remembered is that rejection of misuse is not relaxation of demand.[63] The misuse of law is excoriated in all of Scripture; but the cure for its abuse is not its annulment. Why, then, was Paul seemingly negative in some of his statements about the law?

Cranfield helpfully observes that Paul did not possess a wordgroup in the Greek that was the equivalent of "legalism." One must therefore "be ready to reckon with the possibility that Pauline statements, which at first sight seem to disparage the law, were really directed not against the law itself but against that misunderstanding and misuse of it for which we now have a convenient terminology."[64] For Paul, then, the antithesis of grace is not law—for law does, indeed, reveal both divine demand and divine grace, even in its remedy for failure and disobedience—but, rather, law "as an arrogantly and arbitrarily chosen target of human ambition and as a system of human achievement, that is, legalism."[65]

---

63. Moule, "Obligation in the Ethic of Paul," 393, 403.

64. Cranfield, *The Epistle to the Romans*, 2:853.

65. Moule, "Obligation in the Ethic of Paul," 397. Conceivably, then, if τέλος in Rom 10:4 were to be read as indicating "termination" of the law, it could indicate "the end of the Pharisaic heresy of trying to merit salvation on the basis of legal righteousness"—"Pharisaic merit theology." See Sprinkle, *Biblical Law and Its Relevance*, 10. Thomas R. Schreiner, "Paul's View of the Law in Romans 10:4–5," *WTJ* 55 (1993): 121, also holds this view. Even if one were to concede the validity of this interpretation, the fact remains that *law itself* is not abrogated, but only its misuse.

There is no hint in any of the Pauline discussions that the law, divine demand, has been nullified. Jesus' assertion in Matt 5:17, that he came not to abolish the Law or the Prophets, but to fulfill them, should not be taken to indicate he fulfilled *and thus abrogated it*. His explicit statement goes against that assumption, as also does 5:19, where he declares that annulling even "one of the least of these commandments" renders one "least in the kingdom of heaven." Rather the child of God is to keep and teach the commandments, upon which greatness in the kingdom is predicated.

It would be fair to assert, then, that law as a whole, including the Mosaic law, has not been terminated (Rom 3:31; 8:4; 13:8–10). The phrases "not under law" (6:14) and "die to the law" (7:4) have reference to the *condemnatory role* of the law, as 8:1 confirms. All that was achieved by a faithless keeping of the Mosaic law was the production of "fruit for death" (7:5). Dying to the law does not mean that one is no longer under God's law, his divine demand, but that the condemnation for failure to keep it will no longer be extracted from the child of God who has put his or her trust in Jesus Christ as Savior. The jurisdiction of the law, which Paul describes in 7:1–6 as being curtailed by the believer's "death" to the law in Christ, refers to the dissolution of its punitive power—its condemnation for sin. That makes sense, for the discussion in Rom 7 comes right after the apostle has asserted in 6:23 that the "wages of sin is death." And it also fits well with the proximal references to dying in Christ (6:1–11; 5:6–11, 18–19), which might be considered equivalent to dying to the law, i.e., to its condemnatory power.[66]

All this to say, God's law (divine demand) continues to operate. How exactly does it function in the life of the believer today, in light of the tremendous changes in context between the circumstances of the giving of the law in the ancient day, and the circumstances of the reading of the law in the present one? In other words, how does one interpret biblical law in order to preach it?

Law Functions Theologically

Laws establish a repeatable phenomenon, a predictable reaction for every action—sanctions for disobedience and rewards for obedience. They are intended

---

66. Cranfield, "Has the Old Testament Law a Place?," 115. Likewise, Paul's statement in 1 Cor 9:20 that he considers himself as "not being . . . under the law" means that he is not under law in the way he once was, before coming to faith, succumbing to its condemnation (ibid., 114). In any case, the believer is still under the obligation to meet divine demand.

to direct behavior in times and spaces beyond the origin of the text and its writing. God does not change, neither does his holy character or standard; therefore, divine demand also remains the same across the ages. But with the shifts in context between the time of writing and the time of reading, one encounters the thorny problem of distanciation: How can an ancient law given in one era be applicable in another, when there have been seismic changes in language, culture, institutions, forms, etc., between the two ages? This is where a theological hermeneutic comes into play. Every law of God depicts a facet of the character of the Lawgiver and his relationship to his people—i.e., every law has something theological to offer. It is this theological nugget that must be ascertained. But how does one discern the theological thrust of a pericope of biblical law? In other words what was the author *doing* with what he was *saying* with that particular law? In this section, the contextual shift of OT law will be addressed first, following which a theological hermeneutic for interpreting biblical law will be proposed, a process similar to what has already been discussed in chapter 2. Essentially, it is the rationale of the law that yields the world being projected, the theology of the pericope.

With this theological approach to law, one may fruitfully apply the legal portions of the canon to believers of all times (an operation pertinent to every other genre of Scripture as well). As was detailed in chapter 2, the discerning of pericopal theology, i.e., the precepts, priorities, and practices of the *world in front of the text*, is essential if one is to counter textual distanciation and apply the pericope validly into the lives of believers today.

Contextual Shift of OT Law

Dorsey holds that "legally, none of the 613 stipulations of the Sinaitic covenant are binding upon NT Christians, including the so-called moral laws, while in a revelatory and pedagogical sense all 613 are binding upon us, including all the ceremonial and civic laws."[67] The basic thrust of his argument is that the stipulations of the old covenant were unique and exquisitely contextual—components of a suzerain-vassal treaty that Yahweh made with a particular nation, billeted in a particular geographical location, sojourning in a particular era, maintaining a particular cultic organization, and supporting a particular political configuration. The church today is not regulated by the specifics of that ancient treaty, for

---

67. Dorsey, "The Law of Moses," 325.

the contextual circumstances in which the reading of the law is conducted now are drastically different from the circumstances of its writing then. The original geographical and climatic situations make it difficult for these laws to be duplicated elsewhere (the regulations governing the cultivation of particular plants and husbandry of particular animals, etc.); the cultural milieu was specific and contextual, rendering those ancient practices, institutions, and customs completely foreign in another era (levirate marriage, siege warfare against walled cities, double inheritance of the firstborn, etc.); the cultic organization made Hebrew religious phenomena unique (laws concerning the ephod, altar, sacrifices, etc.); the governmental structure was defined for that particular nation and for no other (rules directing the behavior of kings, the maintenance of the tribes, the establishment of cities of refuge, etc.); and so on.[68] "Nearly all the regulations of the corpus—over ninety-five percent—are so culturally specific, geographically limited, and so forth that they would be completely inapplicable, and in fact unfulfillable, to Christians living throughout the world today. This fact alone should suggest that the corpus is not legally binding upon Christians and that it cannot possibly represent the marching orders of the Church."[69]

It will not do, at this juncture, to dismiss portions of the OT laws as dealing with ceremonial and civic functions and institutions, and to retain only the moral aspects of OT law, making them applicable to believers today. As was noted earlier in this chapter, not only do most of the extremely context-dependent ceremonial and civic laws contain moral elements, many of the moral laws contain time-bound, highly contextual formulations as well. The Decalogue, itself, is stated in culturally specific terms involving Near Eastern cultic elements such as idols, slavery, animals, a uniquely defined nation, and motives and promises particular to Israel (e.g., the rationale for the Sabbath in Deut 5:15, and the inheritance of land in 5:16). The explicitly moral command to imitate Yahweh's own holiness (Lev 19:1) is clearly to be respected even in ceremonial and civic ordinances such as those regulating the Sabbath (19:2), the performance of sacrifices (19:4–8), the practices of harvest (19:9–10), etc. In any case, in modern church praxis, inconsistencies abound in the way certain laws are deemed "moral" and others are not, and how some are considered time-bound

---

68. Dorsey considers, in detail, the specificity of several of these laws, their contexts, and their binding nature upon the ancient Israelites (ibid., 325–29).

69. David. A. Dorsey, "The Use of the OT Law in Christian Life: A Theocentric Approach," *EvJ* 17 (1998): 5.

and dispensable and others not. Dorsey notes that while the condemnation of homosexuality in Lev 20:13 is considered normative for the church, other laws in the same chapter are not, such as the restriction on eating unclean animals and the extreme penalty for those cursing their parents. Loving one's neighbor, in Lev 19:18, is unquestionably appropriate for today, but how about 19:19 that prevents wearing garments made of two different kinds of material, not to mention breeding two kinds of cattle or sowing fields with two kinds of grain?[70]

Neither will it do to protest that Jesus reiterated Lev 19:18 but was silent on 19:19; applying that formula, OT laws that Jesus did *not* discourse upon can conveniently be discarded, including most of the 613 enumerated laws. Moreover, NT writers' monolithic view of OT law (Matt 5:19; Gal 5:3; Jas 2:10; etc.) was mentioned previously—it is all or none. In short, the rather arbitrary categorization of laws into ceremonial, civic, and moral is not helpful, particularly when it comes to preaching and applying pericopes of OT law to contemporary Christians in the pews. Rather, the interpreter is to regard *all* the laws as applicable, for, as was noted, God does not change, neither does his holy standard and demand. And if every law, even in its granular and contextual particularity, tells God's people something about God, each one is a gem of theology that must be scrutinized, interpreted, and applied. The question, of course, is how one might do so, in the light of changes in context between the inscription of the law and the reading of the law.

Law as Imitatio Dei

One clear purpose of ancient laws was to portray the character of the lawgiver, whether human or divine. The Code of Hammurabi, for instance, extols the virtues of this regent in both its prologue and epilogue. In the former, Hammurabi claims to have been called by the gods, "to cause justice to prevail in the land, to destroy the wicked and the evil, to prevent the strong from oppressing the weak, ... to further the welfare of the people." He asserts that he is "the wise and perfect one," "who made justice prevail and who ruled the race with right." The epilogue echoes these sentiments. Other proclamations continue to laud his own wisdom and praise his justice to orphans and widows, his righting of wrongs, his pronouncement of judgments: "My words are precious, my wisdom is unrivaled."[71]

---

70. Dorsey, "The Law of Moses," 321–22, 330–31.
71. *The Code of Hammurabi* (trans. Percy Handcock; New York: SPCK, 1920), 6–9, 41–43.

In not a very different manner, Yahweh is portrayed in the Pentateuch not just in its narratives, but even in its laws and ordinances. For instance, Ex 20–23 shows him as a covenant-keeping God, who seeks a relationship with his people to bless them; he is powerful, holy, jealous, moral, and just. Yet he is also one who loves, and who is full of mercy and compassion not only for his own, but also for the oppressed, the disadvantaged, the foreigner, and, indeed, even for non-human life. Westbrook observes that law codes of the ancient Near East were frequently intended to "illustrate how well the king, in whose name they were published, had established justice throughout his realm."[72] In the case of biblical impera-tives, the greatness of the divine sovereign is not the only motive for such depic-tions. Biblical law consistently demands that Yahweh's people be like him, for the depictions of his character are the "revelation of the standard of holiness for the people of God."[73] Dorsey summarizes it well:

> Each law issued by God to ancient Israel . . . reflects God's mind and ways and is therefore a theological treasure. Moreover the theological insights we gain from a particular OT law will not only enhance our knowledge and under-standing of God but will also have important practical implications for our own lives if we are patterning them after our heavenly Father and modify-ing our behavior and thinking in response to our knowledge of him and his ways.[74]

The *imitatio Dei* is thus a constant focus of OT ethics.[75] For preaching, par-ticularly, the imitation of the divine is a critical hermeneutical concept; this issue will be considered further in chapter 4.[76] At any rate, the revelation of God and his character even in his laws mandates that every pericope of biblical law be attended to, and even preached.

---

72. Raymond Westbrook and Bruce Wells, *Everyday Law in Biblical Israel: An Introduction* (Louisville: Westminster John Knox, 2009), 130.

73. Allen P. Ross, *Holiness to the LORD: A Guide to the Exposition of the Book of Leviticus* (Grand Rapids: Baker, 2002), 62.

74. Dorsey, "The Law of Moses," 332.

75. See Gen 2:1–3; Ex 20:8–11; 22:27; Lev 11:44–45; 19:2; 20:7, 26; 21:8; Deut 10:17–19; 15:14–15; Ps 25:8–10; etc.

76. There, I shall argue that every pericope of Scripture, irrespective of genre, portrays not just "God," but "God-in-Christ," the Second Person of the Trinity—the "goal" and "fulfillment" (τέλος) of the law—into whose image God ultimately seeks to conform his children (Rom 8:29); the importance of *imitatio Dei/ Christi* for preaching and application will be dealt with in chapter 4, as well.

Law as a System of Ethics, than a Code of Rules

Gordon Wenham argues that biblical law is not an exhaustive morality code that specifies every aspect of the lives of God's people, but rather is intended to be an ethical system to portray the Lawgiver. Thus, there is more to OT ethics than mere obedience to rules.[77] Divine demand encompasses more than simply behavioral restriction in the few circumscribed facets of life that are explicitly prescribed by law. Even secular and civil law governs only a few selected aspects of life's complexities and vagaries.[78] The key point is this: "In general, the law prescribes *external* behaviour rather than states of mind and intentions."[79] In other words, "[t]he law sets a minimum standard of behaviour, which if transgressed attracts sanction." Only this minimum standard (the "floor") of behavior is exhorted and enforced; the ideal (the "ceiling") is rarely propounded as specifically as is that minimum standard in all its mind-numbing particularity and contextual detail. In other words, refraining from breaking any of the specified laws does not make one a perfect human in the eyes of God: "[E]thics is much more than keeping the law."[80] While the law of God is good (Neh 9:13; Ps 119:39), not *all* that is good is explicitly listed or specifically detailed in the Mosaic law. The contrary is also demonstrably true: there are far more ways to sin than by simply disobeying God's expressly stated law! That is to say, one might sin by not loving one's neighbor as oneself (not attaining to the "ceiling"), while yet keeping all the specifically formulated laws prohibiting stealing, bearing false witness, and so on, that are integral to loving one's neighbor (successfully abiding by the "floor"). Calvin, likewise, declares:

> Hence the commandment, "Thou shalt not kill," the generality of men will merely consider as an injunction to abstain from all injury and all wish to inflict injury ["floor"]. I hold that it moreover means that we are to aid our neighbor's life by every means in our power ["ceiling"]. And not to assert without giving my reasons, I prove it thus: God forbids us to injure or hurt

---

77. Gordon J. Wenham, *Story as Torah: Reading Old Testament Narrative Ethically* (Grand Rapids: Baker, 2000), 79.

78. This limited role is recognized by Hunter: "At best, the state's role addressing human problems is partial and limited.... [L]aws cannot generate values, or instill values, or settle the conflict over values" (James Davison Hunter, *To Change the World: The Irony, Tragedy, and Possibility of Christianity in the Late Modern World* [New York: Oxford University Press, 2010], 171).

79. Ze'ev W. Falk, *Religious Law and Ethics: Studies in Biblical and Rabbinical Theonomy* (Jerusalem: Mesharim, 1991), 79–80 (emphasis added).

80. Wenham, *Story as Torah*, 80.

a brother ["floor"], because He would have his life to be dear and precious to us; and, therefore, when He so forbids, He, at the same time, demands *all the offices of charity* which can contribute to his preservation ["ceiling"] (*Institutes* 2.8.9 [emphases added]).

Thus there is a gap between "floor" and "ceiling," between the legal and the ideal in the OT. To take another example: merely refraining from idolatry (Ex 20:3; "floor") does not meet the ideal of the divine demand to love Yahweh with all one's heart, soul, and strength ("ceiling"). The avoidance of false worship may have precluded reprimand and retribution, but the ethical goal was far more comprehensive and, involving matters of the mind and heart, impossible to legislate with any useful degree of specificity. "In this sense ethics is not so much a system of obligations [to law] as a way of communion with God...."[81] Wrapped up in the worship of God, and of God alone, is not only demonstrable external loyalty to God ("floor"), but also the intangible love for him with all of one's being ("ceiling"). Obedience to explicit laws is, for sure, an essential expression of such love and allegiance to Yahweh, but one can never reduce love and allegiance to mere compliance with statutes. There is more to loving God than mere adherence to law; the psalmist's exultation demonstrates that abundantly in 42:1–2; 63:1; 84:1–2; etc.[82] There is much in the law about murder, but not as much about anger (Matt 5:21–22); much about adultery, but not as much about lust (5:27–30). In his Sermon on the Mount, Jesus was clearly establishing the "ceiling" above these "floor" demands of the OT: "You have heard that it was said ['floor']..., but I say to you ... ['ceiling']." To reiterate, there is more to meeting divine demand than simply obedience to the letter of the law. That is not to say that the "ceiling" was left to the reader's imagination; it is expressed in the Mosaic law: for instance, Deut 6:5, 13; 10:12–13, 20; 11:1, 13; and 13:4 talk about following, loving, fearing, and serving God in general "ceiling" terms.

Thus, it may well have been that the inclusion of particular, specific, "floor"

---

81. John Barton, "Approaches to Ethics in the Old Testament," in *Beginning Old Testament Study*, by John Rogerson, John Barton, David J. A. Clines, and Paul Joyce (London: SPCK, 1998), 130.

82. Wenham, *Story as Torah*, 81. Needless to say, the explicit expression in the legal code of every single facet of what it means to love God would be an utter impossibility:

"Could we with ink the ocean fill, And were the skies of parchment made,
Were every stalk on earth a quill, And every man a scribe by trade,
To write of loving God above, Would drain the ocean dry.
Nor could the scroll contain the whole, Though stretched from sky to sky"
(with apologies to Frederick M. Lehman, "The Love of God" [1917]).

laws in the Pentateuch and the canon was intended "less as a source for legal action . . . than as a statement of legal policy," less as a code of rules than as syn-ecdoche for ethics, less as a fountain of information on community governance than as an instrument for the depiction of the world the text projects.[83] Daube has convincingly shown how Deuteronomic law functions more as wisdom than as pure legalese. Deuteronomy describes itself as wisdom (חָכְמָה, *hakmah*, Deut 4:6–8) that causes the nations to exclaim: "Surely this great nation is a wise [חָכָם, *hakam*] and understanding people." The word "hear" (שָׁמַע, *shm'*) oc-curs over fifty times in Deut, expressing the standard posture adopted towards a teacher of wisdom (e.g., 4:1, 6, 10, 12, 30, 33, 36). So also the ethical use of "way" (דֶּרֶךְ, *derek*)—another characteristic of "wisdom"—occurs fifteen times in the same book (e.g., 8:6; 10:12; 11:28; 26:17; 30:16; 32:4). As Daube notes, a choice is given to the Israelites as to the "way" they could go: "I command you today to love the LORD your God, to walk in his ways and to obey his commandments and his statutes and his ordinances. Then you will live and multiply, and that the LORD your God may bless you in the land where you are entering to pos-sess it. But if your heart turns away and you will not obey . . ." (Deut 30:16–17). Legislation proper does not generally provide a choice, or even incentives for obedience: "[I]t is wisdom that tries to explain to its audience the consequences of diverse actions and how much depends on taking the right course."[84] All this to say that there is more to the Mosaic law than just law!

Patrick also argues that the law codes of the Pentateuch were *not* consid-ered to be exhaustive, comprehensive revelations of God's will for his people. Instead, the precepts and judgments in the Torah were created "to inculcate the

---

83. Calum Carmichael, *The Spirit of Biblical Law* (Athens, Ga.: University of Georgia Press, 1996), 27. The selectivity of the laws is telling. For instance, the "statute of the law which the LORD has commanded Moses," as referred to by Eleazar (Num 31:21), is not found elsewhere in the Pentateuch; thus, perhaps not even every law given to Moses was included in the corpus. This is also suggested by the observation that the number of laws, 611, is the numerical equivalent of תורה (*trh*, the syllables that when vocalized indicate the *Torah*). The traditional enumeration of 613 considers, in addition, the Shema (Deut 6:4) and Ex 20:2, "I am the LORD your God." Thus, an "artificial" compilation seems to have been the intent, not an exhaustive collection. It is also quite striking that the OT lacks any reference to the judicial use of, or direct appeal to, the written laws during legal disputes, while even Hammurabi calls upon the plain-tiff to "have my inscribed stela read aloud to him, thus may he hear my precious pronouncements and let my stela reveal the lawsuit for him" (Martha T. Roth, *Law Collections from Mesopotamia and Asia Minor* [Atlanta: Scholars, 1995], 134; also see James W. Watts, *Reading Law: The Rhetorical Shaping of the Pentateuch* [Sheffield: Sheffield Academic Press, 1999], 21–22).

84. David Daube, *Law and Wisdom in the Bible: David Daube's Gifford Lectures, Volume 2* (ed. Calum Car-michael; West Conshohocken, Penn.: Templeton, 2010), 27–28. Talking of incentives, I would rather prefer getting a "citation" for all the good driving I have done, rather than a citation when I break the speed limit, but alas, that is not how the law of the land works.

values, principles, concepts, and procedures of Israel's legal tradition, not to decree specific rulings for specific cases." The law books, rather than resembling judicial codes, approximate "moral homilies" in their formulation as addresses: the language of moral suasion pervades the presentation of law (with an abundance of motive clauses; see below), and apodictic commandments resemble moral precepts more than they do legal prescriptions.[85] The allusion to homiletical practice is apropos: biblical law is more of a world-projecting system than a behaviour-governing code, intended to conquer distanciation and enable application by contemporary readers of the text and listeners of sermons on it.

Rationale of Law

Finding the rationale of OT laws that are no longer directly applicable to modern readers is a valid enterprise in the preacher's attempt to apply these laws to the people of God.[86] After all, the goal of the interpreter is to discern the transhistorical intention of the law, where intention is equivalent to rationale. The pragmatic force of an imperative is likely to be reflected in the rationale of that law. In a famous case of the nineteenth century, *Riggs* v. *Palmer*, the Court of Appeals of New York ruled that a nephew who poisoned his uncle, and who was in line to receive an inheritance from the murdered uncle, should *not* be eligible to do so. The judges agreed that the plain sense of the statute called for the nephew to come into his uncle's wealth, but the jurists decided against applying it, grounding their verdict in part on their assessment that the state legislature could never have intended such an immoral result when it promulgated that statute, a clear reversion to the rationale of the law that did not mean to reward homicide.

> It is a familiar canon of construction that a thing which is within the intention of the makers of a statute is as much within the statute as if it were within the letter; and a thing which is within the letter of the statute is not within the statute, unless it be within the intention of the makers. The writers of laws do not always express their intention perfectly, but either exceed it or fall short of it, so that judges are to collect it from probable or rational conjectures only, and this is called rational interpretation.[87]

---

85. Dale Patrick, *Old Testament Law* (Atlanta: John Knox, 1985), 188–89, 198.

86. So it also is in civic legal hermeneutics; see Frederick Schauer, *Playing by the Rules: A Philosophical Examination of Rule-Based Decision-Making in Law and in Life* (Oxford: Clarendon, 1991), 25–28, 74–75 (he calls "rationale" the "justification" of the law).

87. *Riggs* v. *Palmer*, N.Y. 115 (1889): 509.

This is an example of legal interpretation that seeks to understand what the lawmakers were *doing* with the law they were making, what kind of world was being projected by the law, and what its rationale was. It is apparent, here, that *"rationale* of the law" could very well be replaced by *"principle* of the law." The problems with principlizing were discussed in chapter 2; however, there is likely to be a place for discovering principles in the genre of law, which is essentially a genre of principles, so to speak. Westbrook observes that "[the legal system of the ancient Near East] looked to the code, not for an exact, mechanical precedent, but for the principle that the code indirectly laid down through its examples." Such principles, he notes, can be "extracted" and this was what ancient courts sought to do.[88] Sprinkle agrees: for interpretation and application of biblical law in the current era, "it is necessary to look at each law and ask what principle—moral or religious—underlies this regulation."[89] In explaining his methodology of interpretation of the "moral" law (the Decalogue), Calvin declares:

> [T]here is always more in the requirements and prohibitions of the Law than is expressed in words. . . . It is plain that a sober interpretation of the Law must go beyond [the letter of the law], but how far is doubtful, unless some rule be adopted. The best rule, in my opinion, would be, to be guided by the principle [*praeceptum*, "rationale"] of the commandment—viz. to consider in the case of each what the principle [*praecepto*] is for which it was given to us. For example, every commandment either requires or prohibits; and the nature of each is instantly discerned when we look to the reason [*rationem*] as its purpose [*finem*]. . . . So in each of the commandments we must first look to the matter of which it treats, and then consider its purpose [*finis*], until we discover what it properly is that the Lawgiver declares to be pleasing or displeasing to him. (*Institutes* 2.8.8)

---

88. Raymond Westbrook, *Studies in Biblical and Cuneiform Law* (Paris: Gabalda, 1988), 77, and 77 n. 156.

89. Sprinkle, *Biblical Law and Its Relevance*, 20. Notwithstanding this special use of "principle" *behind the text*, what the biblical authors are doing is projecting a *world in front of the text*—a world that functions according to the demand(s) of that particular law—the theology of the pericope. In *Riggs* v. *Palmer*, for instance, the projected world is one in which murderers do not profit from their nefarious activities; no doubt, this could well be rephrased as a principle. Nevertheless differences remain: as was noted in chapter 2, by the theological hermeneutic proposed in this work, the text gives rise to the world *in front of* it/pericopal theology (and the text is not reducible to that world/theology); in the "principlizing" hermeneutic, the principle gives rise to the text (and the text is often considered reducible to the principle *behind* it). However, for the genre of legal literature, biblical or otherwise, the distinction between a law's rationale (the projected *world in front of the text*) and "principle" is admittedly not as sharp as it would be, for instance, for narrative or for hymnody. Therefore the account of this section will concede the use of the term "principle" when employed by authors who are cited here.

Such rationales form part of the world projected by those texts of law—the theology of those pericopes. Admittedly, not all biblical laws have rationales that can be ferreted out. Indeed, there may even be multiple rationales for a given regulation: for instance, the observance of the Sabbath was based upon the rationale of *imitatio Dei* (Ex 20:8–11), it was a sign of the covenant (31:12–17), it was a humane consideration of the plight of servants (Deut 5:14), and it was also a memorial to the exodus (5:15). It is likely that such rationales operated in the formulation of biblical laws; for the most part they were linked to the historical traditions of the nation, and enunciated in response to issues that arose in the arena of their lives and in those of succeeding generations. Interestingly, comparing the laws of the OT with legal collections of Israel's *Umwelt*, the ancient Near East, it appears that motive clauses, including paraenetic exhortations, were a peculiarity of the laws of Israel (motive clauses are found, for instance, in Ex 20:5; 23:32–33; Lev 17:10–11; 26:1; Deut 1:30–31).[90] The presence of these motive clauses further substantiates the conclusion that God's law is primarily intended as an instrument to aid sanctification. "The purpose of motivation in a large degree is to clarify the place of law in sanctification (especially dealing with promise and blessing).... Motivation reveals the character of God and his plan to make us like him," ultimately to be conformed into the image of Christ (Rom 8:29; see chapter 4).[91]

Wright observes correctly:

> Laws in any society are made for a purpose. Laws protect interests. Laws restrict power. Laws try to balance the rights of different and possibly competing groups in society. Laws promote social objectives according to the legislators'

---

90. B. Gemser categorically asserts of non-Jewish legal compilations that "[i]n absolutely none of these law books or -codes or -collections can one single instance of motive clauses be discovered." In Deut and Lev, 60–65 percent of the laws have motive clauses by his reckoning ("The Importance of the Motive Clause in Old Testament Law," in *Congress Volume: Copenhagen* [VTSup 1; Leiden: Brill, 1953], 52). Other studies have generally supported Gemser's findings; in contrast, motive clauses have been found only in 6 percent of the Laws of Hammurabi and in 5 percent of the injunctions of Middle Assyrian Law. That "legal motivation is not a characteristic of cuneiform law" seems clear (Rifat Sonsino, *Motive Clauses in Hebrew Law: Biblical Forms and Near Eastern Parallels* [Chico, Calif.: Scholars, 1980], 86–93, 155–73). Even what appear as "motive clauses" in Hammurabi seem to be merely offering further legal clarification, rather than motivation per se that is grounded elsewhere in the history of the people. "They in no way parallel such motivations as the frequent reference, in Old Testament laws, to Israel's liberation from Egypt." In fact, the biblical motive clauses add a "pleading, preaching, persuading tone" to the mandates of OT law, quite unusual for law codes (Waldemar Janzen, *Old Testament Ethics: A Paradigmatic Approach* [Louisville: Westminster John Knox, 1994], 61, 81 n. 12).

91. Greg Chirichigno, "A Theological Investigation of Motivation in Old Testament Law," *JETS* 24 (1981): 312.

vision of what kind of ideal society they would like to see. So, in the light of our understanding of Israelite society, we need to articulate as precisely as possible the objective of any specific law. In other words, we are trying to understand "Why was this law there?"

Or, what was the author *doing* with what he was saying by that biblical law? Wright further recommends that the interpreter "preserve the objective [rationale] but change the context," in order to bring valid application to bear upon life.[92] This approach explains how Abraham can be said to have kept the "commands, statutes, and laws" (Gen 26:5) even *before* the Mosaic law was given, for what Abraham abided by were not these laws per se, but their underlying rationales—the theology of the text, what the author was *doing* with what he was *saying* in those texts of law. Essentially, the patriarch obeyed in doing what he would have been supposed to do *had the laws been given in his time.* This is quite similar to the situation faced by the current reader, but located in the future with regard to the Mosaic law (unlike Abraham who was located in the past with respect to that law code). The Christian, by attending to the theology of the legal text, can obey, by doing what he would have been supposed to do *were the laws given in his contemporary day.*

A failure to make the theological move in this fashion results either in a denial of the validity of the law in the current age (usually accompanied by alterations of the text to make it palatable to modern sensibilities), or an unthinking attempt to adopt the ancient law exactly as it is, anachronous and incongruous though it may be to a modern audience. David Clark notes that interpreters who are "transformers" fail because of their lack of fidelity to the text, simply changing the text to fit the contemporary cultural landscape (or else they completely abandon such texts). Those who are "transporters," who merely read the text in slavish imitation even in a new situation, fail because of their cultural naïveté: they do not recognize that times and contexts have changed. Clark sees only "translators" as being faithful to the ancient text *and* sensitive to the modern audience. Or, as the Talmud states: "If one translates a verse literally, he is a liar: if he adds thereto, he is a blasphemer and a libeler" (*b. Qidd.* 49a). One could conceivably add to that observation: "But if one translates *theologically,* he tells the truth." This is essentially the position advocated here—a theological hermeneutic ("translation" that grasps the theology of the pericope) is essential

---

92. Wright, *Old Testament Ethics,* 322–23.

if one is to be faithful to the text as well as be relevant to the audience.[93]

For instance, the witness of the Bible is uniformly against lending at interest. One of the characteristics of a just and righteous life, the prophet Ezekiel announces, is that one does not lend money on interest (Ezek 18:8, 13, 17; also 22:12); this is, of course, based upon the ordinances of the Pentateuch prohibiting usury when lending to anyone in need (Ex 22:25; Lev 25:36–37; Deut 23:19–20; also see Ps 15:5). From the early days of the church and into the medieval age, lending at interest had, therefore, always been deemed unbiblical.[94] Reflecting newer economic situations that markedly differed from the earlier agrarian circumstances of the biblical age, later theologians began to make exceptions to the absolute ban on loans at interest: after all, the biblical proscriptions of usury were promulgated to prevent the exploitation of the insolvent, and to enable their recovery and the repayment of their loans—the rationale of the law, or the *world in front of the text*, the theology of the pericope. Thus, the church today reads the law that prohibits interest-bearing loans in light of its rationale not to put burdens on those in dire financial straits. This rationale is considered as having moral force, mandating concern for the penurious and helpless.[95] Thus it is possible to be faithful to the text *and* simultaneously respect current changed circumstances by means of the theological hermeneutic proposed herein.

Dorsey's example of the commandment in Deut 22:12, requiring the wear-

---

93. See David K. Clark, *To Know and Love God* (Wheaton: Crossway, 2003), 56. Also see Abraham Kuruvilla, "Preaching as Translation *via* Theology," *JEHS* 9 (2009): 85–97. Such a translation is similar to the exercise with dates described in chapter 1. One could move from the U.K. to the U.S. and retain the U.K. text "2/12/1991" and read it as "2/12/1991" ("transportation"); or one could read that U.K. text in the new U.S. context as "12/2/1991" ("translation").

94. Along with anathematizing the Arian heresy, the Council of Nicea (325) also advocated that the cleric who loaned money on interest "shall be deposed from the clergy and his name stricken from the list" (Canon 17). The Second Lateran Council about a millennium later (1139) condemned as despicable the "ferocious greed of usurers"—"we sever from them every comfort of the church" (Canon 13).

95. Rationales are, no doubt, hierarchical and are present at multiple levels of specificity in relation to the text. Thus the text's theology may also be considered at various levels as discussed in chapter 2. Behind the immediate purpose of preventing the subjugation of the poor in the credit business, is the scriptural concern for the overall protection of the powerless. This, in turn, is based upon God's identification of himself as the defender of the defenseless (Ps 35:10; Prov 22:23; 23:10–11; etc.), and upon the obligations of God's people to take their cues from the character of God himself who is merciful and gracious (Ps 86:15): they are to be sensitive and generous, willing to help those in need even when they will not stand to gain financially in the process. While there is some flexibility here in choosing the level of theology from which to make valid application, I would strongly recommend abiding by the Plimsoll premise (see chapter 2): *Go as high as you need to; stay as low as you can.* See Charles H. Cosgrove, *Appealing to Scripture in Moral Debate: Five Hermeneutical Rules* (Grand Rapids: Eerdmans, 2002), 34–37. Also see Albert R. Jonsen and Stephen Toulmin, *The Abuse of Casuistry: A History of Moral Reasoning* (Berkeley, Calif.: University of California Press, 1988), 181–94.

ing of tassels on the four corners of the Israelite's cloak, is appropriate for a brief demonstration of this operation.[96] The tassel, as an extension of the garment hem—usually the most ornate part of a Near Eastern garment—was considered an important social statement, "the 'I.D.' of nobility," signifying the special status of the wearers as gods or kings. The blue color that the law required the affixture to be, made this undertaking quite exclusive, for the production of this dye was extremely expensive.[97] However, even a poor Israelite could afford to have four threads of blue in the tassel as mandated in the regulation; thus it was possible for everyone in the community of God to be tagged by the badge of honor. This appendix to clothing, therefore, was to serve as a reminder to the children of the Hebrew nation, one and all, of their unique standing before God on the basis of their redemption, and the resulting obligation to obey him; this was the rationale implied in the law. The tassel commandment that is also found in Num 15:37–41, in fact, makes this explicit, linking the Israelites' distinctive position as those redeemed from Egypt by Yahweh with the demand for obedience to him ("I am the LORD your God who brought you out of the land of Egypt to be your God").[98] Thus, the world projected by this text is one in which those in God's community, those redeemed by God, constantly bear upon their person a reminder of their high status before God and of the priority of a lifestyle commensurate with that privilege. In this ideal world, God's children would be marked in a visible fashion on their clothing with a token of their calling that would remind them of their filial responsibility to God, to follow his commandments. Consequently, for contemporary application, based upon the world the text projects, such a remembrancer of position and responsibility could be any number of tangible objects, not necessarily restricted to blue threads in a tassel on a cloak—a lapel pin, a scarf, etc.

Summary: Law Functions Theologically

In a *forensic* sense, then, it appears that it is not incumbent upon NT believers to obey any of the stipulations of the Mosaic law as such, in light of the drastic

---

96. Dorsey, "The Use of the OT Law," 13–15.

97. See Jacob Milgrom, "Of Hems and Tassels," *BAR* 9 (1983): 61–65. He also suggests that the blue tassel denoted elements of the priesthood as well, in accordance with God's declaration that Israel was a kingdom of priests (Ex 19:6).

98. Stephen Bertman, "Tasseled Garments in the Ancient East Mediterranean," *BA* 24 (1961): 128. Indeed, it appears that obedience to all the commandments of Yahweh was inextricably bound up with this privileged station of the children of Israel as God's possession redeemed from the land of Egypt: see Ex 19:4–6; Deut 4:20; 7:6–8; 26:16–18; etc.

changes in circumstances between then and now that preclude obedience to the laws as explicitly tendered. However, in the *theological* sense that has been propounded in this work, all of those laws—indeed all texts in non-legal genres, as well—are applicable to believers of all times and ages (2 Tim 3:16–17), for every law points to the divine Lawgiver and to some facet of his relationship to his creation. Biblical law, or divine demand, seeks to mold the people of God into the image of God himself. In other words, there is more to law than law itself. It is more a world-projecting system than a behavior-directing statute book—it projects a *world in front of the text* and beckons mankind to abide by this world's precepts, priorities, and practices. Grasping the rationale of the law helps the interpreter discern this projected world and the theology of the text.

In sum, law continues to operate, with the caveat that it be interpreted theologically, in light of the immense contextual shift that has occurred between the writing of the law and its modern-day reading. In so interpreting law for application, the people of God learn about the *world in front of the* legal *text* that depicts God and his relationship with his creation, and how they can inhabit that world— i.e., abide by divine demand. The underpinning of this operation is the powerful truth that a relationship with God precedes responsibility: it is *because* his people are related to him in the first place that God makes demands that they are responsible to fulfill (in the power of the Holy Spirit, as will be discussed below).

Relationship Precedes Responsibility

"The law was given after the redemption from Egypt had been accomplished, and the people had already entered upon the enjoyment of the blessings of the *berith*." Therefore, Vos declared it is "distorted and misleading" to identify the ot with law and the nt with gospel. "The people of God in those days did not live and die under an unworkable, unredemptive system of religion, that could not give real access to and spiritual contact with God. . . . That which we call 'the legal system' [in the ot] is shot through with strands of gospel and grace and faith. Especially the ritual law is rich in them. Every sacrifice and every lustration proclaimed the principle of grace."[99] While it is no doubt true, as has already been mentioned, that a legalistic and salvation-oriented (mis)understanding of the role of law prevailed in at least some strands of Second Temple

---

99. Geerhardus Vos, *Biblical Theology: Old and New Testament* (Grand Rapids: Eerdmans, 1948; repr. 1975), 127–29.

Judaism (to which Paul responded with his polemic), God's plan, all along, was to guide, by his divine demand, the behavior of those who were *already* his children. Relationship always preceded the responsibility of the people of God to meet divine demand and to be holy as God was holy. So also Wright: "The law was not given as a means of salvation, but as a gift of grace to those whom God had already redeemed."[100] In other words, obedience is the response of God's people to his prevenient operations of grace; relationship *precedes* responsibility, but relationship does not *preclude* responsibility!

Kaiser makes the point noted earlier that the relationship between God and his people, Israel, antedated the transactions on Mt. Sinai: "[T]he giving of the law only fixed and settled outwardly a relationship which had already been initiated in the plagues on Israel's behalf and their Exodus." In fact, Jeremiah pinpoints the making of the covenant between sovereign and subjects to "the day I [Yahweh] took them by the hand to bring them out of the land of Egypt" (Jer 31:32; also see Ex 6:2–8). It was God's love that had established the relationship between him and his people, not the latter's obedience, or even their willingness to obey (Deut 4:37; 7:7–9; 10:15; etc.). None of these was a criterion for the relationship—it was entirely a unilateral, divine act of grace, apprehended, from the human side, by faith alone. And once established, nothing could disrupt this relationship, not even breakage of the law, for the law itself made provision for remedying such a contingency by outlining the procedure for the atonement of less-than-perfect obedience. Again, all of this was the product of the grace of Yahweh, "the LORD God, compassionate and gracious, slow to anger, and abounding in lovingkindness and truth, keeping lovingkindness for thousands, forgiving iniquity, and transgression, and sin" (Ex 34:6–7).[101]

Generally (but not without exceptions), the rabbis understood the law this way, too—as a criterion for the maintenance of Israel's relationship with God and not a means of entry thereunto. "R. Joshua b. Karha [140–165 C.E.] said:

---

100. Wright, *Old Testament Ethics*, 316.

101. While there would surely be discipline for disobedience, there would also be provision for forgiveness, for that is the very nature of God. See Walter C. Kaiser, "Leviticus 18:5 and Paul: Do This and You Shall Live (Eternally?)," *JETS* 14 (1971): 21–22. "As for me, if I stumble, the mercies of God shall be my eternal salvation. If I stagger because of the sin of flesh, my justification shall be by the righteousness of God which endures forever. . . . He will judge me in the righteousness of His truth and in the greatness of His goodness He will pardon all my sins. Through His righteousness He will cleanse me of the uncleanness of man and of the sins of the children of men" (1QS 11.11–15; also see 1QM 1.3–4; 1QH 4.30–32).

Why was the section of 'Hear' [Deut 6:4–9] placed before that of 'And it shall come to pass' [Deut 11:13]? So that one should first accept upon himself the yoke of the kingdom of heaven and *then* take upon himself the yoke of the commandments" (*m. Ber.* 2.2 [emphasis added]). In *Sipra* 13.3 on Lev 18:1–4 ("I am the LORD your God . . . you must obey my laws"), the commentator (R. Simeon ben Yohai, mid-second century C.E.) paraphrases: "You have accepted my kingship: [now] accept my ordinances." Likewise, *Mek.* on Ex 20:3: "God said to Israel: 'I am the Lord thy God, thou shalt not have other gods—I am He whose reign you have taken upon yourselves in Egypt.' And when they said to Him: 'Yes, yes,' He continued: 'Now, just as you accepted My reign, you must also accept My decrees: "Thou shalt not have other gods before Me."'" Relationship always precedes responsibility.

It seems fair to say that God's intention from the very beginning was to guide his people to live by the demands he made of them; such a theme resonates through the Pentateuch. God had elected a people; he then required of them obedience to divine demand. "First God redeems Israel from Egypt, *and then* he gives the law, so obedience to the law is a response to God's grace, not an attempt to gain righteousness by works (see Ex 19–20)."[102] In Gen 1:27–28, God blesses Adam and Eve *before* delivering the first imperative for mankind—to reproduce and to rule. So also the similar command to Noah and his sons is preceded by blessing (Gen 9:1). In Ex 19:4, Yahweh recites his deliverance of the Israelites from the Egyptians and how he bore them on eagles' wings and brought them to himself. Then he promises them a special status contingent upon their obedience—they would be his "own possession" and "a kingdom of priests and a holy nation" (Ex 19:5–6). Deliverance came first; subsequent obedience did render them a special people (the blessings/reward of obedience), but the foundational relationship based upon their deliverance was prior to God's placing any demands upon them, which he then proceeded to do in Ex 20 (the Decalogue). Notable is the fact that this code was prefaced by an announcement of relationship: "I am the LORD your God, who brought you out from the land of Egypt, out from the house of slavery" (Ex 20:2). The list of divine demands came afterwards. The relationship between God and mankind

---

102. Thomas R. Schreiner, *Paul, Apostle of God's Glory in Christ: A Pauline Theology* (Downers Grove: InterVarsity, 2001), 117–18.

is the primary incentive for obedience.[103]

In Ex 31:13, the Sabbath command (subsequent responsibility) was given as a "sign" that the Israelites might know that it was Yahweh who was their sanctifier (prior relationship). At the end of the dietary restrictions in Lev 11, Yahweh gave the reason for those commands: "For I am the LORD your God. . . . For I am the LORD who brought you up from the land of Egypt to be your God; thus you shall be holy, for I am holy" (11:44–45). Being the Israelites' God—a relationship inaugurated prior to the giving of the Mosaic law—had significant bearing upon the subsequent responsibility of the people to be holy. Likewise, Lev 18:1–5 ("I am the LORD your God. You shall not do . . . I am the LORD your God. So you shall keep my statutes and my ordinances, by which a man will live if he does them; I am the LORD") suggests that *because* this God was Yahweh, the Israelites' covenantal God, *therefore* the Israelites were to behave in a certain fashion.[104] That God's setting apart of his people (the divine-human relationship) came prior to their responsibility to be holy was asserted in Lev 20:26—"Thus [according to the specifics detailed in 20:1–25] you are to be holy to me, for I the LORD am holy; and I have set you apart from the peoples to be mine" (also see 22:32–33; 23:41–43). A recitation of Israel's special status—as those loved by God—was followed by exhortation to obey (Deut 4:32–40): obedience was the sign of an abiding relationship. By God's affirmation that he would be the Israelites' God and they his people (Ex 6:7; 19:5–6; 20:2; Lev 26:12; Deut 7:6; 14:2; 28:9; 29:13; etc.), a close relationship was envisaged, in turn calling for the responsibility of obedience to be duly discharged.

The *Shema* begins with an exhortation to love Yahweh with heart, soul, and might (the core of the relationship between God and man; Deut 6:5). It then goes on to describe what the responsibility of the Israelite to God's demand ought to

---

103. Rewards are also a powerful biblical motivator to obedience. Blessing as a reward for obedience to divine demand is amply attested in the OT and elsewhere: Lev 20:22–23; 25:18; 26:14–46; Deut 4:25–28, 40; 5:29–33; 6:18, 24; 7:12–16; 8:1; 11:8, 13–15, 22–28; 13:17–18; 27:1–28:68; 29:9; 30:2–3, 9–10, 16; Josh 1:8; *As. Mos.* 12:10; *4 Ezra* 7:21; Philo, *Congr.* 86; *L.A.B.* 23:10. This blessing for obedience included "life"—an abundant temporal life in the land that Yahweh would give his people, a life that blended into eternity: Lev 18:5; Deut 4:1; 6:2, 24; 30:20; Neh 9:29; Prov 3:1–2; 6:23; Sir 17:11 ("law of life"); Bar 3:9 ("commandments of life"); 4:1; also see 1QS 4:6–8 ("plentiful peace in a long life, and fruitfulness, together with every everlasting blessing and eternal joy in life without end"); *Pss Sol.* 3:11–12; 9:5; 14:1–5, 10; *m. 'Abot* 2:7; etc. The concept of rewards will be treated further in chapter 4.

104. Also Lev 19:1–3 ("You shall be holy, for I the LORD your God am holy. . . . I am the LORD your God") and the numerous echoes throughout Leviticus of "I am the LORD" (19:3, 4, 10, 12, 14, 16, 18, 25, 28, 29, 30, 31, 32, 34, 36, 37; etc.).

be: its words were to be on their hearts, bound to their hands and as frontals on their foreheads, inscribed on their doorposts and gates (6:6–9). The Israelites were not to forget Yahweh, but to fear him, worship him, and swear by his name, not following any other, or putting Yahweh to the test (6:10–16). In other words, in light of their prior relationship to God, they had certain responsibilities, the shape of which was spelled out in the covenants, statutes, and ordinances.[105] Deuteronomy 6:20–25 indicates the same sentiment, pictured in the response of the elder to his son when asked about God's statutes and judgments: the relationship with God, exemplified in the exodus rescue, was cited as the reason for obedience. It is only *after* the assertion of relationship between divine regent and people (6:20–23) that the call to obedience is given: "So the LORD commanded us to observe these statutes…" (6:24). Relationship preceded and mandated obedience, the filial responsibility of God's children to meet divine demand. Indeed, the essence of the new covenant is the placement of the law on the hearts of God's people, so that "I will be their God, and they shall be my people" (Jer 31:33). It is not a new law being promulgated here, but the same divine demand that had existed all along. Ezekiel 36:26–28 points to the key aspect of this new covenant— the Holy Spirit's presence that enables believers to obey divine demand. And one day, in the eternal state, this relationship of God to his people will ultimately be consummated: "Behold the tabernacle of God is among men, and He will dwell among them, and they will be His people, and God Himself will be among them" (Rev 21:3). Perfect obedience, perfect alignment with divine demand, perfect inhabitation of the *world in front of the text* will then have been achieved.

Section Summary: Divine Demand

The idea of "divine demand" in each pericope of Scripture requires one to investigate the role of the OT law for the Christian. Traditional approaches (Lutheran, Reformed, and Dispensational) were compared with that of proponents of the NPP. Though divergent in their claims, all generally hold to the inapplicability of the Mosaic law in the current age, excepting the "moral" aspects of the OT law. It was argued that a division of the law into moral and other categories is untenable; *all* of God's demands are moral in essence and theological in function, thus necessarily valid for all of God's people. Therefore, this work takes the stance that *all* OT law continues to operate, howbeit in a theological

---

105. Sprinkle, *Biblical Law and Its Relevance*, 50.

fashion. It is incumbent upon the interpreter to read this genre (and indeed, every other genre) theologically, discerning the segment of the *world in front of the text* projected by the pericope in question, comprehending what the author is *doing* with what he is saying. In other words, a theological hermeneutic of law admits that all pericopes in that genre are applicable—theologically—for God's people everywhere always (the Rule of Application; see chapter 1). "[A]lways remember that the grace of God precedes the law of God. What Yahweh has done comes before what Yahweh demands; he gives redemption before he imposes requirements; he first sets you free, then shows you how a free people are to live. Proper order is crucial."[106] That was what divine demand was intended for: God's people were required to keep the law—not as a condition of entry into, but as a response to, the relationship with God into which they had already entered. Obedience is, and has always been, required of God's people of all time; divine demand is to be met, even in the eternal state. The power and capacity of mankind to obey may differ by situation and station, age and dispensation (for instance, *posse non peccare* ["possible not to sin"] pre-fall, *non posse non peccare* ["not possible not to sin"] post-fall, and *non posse peccare* ["not possible to sin"] in the eschaton[107]), but divine demand does not change, for God's standard of righteousness does not change, simply because God himself does not.

This work also proposes that divine demand is not restricted to the biblical genre of law; a divine demand is implicitly or explicitly borne by every pericope. Second Timothy 3:16–17 addresses the profitability of *all* Scripture and its efficacy in maturing God's children, aligning them progressively to divine demand. Every pericope in every genre in both Testaments of Scripture projects a segment of the canonical *world in front of the text*—the theology of the pericope. This intermediary between text and application bears a transhistorical intention and depicts the precepts, priorities, and practices of the ideal world that God would have his people inhabit. This is to say that implicitly or explicitly, every pericope provides guidelines for ethical behavior before God, dealing with one facet or another of the relationship between God and man. Such imperatives are not salvific in intent or meritorious in performance. They are simply divine demands that God expects his children to obey, that his people may be like him:

---

106. Dale Ralph Davis, *The Word Became Fresh: How to Preach from Old Testament Narrative Texts* (Ross-Shire, U.K.: Mentor, 2006), 81 (italics removed).

107. See Peter Lombard, *The Four Books of Sentences*, 2.25.5, and Augustine, *Corrept.* 33 (both use slightly different wordings than what is given here).

"You shall be holy, for I am holy" (Lev 19:2; 1 Pet 1:16). Relationship precedes responsibility; in fact, to love God will result in the keeping of his commandments (John 14:21; 15:10; 1 John 2:3–5; 3:21–24; 5:3). It is the role of each preacher of Scripture to spell out the particularities of this business of keeping his commandments and being holy, meeting divine demand; and this is accomplished in the power of the indwelling Spirit (see below). The theology of the pericope provides this transhistorical direction for holiness; the preacher's task, in the second step of preaching, is to apply this theology into the concrete specificities of the lives of the congregants. Their obedience would be a response to their already belonging to God, an expression of the covenantal relationship they already had with their Creator. And through believers' obedience, God is glorified as they manifest his holiness and represent him to the world.

FAITHFUL OBEDIENCE

In Rom 9:30–10:8, law is an entirely legitimate goal, if pursued the right way, by faith (see discussion above). "Israel's mistake was not that they pursued the law, but that they did so as though that goal was to be achieved in terms of works; whereas it could only be achieved 'from faith.'"[108] Law, thus pursued in the right manner, becomes the "law of faith"—i.e., obedience (as always required by every divine demand) pursued in faith, by faith. Faith is thus a descriptor of obedience, the "faithful obedience" that Paul talks about in Rom 1:5—ὑπακοὴ πίστεως (*hupakoē pisteōs*, "obedience of faith"). What exactly is this species of obedience?

Hupakoē Pisteōs

Garlington lays out the various options for ὑπακοὴ πίστεως: the genitive in question could be objective (obedience to the faith—i.e., obedience to a body of doctrine), subjective (obedience worked by/springing from faith), qualitative (believing/"faith-full" obedience or obedience characterized by faith), or appositional (obedience which consists in faith and/or is equivalent to faith).[109]

---

108. James D. G. Dunn, "'The Law of Faith,' 'the Law of the Spirit' and 'the Law of Christ,'" in *Theology and Ethics in Paul and His Interpreters: Essays in Honor of Victor Paul Furnish* (eds. Eugene H. Lovering and Jerry L. Sumney; Nashville: Abingdon, 1996), 67.

109. Don B. Garlington, *Faith, Obedience and Perseverance* (WUNT 79; Tübingen: J. C. B. Mohr [Paul Siebeck], 1994), 14. Also see James C. Miller, *The Obedience of Faith, the Eschatological People of God, and the Purpose of Romans* (SBLDS 177; Atlanta: SBL, 2000), 42.

The genitival structure, ὑπακοὴ πίστεως, is an unexpected way of indicating obedience to a body of doctrine as the very different syntax of verses dealing with that issue indicates: Acts 6:7; Rom 10:16; 2 Thess 1:8; and 3:14, where the object of obedience is in the dative—"obedience *to*. . ." Thus the sense of the objective genitive is unlikely.[110]

With Garlington, I hold that the genitive of apposition, that equates faith and obedience (obedience = to have faith), does not exhaust the meaning of "obedience of faith."[111] In other words, obedience is not merely an exercise of faith, a cognitive undertaking. Indeed, obedience for Paul is largely in reference to the behavior of believers: Rom 6:12, 16, 17; 1 Cor 14:34; 2 Cor 2:9; 7:15; 10:5, 6; Eph 6:1, 5; Phil 2:12; Col 3:18, 20, 22; Titus 2:5, 9; 3:1; Phlm 1. In consonance with this conclusion, the Roman *Christian* readers of Paul's Epistle are seemingly included among the Gentiles whose "obedience of faith" Paul was attempting to bring about (Rom 1:6), suggesting that this obedience was something that those already in Christ also needed to exhibit. In fact, the apostle's desire to come to the city "to preach the gospel even to you who are in Rome" (1:15; including believers) hints at this "obedience of faith" being a practice that begins with conversion and extends through the Christian life, the whole spectrum of Christian maturity (the broad sense of "gospel"). And this process operates by the instrumentality of faith, from beginning to end, from justification through sanctification to glorification ("from faith to faith," 1:16–17).[112] One also notes that the phrase "obedient from the heart" in 6:17 has the same connotation as our phrase of interest, "obedience of faith." This might either indicate a heartfelt/"faith-full" obedience (the qualitative sense) or a heart-sourced/faith-generated obedience (the subjective sense). In any case, it appears that the passages that speak of faith and obedience can be interpreted to have a more

---

110. First Peter 1:22 appears to be an exception, being in the genitive (ὑπακοῇ τῆς ἀληθείας, *hypakoē tēs alētheias*), but here, as with the dative instances listed, the object of obedience bears an article, unlike in Rom 1:5. See Garlington, *Faith, Obedience and Perseverance*, 14–15.

111. Ibid., 17. This is "evaporating 'obedience' into faith" (Douglas J. Moo, *The Epistle to the Romans* [NICNT; Grand Rapids: Eerdmans, 1996], 52).

112. While there is no doubt that "unbelief" in Christ is disobedience (compare Rom 10:16a with 10:16b; and 11:23 with 11:30–31; also John 3:36; 2 Thess 1:8, 10; and Heb 3:18–19), obedience is not solely focused upon the initial coming to faith in Christ of unbelievers (though, of course, that preliminary movement is part of the larger continuum of obedience as viewed by Paul). To have salvific faith in Christ is certainly *part* of what it means to be obedient. This is justifying faith—the first step of obedience. But justifying faith alone does not constitute the totality of Christian obedience. There is to be, in addition, a worked-out faith: sanctifying faith—the "obedience of faith."

comprehensive dimension than a simple equation of obedience with faith (the appositional genitive).

In sum, the evidence appears to indicate that the syntax of ὑπακοὴ πίστεως is either a subjective genitive ("obedience worked by/springing from faith") or a qualitative one ("believing/'faith-full' obedience"), or both. For the purposes of this work, not much will be made of the distinction between the subjective and qualitative interpretations of ὑπακοή πίστεως. In either case there is the sense that every act of obedience to divine demand springs from faith, is characterized by faith, and is carried out in faith—i.e., aspects of *both* subjective and qualitative senses of the genitive operate in such an understanding.

The special case of two pairs of verses—Rom 1:5 ("obedience of faith among all the Gentiles") with 15:18 ("obedience of the Gentiles"), and Rom 1:8 (the Romans' faith being widely proclaimed) with 16:19 (the Romans' obedience being widely reported)—will be considered in more detail next.

Romans 1:5/15:18 and 1:8/16:19

The issue in Rom 1:5/15:18 is whether the "obedience of the Gentiles" in the latter passage is equivalent to "obedience of faith among all the Gentiles" in the former. Particularly, is "obedience of the Gentiles" simply referring to the faith they exercised at their conversion (the appositional sense of ὑπακοὴ πίστεως)? It must be remembered that 15:18 belongs in (and serves to close out) the paraenetic section of the Epistle that began at 12:1, especially the portion from 15:1 onward that focuses upon the imitation of Christ (15:3, 5, 7–8). Romans 15:13 records Paul's wish that God may fill the Romans with "all joy and peace by believing [ἐν τῷ πιστεύειν, *en tō pisteuein*[113]]"; this does not sound as if the "believing" were a one-time event in the past with the once-and-forever consequences of "all joy and peace." Instead, Paul wishes for them to be continually filled with joy and peace *as they continue to exercise faith*—an ongoing state that extends beyond their initial salvific exercise of faith in Christ. Also, while Paul prays in 15:13 that their "joy and peace by believing" may result in hope, in 15:4 it is the "perseverance and encouragement of the Scriptures" that results in hope. Thus the "believing" appears to be related to a continuing transaction

---

113. This is an infinitive of means, "the way in which the action of the controlling verb [πληρῶσαι, *plērōsai*, "may he fill"] is accomplished [i.e., ἐν τῷ πιστεύειν, "by faith"]" (see Daniel B. Wallace, *Greek Grammar beyond the Basics: An Exegetical Syntax of the New Testament* [Grand Rapids: Zondervan, 1996]), 597–98).

linked to the Romans' "perseverance and encouragement" through the word of
God—i.e., an ongoing process of growth into maturity. That also explains the
apparent inclusion of the Roman *Christians* within the purview of "Gentiles"
(15:7–12, and 15:15–17), just as in 1:6–7 ("among whom you also"). "Therefore,
Paul's promotion of [the Roman Christians'] obedience assumes wider dimension than the conversion experience. Hence, when 15:18 speaks of Paul's aim
to win obedience from the Gentiles, such obedience, by the nature of the case,
must be subsequent to their initial response to his gospel"—equivalent to "obedience of faith" in 1:5.[114]

And this ongoing, faithful "obedience of the Gentiles" is what Paul would
rather boast about (15:17), not his own qualifications and credentials (15:15–
16). In other words, the "obedience" that the apostle has been working for all
along, accomplished through him by Christ, is the culmination of his mission,
his only reason for boasting. Hence he can claim, with pride, "I have fulfilled the
gospel of Christ" (15:18–19): a comprehensive lifelong undertaking had been
discharged. The obedience of 15:18, then, was the Romans' slavery to righteousness (6:18), their ongoing growth and maturity in Jesus Christ, their "obedience
of faith" (1:5). In short, obedience of faith epitomizes the comprehensive and
overarching goal of Paul's endeavors for the cause of Christ in every place.[115]
Thus the phrase "obedience of faith" in 1:5 and "obedience of the Gentiles" in
15:18 are equivalent and stand for "faith-full" obedience.

The issue with Rom 1:8/16:19 is whether the Romans' *faith* that was "being
proclaimed throughout the whole world" (1:8) was equivalent to the Romans'
obedience, the report of which "has reached to all" (16:19). This "faith" in 1:8 is
quite likely to be related to "faith" in 1:5—the faith that undergirds, enables, and
characterizes obedience. And the "obedience" applauded by Paul in 16:19 is in
contrast to the behavior of those who are "slaves of their own appetites," the flat-
terers and deceivers of 16:18, who create disunity "contrary to the teaching" the

---

114. Garlington, *Faith, Obedience and Perseverance*, 26–27. Garlington also notes the echo of Rom 12:1–2
in 15:15b–16 (concepts of liturgical offering, acceptability, and holiness): "one cannot help but see
something more than a forensic [justificatory] dimension to the outcome of his ministry" (ibid., 27).
Thus the "gospel" Paul ministered (15:16) likely consisted in more than the message of justifying faith
in Christ.

115. Ibid., 11. The phrase "obedience of faith" is repeated in Rom 16:26. The textual problem of Rom 16:25–
27 will not be addressed here; for a succinct summary of the issues see Moo, *The Epistle to the Romans*,
936–37n2. He is "slightly inclined" to accept its authenticity. In any case, the outcome does not affect
the argument here, though its authenticity would strengthen it.

Romans had received (16:17). "Obedience" in Rom 16, then, appears to be a pattern of life that Paul recommends and credits, in accordance with the Scripture. Garlington also points out the intriguing connection between what follows (16:19–20) and the account of the fall in Gen 3.[116] Romans 16:19 has Paul exhorting his readers to further improve their obedience by being "wise in what is good, and innocent in what is evil." "Good" and "evil" evoke echoes of the forbidden fruit (Gen 2:17; 3:5, 22), as well as the choices proffered to the ancient Israelites—"life and good, death and evil" (Deut 30:15). Unlike Adam and Eve, and unlike the Israelites, Paul would have the Romans be wise with regard to good and innocent with regard to evil, so that the deceivers' schemes would be thwarted (16:17–19). Indeed, these devious ones are likened to the serpent in the Garden in Rom 16:20: "And the God of peace will soon crush Satan under your feet." Once again, the obedience of the Romans appears to be more than simply the faith that justifies. It is the ethical consequence/accompaniment of the Romans' ongoing faith (that was "widely proclaimed," 1:8) that is being lauded in 16:19, expressing either the subjective sense of the genitive of ὑπακοὴ πίστεως: "obedience worked by/springing from faith," or the qualitative sense: a "believing/'faith-full' obedience." Both senses are likely operating, and it was this "faith-full" obedience of the Gentiles that Paul applauded (1:8 with 16:19); and bringing all mankind to such an obedience of faith was Paul's divine commission in its essence (1:5 with 15:18).

"Faith-full" Obedience and the Law of Christ

Faithfulness is described in Ps 78:7–8 as putting one's confidence in God, and not forgetting his works, but keeping his commandments, unlike the Israelites' "stubborn and rebellious" forebears, "whose spirit was not faithful [LXX—οὐκ ἐπιστώθη (*ouk epistōthē*, "they did not come to believe"), from πιστόω, *pistoō*, "believe"] to God." On the other hand, faithlessness (equated with disobedience) is described as the Israelites' forgetting God's great deeds (78:11), their continuing to sin and rebel against God, putting him to the test and speaking against him (78:17–19, 32), attempting to deceive and lie to God (78:36). Indeed, "their heart was not steadfast toward him, nor were they faithful [οὐδὲ ἐπιστώθησαν, *oude epistōthēsan*] in his covenant" (78:37 LXX), and they rebelled against God, grieved God, tempted God, and pained God, not remembering his power and

---

116. Garlington, *Faith, Obedience and Perseverance*, 23.

his redemption of them, not keeping his testimonies, and acting treacherously, turning aside, provoking God and arousing his jealousy (78:40–42, 56–58).[117] This is the essence of "faith-full" obedience, and its contrary, faithless disobedience.[118] In fact, "whatever is not from faith is sin" (Rom 14:23)—this "faith" clearly includes more than justifying faith; a sanctifying faith that is part of the obedient lifestyle of the believer is also meant.

In essence, then, there are two kinds of *approaches* to the law—by faith, and without faith (as Rom 9:30–32 describes; see above). The latter is the "law of sin and of death" in Rom 8:2, the law operating in a fleshly and faithless person resulting in condemnation. It is still "the good law of God, but defeated" by the combination of sin's power and the flesh—law unfulfilled (disobedience/faithlessness). The former, the approach to law by faith, is "the law of the Spirit of life in Christ Jesus" (Rom 8:2), the same, single law of God, but approached "faith-fully" and empowered by God's Holy Spirit (it is a "spiritual" law, after all; 7:14)—law fulfilled (the obedience of faith). And then Rom 8:3–4 proceeds to state the purpose for God sending his own Son: that the law's requirements may be fulfilled, that God's divine demand would be met and his will be done, by the power of the Holy Spirit given to believers. "It would appear, then, that 'the law of the Spirit' is simply a summary way of speaking of the requirement of the law fulfilled by those who walk in accordance with the Spirit"—an obedience enabled and empowered by the Holy Spirit, through the instrumentality of faith, i.e., the obedience of faith.[119]

> Clearly there is also a link between the "law of the Spirit" and the . . . "law of faith" (Rom 3:27). In both cases Paul uses the term "law" because he wanted to underline the vital importance of doing, obeying God's will. And in both cases the qualifier, "of faith," "of the Spirit," indicates in a summary way how that obedience is made possible. In Paul's solution to the problem of human weakness and sin's power, faith and Spirit are the two sides of the same coin. The human trust is met by the power of the Spirit. The obedience that God looks for and makes

---

117. Despite these gross failures on the part of God's people, "He, being compassionate, forgave their iniquity, and did not destroy them; and often he restrained his anger, and did not arouse all his wrath. Thus he remembered [while his people forgot, 78:11, 42] that they were but flesh" (78:38–39).

118. Ps 78:8 and 37 LXX contain two of the three instances of πιστόω in the Psalms; there are only eleven uses of the word in the LXX.

119. Dunn, "The Law of Faith," 72–73.

possible is, in a phrase, human receptiveness (faith) to divine enabling (Spirit).[120]

Galatians 6:2 exhorts believers to bear one another's burdens—this is the fulfillment of the "law of Christ." This exhortation is preceded by Gal 5:13–14, citing Lev 19:18 on loving one's neighbor—the fulfillment of the "whole Law." It appears then that fulfilling the "law of Christ" by bearing one another's burdens (Gal 6:2) is equated to fulfilling the "whole Law" by loving one's neighbor (Gal 5:13–14).

GALATIANS 5:13–14	GALATIANS 6:2
fulfill law	fulfill law of Christ
love neighbor (Lev 19:18)	bear one another's burdens

This means that the "law of Christ" is not a new law, or even a new code that is established in the new dispensation. It is the single law (broadly: "divine demand") that has always been binding upon mankind—though, of course, changes have taken place in the new dispensation (see below on what Christ has accomplished, particularly the sending of the Spirit who empowers).[121] The same pattern operates in Rom 13:8–10 and 15:1–3: both texts deal with the believer's neighbor, with the former passage stating that to love one's neighbor is to fulfill the law (also citing Lev 19:18). The latter passage, adducing the example of Christ who did not please himself, exhorts the Romans likewise to please their neighbors for their good and edification. As with the Gal texts, this pair of passages appears to equate Jesus' self-sacrificial example (in a sense, the "law of Christ," Gal 6:2) to the fulfilling of the law.

ROMANS 13:8–10	ROMANS 15:1–3
fulfill law	follow example of Christ
love neighbor (Lev 19:18)	please one's neighbor

120. Ibid., 74. The parallel statements of Gal 5:6 ("For in Christ Jesus neither circumcision nor uncircumcision means anything, but faith working through love") and Gal 6:15 ("For neither is circumcision anything, nor uncircumcision, but a new creation") acknowledge that "faith working through love" is a characteristic of the "new creation," freed and enabled to obey divine demand. See Cranfield, "Has the Old Testament Law a Place," 119.

121. Dunn, "The Law of Faith," 76, 76n37.

All of this leads one to conclude that the "law of Christ" is equivalent to the divine demand of God constant throughout Scripture and throughout the ages, and echoed in the teachings of Jesus and exemplified in his life (the example of Jesus is particularly emphasized in Rom 15:1–3). Dunn is worth quoting at length:

> [T]he clear implication of Rom 13:8–10 and Gal 5:13–14 is that Paul had *not* discarded the law or abandoned the law or broken with the law. In both passages he talks about the "fulfilling" of the law as something obviously desireable on the part of Christians. . . . Not just the moral commands within the ten commandments are in view, but "any other command" too (Rom 13:9). His concern was not just with the particular command to love the neighbor, understood as abstracted or separated from other commands, but the "whole law" was in mind as worthy and necessary of fulfillment (Gal 5:14). To fulfill the law of Christ is to fulfill the law. . . . Paul still saw a positive role for the law in Christian conduct.[122]

The divine demand of God remains unchanged for all time; Jesus taught it and lived it. And so believers, too, are to respond to divine demand in faithful obedience. Both the Gal and Rom texts above, in parallel fashion, indicate that the law of Christ is not a different entity than the law once given (both include citations of Lev 19:18). Thus the law of Christ (and the parallel "law of God," 1 Cor 9:21) and the elements of the Mosaic law all deal with the divine demand made on humankind. This is a unitary law—God's character and standard are always the same; therefore God's demands of his people always remain the same. What is critical is *how* the law is kept: the law of Christ describes law-keeping that is spiritual/Spirit-led (Rom 8:2–4)—the obedience of faith.[123] It is also what it means to "follow in the steps of the faith of our father Abraham" (4:12); of course, Heb 11 offers numerous examples of those whose faith was inextricably linked with their obedience. All such obedience is rightly considered post-salvific, and it is the proper response of one already rebirthed into the family of God; this is evident in the OT itself (Deut 4:6, 8; Pss 1:2; 19:7–11; 119:97; etc.).[124]

---

122. Ibid., 76, 77.

123. This obedience of faith is also likely to be equivalent to the ἔργον τῆς πίστεως (*ergon tēs pisteōs*, "work of faith") that Paul mentions in 1 Thess 1:3 and 2 Thess 1:11.

124. "Obedience of faith" thus encompasses both the exercise of justifying faith as one is placed in Christ, as well as sanctifying faith as one continues in faith to obey divine demand. Our focus in this work is primarily on the latter aspect of this obedience. Needless to say, that initial "obedience" of conversion, too, is a response to, and enabled by, God's grace and the working of his Spirit (Eph 2:10).

In sum, the law of Christ is the demand God makes of his children, a law that is obeyed by faith (thus "law of faith," Rom 3:27) in the power of the Holy Spirit (thus "law of the Spirit," Rom 8:2). As the Galatian Epistle indicates, the "law of Christ" (Gal 6:1) can be fulfilled only by those who are "spiritual" (6:1), who "walk by the Spirit" (5:16, 25), are "led by the Spirit" (5:18), "live by the Spirit" (5:25), who "sow to the Spirit" (6:8), and are bearing "the fruit of the Spirit" (5:22–23). This renders law-keeping far from being a legalistic, self-justifying enterprise (see "Excursus" below).[125]

Section Summary: Faithful Obedience

Dunn is quite correct—unfortunately so: "Despite the thousands of pages devoted to the subject, too little attempt has been made to integrate the undeniably positive affirmations Paul . . . makes concerning the continuing role of the law in the life of the believer."[126] What has been proposed in this section is that the law is altogether positive in Paul's eyes; the negativity noted is narrowly circumscribed and limited to the *means* by which (and, no doubt, the *attitude* with which) its keeping was being wrongly attempted, as well as to its negative consequences—the condemnation that it registers for those without Christ, and the failure of those who attempt to keep the law faithlessly and legalistically. A misguided effort to keep divine demand by one's own resources and for one's own glory, under the faulty assumption that one can keep God's standard perfectly, is at the root of legalism. Paul's deprecatory remarks are directed against this sinful attitude and activity, the product of the power of sin and the flesh, producing a self-justifying, faithless pursuit of righteousness. Such a misconception of the law as divine demand that may be humanly met, without any divine aid, for the purposes of exalting self, is what meets with Paul's (and God's) extreme disfavor. "As many, therefore, as are led by their own spirit, trusting in their own virtue, with the addition merely of the law's assistance, without the help of grace, are not the sons of God" (Augustine, *Grat.* 24.12).

On the other hand, Spirit-enabled obedience to God's law is the faithful response of God's people to his divine demand, acknowledging their own incapacity to meet it, and seeking his forgiveness and mercy in Christ when they fail

---

125. Thomas R. Schreiner, *The Law and Its Fulfillment: A Pauline Theology of Law* (Grand Rapids: Baker, 1993), 159.

126. Dunn, "The Law of Faith," 80–81.

to obey. This is the essence of ὑπακοὴ πίστεως that, not surprisingly, yields the fruit of the Spirit (Gal 5:22). That this obedience, too, like everything else in the Christian life, is God's doing, his operation by grace, through the instrumentality of the believer's faith, is made clear in Rom 5:15–17; 6:23; Eph 2:8–10; Phil 2:13; etc.

> Paul called men and women into a faith that was always inseparable from obedience—for the Savior in whom they believe is nothing less than our Lord—to an obedience that could never be divorced from faith—for we can only obey Jesus as Lord when we have given ourselves to him in faith. Viewed in this light, the phrase ("obedience of faith") captures the full dimension of Paul's apostolic task, a task that was not confined to initial evangelization but that included also the building up and firm establishment of churches.[127]

The question may be asked at this point: If God's people of *all* time have to obey all of God's laws (the divine demand), then what, if anything, changed with Christ and his salvific work? The answer has been given in brief in earlier sections, but here it will be gathered together in some detail.

Excursus: What Christ Hath Wrought

God's righteousness, his own standard of holiness, is, objectively, the sum of the demands he makes upon mankind that they may live up to that divine standard. Ultimately, of course, God's righteousness is epitomized in Christ—his life that was sinless (1 Cor 1:30; 2 Cor 5:21; 1 Pet 2:22–24; 2 Pet 1:1; 1 John 3:7), and his redemptive work that atoned for sin (Rom 1:17; 5:18). Jesus Christ, by his life and work, enabled God's righteousness to be available by faith to all who believe (Rom 3:21–26; Phil 3:9)—positional sanctification—and also made available the indwelling Holy Spirit who now empowers believers to obey divine demands—practical sanctification.

Wenham's concept of law's "floor" and "ceiling" were noted earlier, and it was observed that not every aspect of living by God's standard was explicitly spelled out in the law.[128] By that same token, not everything that God does *not*

---

127. Moo, *The Epistle to the Romans*, 52–53.

128. Everything God demands of his people *is* in Scripture, but not necessarily *explicitly*. General statements abound, but not every specific detail about how to apply those generalities in any specific situation for any specific person is provided. That, of course, would be an impossibility, for any system of law, sacred or otherwise. This "spottiness"—the non-exhaustive nature—of the biblical genre of law is obvious (Patrick, *Old Testament Law*, 199).

want his people to do is spelled out either. As was noted, attitudinal sins, for instance, are only sparsely covered in the Mosaic law: coveting (Ex 20:17); hatred (Lev 19:17–18); etc. Atonement for such attitudinal sins is also not specifically stated, except for a blanket offering for infractions, intentional or otherwise, individual or corporate, of "the commandments of the LORD which must not be done" (Lev 4:2–3; 5:17–19; also see Num 15:22–31).[129] In other words, for the most part, the sacrificial atonement provided for in the Mosaic law covered the sins specified therein—the "floor" violations, not necessarily those violations between "floor" and "ceiling." Therefore the author of Hebrews can assert that "it is impossible for the blood of bulls and goats to take away sins" (10:4), and that such can only "sanctify for the purification of the flesh" (9:13). A greater sacrifice was needed to "cleanse [the] conscience" (9:14)—a single sacrifice (9:25–29; 10:10–15), unlike the OT sacrifices that needed to be repeated (10:1–3), for they were only a temporary staving off of the consequences of sin.

This is the major change wrought by the work of Christ. Without Christ, the law is shown up for all its incapacities: it can do nothing to justify the sinner, it has no expiatory provision, it exercises no forgiving grace, and it cannot empower obedience to its own demands. All it can do is pronounce sentence upon the sinner. But with Christ, all has been made anew. Forgiveness is now complete and final, attained forever, and freely available for the one who believes in Christ's atoning work on the cross. The condemnation that the law pronounces is no more, for Jesus paid it all (Rom 8:1), condemning sin instead (8:3–4), so that God's divine demands ("righteous requirement," δικαίωμα, *dikaiōma*, 8:4) may be fulfilled in his Spirit-indwelt and Spirit-empowered children.

This newness of creation post-Christ obviously does not nullify the divine demand made through the various codices of the law, Mosaic or otherwise, and, indeed, in every pericope of Scripture. Sanctification is an ongoing process, and vital to this process is the obedience of the believer: relationship demands responsibility. In this operation also, the work of Christ has brought significant benefits to the people of God in this dispensation—the Holy Spirit now indwells

---

129. Perhaps "thank" offerings and "peace" offerings come closest to a ritual that is based upon the attitudes of the sacrificer (Lev 7). In this connection, it is interesting to note Yahweh's frequent diatribes *against* sacrifices and offerings, in favor of correction of heart attitudes: Ps 40:6; Ps 50:7–15; Isa 1:11; 56:7; 66:2–3; Jer 14:10–12; Hos 6:6; Amos 5:21–24; Mic 6:6–8; etc. Those "ceiling" demands were evidently more important than the "floor" ones. Jesus also approved of a scribe's remark to that effect (Mark 12:32–34).

the believer and enables him/her to overcome the flesh (Rom 8). As a result of Christ's atoning work and the justification of the believer, the power of the Holy Spirit is made accessible; this, too, is part of the work of the Son, the Spirit's sender (John 14:16; 15:26; 16:7). Thus God is able to both command what he wills (divine demand) and give what he commands (the empowerment to meet divine demand).[130] With the indwelling of the Holy Spirit a new life is begun, and the believer is enabled to walk, not according to the flesh, but according to the Spirit, to fulfill the demands of God in the law and in all of Scripture (8:4, 12–16).[131] The child of God is never to attempt obedience without faith, in self-justification, with self-resources, for self-glory; rather, with a faith-filled dependence upon the Holy Spirit, the flesh is to be defeated: this is the obedience of faith. In other words, it is God's grace through Jesus Christ and by the Holy Spirit that empowers believers to keep the law.

> Accordingly, by the law of works, God says to us, "Do what I command thee"; but by the law of faith we say to God, "Give me what Thou commandest." Now this is the reason why the law gives its command—to admonish us what faith ought to do, that is, that he to whom the command is given, if he is as yet unable to perform it, may know what to ask for; but if he has at once the ability, and complies with the command, he ought also to be aware from whose gift the ability comes (Augustine, *Spir. et litt.* 22.13).

That it is the Holy Spirit who gives the ability to obey and to gain victory over the flesh is clear from Rom 8; it is also established from the OT: Deut 30:6; Jer 31:31–34; Ezek 36:26–28; 37:1–28; etc. No wonder we are told that our works are, in fact, *God's* works: "For we are his workmanship, created in Christ Jesus for good works that God prepared beforehand, so that we may walk in them" (Eph 2:10); and "He who began a good work in you will perfect it until the day

---

130. That was Augustine's prayer: *Domine, da quod iubes, et iube quod vis* ("Lord, give what you command and command what you will" [*Conf.* 10.29.40]). John 4:15, 21; 15:10, 12; 1 John 2:3, 4; 3:22–24; 4:21; 5:2–3; and 2 John 6, all exhort the keeping of God's commands, focusing particularly on the love disciples are to have for one another. While Jesus called this a "new" commandment (John 13:34), 1 John 2:7–11 calls it an "old" one, perhaps referring to the OT mandate to love one's neighbor (Lev 19:18). The *newness* of this command reflects not only the consequences of what Jesus Christ has accomplished—the removal of the condemnation of law—but also the power endowed by the Holy Spirit to obey divine demand, not to mention Christ's continuing intercession for the believer before the Father (Rom 8:34; Heb 7:25; 9:24; 1 John 2:1).

131. "The Christian is still under solemn obligation to keep the law of God, but with this vital difference, that he now has the power, the power of Christ by the Holy Spirit within himself, to keep it" (Philip Edgcumbe Hughes, *Paul's Second Epistle to the Corinthians* [NICNT; Grand Rapids: Eerdmans, 1962], 90).

of Christ Jesus" (Phil 1:6); and, yet again, "It is God who is at work in you, both to will and to work for his good pleasure (Phil 2:13). Of course, there is also the declaration of Jesus: "Apart from me you can do nothing" (John 15:5).[132] The power of God is explicitly said to be at work in the believer (Eph 3:16; Phil 4:13; Col 1:9–11). The old covenant, "faulty," unable to empower the children of God for obedience (Heb 8:7–13), is now replaced with a new covenant, the Maker of which is also an equipper of his people: "Now may the God of peace, who, through the blood of the eternal covenant, brought back from the dead the great Shepherd of the sheep, Jesus our Lord, equip you in every good thing to do His will, working in us what is pleasing before Him, through Jesus Christ, to whom be the glory forever. Amen!" (Heb 13:20–21).

In conclusion, it must be underscored that there is no diminution of the atoning work of Christ on the cross in the accomplishment of this obedience of faith. Because this "faith-full" obedience is a work of the indwelling Spirit in those who are in Christ—the new creation—the cross remains the ground for this powerful work of the Spirit that enables the Christian to meet divine demands. Relationship always precedes (but does not preclude) responsibility.

> It is of the utmost importance that we do not underestimate the newness of the Christian's understanding of, and relation to, the law. He understands it in the light of Christ, in the light of his perfect obedience to it and of his clarification of its intention by his life and work and teaching. He has been freed from the illusion that he is able so well to fulfill it as to put God in his debt. He knows that, while it shows him the depth of his sinfulness, it no longer pronounces God's condemnation of him, since Christ has borne that condemnation for him. He no longer feels its commands simply as an obligation imposed on him from without, but is being set free by the Holy Spirit to desire wholeheartedly to try to obey and thereby to express his gratitude to God for his mercy and generosity. So he receives the law's commands as God's fatherly guidance for his children—not as a burden or an infringement of his liberty, but as the pointing out of the way to true freedom.[133]

As Calvin stated: "the doctrine of the Law has not been violated [*inviolabilis*] by Christ, but remains [*manet*], that, by teaching, admonishing, rebuking, and correcting, it may fit and prepare us for every good work" (*Institutes* 2.7.14).

---

132. Also see Gal 6:3; 1 Cor 4:7; 2 Cor 3:5; 4:7; 8:1 with 8:7 (the grace of God becomes the Macedonians' work of grace); 12:9–10; Eph 4:7; 1 Thess 5:24; 1 Pet 4:10–11; etc.
133. Cranfield, "Has the Old Testament Law a Place?" 122–23.

SUMMARY: DIVINE DEMAND AND FAITHFUL OBEDIENCE

This chapter has addressed the issue of "divine demand" broached in chapters 1 and 2. The explicit divine demands of Scripture are, of course, in its genre of law. Is biblical law, particularly that in the OT, then, valid for the Christian today? Traditional approaches (Lutheran, Reformed, and Dispensational) were examined and compared with that of adherents of the NPP. In all these, broadly speaking, the Mosaic law is considered inapplicable for the contemporary Christian, with the exception of the "moral" aspects of the law (a distinction of law not very sustainable). As against these approaches, this work posits that OT law continues to operate today—theologically: every legal pericope of Scripture says something about the Lawgiver and his relationship to his creation. Or, to put it in terms borrowed from chapters 1 and 2, every pericope of Scripture projects a segment of the canonical *world in front of the text* (what the author is *doing* with what he is *saying*); such worlds, the theology of the pericopes, portray God and facets of his relationship with his creation. Implicit in pericopal theology, therefore, are divine demands. With regard to biblical law, it was shown that the dichotomy of law/works vs. faith/grace was unnecessary, at least for preaching purposes. Divine demand, or law, is intended for those already within the community of God; law is not a condition for salvation. Instead, it provides direction for sanctification, that the children of God might become as holy as God himself is. Needless to say, both in biblical history, and in the millennia thereafter, this has oft been misunderstood, and legalism has tended to be the order of the day: an attempt to please God and win merit before him by striving for obedience with one's own resources and for one's own glory.[134]

Several critical texts of Scripture were examined that show that law, divine demand, continues to operate: neither God's holiness nor his demands change. But what has changed—and changed significantly—are the contexts and circumstances of the original giving of the OT law. The only way, then, that divine demand in OT law (or, for that matter, in any biblical genre) may be faithfully met is by accounting for and allowing for those contextual shifts. A theological approach to OT law was recommended, that sees the rationale of the law (integral to the theology of the pericope) as binding upon God's people. The keeping of divine demand, thus, is the result of a prior relationship between God and his chil-

---

134. It was when mankind began to take credit for its "obedience," that legalism reigned (it not only reigned, it poured)!

dren: obedience, then, is a filial responsibility. It does not qualify one to *become* a child of God, but it behooves a child to align himself or herself to the demands of God, *because* he or she is already a child of God by grace through faith.

Relationship demands responsibility. That responsibility, this chapter has demonstrated, is the believer's obedience of faith, ὑπακοή πίστεως ("faith-full" obedience or obedience characterized by faith). This is not legalism in another guise: such obedience springs from faith, is characterized by faith, and is carried out in faith. The power for such obedience is the work of the indwelling Holy Spirit. Unlike legalism—an attempt to gain merit with God and glory for self, relying on one's own resources to obey—obedience of faith is a matter of God's grace. The believer who is faithfully obedient also recognizes that there is no longer eternal condemnation for falling short of God's glory—the price of sin has been paid through the atoning work of Christ. The child of God acknowledges that failure does occur; but forgiveness is freely available through God's grace in Jesus Christ. All this to say, faithful obedience rests in God's grace and his provision through Christ and his Spirit, but without neglecting the Christian responsibility to meet divine demand to be "holy, for I [God] am holy."

One of the features of such a theological approach to pericopes for preaching is its concentrated focus upon the particular text being considered for that sermon event. When dealing with pericopes from the OT, such a focus raises the inevitable question: How does one find Jesus Christ in these texts? If one is attending closely to the text, privileging it and the theology of the pericope, would that not preclude a biblical-theology operation that sees Christ in the OT? One might remember the Rule of Centrality, one of the Rules of Reading propounded in chapter 1: *The Rule of Centrality focuses the interpretation of canonical texts for applicational purposes upon the pre-eminent person of Christ and his redemptive work that fulfills the will of the Father in the power of the Spirit.* How does this rule operate in the discernment of pericopal theology? In other words, where is Jesus Christ in an OT pericope? That issue will be tackled in chapter 4, which begins by examining a narrative text, Gen 22 (the *Aqedah*), that has historically been interpreted in christocentric fashion. A new way of reading, *christiconic* interpretation, will be proposed as the goal of the theological hermeneutic described in this work.

CHAPTER 4

The *AQEDAH* and CHRISTICONIC INTERPRETATION

... συμμόρφους τῆς εἰκόνος τοῦ υἱοῦ αὐτοῦ.
(... summorphous tēs eikonos tou huiou autou)
... conformed to the image of his Son.

ROMANS 8:29

A fter establishing, in chapters 1 and 2, that the biblical canon projects a *world in front of the text*—what authors *do* with what they *say* (the pragmatics of the text)—it was shown that this segment of the canonical world was the theology of the pericope, bearing a divine demand: how God would have his people live, i.e., by the precepts, priorities, and practices of the projected world. Chapter 3 examined the genre of biblical law and showed that even pericopes in this genre carry divine demands applicable for the Christian today. Each pericope projects a segment of the canonical *world in front of the text*, i.e., the theology of that pericope, that portrays an aspect of God and his relationship with his creation. Thus, each text bears a divine demand intended to be obeyed, not as a condition for salvation, but as a call to sanctification. Grounded in a prior relationship with God, the believer has a filial responsibility to obey. A theological hermeneutic for the interpretation of OT law was proposed, that is guided by the rationale of the law implicit in the theology of the pericope.

PREVIEW: THE *AQEDAH* AND CHRISTICONIC INTERPRETATION

The potential applicability of every pericope of Scripture, even those in the genre of OT law, raises an important question: Where is Christ in these texts? How does the interpreter do justice to the Rule of Centrality that calls for focusing all interpretation upon Christ (see chapter 1), particularly when handling an OT pericope? This chapter will address these questions. It begins with the study of a text that, over the last two millennia, has been extensively mined for christological elements—the narrative of Gen 22. The christocentric readings will be critiqued; arguments for and against such an interpretation will be analyzed. Subsequently an examination of this narrative text will be conducted to yield the theology of the pericope according to the hermeneutic propounded in this work. This chapter will close with the proposal for a new model for the christological reading of Scripture—*christiconic* interpretation, one which "sees" Christ in every pericope of Scripture, OT and NT, a hermeneutic that *does* abide by the Rule of Centrality. In brief, the plenary text of Scripture projects an image (εἰκών) of Christ, with each pericope portraying a facet of this image: what it means to be Christlike.

THE *AQEDAH* (GENESIS 22)

For millennia, Bible scholars, both Jewish and Christian, have exerted themselves at the task of interpreting Gen 22, the *Aqedah*.[1] The first part of this chapter will revisit these interpretations and discover the theology of the pericope by means of a focused exegesis that privileges the text.[2]

Traditional Views

The perplexities of this narrative are many. Elie Wiesel, the Holocaust survivor and Nobel prize-winning author, called this story "terrifying in content."[3] How could God test/tempt someone in so gruesome a fashion, seemingly contradicting his own promises? How could Abraham agree to this gory transaction? What did Sarah—or for that matter, Isaac—think about the whole deal? And, of course, the question of how Christ fits into the scheme has kept Christian interpreters busy.

---

1. *Aqedah* comes from עקד, *'qd*, "bind" (Gen 22:9)—a *hapax legomenon*.

2. Portions of this section were presented at the 63rd Annual Meeting of the Evangelical Theological Society, San Francisco, Calif., November 16–18, 2011, and published in Abraham Kuruvilla, "The *Aqedah*: What Is the Author *Doing* with What He Is *Saying*?," *JETS* 55 (2012): 489–508.

3. Elie Wiesel, *Messengers of God* (New York: Random House, 1976), 69.

God's Joke?

The account is so unimaginable as it stands, that some have thought God must have been joking! Woody Allen thinks it happened this way:

> And Abraham awoke in the middle of the night and said to his only son, Isaac, "I have had a dream where the voice of the Lord sayeth that I must sacrifice my only son, so put your pants on."
>
> And Isaac trembled and said, "So what did you say? I mean when He brought this whole thing up?"
>
> "What am I going to say?" Abraham said. "I'm standing there at two a.m. in my underwear with the Creator of the Universe. Should I argue?"...
>
> And Sarah, who heard Abraham's plan, grew vexed and said, "How doth thou know it was the Lord and not, say, thy friend who loveth practical jokes...?"
>
> And Abraham answered, "Because ... [i]t was a deep, resonant voice, well-modulated, and nobody in the desert can get a rumble in it like that."...
>
> And so he took Isaac to a certain place and prepared to sacrifice him, but at the last minute the Lord stayed Abraham's hand and said, "How could thou doest such a thing?"
>
> And Abraham said, "But thou said—"
>
> "Never mind what I said," the Lord spake. "Doth thou listen to every crazy idea that comes thy way?"
>
> And Abraham grew ashamed. "Er—not really ... no."
>
> "I jokingly suggest thou sacrifice Isaac and thou immediately runs out to do it."
>
> And Abraham fell to his knees. "See, I never know when you're kidding."
>
> And the Lord thundered, "No sense of humor. I can't believe it."
>
> "But doth this not prove I love thee, that I was willing to donate mine only son on thy whim?"
>
> And the Lord said, "It proves that some men will follow any order no matter how asinine as long as it comes from a resonant, well-modulated voice."
>
> And with that, the Lord bid Abraham get some rest and check with him tomorrow.[4]

---

4. Woody Allen, "The Scrolls," in *The Insanity Defense: The Complete Prose* (New York: Random House, 2007), 137–38.

Was God just kidding? Unlikely. The particle נָא (*na*'; an interjection of entreaty usually translated as "pray," "now," or "then") that is linked to God's command to Abraham to "take" (Gen 22:2; קַח־נָא, *qah na*', "take now") is found over sixty times in Gen. However, it is employed in divine speech only five times: Gen 13:14; 15:5; 22:2; Ex 11:2; Isa 7:3, and in each of these instances, God demands something incredulous of the individual, "something that defies rational explanation or understanding."[5] No, there could be no question but that God *was* aware of the magnitude of what he was asking Abraham to do in Gen 22. He was not joking; that he did mean "sacrifice" is clear from the reference to "burnt offering" in 22:2.

In a similar vein, but rather than make the Almighty a prankster, the rabbis concluded Abraham had simply heard God wrong.

> Said R. Aha:
>
> [Abraham said to God] "Are there jokes even before You? Yesterday You said to me, 'For in Isaac shall seed be called to you.' And then You went back on Your word and said, 'Take your son.' And now: 'Do not lay your hand on the lad or do anything to him.' [What's next?] . . ."
> [God to Abraham] "True, I command you, 'Take now your son.' I will not alter what has gone out of My lips. Did I ever tell you to kill him? No, I told you, 'Bring him up.' Well and good! You did indeed bring him up. Now take him down." (*Gen. Rab.* 56:8)[6]

So, God is off the hook. It was all Abraham's fault. He had misunderstood God.

Kant deprecated this whole idea of God conversing with Abraham. According to him, one could be sure that the voice that commanded sacrifice was *not* God's and, Kant advised, Abraham ought to have repudiated this supposedly divine command: "'That I ought not to kill my good son is quite certain. But that you, this apparition, are God—of that I am not certain, and never can be, not even

---

5. Victor P. Hamilton, *The Book of Genesis, Chapters 18–50* (NICOT; Grand Rapids: Eerdmans), 101.

6. The verb in Gen 22:2 translated "offer," derived from עלה ('*lh*, "to go up," "to rise," or "to ascend"), could conceivably mean "bring up" (as a noun, עֹלָה, '*olah*, means "whole, burnt sacrifice"). See Laurence H. Kant, "Restorative Thoughts on an Agonizing Text: Abraham's Binding of Isaac and the Horror on Mt. Moriah (Genesis 22): Part 2," *LTQ* 38 (2003): 173–74. A burnt offering expressed the giving of the offerer completely to God, the animal taking the place of the person. Biblical law considered every firstborn son to be so dedicated to God, but that "offering" was to be substituted in the actual sacrifice by an animal (Ex 22:29; 34:20). Later, Levites took on that role of being substitutes consecrated entirely to God, in lieu of Israel's firstborn male children (Num 4:45–49). See Wenham, *Genesis 16–50*, 105.

if this voice rings down to me from (visible) heaven.'"[7] In other words, Abraham should not have been taken in by the "resonant, well-modulated voice." This argument will not be countered here; I accept the veracity of the biblical account as a starting premise, construing it as part of Scripture: it *was* God speaking. The goal here is to unravel the speech-action of the author, and for that purpose, this account will be dealt with as it stands, without undermining it.[8]

Satanic Influence in the Test?

There is a whole array of rabbinic exposition that dwells on the role of evil angels in the *Aqedah*. They are said to have instigated the test of the patriarch after the manner of Job's trial. *Jubilees* 17:16 and 4Q225 (pseudo-Jubilees) propounds a satanic character, Mastema, inciting God to test Abraham; *m. Sanh.* 89b assumes it was Satan himself behind all of this.[9] Another account thinks jealous demons had something to do with this frightful test—jealous because Abraham had a son (Pseudo-Philo, *L.A.B.* 32:1–4).[10] None of these ideas has any biblical basis.

Isaac—Ignorant Victim or Willing Partner?

Given that this was actually a test—rather than a joke or a misunderstood command or a demonically instigated enterprise—how does one explain Abraham's willingness to go through with the sacrifice? The rabbis tried hard to blunt the force of the horrific narrative by speculating that Isaac was a willing participant

---

7. Immanuel Kant, "The Conflict of the Faculties," in Immanuel Kant, *Religion and Rational Theology* (trans. Mary J. Gregor and Robert Anchor; Cambridge: Cambridge University Press, 1996), 283 (7:63), and the unnumbered footnote on the same page.

8. While not considering this episode a joke, Elie Wiesel's accounting of the event is unique: Abraham actually twisted God's arm and forced the test back upon God, as if to say: "I defy You, Lord. I shall submit to Your will, but let us see whether You shall go to the end, whether You shall remain passive and remain silent when the life of my son—who is also Your son—is at stake!" And of course, God blinked! Abraham won. Wiesel thinks *that* was why, at the conclusion of this tussle of wills, God sent an angel to rescind the order and to congratulate him: because God was too embarrassed to do so personally, having lost this battle of bluffs (*Messengers of God*, 91).

9. Mastema is a cryptic and esoteric evil being frequently found in the Qumran literature: 1QS, 1QM, CD, 4Q286, 4Q387, and 4Q390, in addition to 4Q225. The word משטמה (*mstmh*) is a feminine abstract noun meaning "opposition," an etymology similar to that of שָׂטָן (*satan*). See Moshe J. Bernstein, "Angels at the Aqedah: A Study in the Development of a Midrashic Motif," *Dead Sea Discoveries* 7 (2000): 263–91.

10. There are other florid stories of angels as well: watching and weeping angels (*Gen. Rab.* 56:7 speculates that the tears of angels dissolved Abraham's knife; elsewhere, in *Gen. Rab.* 65:10, it is said that their tears, falling into Isaac's eyes, blinded him), and singing angels (they sang, apparently when Isaac was finally spared, *t. Soṭ.* 6:5).

in the affair, colluding with his father. The seemingly passive Isaac of Gen was reinterpreted by later Jewish scholars to depict a "mature, active, and virtuous volunteer, the perfect offering."[11] In *Tg. Ps.-J.* on Gen 22:10, the son exhorts his father, "Bind me well that I may not struggle in the agony of my soul and be pitched into the pit of destruction and a blemish be found in your offering" (so also *Tg. Neof.* and *Gen. Rab.* 56:8). Josephus even has Isaac being so "pleased" with the news of his fate that he "went immediately to the altar to be sacrificed" (*Ant.* 1.13.4). Later in the history of interpretation, Isaac is also supposed to have bound himself (*Sipre* Deut 32).

We do best to remain as restrained as the biblical account is about Isaac's willingness. There is no record of any conversation between father and son, beyond the cryptic remarks of each in Gen 22:7–8. Luther, however, thought there was more chatting between father and son, and he gave in to his speculative tendencies:

> The father said: "You, my dearly beloved son, whom God has given me, have been destined for the burnt offering." Then the son was undoubtedly struck with amazement and in turn reminded his father of the promise: "Consider, father, that I am the offspring to whom descendants, kings, peoples, etc., have been promised. God gave me to my mother Sarah through a great miracle. How, then, will it be possible for the promises to be fulfilled if I have been killed? Nevertheless, let us first confer about this matter and talk it over." All this should have been recorded here. I do not know why Moses omitted it.[12]

But despite all these heroic efforts, the text remains inscrutable. There is hardly any concern for the details of the event that Luther and others are grasping for. Rather, as I will demonstrate, authorial interest is theological; the writer has an agenda and therefore is selective about what is detailed in the text. It is those details that the interpreter must attend to—it is the text that must be privileged, not the events *behind* the text.

Typology of the Passover?

Over the millennia, one of the more common avenues of exploration of the *Aqedah* has been the identification of the typology within the narrative. The purported willingness of Isaac to go to the altar rendered him a virtuous sacrifice

---

11. Kenneth A. Mathews, *Genesis 11:27–50:26* (NAC 1B; Nashville: Broadman & Holman, 2005), 301.

12. Martin Luther, *Lectures on Genesis Chapters 21–25: Luther's Works*, vol. 4 (trans. George V. Schick; ed. Jaroslav Pelikan; St. Louis: Concordia, 1964), 112–13.

that was seen by Jewish interpreters as efficacious for future generations of Is-raelites. For instance, *Mek. R. Ishmael* (*Pisha* 7 on Ex 12:13) interprets God's "When I see the blood I will pass over you" as, in fact, concerning the blood of the sacrifice of Isaac, anachronistic as it may be. In similar fashion, the account of the *Aqedah* in *Jubilees* makes it coincident with the (pre)anniversary of the Passover. As *Jub.* 18:3 has it, God's command to Abraham regarding Isaac was issued on the twelfth day of Nisan; the sacrifice party then travels for three days, making the sacrifice on "Mt. Zion" occur on the fifteenth of Nisan, the exact date of the Passover ritual. Subsequently, returning to Beersheba, a seven-day fast is observed by Abraham (*Jub.* 18:18–19), corresponding to the only seven-day feast in the Bible—that of Passover (Lev 23:6 and Num 28:17). The *Aqedah* thus becomes the "etiology of Passover."[13] One is hard-pressed to see how this line of typological thinking is substantiated in the canonical Scriptures.

Typology of the Atonement?

It is understandable why the substitutionary sacrifice of Jesus Christ, the Son of God, has been oft linked to the *Aqedah*. The concepts of "sacrifice" and "son" and "substitute" in Gen 22 have obvious parallels in the theology of the atonement; the resulting enterprise of finding typological elements in Gen 22 has been un-paralleled in the history of biblical interpretation. The identification of Abraham with God the Father and Isaac with God the Son was articulated by numerous patristic and medieval interpreters.[14] Barnabas (second century) was perhaps the earliest to advance on this path: "He himself [Jesus Christ] was going to offer the vessel of the spirit as a sacrifice for our sins, in order that the type [ὁ τύπος, *ho tupos*] established in Isaac, who was offered upon the altar, might be fulfilled [τελεσθῇ, *telesthē*]" (*Barn.* 7.3). Clement of Alexandria (ca. 150–215) also explicitly labeled Isaac as a "type" of the Christ—both were sons, both were victims, both bore wood (*Christ the Educator* 1.5.23).[15] Tertullian (ca. 160–220) contributed to

13. Leroy Andrew Huizenga, "Obedience unto Death: The Matthean Gethsemane and Arrest Sequence and the Aqedah," *CBQ* 71 (2009): 510–11. Other parallels in *Jubilees*: both the *Aqedah* and the Passover celebrations involved rejoicing (18:18–19 and 49:2, 22); Mastema (the mysterious evil heavenly being) showed up in both accounts (17:16; 18:9, 12; and 48:2, 9); and he was ultimately shamed (18:9–12; and 48:13; 49:12).

14. See Jon Balserak, "Luther, Calvin and Musculus on Abraham's Trial: Exegetical History and the Trans-formation of Genesis 22," *RRR* 6 (2004): 364–65, for an extensive list and bibliography.

15. Cited in Thomas C. Oden and Mark Sheridan, eds., *Genesis 12–50* (Ancient Christian Commentary on Scripture: Old Testament, vol. 2; Downers Grove: InterVarsity, 2002), 105.

this line of thought, too: "Isaac, on the one hand, with his 'wood,' was saved, the ram being offered which was caught by the horns in the bramble. Christ, on the other hand, in His times, carried His 'wood' on His own shoulders, adhering to the horns of the cross, with a thorny crown encircling His head" (*Adv. Jud.* 13). Origen (ca. 185–254) came to the same conclusion: "We said . . . that Isaac represented Christ. But this ram no less also seems to represent Christ" (*Homilies on Genesis* 8.9).[16] Irenaeus (second century) declared: "For Abraham, according to his faith, followed the command of the Word of God, and with a ready mind delivered up, as a sacrifice to God, his only-begotten and beloved son, in order that God also might be pleased to offer up for all his seed His own beloved and only-begotten Son, as a sacrifice for our redemption" (*Haer* 4.5.4). Caesarius of Arles (ca. 470–542) observed that "[w]hen Abraham offered his son Isaac, he was a type of God the Father, while Isaac prefigured our Lord and Savior" (*Sermon* 84.2). He went further: the two servants of Abraham, left below the mountain, represented the Jewish people, who could not ascend or reach the place of sacrifice because of unbelief in Christ; the donkey, inexplicably, indicated the synagogue.[17] Thus Abraham represents the believer and his faith, Isaac represents the believer's self-denial, *and* Isaac also represents Jesus Christ, creating no small confusion, not to mention the typology of wood and thorns, ram and donkey.

Typical of modern-day interpreters who focus on OT typology is Clowney[18]:

> When God provided the ram, he not only spared Isaac (and Abraham!) but showed Abraham that the price of redemption was greater than he could pay. The Lord himself must provide the offering that brings salvation. . . . The One descended from Abraham must come, in whom all the families of the earth will be blessed. "The Lord Will Provide" promises the coming of Christ. . . . Not Isaac but the Lamb of God was the Sacrifice that the Father would provide.

16. Cited in Oden and Sheridan, *Genesis 12–50*, 109. Chrysostom (ca. 349–407) asserted: "All this, however, happened as a type of the cross. . . . an only-begotten son in that case, an only-begotten son in this; dearly loved in that case, dearly loved in this" (*Homilies on Genesis* 47.14; cited in Oden and Sheridan, *Genesis 12–50*, 110). Jerome (ca. 347–420) described "Isaac who in his readiness to die bore the cross of the Gospel before the Gospel came" (*Ep. ad Pammachium*, 7).

17. Cited in Oden and Sheridan, *Genesis 12–50*, 102. So also Melito of Sardis (see Fragments 1 and 3, translated in Robert L. Wilken, "Melito, the Jewish Community at Sardis, and the Sacrifice of Isaac," *TS* 37 [1976]: 64, 66, 67), and Theodoret (*Dialogues* [III: "The Impassable"]). Later commentators followed suit, blending the types of Isaac and the ram into the antitype of Christ, among them Augustine (see *City of God* 16.32, and *De Trinitate* 6.11).

18. Edmund P. Clowney, *Preaching Christ in All of Scripture* (Wheaton: Crossway, 2002), 76–77.

There is no mention at all about the "fear of God" for which Abraham was commended (see below). According to Sidney Greidanus, another proponent of the redemptive-historical (RH) approach to OT interpretation, "[c]learly, the theme of God providing a lamb leads directly to Jesus Christ and the sacrifice he makes so that his people may live."[19] His resulting sermon on this text has the goal "[t]o assure God's people that their faithful covenant LORD can be trusted to provide their redemption."[20]

Despite these christocentric assertions, ancient and modern, Moberly makes it clear that שֶׂה (*seh*), translated "lamb" in Gen 22:7, is "a generic term for an animal from a flock." Indeed even the LXX of Gen 22:7 has πρόβατον (*probaton*, and not the christological "lamb [ἀμνὸς, *amnos*]" of John 1:29 that one might expect); the precise Hebrew word for lamb is כֶּבֶשׂ (*kebes*, as in the "lamb" of the "continuous" offering, Ex 29:38), and not שֶׂה. Thus there appears to be little basis for drawing out any ovine typology from Gen 22.[21] Calvin is honest about these conjectures: "I am not ignorant that more subtle allegories may be elicited; but I do not see on what foundation they rest" (*Commentary on Genesis*, on 22:13). All of these typological explorations render the narrative a tangled skein of anachronistic references, especially for preachers. Rather than immediately fling out a lifeline from the NT to accomplish a christocentric rescue of the *Aqedah*, I suggest that the interpreter privilege the text and its immediate context to figure out what the A/author was *doing* with what he was saying (the theology of this pericope). For there is the "strong danger of ultimate superficiality" when the ancient text is not allowed to speak for itself and express its primary message. "If the Old Testament no longer says something to the Christian in its own right, to which the Christian still needs to attend and on which Christian faith necessarily builds, its actual role within Christian faith will tend to become marginal and optional, no matter what rhetoric is used to urge its importance."[22] A sound warning, indeed.

19. Sidney Greidanus, *Preaching Christ from the Old Testament: A Contemporary Hermeneutical Method* (Grand Rapids: Eerdmans, 1999), 311. He does admit that "there is no agreement" as to which character of the story is a type of Christ—Abraham, Isaac, or the ram (Sidney Greidanus, *Preaching Christ from Genesis* [Grand Rapids: Eerdmans, 2007], 202, 203).

20. Ibid., 205 (italics removed). For a review of Greidanus's work on Genesis, see Abraham Kuruvilla, "Book Review: *Preaching Christ through Genesis*, Sidney Greidanus," *JEHS* 8 (2008): 137–40.

21. R. W. L. Moberly, *The Bible, Theology, and Faith: A Study of Abraham and Jesus* (Cambridge: Cambridge University Press, 2000), 107n52.

22. Ibid., 140.

It is certainly not universally accepted that Isaac and the ram represent God the Son, and Abraham, God the Father. Even in the late first-century interpretation of Gen 22 by Clement of Rome (*1 Clem.* 10:7), there is no indication of typology: "By obedience he [Abraham] offered him a sacrifice unto God on one of the mountains which he showed him."[23] Clement instead pronounces on Abraham's righteousness and faith as aspects of the narrative that ought to be exemplary for the Christian. In fact, the NT does not specifically refer to the *Aqedah* at all.[24] Kessler remarks on the unusual lack of references to the *Aqedah* in the NT, suggesting that "the biblical story was either not of special importance and/or lacked significance to Jesus and his first followers." This is especially telling, in light of the fact that OT quotations are, as a rule, frequently employed in the NT to substantiate atonement themes. Yet there appears to be no evidence that the earliest Christians viewed Gen 22 as christologically significant. Even though Paul uses a phrase in Rom 8:32 (τοῦ ἰδίου υἱοῦ οὐκ ἐφείσατο, *tou idiou huiou ouk epheisato*) that is perhaps an allusion to Genesis 22:12 and 16 (οὐκ ἐφείσω τοῦ υἱοῦ σου ἀγαπητοῦ, *ouk epheisō tou huiou sou agapētou*), "he makes little theological capital of it," neither is there any obvious portrayal of Isaac as a type of Christ elsewhere in Paul.[25] In Rom 8:32, "the typology is purely implicit, a by-product of the imaginative application to God of a clause that pertains to Abraham in the Greek Bible tradition."[26] This is a critical observation, often missed by those examining quotes of the OT in the NT. Not every NT citation or allusion or oblique reference to the OT is an *exposition* of the older text that adheres to literary, historical, and grammatical constraints. Rather, they are often imaginative

---

23. Where the patriarch was commanded to make his burnt offering apparently was the same location where the children of Abraham were called to do so—at the Temple mount (see the use of "Moriah" in Gen 22:2 and 2 Chron 3:1; also note the use of הר [*har yhwh*, "mountain of Yahweh"] in Gen 22:14 and in Ps 24:3; Isa 2:3; etc.). This does not necessitate a connection with the atonement; rather the nexus is with faith. The faith of Abraham (or "fear of God"; see below) in the *Aqedah* was the attitude God's people were to have as they approached him, in the Temple or elsewhere. Any approach to God, any relationship with God, is to be undergirded with faith; hence the subtle link between the Temple (the place where God was encountered) and the *Aqedah* (the paradigmatic biblical demonstration of faith).

24. P. R. Davies and B. D. Chilton, "The Aqedah: A Revised Tradition History," *CBQ* 40 (1978): 532.

25. If he were referring to Gen 22, Paul would surely have employed the LXX's ἀγαπητοῦ. Hebrews 11:17 also refuses to use this potent adjective, preferring μονογενής (*monogenēs*, "only") instead. Edward Kessler, *Bound by the Bible: Jews, Christians and the Sacrifice of Isaac* (Cambridge: Cambridge University Press, 2004), 60–61, 121. The "typology" in Heb 11:19 refers to the reception of Isaac symbolically/figuratively back from the dead (thus, παραβολή, *parabolē*, "symbol/figure"). Rather than being a definitive statement of the meaning of the *Aqedah*, this NT verse simply underscores Abraham's incredible faith in a trustworthy God, as a result of which, "*in a sense/so to speak* [ἐν παραβολῇ] he received him [Isaac] back from the dead."

26. Davies and Chilton, "The Aqedah," 533.

applications and creative re-employments of a pithy phrase—a hijacking, if you will, of a recognizable commonplace, slogan, or bromide: an intertextual pun.[27]

Genesis 22 and the Author's *Doings*

What, then, was the author *doing* with what he was saying? And, with particular regard to Christology, where does Christ fit in this account?

A Necessary Test of Faith

The account begins with a time-stamp: "Now it came about *after these things*, that God tested Abraham" (Gen 22:1, emphasis added). What exactly were "these things"? A review of the Abrahamic saga is helpful for arriving at the speech-act of the narrator.

Bergen observes that "[t]his most prominent theme—that of Abraham's search for a proper heir—ties the diverse stories of the Abraham cycle together more securely than any other."[28] Indeed! In Gen 12 we have God commanding Abraham to leave his relatives and father's house in order to secure a blessing that would, in great part, come through an heir (12:1–3).[29] And, yes, Abraham showed faith in stepping out as commanded, but one notices that he took Lot his nephew with him, even though the divine word called for a separation from relatives and father's house. Was Abraham thinking of Lot as the likely heir,

---

27. Recently, criticizing the trend in administration circles to weigh, measure, and count everything that is weighable, measurable, and countable, I recommended to a fellow committee member at my institution that our committee motto ought to be *mene, mene, tekel, upharsin.* Yes, I wanted the biblical reference recognized. Yes, I wanted the literal meaning of the arcane terms understood. But I also wanted it known that I was trying to be creative and clever, while at the same time poking fun at (and condemning) our inclination towards the idolatry of numbers that makes us devotees of metrology. In other words, I was making an *intertextual pun!* My intention was hardly congruent with that of the venerable prophet: the "hijacking" of Daniel's Aramaic report of what was inscribed on Belshazzar's wall was not intended to be an exposition of Dan 5:25–28. While there were connections between my utterance and Daniel's—connections actually meant to be recognized—there was no intention to pass off my wisecrack as a literary-historical-grammatical gem of interpretation. One must bear in mind that OT-in-the-NT is not a monolithic transaction. There is clearly a vast diversity of purposes in the use of OT texts in the NT: illustrations and analogies and intertextual puns, in addition to prophetic, typological, and allegorical usages. Rather than seeking the *hermeneutical* bases of these NT uses of OT texts, I suggest that one must seek the *rhetorical* bases of their uses. What was the NT author trying to do in/with the writing of *his* text—OT quotes and all? At least for preaching purposes, the interpreter must privilege the text itself, not the hermeneutical method the author employed to bring the text into being (see below for further discussion on this point).

28. Robert D. Bergen, "The role of Genesis 22:1–19 in the Abraham Cycle: A Computer-Assisted Textual Interpretation," *CTR* 4 (1990): 323.

29. "Abraham" is, of course, "Abram" in Gen 12, but for ease of expression his final name (and that of his wife, "Sarah," not "Sarai") will be used throughout, despite the anachronism.

seeing that he himself was already seventy-five years old, and his wife sixty-five (12:4)? That certainly was not an attitude of faith in God's promise. Later, perhaps still holding on to the hope that his nephew Lot would be the chosen heir, Abraham gives him the choicest portion of the land; Lot goes east and Abraham west (13:10–11). God appears to Abraham soon thereafter, renewing the promise to his descendants (13:16) as if to assert that he, Abraham, had been mistaken in his reckoning of Lot as his heir. The patriarch *was* wrong, for the descendants of Lot would become sworn enemies of the descendants of Abraham (19:38).

Soon after he left his father's household and homeland, as Abraham stepped into the Negev, his caravan was hit by a famine (12:9–10). He promptly decamped to Egypt "to sojourn there," despite the fact that Yahweh had just appeared to him and promised, "To your descendants I will give this land," upon which Abraham had immediately built an altar (12:7). There appears to have been a hint of faithlessness in his fleeing to Egypt during the famine. Surely he knew God would keep his promise? Of course, one knows what happened in that land of refuge—Abraham was willing to pass off his wife, Sarah, as his sister, lest he got killed by Pharaoh for that "very beautiful" woman (12:12–14). Would not God keep his promise about the seed? Why then did he have to worry about his own life, and even put his wife's well-being in jeopardy?

In Gen 15, Yahweh's promise to Abraham was renewed (15:1). But Abraham was still childless, and so the heir, he figured, had to be Eliezer, his steward (15:2–3). God completely negated that suggestion: Abraham's heir would be "one who comes forth from your own body" (15:4), a promise set forth in covenant form (15:5–21). Yet Sarah continued to remain barren (16:1). Abraham then resorted to a compromise: perhaps the chosen heir, "from your own body," was to come through the maternal agency of a concubine (16:2). Acting on this misconception, Abraham fathers Ishmael through Hagar, the Egyptian. God reappeared to Abraham in Gen 17 and once again spelled out his promise to the patriarch. The divine word was crystal clear: *Sarah* would be the mother of the heir (this was iterated thrice this time: 17:16, 19, 21), not the maid, Hagar. And just as in the case of Lot, Ishmael's descendants (25:12–18) would turn out to be enemies of the descendants of Abraham. Again, faithlessness characterized Abraham's response to God.

Then, to make matters worse, in Gen 20, Abraham palmed his wife off as his sister . . . again! This time to Abimelech (20:2), but for the same reason that he had conducted his subterfuge in Gen 12—out of fear for his own life (20:11), and that despite the extended account of Yahweh's appearance and re-promise to Abraham and his wife that an heir would be born to them (Gen 19). As in Gen 12, God had to intervene to set things straight (20:6–7).

Thus, all along, Abraham is seen rather clumsily stumbling along in his faith. All of his attempts to help God out with the production of an heir had come to naught. None of his schemes had worked; in fact, they had only created more trouble for himself and, in the future, for his descendants. Genesis 12–20, then, is not the account of a pristine faith on the part of the patriarch.

Finally, in Gen 21, the heir is born, and the account makes it very clear that God had done what he had promised to do all along. Three times in two verses, Yahweh's faithfulness is established: "Yahweh visited Sarah *as he had said*" (21:1a); "Yahweh did for Sarah *as he had promised*" (21:1b); "Sarah conceived and bore Abraham a son . . . at the appointed time *of which God had spoken to him*" (21:2, emphasis added to all). This threefold iteration was almost a rebuke to Abraham's faithlessness thus far. God had been faithful; and he had done as he had promised. Abraham could surely trust him! The thorny issue of "seed," a problem that Abraham had been trying to solve on his own (or at least "help" God in solving it), had now been settled, as God had promised.

And then, in the very next chapter, Gen 22, Abraham is tested.[30] It was almost as if this test was a necessary one. Had Abraham learned his lessons? Would he come around to realizing, finally, that God was faithful? Would he now acknowledge that even against all odds and despite all unfavorable circumstances God's promises *would* come to pass? A test was necessary—not for God's benefit, of course, but for Abraham's, and for the benefit of all succeeding generations of readers of the text, to demonstrate what it meant to trust God fully, to take him at his word.[31]

---

30. "Testing" (נסה, *nsh*) as an act of God for the good of his people is found in Deut 8:2, 16; Ex 15:25; 16:4; Jdg 2:22; 2 Chron 32:31; Ps 26:2. Both "fear of God" and "test" show up in Ex 20:20, where Moses reassures his people: "Do not fear, for God has come to test you, that the fear of him may be before you, so that you might not sin."

31. Both in structure and concept, this test in Gen 22 was strikingly similar to the "test" in Gen 12:1–7. The latter was the first time God spoke to the patriarch; the former, the last. Both speeches contained the same initial command, found nowhere else in the Bible (לֶךְ־לְךָ, *lek-lka*, "go forth/go out," Gen 12:1; 22:2). The first called for a break with Abraham's past; the second, with Abraham's future. Both stressed a journey, an altar, and promised blessings. Thus Gen 12 and 22 form an appropriate commencement and conclusion, respectively, of the Abrahamic saga.

Kass speculates on the test: "Will you, Abraham, walk reverently and wholeheartedly before God even if it means sacrificing all benefits promised for such conduct? Do you, Abraham, fear-and-revere God more than you love your son—and through him, your great nation, great name, and great prosperity—and more even than you desire the covenant with God?"[32] As will be seen, Abraham passed his test in Gen 22 with flying colors. How he did, and what the A/author was *doing* in the recounting of that successful examination, will be addressed next.

> **THEOLOGICAL FOCUS**[33]
>
> *Faith in God's promises and his word is required from the child of God, a faith liable to be tested.*

Abraham's Fear of God

Notice the key phrase in the acclamation of the angel of Yahweh in Gen 22:12: "Now I know that you *fear God*" (emphasis added). Abraham's fear of God had, through this test, been proven. This "fearing of God" is a critical element in the account. The last time fear of God was mentioned in the Abrahamic saga was in 20:11 (in fact these are the first two occurrences of "fear of God" in the Bible: יִרְאַת אֱלֹהִים [*yir'at elohim*] in 20:11; and יְרֵא אֱלֹהִים [*yre' elohim*] in 22:12). When Abimelech confronted Abraham with his wife/sister deception, Abraham's excuse was: "Surely there is no fear of God in this place; and they will kill me because of my wife" (20:11). "No fear of God in this place"—the reader immediately catches the irony. Abimelech was terror-stricken at the possibility of having run up against God; the text explicitly tells us so: "And the men were greatly frightened [וַיִּירְאוּ ... מְאֹד, *wayyir'u ... m'od*]" (20:8). On the other hand, it was *Abraham* who did not fear God enough to trust him to take care of him when God had promised him descendants. Surely his life would not be in danger before he produced progeny.

But here, in Gen 22, Abraham appeared to have learned his lesson in trusting God as indicated in his response to Isaac: "Yahweh will provide" (22:8). In-

---

32. Leon R. Kass, *The Beginning of Wisdom: Reading Genesis* (New York: Free Press, 2003), 337.

33. At the end of each section, the "Theological Focus" will summarize the theological thrust developed in that section; the exploration of the pericope will conclude with an integrated statement of the theology of the pericope ("Comprehensive Theological Focus").

deed, the entire account of Gen 22 is carefully framed around this momentous declaration:[34]

A Divine call to Abraham (22:1a)

  B Abraham's response: "Here I am" (הִנֵּנִי, *hinneni*, 22:1b))

    C Divine command (22:2)

      Abraham's response (22:3–4);
    D raising eyes/seeing (וַיִּשָּׂא אַבְרָהָם אֶת־עֵינָיו וַיַּרְא, *wayyissa' Abraham 'et-'enayw wayyar'*, 22:4)

      E Worship (22:5)

Preparation for sacrifice (22:6)

Abraham's response to Isaac (22:7): "Yahweh will provide" (22:8)

Preparation for sacrifice (22:9–10)

A' Divine call to Abraham (22:11a)

  B' Abraham's response: "Here I am" (הִנֵּנִי, 22:11b)

    C' Divine command (22:12)

    D' Abraham's response (22:13–14);
      raising eyes/seeing (וַיִּשָּׂא אַבְרָהָם אֶת־עֵינָיו וַיַּרְא, 22:13)

      E' Worship implied (22:14)

From the way the story is discoursed, it seems clear that Gen 21, with the birth of Isaac and Yahweh's triple assertion of his faithfulness (21:1–2), had something to do with that change of heart. Apparently, after many blunders and fumbles, Abraham had finally come around to trusting God. And in Gen 22, the divine declaration "Now I know that you fear God" (22:12) gave proof to the fact that Abraham now feared God, trusting him enough to obey without question. Surely a God who could give him an heir from a dead womb could bring back that one from a charred altar. No wonder God could affirm Abraham's fear of God after this momentous test. "Now I know," the assertion that prefaces God's announcement in 22:12, was often used in the OT to describe solemn declarations (Ex 18:11; Jdg 17:13; 1 Sam 24:20; 1 Kgs 17:24; Ps 20:6). Targumic interpretation put it this way in the mouth of God: "I credit the merit

---

34. From Kass, *The Beginning of Wisdom*, 341–42n48; and Stanley D. Walters, "Wood, Sand and Stars: Structure and Theology in Gn 22:1–19," *TJT* 3 (1987): 314. After "and he said," and "and he said," and "and he said," and "and he said" (וַיֹּאמֶר, *wayyo'mer*)—the dialogue between father and son in 22:7—we suddenly have the pointed "and *Abraham* said" in 22:8 (וַיֹּאמֶר אַבְרָהָם, *wayyo'mer Abraham*), signifying that what he was going to say was of great importance: the assertion of his faith, the manifestation of his fear of God.

to you for this action as though I had said to you, 'Offer me yourself,' and you did not hold back" (*Gen. Rab.* 56:7).[35] Indeed, this was a sacrifice not of Isaac, but of Abraham himself—all he hoped for, his future, his life, his seed.[36] A cascade of six imperfect verbs marked Abraham's obedience at the outset of the narrative: he rose, he saddled, he took, he split, he arose, he went (Gen 22:3). Approaching the place of sacrifice, another six imperfect verbs again point to his obedience: he built, he arranged, he bound, he placed, he stretched, he took (22:9–10). Earlier he had countered God's proposals, attempting to substitute Lot (Gen 12–13), Eliezer (15:2), and Ishmael (17:18), in place of Isaac. Here he is totally silent, a silence that is deafening: "his only words are absolute compliance and a confidence in the Lord's final provision."[37]

Ironically, when Abraham understood that "*God* sees/provides" (אֱלֹהִים יִרְאֶה, *elohim yir'eh,* Gen 22:8), God in turn acknowledged that *Abraham* "fears God" (יְרֵא אֱלֹהִים, *yre' elohim,* 22:12); the paronomasia is obvious.[38] One might say that "fear of God" is equivalent to the intense degree of faith that Abraham exhibited. Here, in Gen 22:12, the verb יָרֵא is used substantively to denote Abraham as a "fearer" of God—a (now-proven) characteristic of this patriarch. "Fear of God" is the fundamental OT term for depicting the appropriate human

---

35. So also *Jub.* 18.16 (and 4Q225), quoting God: "'I [God] have made known to all that you [Abraham] are faithful to me in everything which I say to you.'"

36. So also Ross: "[T]he real point of the act was Abraham's sacrifice of himself, that is, of his will and his wisdom with regard to his son Isaac" (Allen P. Ross, *Creation and Blessing: A Guide to the Study and Exposition of Genesis* [Grand Rapids: Baker, 1997], 393). Appropriately enough, Gerhard von Rad's booklet on Gen 22 is titled *Das Opfer des Abraham* ("The Sacrifice of Abraham")—not that of Isaac (Kaiser Traktate 6; Munich: Kaiser, 1971).

37. Mathews, *Genesis 11:27–50:26,* 291.

38. The verb רָאָה (*ra'ah,* "to see/provide") echoes through the account: Gen 22:8, 13, 14 (×2). In fact, "Moriah" (מֹרִיָּה, *moriyah,* 22:2) also may quite likely be related to this root: thus, the "place of seeing." Moreover, one could also read בְּהַר יְהוָה יֵרָאֶה (*bhar yhwh yera'eh,* 22:14b) as "in the mount, the LORD will be seen" (or "in the mount of the LORD, he will be seen"), thus providing an etiology for what might have been the site of the Temple. The various uses of רָאָה in the story form a chiastic structure, centered on Abraham's faith in God's provision for a substitute for his son, and his discovery of that provision.

A	God announces the name of the mountain (הר, *har*): land of "the place of seeing" (מֹרִיָּה, *moriyah,* "Moriah", 22:2)
B	Abraham sees (ראה) the place (מָקוֹם, *maqom*) of sacrifice (22:4)
C	Abraham asserts God will see/provide (ראה, 22:8)
C'	Abraham sees (ראה) God's provision (22:13)
B'	Abraham names the place (מָקוֹם): "God sees/provides" (ראה, 22:14a)
A'	Narrator announces maxim about the mountain (הר): where "God will be seen" (ראה, 22:14b)

Rather than an Atonement analogy, this play of words and structure strongly emphasizes Abraham's faith in a faithful God: he sees (with the eyes of faith)—and God sees (to it).

response to God—the Hebrew equivalent to the Christian "faith" (see Deut 10:12; Eccl 12:13, in addition to Pss 103:11, 13, 17; 112:1; 128:1; Prov 31:30; Luke 1:50). Moberly asserts that "Genesis 22 may appropriately be read as a, arguably the, primary canonical exposition of the meaning of 'one who fears God,'" entailing "obedience of the most demanding kind" grounded in a deep trust in God.[39] In other words, the *Aqedah* defines the meaning of יְרֵאת אֱלֹהִים— "obedience which does not hold back even what is most precious, when God demands it, and commits to God even that future which he himself has promised."[40] Abraham's sacrifice thus becomes "a paradigm for his successors," in his "wholehearted devotion to God" expressed in his obedience.[41] Maimonides would have agreed with this assessment; according to Rambam, one of the great principles of the Jewish faith that is taught in the *Aqedah* is

> the extent and limit of the fear of God. . . . The angel, therefore, says to [Abraham], "For now I know," etc. [Gen 22:12], that is, from this action, for which you deserve to be truly called a God-fearing man, all people shall learn how far we must go in the fear of God. This idea is confirmed in Scripture; it is distinctly stated that one sole thing, fear of God, is the object of the whole Law with its affirmative and negative precepts, its promises and its historical examples. . . . (*Guide for the Perplexed* 24)

And faith is an integral part of that "fear." Abraham's faith in God is underscored in Gen 22:5, where in a series of first person plural verbs, the result that Abraham expected as the final outcome of the incident is implied: "I and the lad—we shall go . . . , and we shall worship, and we shall return." It is this faith of the patriarch in God, despite insurmountable odds, that is emphasized in Heb 11:17–19. James 2:21 points to the "justification" (or "proving") of Abraham by the specific "work" of his offering up Isaac, thus consummating his faith. James

---

39. Moberly, *The Bible, Theology, and Faith*, 79, 96. Also see R. W. L. Moberly, "What is Theological Interpretation of Scripture?" *JTI* 3 (2009): 176.

40. Hans Walter Wolff, "The Elohistic Fragments in the Pentateuch" (trans. Keith R. Crim), *Int* 26 (1972):163–64. As Chisholm put it, "[f]earing God is a metonymy for reverence that results in obedience" (Robert B. Chisholm, "Anatomy of an Anthropomorphism: Does God Discover Facts?" *BSac* 164 [2007]: 13).

41. Gordon J. Wenham, "The Aqedah: A Paradigm of Sacrifice," in *Pomegranates and Golden Bells: Studies in Biblical, Jewish, and Near Eastern Ritual, Law, and Literature in Honor of Jacob Milgrom* (eds. David P. Wright, David Noel Freedman, and Avi Hurvitz; Winona Lake, Ind.: Eisenbrauns, 1995), 102. Notice also in Exod 20:20 where the Israelites are said to be tested (נסה, *nsh*, as in Gen 22:1) by God so that they may "fear" him (יראה, *yr'h*, as in Gen 22:12).

asserts that this was why Abraham was called "the friend of God."[42] The *Aqedah*, thus, is an account that teaches God's people what fearing God is all about—the willing sacrifice of *everything*![43]

> **THEOLOGICAL FOCUS**
> *The fear of God is an attribute to be demonstrated by God's children, involving self-sacrificial trust in God's promises and wholehearted obedience to his word.*

Abraham's Love for Isaac

The extent of Abraham's willingness to sacrifice "everything" and the depth of his wholehearted obedience is indicated in Gen 22 by the emphasis on the father-son relationship: "father" and/or "son" is mentioned fifteen times in Gen 22:1–20 (in 22:2 [×2], 3, 6, 7 [×3], 8, 9, 10, 12 [×2], 13, 16 [×2]). The readers are never to forget the relationship. In the only conversation recorded in the Bible between Abraham and Isaac, the latter's words begin with "my father" and the former's words end with "my son" (22:7–8)—this is also Abraham's last word before he prepares to slay Isaac (בְּנִי, *bni*, "my son," is a single word in the Hebrew). The narrator is explicitly creating an emotional tension in the story; no matter what the typological lens with which this account is viewed, one thing is clear: a father is called to slay the son he loves.

Gregory of Nyssa exclaimed: "See the goads of these words, how they prick the innards of the father; how they kindle the flame of nature; how they awaken the love by calling the son 'beloved' and 'the only one.' Through these names the affection towards him [Isaac] is brought to the boil."[44] In a sense, Mastema's sentiments were right on the money: "And the prince Mastema came and said before God, 'Behold, Abraham loves Isaac his son, and he delights in him above all things else; bid him offer him as a burnt-offering on the altar, and Thou wilt

---

42. Second Chronicles 20:7 and Isa 41:8 call the patriarch "beloved" of God (participle of אהב, *'hb*; the LXX of Isa 51:2 adds ἀγαπάω, *agapaō*, to point to God's love for Abraham (also see Jas 2:23). The "faith" of Abraham (אמן and, in the LXX, πιστός, *pistos*) is specifically noted in Neh 9:7–8.

43. On the other hand, the reversion to typology and a focus on parallels between the *Aqedah* and Christology diminishes the value of the story in its exhortation of the kind of "fear of God" that God desires from his people.

44. *Deit.*, translation from Kessler, *Bound by the Bible*, 49.

see if he will do this command, and Thou wilt know if he is faithful in everything wherein Thou dost try him'" (*Jub.* 17:16). It is therefore highly significant
that the first time the word "love" (אהב, *'hb*) occurs in the Bible is in Gen 22:2.
With the entry of this new word into Scripture came an implicit question: Was
Abraham's love for Isaac so strong that his allegiance to God had diminished?
It appears, then, that this love of Abraham for Isaac was a crucial element in the
test—it was this love that was being tested. Would Abraham be loyal to God, or
would love for the human overpower trust in the divine?

Without even perusing the details of Abraham's test, one can find the answer
to that question of Abraham's loyalties when one compares the unique descriptors of Isaac. There are three heavenly announcements to Abraham (22:1–2,
11–12, 14–16) with three corresponding descriptors of the (proposed/putative)
sacrifice, Isaac. These three descriptors contain three of the ten instances of בֵּן
(*ben*, "son") in the account; but these three alone are inflected with the second
person singular possessive pronoun (בִּנְךָ, *binka*, "your son") and fitted into a
patterned construction. However, there is a significant alteration, before and
after the test, in how God/angel of Yahweh described Isaac.

Pre-test:

    22:2   "your son, your only son, *the one you love*"

Post-test:

    22:12   "your son, your only son"

    22:16   "your son, your only son"

The narrative omissions in 22:12 and 16 help clarify the reason for the test.
The trifold description of Isaac in Gen 22:2 was to emphasize that this son, this
particular one, was the one Abraham *loved*, with a love that potentially stood in
the way of his allegiance to, and faith in, God. The subsequent, post-test deletion
of the phrase, "the one you love," was clear indication that Abraham had passed
the examination. The three-part description of Isaac *before* the test ("son/only
son/one you love") becomes, *after* the test, two-part ("son/only son"). The *Aqedah*
was, in reality, a demonstration of love for God over and against anything that advanced a rival claim to that love. "[T]he story has to do with idolatry—the idolatry of the son. Once God had given the gift of Isaac to Abraham, does Abraham
focus on Isaac and forget the Giver? The climactic line is 'Now I know that you

worship [fear] God,' with the implied 'and that you do not worship your son.'"[45]

Four Maccabees 13:12 agrees with this reading of Abraham's shift in loyalties from Isaac to God: "Remember whence you came, and the father by whose hand Isaac would have submitted to being slain for the sake of devotion [to God; εὐσέβειαν, eusebeian]."[46] Philo, too, was on the right track when he noted that though Abraham was "attached to his child by an indescribable fondness," because he was "wholly influenced by love towards God, he forcibly repressed all the names and charms of the natural relationship," "inclining with his whole will and heart to show his devotion to God" (On Abraham, 32.117; 35.195).[47] Though Abraham's son was "well-beloved," "the commands of God are loved still more." Therefore, Ambrose exhorts, "Let us then set God before all those whom we love, father, brother, mother.... Let us, then, imitate the devotion of Abraham" (On the Decease of His Brother Satyrus, 2.97, 99).[48] Origen expressed it this way: "For Abraham loved Isaac his son, the text says, but he placed the love of God before love of the flesh ...."[49] In sum, the test "proved" the patriarch's absolute allegiance to God—his unadulterated love for, and loyalty to,

---

45. Phyllis Trible, Genesis: A Living Conversation (ed. Bill Moyers; New York: Doubleday, 1996), 227.

46. Sirach 44:20 and 1 Macc 2:52 declare that Abraham was "found to be faithful in his testing" (ἐν πειρασμῷ εὑρέθη πιστός, en peirasmō heurethē pistos). "Hence in the pre-Christian Jewish tradition reflected here, the basis of Abraham's uprightness is no longer his 'faith,' but his stalwart fidelity" (also see Jas 2:21, 23). Joseph A. Fitzmeyer, "The Interpretation of Genesis 15:6: Abraham's Faith and Righteousness in a Qumran Text," in Emanuel: Studies in Hebrew Bible, Septuagint, and Dead Sea Scrolls in Honor of Emanuel Tov (Supplements to Vetus Testamentum 94; eds. Shalom M. Paul, Robert A. Kraft, Lawrence H. Schiffman, and Weston W. Fields; Leiden: Brill, 2003), 259.

47. So also Josephus: Abraham "preferred what was pleasing to God, before the preservation of his own son," proving his "piety" (θρήσκεια, thrēskeia; Ant. 1.13.1).

48. Ambrose also declared that Abraham did not "put love for his son before the commands of his Creator," thus demonstrating his "devotion to God" (On the Duties of the Clergy, 1.25.119). Calvin, while agreeing with Abraham's agonies, thought it was directed elsewhere and not primarily a paternal anguish. "For the great source of grief to him was not his own bereavement ... but that, in the person of this son, the whole salvation of the world seemed to be extinguished and to perish" (Calvin, Commentary on Genesis, 22:1). It is a little hard to imagine a father with a knife poised to strike his beloved son being more worried about his posterity than about his bound child lying helpless before him on the altar. Kierkegaard depicts the pathos well: "There was many a father who lost his child; but then it was God, ... it was His hand took the child. Not so with Abraham. For him was reserved a harder trial, and Isaac's fate was laid along with the knife in Abraham's hand" (Søren Kierkegaard, Fear and Trembling [trans. H. Honig and E. Honig; Princeton: Princeton University Press, 1983], 36).

49. Origen, Homilies on Genesis 8.7 (cited in Oden and Sheridan, Genesis 12–50, 106–7). And likewise, "[U]nless you are obedient to all the commands, even the more difficult ones, unless you offer sacrifice and show that you place neither father nor mother nor sons before God [Matt 10:37], you will not know that you fear God. Nor will it be said of you, 'Now I know that you fear God'" (Origen, Homilies on Genesis 8.8 [cited in Oden and Sheridan, Genesis 12–50, 107]).

deity. Nothing would stand between Abraham and God and, in a circumspect way, the text actually tells us that (see below).

Isaac's Disappearance

One element of the account that has perplexed interpreters throughout the ages is the apparent disappearance of Isaac from the Abraham stories after the mention of "son" in Genesis 22:16. Indeed, father and son are never shown speaking to each other again after this narrative; Isaac does not even show up in the account of Sarah's death and burial (Gen 23). The only mentioned contact between father and son after the stunning episode of the *Aqedah* is at Abraham's funeral (25:9).[50] In fact, in the Gen 22 account itself, it appears that Isaac, after the aborted sacrifice, has vanished. Abraham, we are told, returned from his test, apparently *without* Isaac: "Then Abraham returned to his young men, and they arose and went together to Beersheba; and Abraham lived in Beersheba" (22:19). The use of the same phrase, "went together," used to describe the trip of father and son (22:6, 8), is now used of the return journey of master and servants (22:19), making it all the more strange that Isaac is nowhere visible.

The rabbis recognized the strangeness of this omission in Gen 22:19 and responded with some even stranger solutions. "'And where was Isaac?' R. Berekhiah asserted: 'He had sent him to Shem to study Torah with him.' R. Yose bar Haninah said, 'He sent him away by night, on account of the evil eye.'" And, equally confusingly, R. Levi explained, "He took him and hid him away. He thought, 'Lest that one who tried to seduce him [Satan] throw a stone at him

---

50. Moreover, "[a]fter the *Aqedah*, there is no more direct divine revelation to Abraham and *vice versa*, no contact of Abraham with God in the rest of Abraham's stories in the book of Genesis" (Isaac Kalimi, "'Go, I Beg You, Take Your Beloved Son and Slay Him!' The Binding of Isaac in Rabbinic Literature and Thought," *Review of Rabbinic Judaism* 13 [2010]: 16). All this despite Abraham's endeavors to find a bride for Isaac (24:1–9, 62–67), and his giving his all to Isaac (25:6)—but there is no interpersonal contact or conversation between father and son explicitly noted in these texts.

and render him unfit for use as an offering'" (*Gen. Rab.* 56:5).[51]

When the documentary hypothesis (with its many refinements) was in vogue—dividing the Pentateuch between sources J, E, D, and P—Gen 22 was usually ascribed to E on the basis of the employment of אֱלֹהִים (*elohim*) in 22:1, 3, 8, 9, and 12. The appearance of יְהֹוָה (*yhwh*) in 22:11 and 14 was then attributed to faulty redaction, as was also this return of Abraham *alone*.[52] The speculation was that perhaps the sacrifice of Isaac actually did happen, but the redactor(s), in a bit of sloppy editing while attempting to valorize Abraham and concoct an account of an averted sacrifice, neglected to tweak the original conclusion of the return journey of the patriarch *sans* sacrificed son.[53] This oversight resulted, it is surmised, in the awkward stitching together of the story of an abandoned sacrifice with the absence of Isaac at the end of the account. However, none of these explanations is satisfactory for the one who wants to preach the final form of the text and accepts it as it is (see Rule of Finality in chapter 1).

Because of this seeming inconsistency regarding the presence/absence of Isaac in Gen 22:15–18, the conclusion of the narrative has often been considered an addendum to the main story: there appear to be stylistic differences between the two parts (economy of wording and heavy background in the latter, and repetitiveness and the use of synonyms and similes in the former), as well as vocabulary distinctions (two phrases in 22:15–18 are unparalleled in Gen but common in prophetic literature: "By myself I have sworn," and "declares Yahweh" (22:16). Yet, the story's opening in Gen 22:1 is neatly concluded in 22:18, and the recurrent motif of "only son" (22:2, 12, 16) further strengthens the unity of the whole account. Moberly is right in proposing that Gen 22:15–18, integral to the main account, "should be described as the earliest and canonically recog-

---

51. Other creative speculations as to the fate of the missing son are collected in Shalom Spiegel, *The Last Trial: On the Legends and Lore of the Command to Offer Isaac as a Sacrifice: The Aqedah* (trans. Judah Goldin; Philadelphia: Jewish Publication Society of America, 1967, 3–8). They include: Isaac out of weariness, from the shock of the whole affair, fell behind in his walking; Abraham sent him back home by another route to bear the glad tidings to Sarah; God took Isaac to the Garden of Eden where he remained for three years to be healed (of the wound inflicted by his father?); etc. Spiegel labels all this "paradoxical haggadic lore"—a "deviation from the patent sense of Scripture." He asks rhetorically, "The story of the Aqedah—is it possible that these pious generations failed to be affected by the plain meaning of the words of Scripture?" (ibid., 8). Good question!

52. See Robert Crotty, "The Literary Structure of the Binding of Isaac in Genesis 22," *ABR* 53 (2005): 32.

53. So, according to Coats, "[T]he Yahwist has appropriated an ancient story of child sacrifice, altering it so that it becomes an example of Abraham's faith and an occasion for God's renewing the promise for great posterity, for possession of land, and for blessing open to all the nations of the earth" (George W. Coats, *Genesis: With an Introduction to Narrative Literature* [FOTL 1; Grand Rapids: Eerdmans, 1983], 161).

nized commentary on the story"—a commentary from God himself.[54]

But one is still left with the burden of explaining the disappearance of Isaac. What happened to the lad after the sacrifice of the ram and the reissuing of God's promises?

As was noted earlier, there is one significant difference in the description of Isaac in the pre-test and post-test accounts (22:2 vs. 22:12, 16)—the "love" motif, missing after the abandoned sacrifice (see above). Quite interestingly, in parallel, while there are three assertions of Abraham being accompanied by one or more companions (וַיֵּלְכוּ . . . יַחְדָּו, *wayyelku . . . yahdaw,* "they walked on together," 22:6, 8, 19), the last such statement—the post-test version—is significantly different from the other two: in 22:6 and 8, "them" indicates Abraham and Isaac; in 22:19, Isaac is missing—"they" indicates Abraham and his two young men.

Pre-test:

22:6	"so the two of them [Abraham and Isaac] walked on together"
22:8	"so the two of them [Abraham and Isaac] walked on together"

Post-test:

22:19	"they [Abraham and his young men] . . . walked on together"

After the test, it was as if Isaac had altogether vanished; the narrator apparently took an eraser and wiped out any mention of Isaac after the "sacrifice." But there was a purpose behind this: the author was *doing* something with what he was saying (in this case, with what he *failed* to say, creating a striking gap in the narrative, but that, too, is to "say" something). No more would the account portray father and son speaking to each other or even being in one another's presence until the older one dies (25:8–9). When one remembers that the test was actually an examination of Abraham's loyalties—to God or to son, "the one you love"—one understands what it was the author was doing in Gen 22:19; he was describing, in yet another way, Abraham's success in this critical test. The author was depicting a line drawn; the relationship between father and son had been clarified, the tension between fear of God and love of son had been resolved. One might almost say: *For Abraham so loved God that he gave his only begotten son. . . .* This test had shown that Abraham loved God more than any-

---

54. R. W. L. Moberly, "The Earliest Commentary on the Aqedah," *VT* 37 (1988): 307–8, 314.

one else.[55] And to bring that home to readers, father and son are separated for the rest of their days—*literarily* separated, that is, for the purpose of achieving the narrator's theological agenda.[56] He was *doing* something with what he was *saying*.

THEOLOGICAL FOCUS

The love of God/the fear of God trumps every other allegiance.

Consequences of Abraham's Success

The consequences of Abraham's action, as depicted in the narrative of Gen 22, also give credence to the interpretation of the story as one that teaches what it means to fear God. That Abraham successfully passes this test is not only expressly depicted, but it is also strongly implied: the narrative is both the zenith of the Abrahamic saga and the climax of Abraham's worship. Of the three altars in the patriarch's story (12:8; 13:18; and 22:9), the one in Gen 22 is the only one with a sacrifice; with the others, Abraham only calls on the name of Yahweh (12:8; 13:4). At any rate, the satisfactory completion of the test ensures God's promise to Abraham; in fact, it *enhances* God's promise.

Scholars have generally held that the Abrahamic promises (in Gen 12, 15, 17, 18, and 22) are unconditional.[57] Yet, upon examination of the promise made to the patriarch at the conclusion of the momentous events of Gen 22, one cannot but notice contingency: the clauses "because you have done this thing and have not withheld your son, your only son" and "because you have obeyed my voice" (*A* and *A'* below) bookend the promised blessing (Gen 22:16c–18).

---

55. The equation of "fear of God" and "love for God" is not illegitimate: Deut 6:2, 13 command fear, while the *Shema* calls for love (6:5); Deut 10:12 and 13:3–4—each has both elements; also see Deut 10:20 with 11:1; as well as Pss 31:19, 23; and 145:19–20. There is considerable overlap between these two concepts, as is evident in the *Aqedah* itself.

56. As to whether they were *actually* separated, that is an issue *behind* the text that need not concern the interpreter.

57. However, for more recent doubts about that assumption, see Gary Knoppers, "Ancient Near Eastern Royal Grants and the Davidic Covenant: A Parallel?" *JAOS* 116 (1996): 670–97; Richard S. Hess, "The Book of Joshua as a Land Grant," *Bib* 83 (2002): 493–506; and Steven McKenzie, "The Typology of the Davidic Covenant," in *The Land that I Will Show You: Essays on the History and Archaeology of the Ancient Near East in Honor of J. Maxwell Miller* (eds. J. Andrew Dearman and M. Patrick Graham; London: Continuum, 2001), 152–78.

A	because you have done this thing and have not withheld your son, your only son,
B	indeed I will greatly bless you (בָּרֵךְ אֲבָרֶכְךָ, *barak 'abarekka*)
C	and I will greatly multiply your seed (זֶרַע, *zera'*)
D	as the stars of the heavens and as the sand which is on the seashore;
C'	and your seed (זֶרַע) shall possess the gate of their enemies.
B'	In your seed all the nations of the earth shall be blessed (הִתְבָּרֲכוּ, *hitbaraku*)
A'	because you have obeyed my voice.

This reiterated promise is quite different from the earlier promises in several ways: Gen 22:17a has "greatly bless" (*B* above; בָּרֵךְ אֲבָרֶכְךָ, emphatic and in the infinitive absolute, unique in Gen[58]); likewise, "greatly multiply" (*C*; וְהַרְבָּה אַרְבֶּה, *wharbah 'arbeh*, is also found in Gen 16:10, but 22:17b is the only instance of this promise to the Abraham-Isaac-Jacob lineage). Moreover, 22:17c employs two similes—stars of the heavens, and sand of the seashore (*D*)—used elsewhere in Gen singly, but never together (Gen 15:5; 26:4; 32:12; also Ex 32:13); and the possession by Abraham's seed of "the gate of their enemies" (*C'*; 22:17d) is unusual in the promises in Gen.[59] The nations being blessed "in your seed" (*B'*; 22:18a and 26:4; 28:14) is also new—thus far the blessing of the nations had been explicitly "in Abraham" (12:3; 18:18). This focus on descendants is appropriate given that the *Aqedah* deals with the "saving" of a descendant.[60] Thus, there are significant differences—*contingent enhancements*—to the promises already given to Abraham in Gen 12, 15, 17, and 18. While the essence of the blessing remains the same in its various iterations, the attachment of the contingency of obedience (though there was already a hint of this in Gen 17:1–2 and 18:19), along with the enhancements, is certainly striking.[61]

Origen disagrees: "I see nothing additional. The same things are repeated which were previously promised" (*Homilies on Genesis* 9.1). He explains that the first promises were given at the time of Abraham's circumcision to the "people of circumcision" (those of the flesh), and the second promises, at the time of the "passion of Isaac," to "those who are of faith and who come to the inheritance through the passion of Christ."[62] Thus Origen employs the story to create a dis-

---

58. This construct is also found in Num 23:11, 25; Josh 24:10; Deut 15:4; Ps 132:15; 1 Chron 4:10.

59. This phrase also occurs in Gen 24:60, with the blessing of Rebekah by her family.

60. Moberly, "The Earliest Commentary on the Aqedah," 316–17.

61. This "enhancement" of the promise is more like an unexpected bonus, which, of course, is what grace is all about.

62. Cited in Oden and Sheridan, *Genesis 12–50*, 112–13.

junction between Israel and the church. Likewise, Calvin asserts: "Certainly, before Isaac was born, this same promise had been already given; and now it receives nothing more than confirmation" (*Commentary on Genesis,* on 22:15).

But this is not what one infers from the divine (re)promise in this account (22:16–18). Every element of the original promise is fortified here, ratcheted up a notch, *because of obedience.* It is an enhancement of the earlier promise, especially solidified in Yahweh's unique swearing by himself ("By myself I have sworn," 22:16)—the first and only such divine oath being made in the patriarchal stories, though that oath is frequently referred to elsewhere (24:7; 26:3; 50:24; Ex 13:5; Num 14:16; Deut 1:8; etc.).[63] The oath is validated further by the addition of "declares Yahweh" (נְאֻם־יְהוָה, n'um yhwh), which echoes often in the prophetic corpus (Isa 45:23; Jer 22:5; 49:13) but, in the Pentateuch, is only found in Gen 22:14 and Num 19:28. Thus this promise in Gen 22 is made far more definitive than all the preceding ones, and carries added solemnity and gravitas. Abraham's possession of the land was promised earlier in Gen 12:7; 13:14–17; 15:7–21; and 17:8; but here in 22:17, we find the most militant and triumphant version of that promise ("your seed will possess the gate of their enemies" = conquer their enemies' cities). And, correspondingly, the blessing is focused upon all the *nations* of the earth, not just the *families* as in 12:3. Contingent upon his obedience, every aspect of the earlier promises to Abraham is now "augmented and guaranteed by the LORD unreservedly."[64]

Moberly understands the changes in the promise of Gen 22 this way: "A promise which previously was grounded solely in the will and purpose of Yahweh is transformed so that it is now grounded *both* in the will of Yahweh *and* in the obedience of Abraham. It is not that divine promise has become contingent upon Abraham's obedience, but that Abraham's obedience has been incorporated into the divine promise."[65] While this is a reasonable explanation of the theological worth of human obedience, it does not take the textual evidence into account: there *are* actual changes in the elements of the promised blessing— significant changes in degree of their fulfillment. Thus, in my accounting, human obedience has greater value than merely being incorporated into divine plan, and the resulting blessing is more than just a confirmation of what God has already promised. There is, indeed, a *contingent* divine response to human

---

63. Wenham, *Genesis 16–50,* 111. The phrase, "by myself," is also unique in Genesis, but is found in Jer 22:5; 49:13; Amos 4:2; 6:8; and in the NT, in Heb 6:13–18.

64. Ibid., 116.

65. "The Earliest Commentary on the Aqedah," 320–21.

obedience—in a sense, a divine reward for the latter. So Wenham concludes: "God's test had put Abraham on the rack. Yet torn between his love for his son and his devotion to God, he had emerged victorious with his son intact and his faithful obedience rewarded beyond all expectation."[66] It is exactly this divine reward that is emphasized in the promise to Isaac in Gen 26:2–5, where the blessing is expressly based upon the obedience of Abraham ("because Abraham obeyed me and kept my charge, my commandments, my statutes, and my laws," 26:5). This contingency of faithful obedience heightens the *degree of blessing*, not that the blessing itself is changed in character, but that, in some sense, the quantum of blessing is supplemented and its quality intensified. Obedience *does* result in reward (the concept of obedience resulting in rewards will be addressed later).

THEOLOGICAL FOCUS
Demonstration of faith in God's promises and his word results in divine blessing/reward.

Putting the various theological foci together, one arrives at the comprehensive version of the pericopal theology of Gen 22.

COMPREHENSIVE THEOLOGICAL FOCUS[67]
Faith in God's promises and his word is required from the child of God, and such a faith is liable to be tested (precepts of the world in front of the text). This faith, equivalent to a supreme love/fear of God that trumps every other allegiance (priorities of the world in front of the text), is manifest in self-sacrificial obedience to his word (practices of the world in front of the text). Such faith in God (love/fear of God), God sees fit to reward with blessing (precepts of the world in front of the text).

---

66. Wenham, *Genesis 16–50*, 116. Also see idem, "The Aqedah," 101. This, then, is God's gracious reward upon seeing his child's "fear of the Lord" (obedience): notice the use of שָׂכָר (*sakar*, "reward") in the promise of God to Abraham in 15:1.

67. Elements of the "Theological Focus" discovered earlier in the analysis are brought together here in a "Comprehensive Theological Focus" of the pericope (a summary statement of the theology of the pericope). It is not always the case that this "Comprehensive Theological Focus" will have all three elements—precepts, priorities, and practices of the *world in front of the text*. In fact, quite frequently, there is a blurring of the boundaries between those three facets. Needless to say, labels are not what is important; rather it is what the author is *doing* with what he is saying that ought to be attended to, no matter what the nomenclature adopted or category created.

"What, then, does Abraham teach us? To put it briefly, he teaches us not to prefer the gifts of God to God. . . . Therefore, put not even a real gift of God before the Giver of that gift" (Augustine, *Serm.* 2). Thus the intent of the author was to call for an identification of the readers with the protagonist of this story—Abraham, the paragon of faith. God's people everywhere are to exercise the kind of faith in God that Abraham had, the kind of love for God that Abraham demonstrated, the kind of fear of God that Abraham exhibited: nothing comes between God and the believer. *Nothing!* This is the lesson the preacher must proclaim; this is what the reader must do. Calvin recognized the exemplary features of Abraham's action: "This example is proposed for our imitation. . . . [W]e pay Him the highest honor, when, in affairs of perplexity, we nevertheless entirely acquiesce in His providence" (*Commentary on Genesis,* on 22:7).[68] That is no less a christological understanding of Gen 22 than any other interpretive option, for part of what it means to be Christlike is to exercise the kind of faith, demonstrate the kind of love, and exhibit the kind of fear that Abraham did (see below for the development of the concept of *imitatio Christi*).

The interpretation of Gen 22 proposed in this work, discovering the theology of the pericope, gives direction to the preacher as to the divine demand propounded in the text—what the A/author was *doing* with what he was saying, the theology of the pericope. However, that does not answer the question of how such a theology abides by the Rule of Centrality proposed in chapter 1: *The Rule of Centrality focuses the interpretation of canonical texts for applicational purposes upon the pre-eminent person of Christ and his redemptive work that fulfills the will of the Father in the power of the Spirit.* How is Christ to be seen in this text and its interpretation? In the next section, this issue will be addressed and a new hermeneutic proposed, one that respects both the specific theology of an OT pericope *and* the Rule of Centrality.

CHRISTICONIC INTERPRETATION

One of the questions raised by the method described so far is regarding christocentric interpretation. In the scheme of pericopal theology, as propounded in this work, where does Christ fit in, particularly in the preaching of OT texts? This section, the concluding portion of this work, will address some

---

68. "Abraham alone ought to be to us equal to tens of thousands if we consider his faith, which is set before us as the best model of believing, to whose race also we must be held to belong in order that we may be the children of God" (Calvin, *Institutes,* 2.10.11).

of the issues of christocentric interpretation and preaching, assessing the arguments of some of the major proponents in that camp. Subsequently, a solution will be propounded—*christiconic* interpretation—that respects both the specificity of pericopes and a canonical vision of Jesus Christ in Scripture.

Christocentric Interpretation

Christocentric interpretation—particularly as it deals with the hermeneutic of preaching—is the interpretation of a biblical text in such a way that its main theme is directly and explicitly related to the Second Person of the Trinity: it is "appreciating the Old Testament as it is in the design of God: a witness, foreshadowing, anticipation, and promise of salvation as it has now been accomplished by the work of the triune God in Jesus Christ Incarnate."[69] As is obvious, such an operation is firmly based upon a canonical, bird's-eye view of biblical history; the focus is upon the work of God in redemption across a historical timeline, centered upon Jesus Christ, the Author of salvation. Thus "redemptive-historical" (RH) is an alternative descriptor for "christocentric" interpretation. The NT, of course, maintains an obvious focus on Jesus Christ; the complexity of christocentric interpretation relates particularly to the preaching of OT pericopes.

Greidanus's solution is for preachers to "interpret the Old Testament in the light of its fulfillment in the New Testament."[70] The potential problem with this approach is that the specific thrusts of individual OT texts may get neglected in the rush to correlate the OT with the NT, making the value of preaching from the OT doubtful, at best. For example, when preaching the seventh commandment of the Decalogue that prohibits adultery, Clowney wants the "biblically grounded preacher" to connect this command with Jesus' statement on adultery and, even further, his commandment to love. "Love for neighbor flows from love of God, and love for God is our response to His love for us," which leads Clowney to the cross: "Only at the cross do we know the real meaning of love—of God's redeeming love."[71] But one does not need the seventh commandment to arrive at this NT summit.

---

69. Vern S. Poythress, *The Shadow of Christ in the Law of Moses* (Phillipsburg, N.J.: Presbyterian and Reformed, 1991), 285.

70. Sidney Greidanus, *The Modern Preacher and the Ancient Text: Interpreting and Preaching Biblical Literature* (Grand Rapids: Eerdmans, 1989), 119.

71. Edmund P. Clowney, "Preaching Christ from All the Scriptures," in *The Preacher and Preaching: Reviving the Art in the Twentieth Century* (ed. Samuel T. Logan; Phillipsburg, N.J.: Presbyterian and Reformed, 1986), 183–84. The eventual product of such an approach is a topical sermon on adultery or "love."

When preaching on the commandment against murder, following Clowney's method one could conceivably move to Christ's command against hatred. In turn, one could once again ascend to love and the cross of Calvary, the acme of love. Such an operation culminating in love could be conducted for any pericope, but it would deny the specificity of the particular pericope and what the author was *doing* with what he was saying. This work defends the thesis that divine demand is found in pericopes across the breadth of the canon; every one of them is "profitable for teaching, for reproof, for correction, for training in righteousness" (2 Tim 3:16). And, for preaching purposes, the specific voice of each one must be heard and respected, without being drowned out by the sounds of other texts in the canon.

For Carson, christocentric preaching is based upon "strong biblical theology" that comes from examining the canonically interweaving threads of ideas, tracking such biblical themes as kingdom, priesthood, temple, or sacrifice. According to him there are roughly twenty such broad canonical themes that enable the preacher to trace Christ from any text, "without making a wild leap."[72] Biblical theology does help place the particular event of a narrative pericope against the backdrop of God's deeds in history, and there is, of course, a place for this in the teaching program of the church. The contention of this work, however, is that the sermon is not the place for such a display; rather, preaching is the event where the specific message of a particular text—its divine demand—is exposited and brought to bear upon the life of the children of God to transform them for the glory of God. If the preacher relates every text every Sunday to the larger theme of redemption, or perhaps to the even broader theme of the glory of God, it reduces preaching to painting these big pictures every week—the same twenty-odd vistas recommended by Carson. In such biblical-theology transactions, the specifics of the pericope being preached—the miniatures—tend to get swallowed up in the capacious canvas of RH interpretation.

---

72. D. A. Carson, "Of First Importance (part 1): Eight Words that Help Us Preach the Gospel Correctly," n.p. [cited June 3, 2012]. Online: http://www.preachingtoday.com/skills/themes/gettinggospelright/offirstimportance1.html (access is restricted to subscribers). Goldsworthy, too, asserts that "[t]he riches in Christ are inexhaustible, and biblical theology is the way to uncover them" (Graeme Goldsworthy, *Preaching the Whole Bible as Christian Scripture: The Application of Biblical Theology to Expository Preaching* [Grand Rapids: Eerdmans, 2000], 30). However, for Mohler, also firm in the RH tradition, systematic theology takes precedence: "preaching is an exercise in the theological exposition of Scripture"—by "theological" he means concepts of Trinity, deity and humanity of Christ, atonement, ecclesiology, eschatology, etc. (R. Albert Mohler, *He Is Not Silent: Preaching in a Postmodern World* [Chicago: Moody, 2008], 111 [also see 109–10]).

Indeed, preaching in the RH tradition is often comparable to a ride in a Boeing 747 high above the landscape with its hot deserts, its snowpeaked mountains, its wide rivers, its dense forests, its open prairies, its craggy hills, and its deep lakes. The view is panoramic, majestic, impressive, breathtaking, and always comfortable. But there is one problem. The Christian is not "above" things. He is in the middle of things. He is trekking through the landscape.[73]

This move away from the specifics of a text to a level of canonical abstraction, as biblical theology envisages, is counterproductive for preachers. With such reduction (or abstraction) to biblical theology, a tedious repetition of sermonic themes is inevitable, to the detriment of the faith and practice of God's people. Robinson points out that "[w]hen we shove a passage under some broad theological abstraction without interacting with its specificity, we will end up with sermons as much alike as the repeated patterns on wallpaper."[74] On the other hand, in drilling down to the specifics of a text, the theology particular to that pericope may be discretely and sequentially preached week by week. It is by this privileging of the text and its specific theology that one can preach for concrete life change in small increments, pericope by pericope, sermon by sermon.

Lest it be assumed that preaching employing pericopal theology is a means to godliness apart from Christ, let me reiterate what was stated in chapter 3: one can preach only because of Christ, who made possible salvation; because of Christ there is therefore no condemnation for sin; because of Christ the indwelling of the Holy Spirit is made possible, and it is that indwelling Spirit who empowers the child of God to obey divine demand wherever in Scripture it may be. In other words, what is called for in any given pericope is the obedience of faith, the meeting of divine demand, *by the grace of God, through the power of the indwelling Holy Spirit, all made possible by the redeeming work of the Son.* Sermons are to exhort believers to fulfill the human responsibility aspect of each divine demand, by the grace of God, in the power of the Holy Spirit, in light of what Christ has accomplished.

---

73. Hendrik Krabbendam, "Hermeneutics and Preaching," in *The Preacher and Preaching* (ed. Samuel T. Logan, Jr.; Phillipsburg, N.J.: Presbyterian and Reformed, 1986), 235.

74. Haddon W. Robinson, "The Relevance of Expository Preaching," in *Preaching to a Shifting Culture: 12 Perspectives on Communicating that Connects* (ed. Scott M. Gibson; Grand Rapids: Baker, 2004), 83. This is discernible in Greidanus's treatment of Genesis. As one glances at his "Sermon Goals" for each passage, it becomes immediately apparent that these goals look remarkably similar, pericope after pericope. See Greidanus, *Preaching Christ from Genesis*, 288, 306, 347, 368, 386, 420–21, 441, etc.

Christ in Every Pericope?

There does not seem to be much ground to the claim that Christ must be proclaimed from every pericope of Scripture, as RH interpreters advocate. Instead, the evidence actually shows otherwise: OT exemplars are employed liberally in the NT; every biblical genre conducts ethical instruction, rather than serving exclusively as RH treatises; the history of biblical interpretation in the church points to a rich and edifying tradition of preaching for life change; and adverting to hypothetical apostolic hermeneutics is insufficient ground for preaching in a christocentric manner. These arguments are considered individually below, following which several biblical passages cited in support of christocentric interpretation will be examined.[75]

Exemplars Galore

Contrary to what christocentric interpreters assert ought to be the case, various OT characters (and events) are employed as exemplars for believers in the NT itself—Rom 15:4 and 1 Cor 10:6 explicitly provide the warrant for such a transaction. Note also Luke 4:23–27 (1 Kgs 17:8–24); Rom 4, 9 (Gen 15, 17, 18, 21, 25; etc.); 1 Tim 2:12–15 (Gen 2–3); Heb 3:7–4:11 (Num 14–21); and Jas 2:12–26; 5:10–28 (employing Elijah, noted to be "a man with a nature like ours"). Hebrews 11 has a catena of OT *dramatis personæ* paraded as examples for Christians in every age (also see Heb 13:7). Moreover, Jesus frequently exhorted his listeners to imitate characters in his stories and parables: for example, the wise builder (Matt 7:24–27), David (Mark 2:23–28), and the Good Samaritan (Luke 10:25–37, which concludes with the express injunction: "Go and do the same"). Jesus, himself, is used as an exemplar (Heb 12:1–3; also Rom 15:2–7; Eph 5:2; Phil 2:5–11; 1 Pet 2:18–25; 4:1); likewise, Paul offers himself as a model (Acts 20:33–35; 1 Cor 4:17; 11:1; Gal 4:12; Phil 4:9; 1 Thess 1:6–7; 2 Tim 1:13; 2:2–3; 3:10–17). Thus, the use of exemplars in the NT counters the argument of RH interpreters against "moralizing," the employment of biblical characters as examples for God's children.

Moralizing, according to Greidanus, "undercuts the Bible's own purpose and replaces it with the preacher's agenda." So also Goldsworthy, who condemns

---

75. See Jason Hood, "Christ-Centred Interpretation Only? Moral Instruction from Scripture's Self-Interpretation as Caveat and Guide," *SBET* 27 (2009): 59–65, for further details on these arguments against a christocentric interpretation.

such a sermon as "at worst demonic in its Christ-denying legalism."[76] I suggest that, *pace* Greidanus and Goldsworthy, in many instances the Bible itself makes examples (positive or negative) of its characters, as the study of Gen 22 earlier in this chapter has shown. That, of course, is not to deny that there are "moralistic" preachers who launch into an indiscriminate imitation of biblical characters, routinely moving from text to application without any consideration of what the author was *doing* with what he was saying (i.e., without attending to the theology of the pericope). Rather than their random and haphazard use of exemplars in a "Be-like-*X*" hermeneutic, this work calls for the theology of the pericope to be isolated and applied. But to label *all* preaching based on biblical characters "moralizing" is not only hermeneutically suspect, it is also homiletically naïve.[77]

Consistent Moral Instruction

All biblical genres in the OT engage in moral and ethical instruction; they do not serve exclusively as adumbrations of the Messiah, and neither do they solely establish salvific truths.

As has already been detailed in chapter 3, the legal aspects of the OT are not to be discarded, for *all* Scripture is profitable for edification. The law, Paul says, is holy and righteous and good, it is spiritual, and he joyfully concurs with it (Rom 3:31; 7:12, 14, 22); moreover, NT writers quoted from the law frequently (Eph 6:1; Jas 2:8, 11; 1 Pet 1:15). Thus the law is still *theologically* valid for believers in every dispensation, as the NT application of such commands shows (1 Cor 9:9–10; 1 Tim 5:17–18). The same situation pertains to other genres of the OT, as well. For instance, while not denying the employment of the psalms for messianic purposes, they are often applied to believers: Ps 2, for instance, is applied both to Christ and to Christians (Acts 4:25–27; 13:33; Heb 1:5; 5:5; Rev 2:26, 27; 12:5; 19:15); also see Ps 44:22 (Rom 8:36); Ps 95:7–11 (Heb 3:7–11, 15; 4:3, 5, 7); etc. Prophecy, too, is applied to the believer: Gen 3:15 (Rom 16:20); both Jesus and believers are called "light of the world" (Matt 5:14 and John 8:12; 9:5; from Isa 49:6; 60:3); and Isa 45:23 is used both of Jesus' ultimate victory (Phil 2:10) as well as to motivate believers to remember the final accounting

---

76. Greidanus, *Preaching Christ from the Old Testament*, 293; idem, *The Modern Preacher*, 117; Goldsworthy, *Preaching the Whole Bible*, 124.

77. I suspect what is happening in RH interpretation is an over-reaction to the inadequately text-grounded operation of the "Be-like-*X*" hermeneutic. This work suggests a more legitimate hermeneutic that, taking into careful account the specificity and demand of the text, does not veer towards either extreme.

and, therefore, to treat one another decently (Rom 14:11). Wisdom literature is also employed in the NT for instruction in godly living—the book of Prov, for instance: Prov 3:7 (2 Cor 8:12); Prov 3:11–12 (Heb 12:5–6); Prov 3:34 (Jas 4:5; 1 Pet 5:5); Prov 11:31 (1 Pet 4:18); Prov 25:21–22 (Rom 12:20); etc.

In other words, Scripture is more than just a witness to the fulfillment of messianic promises; there are ethical demands therein as well that must be brought to bear upon the lives of God's people. Christocentric preaching tends to undermine the ethical emphasis of individual texts. Surprisingly, an RH interpreter like Goldsworthy goes to great lengths to make an excuse for those NT writings that apply the OT to believers for ethics, as does, for example, 1 Tim 5:18: "the connection through Christ does not have to be indicated in every instance once the principle is established in the wider text."[78] Why, then, does every *sermon* have to have that connection and reestablish that principle? Chapell, too, excuses NT writers who "commend moral behaviors with no mention of the cross, the resurrection, the Holy Spirit, or God's enabling grace," on grounds of the "context" of the "overarching biblical message."[79] I would heartily agree that context is key, and this is true for sermons as well: the immediate context of a sermon delivered in a worship service that mentions Jesus Christ in prayers, hymns, ordinances, Scripture readings, etc., as well as the long-term context of the weekly ministry of a preacher to his congregation, where Christ is exalted in counseling, prayer meetings, small group gatherings, discipline, funerals, weddings, etc. Therefore, in preaching, perhaps it is not an absolute essential that every sermon be christocentric, especially if the chosen pericope does not actually point to Christ in that fashion.

Historical Evidence

Hood also argues that historically, expositors have employed "more than a bare Christ-centred approach."[80] Luther was largely responsible for the emphasis on christocentric preaching in the Protestant church. On Rom 10:4, Luther

---

78. Goldsworthy, *Preaching the Whole Bible*, 117.

79. Bryan Chapell, *Christ-Centered Preaching: Redeeming the Expository Sermon* (2nd ed; Grand Rapids: Baker, 2005), 275.

80. Hood, "Christ-Centred Interpretation Only?" 65. Early Judaism clearly employed Scripture for the purposes of moral instruction. "Virtually without exception, Judaism presents a powerful demonstration of Paul's notion that Scripture was written to teach us how to live. . . . In general, therefore, scholars agree that all Jews expected Scripture to supply rules for living" (Brian S. Rosner, "'Written for Us': Paul's View of Scripture," in *A Pathway into the Holy Scripture* [eds. D. Wright and P. Satterthwaite; Grand Rapids: Eerdmans, 1994], 102).

declared that "every word in the Bible points to Christ," and that "the whole Scripture, if one contemplates it inwardly, deals everywhere with Christ."[81] For Luther, Christology blended into christocentric preaching of Scripture, with Christ explicitly found in OT texts and expressly preached in OT sermons. Indeed, the dual nature of Christ was deemed analogous to a similar duality of Scripture: "Scripture is God's word lettered and put into the form of letters just as Christ is the eternal Word of God incarnate in the garment of his humanity."[82] Such an application of the Chalcedonian formula to the Bible naturally inclined him to seeing Christ everywhere in Scripture: "[Christ] is the man to whom it [Scripture] all applies, every bit of it."[83]

Calvin's sermons on the OT, on the other hand, were more *theo*centric than *christo*centric. He did not hesitate to use OT characters as examples for his flock: "[I]t is good for us to have such examples as show unto us how there have been other men as frail as we, who nevertheless have resisted temptations, and continued steadfastly in obedience unto God. . . . Thus have we here [in Job] an excellent mirror" (*Sermons on Job*, on Job 1:1). However, Greidanus excuses Calvin for this apparent neglect of Christology: the Reformer, Greidanus says, understood "God" always as encompassing the three Persons of the Trinity, "[t]herefore, whenever the name of God is mentioned without particularization, there are designated no less the Son and the Spirit than the Father." Thus, Calvin's God-centered sermons are "implicitly Christ-centered." Greidanus plunges on: "Still another reason is probably Calvin's view of expository preaching as limiting the sermon to the text for the day." But most surprising is his final escape clause: "[W]e must remember that in Geneva Calvin preached from the Old Testament in homily style on consecutive verses (*lectio continua*) and usually on consecutive weekdays when committed Christians were in attendance. Thus he may not have thought it necessary to preach Christ explicitly each time."[84] I submit that

---

81. Martin Luther, *Luther: Lectures on Romans* (Library of Christian Classics 15; trans. Wilhelm Pauck; Philadelphia: Westminster, 1961), 288.

82. Martin Luther, *D. Martin Luthers Werke: kritische Gesammtausgabe (Weimarer Ausgabe*; 121 vols.; Weimar: H. Böhlaus Nachfolger, 1883–2009), 48:31 (translation modified from A. Skevington Wood, *Captive to the Word: Martin Luther: Doctor of Sacred Scripture* [London: Paternoster, 1969], 178).

83. Martin Luther, "Prefaces to the Old Testament," in *Luther's Works*, vol. 35 (trans. Charles M. Jacobs; rev. E. Theodore Bachmann; Philadelphia: Muhlenberg, 1960), 247.

84. Greidanus, *Preaching Christ from the Old Testament*, 147–48. Even while excusing Calvin, Greidanus remains unsatisfied with that worthy's homiletical exertions: "[F]rom our perspective Calvin did not sufficiently focus on producing explicitly Christ-centered sermons in the context of the whole of Scripture" (ibid., 149).

these benefits should be extended to modern-day preachers as well, who are no less Trinitarian in their concept of "God," no less focused on a given pericope in each sermon, and no less committed to *lectio continua*.

Apostolic Hermeneutics

According to Mohler, one should preach the cross in every sermon, no matter what the text. "As Charles Spurgeon expressed this so eloquently, preach the Word, place it in its canonical context, and 'make a bee-line to the cross.'"[85] It is often claimed that the pattern of apostolic preaching validates a christocentric approach: the apostles were "consistently preaching the death, burial, and resurrection of Jesus Christ."[86] While this may certainly be true of most (though not all) of the *recorded* sermons available to us in the NT, one should be careful about creating a comprehensive apostolic hermeneutical model out of scant data.[87] The sermons we have in the NT are but few in number, and all of them, without exception, are evangelistic—of course, they *would* be presenting the gospel: "the death, burial, and resurrection of Jesus Christ."[88]

In any case, what is important is not the apostolic hermeneutic *behind* the text, but what is actually *in* the text and what is thereby projected *in front of* the text: what the authors were saying and what they were *doing* with what they were saying—OT citations, allusions, and all. Elements that are behind the text, including hermeneutical methodology, mechanics of revelation (divination, dreams,

---

85. Mohler, *He Is Not Silent*, 21. Spurgeon quotes an "old divine" advising a young preacher: "From every text in Scripture, there is a road to the metropolis of the Scriptures, that is Christ. . . . I have never yet found a text that had not got a road to Christ in it, and if I ever do find one that has not a road to Christ in it, I will make one." See Charles H. Spurgeon, "Christ Precious to Believers," n.p. [cited June 3, 2012]. Online: http://spurgeon.org/sermons/0242.htm. The sermon was delivered on March 13, 1859.

86. Mohler, *He Is Not Silent*, 21.

87. One must also bear in mind that what we have in the NT are unlikely to be verbatim sermons; undoubtedly these were edited by the respective authors to further the Spirit-inspired agendas of their writings. Thus, we are not examining sermons *in toto*, but portions thereof, already raising the potential for skewing our analyses.

88. Presenting the good news of salvation in Jesus Christ is obviously an essential practice for preachers. Whether the benefits of Christ's redemptive work must be enumerated week after week is, in my opinion, a *pragmatic* issue, not a *hermeneutical* one, for the decision must be made on the basis of what one's listeners already know or do not know, or who may be in the listening audience—quite possibly several who do not know Christ as Savior. There is no hermeneutical imperative emerging from each pericope that constrains one to recite redemption history and its glorious benefits in every sermon (unless, of course, the theology of the specific pericope actually demands it). What is hermeneutically constrained in a specific text is the specific guidance for moral living in a specific area of life—how to meet divine demand (by an obedience of faith).

Urim and Thummim, braying of donkeys, casting of lots), scribal material employed (skin and papyrus, quill and ink), form of corpus (codex and scroll), methods of illustration (parabolic material, words of ancient Greek seers), etc., are not inspired and thus not profitable for doctrine, reproof, correction, and instruction in righteousness (2 Tim 3:16–17). And for that matter, neither are the events behind the text; while these may be revelatory, they are not inspired (see chapter 2).[89] What is inspired is the biblical *account* of those events, the final scripted product of those behind-the-text hermeneutical methodologies, revelational mechanics, real-life events, and rhetorical strategies. Therefore, the interpreter must *privilege the text,* not what lies behind it.

Reflecting this, Johnson, even as he calls for adoption of apostolic hermeneutics, seems to be hedging: "In proposing, therefore, that we follow the apostles' hermeneutic lead by interpreting OT passages in the context of Jesus, I am *not* suggesting that we may take the liberty to modify, amplify, or conflate OT passages as they did" (as for instance in Isa 59:20/Rom 11:26; Ps 95:7–11/Heb 3:7–11; Ps 68:18/Eph 4:8, 11; Gen 2:7/1 Cor 15:45; etc.).[90] One wonders why not, for such modification, amplification, and conflation were also integral to the apostles' hermeneutic. Here, Longenecker is better positioned than the RH interpreters, as he emphasizes *what* the apostles taught as they cited the OT (privileging the text), rather than focusing on *how* they cited the OT (a methodological element *behind* the text). "Our commitment as Christians is to the reproduction of the apostolic faith and doctrine, and not necessarily to the specific apostolic exegetical practices."[91] In other words, it is not the method of the authors of Scripture that was inspired, but their actual textual affirmations. It must be noted that "not inspired" does not mean "wrong," or even "right," for that matter. In this formulation, no value is being placed, positive or negative, upon the elements *behind* the text, except that, for preaching purposes, non-inspired elements of the text, details of provenance and production, and matters of style and strategy are not "profitable." And these were not intended to be reproduced in pulpits today.

---

89. This, of course, is not to say that the NT writers were insincere or deceptive in their writings, but that, like the other elements, such events, too, are *behind* the text—antecedent to and preceding it.

90. Dennis E. Johnson, *Him We Proclaim: Preaching Christ from All the Scriptures* (Phillipsburg, N.J.: Presbyterian & Reformed, 2007), 146n21.

91. Richard N. Longenecker, *Biblical Exegesis in the Apostolic Period* (Grand Rapids: Eerdmans, 1975), 219.

Do Biblical Passages Support Christocentric Preaching?

The biblical passages commonly canvassed to support claims for christocentric preaching are: Luke 24:13–27, 44–48; 1 Cor 1:22–23; 2:2; and 2 Cor 4:5.

Luke 24:13–27, 44–48

Mohler's remarks typify the christological tendencies of RH interpreters: "Every single text of Scripture points to Christ. He is the Lord of all, and therefore He is the Lord of the Scriptures too. From Moses to the prophets, He is the focus of every single word of the Bible. Every verse of Scripture finds its fulfillment in Him, and every story in the Bible ends with Him."[92] It is hard to defend a stance that locates Christ in every word, verse, and story, without the interpreter engaging in some hermeneutical acrobatics. Mohler's assertion is in reference to Luke 24:13–27, 44–48, a passage that Clowney calls the "key, one that unlocks the use of the Old Testament by the New."[93] This Lucan text is frequently cited to further christocentric preaching.

Examining that text, one must ask what the extent of "in all the Scriptures" (ἐν πάσαις ταῖς γραφαῖς, *en pasais tais graphais*, 24:27) actually is: Is it every portion of Scripture, or every book, or every pericope, or every paragraph, or every verse, or every jot and tittle? The subsequent statements by Jesus to the Emmaus disciples suggest that what is meant is every *portion* of Scripture—a broad reference to its various parts, primarily the major divisions: Law, Prophets, and Psalms (writings). The parallelism between 24:27 and 44 (and the parallels even within each verse) make this clear.

---

92. Mohler, *He Is Not Silent*, 96.

93. Clowney, "Preaching Christ," 164. And so "[a]ll the Old Testament Scriptures, not merely the few passages that have been recognized as messianic, point us to Christ" (ibid., 166).

24:25		πᾶσιν οἷς ἐλάλησαν οἱ προφῆται **pasin** hois elalēsan hoi prophētai "**all** that the prophets spoke"	
24:27	Μωϋσέως καὶ ἀπὸ πάντων τῶν προφητῶν Mōuseōs kai apo pantōn tōn prophētōn "with Moses and with all the prophets"	=	ἐν πάσαις ταῖς γραφαῖς en **pasais** tais graphais "in **all** the Scriptures"	τὰ περὶ ἑαυτοῦ ta peri heautou "things concerning Himself"
24:44	Μωϋσέως καὶ τοῖς προφήταις καὶ ψαλμοῖς Mōuseōs kai tois prophētais kai psalmois "law of Moses and the prophets and psalms"	=	πάντα τὰ γεγραμμένα **panta** ta gegrammena "**all** that was written"	περὶ ἐμοῦ peri emou "concerning Me"

Thus "Moses and all the prophets" is equated with "all the Scriptures" (24:27); and "law of Moses and the prophets and the Psalms" with "all that was written" (24:44). The two verses balance each other precisely. In addition, "all that the prophets spoke" (24:25) is likely parallel to the corresponding elements in 24:27 and 44, as shown above. All three are linked by πᾶς (*pas*, "all"; see the center column above).[94] Thus "prophets" in 24:25 (i.e., what they spoke) functions as a metonym for all of written Scripture; after all, Israel's Scriptures as a whole were the product of prophetic witness to Yahweh's will.[95] Thus Luke's use of "Moses," "prophets," and "Psalms" indicates that the major portions of Scripture—specific verses therein—are christologically focused, and not that every word, verse, and story is. Dale Ralph Davis expresses a balanced view of this text:

> [T]he whole Old Testament bears witness to Christ; and, the Old Testament does not bear witness only to Christ. . . . I agree with making an *extensive* inference from Luke 24:27 and 44 but hold that an *intensive* inference is illegitimate. . . . I think Jesus is teaching that *all parts* of the Old Testament testify to the Messiah in his suffering and glory, but I do not think Jesus is saying that *every* Old Testament passage/text bears witness to him. Jesus referred to the

---

94. One could also add "Scriptures" in 24:45 (τὰς γραφάς, *tas graphas*) to the other equivalent elements.

95. The fact that the similar phrase, "Moses and the prophets," is found in Luke 16:29–31, in the story of Lazarus and the rich man, hints that Jesus' exposition of the portion of Scripture at Emmaus also dealt with the shared theme of resurrection found in Luke 16 and 24. See also Acts 26:22–23.

things written about him *in* the law of Moses, the prophets, and the psalms—he did not say that every passage spoke of him (v. 44). Therefore, I do not feel compelled to make every Old Testament (narrative) passage point to Christ in some way because I do not think Christ himself requires it.[96]

Indeed, in 24:27, Jesus mentions only those matters from the OT *that actually concern himself* (τὰ περὶ ἑαυτοῦ, *ta peri heautou;* "the things concerning himself"); so also in 24:44 (περὶ ἐμοῦ, *peri emou*, "all things which are written about me"). Thus a selectivity and choice of material is explicit in the text. Jesus is not finding himself in *all the texts* of Scripture, but rather finding *just those texts that concern himself* in all the major divisions of Scripture. What is striking is that Jesus is not recognized by the two Emmaus disciples as a result of a christocentric lecture from the OT, one delivered by the Lord himself. Instead, what sparks recognition is the sharing of a meal (24:30–31)![97]

In any case, explicit messianic promises and adumbrations in the OT are few in number, in relation to the total number of verses in Scripture: Gen 3:15; 12:3; Num 21:9; Deut 18:15 (as Jesus claims in John 5:46—"he [Moses] wrote about me"); and an assortment of other texts, such as Pss 2, 16, 22; Isa 53; etc. Therefore, Jesus' assertion that the Scriptures "testify about me" could not mean that every pericope, paragraph, and verse must be explicitly referring to Christ.

1 Corinthians 1:22–23; 2:2; 2 Corinthians 4:5

It is asserted by those in the RH camp that "[w]hen Paul preached, his message was centered on the cross as the definitive criterion of preaching."[98] As a

---

96. Dale Ralph Davis, *The Word Became Fresh: How to Preach from Old Testament Narrative Texts* (Ross-Shire, U.K.: Mentor, 2006), 134–35.

97. In true Passover meal fashion, Jesus broke the unleavened bread (Luke 24:30); the broken piece was the *afikoman* (אפיקומן, ἀφικόμενος, *aphikomenos,* "he who comes"). While the antecedents of this particular ritual are unclear, the *afikoman* in Jewish tradition possibly represented the Messiah himself—still true of Sephardic and Ashkenazi Seder rituals. See Arvid Nybroten, "Possible Vestiges of the *Afikoman* in the Elevation of the *Panagia,*" *GOTR* 43 (1998): 106, 126n6. In the Synoptic Gospels, as Jesus distributed this symbolic element of the Messiah, he also identified it with his body, virtually claiming that he himself was the Messiah (Matt 26:26; Mark 14:22; Luke 22:19). Such an understanding of Jesus' claim and what he was doing at the Last Supper was prevalent in the early church. The second-century bishop of Sardis, Melito, in his paschal homily, specifically called Jesus the ἀφικόμενος (*Peri Pascha* 66, 86). This messianic significance of bread-breaking thus might very well have been what prompted the instant recognition of Jesus by those disciples at Emmaus at the precise moment he is said to have given them the broken bread (Luke 24:30–31): perhaps he even uttered the same words "This is my body" (= "This is I"). Also see Deborah Bleicher Carmichael, "David Daube on the Eucharist and the Passover Seder," *JSNT* 42 (1991): 59–60.

98. Mohler, *He Is Not Silent,* 43.

matter of fact, Paul himself did not preach Christ in every sermon recorded in Scripture. At least in the one delivered on Mars Hill (Acts 17:22–31, and, perhaps, in his defense in Acts 14:8–18), neither Jesus nor the cross is mentioned.[99] Nevertheless, the apostle's declarations in 1 Cor 1:22–23; 2:2; and 2 Cor 4:5 have often been used to lend credence to christocentric/cruciform interpretation and preaching. On closer examination, however, this credence is found to be misplaced. The context of 1 Cor 1:22–23 is hard to escape: Paul clearly has an evangelistic purpose in mind; the mention of Jews and Greeks in 1:22–23 (and 24) makes this evident.

	ask for	but think they get	when Christ actually is
JEWS	signs	a stumbling block	the power of God[100]
GREEKS	wisdom	foolishness	the wisdom of God

Just prior, in 1:21, Paul had stated that "God was well-pleased through the foolishness of the message preached to save those who believe [πιστεύω, pisteuō]"—obviously an evangelistic goal.[101] So, too, in 1 Cor 2:2, when Paul asserts that he "decided to know nothing among you except Jesus Christ, and him crucified." Here he appears to be reminiscing about his earlier visit to Corinth (2:1), the occasion of the establishment of that local church; and 3:10–11 mentions the laying of the church's foundation by Paul.[102] Here also, the thrust is on his preaching for the conversion of non-Christian Corinthians. It was in the service of this goal of conversion that Paul announced divine wisdom employing divine power. Both "power of God" and "wisdom of God" in 2:5–7 are carryovers from 1 Cor 1:22–24, linking the units and the evangelistic themes and purposes they share.[103]

Likewise, regarding 2 Cor 4:5, it seems that Paul's declaration "we do not

---

99. Again, the same cautions mentioned earlier apply: what is biblically inscribed are edited snippets of sermons, making the derivation of hermeneutical and homiletical methodologies tenuous, at best.

100. "Signs" are often associated with power: Acts 6:8; Rom 15:19; 2 Thess 2:9.

101. Acts 5:42–6:1, that describes the disciples "teaching and preaching Jesus as the Christ," is also clearly evangelistic, as evidenced by the context of Pentecost, the increase in the number of disciples, etc.

102. Raymond Pickett, *The Cross in Corinth: The Social Significance of the Death of Jesus* (JSNTSup 143; Sheffield: Sheffield Academic Press, 1997), 69, 74.

103. Ephesians 3:8 also makes clear this evangelistic mandate of the apostle: Paul was preaching the "riches of Christ" to the Gentiles to move them to salvific faith.

252 PRIVILEGE THE TEXT!

proclaim ourselves but Christ Jesus as Lord" is also evangelistic, harking back to the days when the church in Corinth was being established. Note the references to the gospel being veiled to those who are perishing (4:3), and to the blinding of unbelievers' eyes by "the god of this world" so that they fail to see the light (4:4), as well as the repetition of the darkness/light theme in 4:6. There is also the theme of "weakness" in 2 Cor 4 that parallels the similar motif in 1 Cor 1:18–2:5: the powerlessness of the messenger. "We have this treasure in earthen vessels, that the extraordinary power may be of God and not from ourselves" (2 Cor 4:7), and this declaration is followed by a litany of Paul's ministry-related woes (4:8–18). The general point of the discussion in 2 Cor is, of course, the vindication of the apostle's ministry; 2 Cor 4 is part of that argument, referring the readers to the credentials of his evangelistic ministry amongst them and also to others.[104]

In a nutshell, the biblical arguments for christocentric preaching are weak. Before proposing a new hermeneutic for seeing Christ in Scripture, the priority of divine demand and the responsibility of human obedience must be established, for these form the foundation of the christiconic interpretation to be described.

Divine Demand and Human Obedience

This work holds that every pericope of Scripture bears an implicit divine demand, and that the children of God are to fulfill their filial responsibility to God by meeting that demand. To be sure, this obedience is grounded upon the grace of God, the forgiveness of Christ, and the power of the Holy Spirit. That, however, does not diminish the force of the imperative of Scripture that his people be holy, even as God himself is holy.

---

104. In light of 1 Cor 1:22–23 and 2:2, RH interpreters often advance the thesis that christocentric sermons serve to distinguish Christian sermons from "synagogue sermons": "Preaching Christ from the OT means that we preach, not synagogue sermons, but sermons that take account of the full drama of redemption, and its realization in Christ" (Clowney, *Preaching Christ*, 11; so also Greidanus, *The Modern Preacher*, 220). To follow this advice would mean that in one's brief (30 minutes or so) homiletical exercise each Sunday, the preacher must carefully distinguish that sermon from every potential non-Christian exposition of the Bible. But a sermon is not the place for apologetics week after week, not when there is an abundance of pericopal theology that needs to be—that *must be*—preached to the people of God so that lives may be changed in specific ways for the glory of God. Ott put it well about half a century ago: "We ought to feel uneasy about those critics who declare that they 'miss' references to the 'cross' or the 'resurrection' in some particular sermon. . . . As though it were [the preacher's] duty at any and every cost to push into his sermon every article of Christian doctrine!" (Heinrich Ott, *Theology and Preaching* [trans. Harold Knight; Philadelphia: Westminster, 1965], 27).

Value of Obedience

Johnson asserts that "[t]he purpose of Old Testament historical narrative is not to teach moral lessons, but to trace the work of God, the Savior of his people, whose redeeming presence among them reaches its climactic expression in Christ's incarnation."[105] If the purpose of the OT is only informational and historical, "to trace the work of God," is there nothing in it that tells us what God wants of us, how God would have us live, what it means to be Christlike in specific facets of life?

Redemptive-historical interpreters generally believe that "to teach that there is merit in obedience is ungracious. . . . To imply there is merit in moral behavior is against the Scriptures."[106] Of course there *is some* merit in obedience—though certainly not salvific merit. Surely God takes pleasure in the obedience of his children, and surely there are benefits that accrue from his pleasure, even if the obedience is a consequence of God's own gracious operation in those believers.[107] Indeed, Col 1:10 encourages the believer to "live worthily of the Lord, to please him in all respects, bearing fruit in every good deed." Take, for instance, the blessing of God's love: though God loves all of his children fully, perfectly, completely, and unconditionally, all of the time, the believer's *experience* of that love is conditional and one can remove oneself from that experience of blessedness, a contingency the author of Jude was fully aware of, as he exhorted Christians: "Keep yourselves in the love of God" (Jude 21).[108] Jesus himself declared, "If you keep my commandments, you will abide in my love; just as I have kept my Father's commandments, and abide in his love" (John 15:10; also see 1 John 2:5; 4:12). Walking in fellowship with the Father is urged upon the child of God, and that in itself brings blessings. I would, therefore, assert that there is much to be gained by obedience—not salvation, but the enjoyment of a filial relationship with God,

---

105. Johnson, *Him We Proclaim*, 50–51.

106. Bryan Chapell, "Application without Moralism: How to Show the Relevance of the Text," 3, cited June 3, 2012. Online: http://www.preachingtoday.com/skills/themes/application/200203.25.html?start=3. The essay has a total of 7 pages, and the different pages may be accessed by altering the last digit of the hyperlink; what is provided is the link to page 3.

107. Both divine sovereignty and human responsibility operate in sanctification, and one must simply accept the biblical tension.

108. The self-removal from the experience of divine love warned by Jude is not loss of salvation, but departure from the sphere of divine blessedness in sanctification. Chapell does admit that "there are blessed consequences to moral behavior," and that "[l]oving service offered in Christ to God in response to his mercies . . . pleases him" (*Christ-Centered Preaching*, 315).

innumerable blessings here, and eternal blessings of rewards in the hereafter.

Incentives Now

"'Ye shall therefore keep my statutes and my ordinances which if a man do, he shall live by them' [Lev 18:5], which means that one who desists from transgressing is granted reward like one who performs a precept," declares the Mishnah, and such a one "acquire[s] merit for himself and for generations and generations to come, to the end of all generations" (*m. Mak.* 3.15). However, there is a general aversion to acknowledging temporal blessings from the hand of God for obedience; perhaps it is a fear that such inclinations may lead to abuses of the kind widely on display in the mercenary teachings of those who peddle Jesus Christ, guaranteeing ample gain (mostly financial) for their listeners (and for themselves). That fear, though valid, should not preclude the believer from acknowledging the promises of God. Blessings and rewards (and the corollary, chastisement and discipline) are valid motivators of behavior and lifestyle. The Bible is clear, in all of its various parts, that the one who walks with God is blessed—and not just in eternity (Prov 3:1–12): for instance, the promises of peace (in Rom 8:6; 2 Cor 13:11; Gal 6:16; Phil 4:6–7) are fulfilled when the child of God adopts certain kinds of behaviors. Any positive consequence from any divinely prescribed behavior is, in the end, an act of grace—hence, "blessing."

The number of Paul's hortatory greetings and benedictions, that God may grant his readers grace, mercy, and peace, suggest that these blessings were not automatic, but contingent upon godliness.[109] Now the shape such blessings might take, and what species they might be—that is entirely the prerogative of God: they may be physical, emotional, spiritual. . . . About the *kind* of blessing for obedience we must confess ignorance, but the *fact* of blessing for obedience cannot be disputed; it is guaranteed by Scripture.[110] Calvin argues that part of the reward from God in this age includes the fact that the believer's works, though "not estimated by their own worth, He, by his fatherly kindness and indulgence, honors, so far as to give them some degree of value." Moreover, God overlooks "the imperfection by which they are all polluted"—another form of his gracious

---

109. See Rom 1:7; 1 Cor 1:3; 2 Cor 1:2; Gal 1:3; Eph 1:2; Phil 1:2; Col 1:2; 1 Thess 1:1; 2 Thess 3:16; 1 Tim 1:2; 2 Tim 1:2; Titus 1:4; Phlm 3; 1 Pet 1:2; 2 Pet 1:2; 2 John 3; 3 John 15; Jude 2; Rev 1:4.

110. See Deut 4:4, 29–31, 40; 5:16, 29, 33; 6:3, 10–12, 18, 24; 11:8–15, 18–25; 12:28; 16:19–20; 28:1–14; 30:1–10, 15–16, 20; 32:46–47; etc. The Psalter and Wisdom literature abound in these promises as well: Pss 1, 23, 37, 41, 91, 112, 128; Prov 2:1–12; 3:1–12; etc. Neither is the NT lax in recounting such guarantees: Matt 6:31–33; 7:24–27; 11:28–30; Mark 8:14–21; 10:29–30; John 14:21; 15:5, 10; 2 Cor 9:6–15; Eph 6:1–3; 1 Tim 5:17–18; Titus 3:8; Jas 5:13–18; 1 Pet 3:1–2; 1 John 3:21–24; etc.

reward (Calvin, *Institutes* 3.17.3). God's blessings are, indeed, manifold, and he does not—thankfully—deal with his children in proportion to their deeds or misdeeds, which in itself is blessing divine. Thus, God's blessings are never earned, in the sense of contractual recompense, but are always the result of his grace that includes the empowerment of his children by the Spirit for obedience (see chapter 3); rewards are bestowed upon those who walk with him.[111]

It must also be readily admitted that what is promised to the believer in this age is a paradoxical combination of suffering and blessing. Mark 10:29–30 has Jesus explicitly promising his followers: "[T]here is no one who has left house or brothers or sisters or mother or father or children or farms for my sake and for the sake of the gospel who will not receive hundredfold now in this age—houses and brothers and sisters and mothers and children and fields, *with persecutions*— and in the age to come, eternal life." Perhaps 2 Cor 12:10 explains this paradox: in any situation, the grace of God transcends the "momentary light affliction" (2 Cor 4:17), and this blessing of grace is sufficient for every circumstance, however dire it may be: that, too, is a reward for faithful obedience. Joseph's story provides a shining example. At either end of Gen 39, the account is explicit about Yahweh being with that young man, blessing him and the household and jail he was living in (39:1–5, 21–23). The terms used to describe Joseph's blessings are parallel at either end of this chapter, emphasizing that no matter how perilous, dark, and hopeless the situation, for the child of God, God's blessings would come through—in some shape, form, or fashion—even in, with, and through the desperate and agonizing conditions of tribulation. On the other hand, if one believes there are no blessings at all that the believer obtains from God in this life, whither thanksgiving for daily mercies/blessings so abundant, so rich, and so free? The basis for gratitude, moment by moment and hour by hour, for each and every one of God's innumerable blessings, is thereby eliminated.

After warning us that there is no merit in obedience, Chapell issues another admonition: "[T]o teach that God rejects for disobedience is ungracious."[112] To be sure, for the child of God who has placed his/her trust in Christ and his atoning work, there will never be the rejection of eternal condemnnation (Rom

---

111. As has been noted earlier, obedience is, after all, a response to what God has *already* done for his people: relationship precedes responsibility. See Deut 11:1—"You shall *therefore* [i.e., because of God's redemption of his people, 10:22] love the Lord your God, and always keep his charge, his statutes, his ordinances, and his commandments."

112. Chapell, "Application without Moralism," 3.

8:1). But *some* kind of "rejection" there must be, for there *are* consequences, even for—and perhaps, particularly for—the child of God: divine discipline.[113] All this, notwithstanding the fact that God is a forgiving God. That he shows mercy upon his prodigal children does not obviate his disciplinary actions.[114] The Bible is replete with warnings for disobedience (again, this is not loss of salvation). Such discipline for believers can take the form of disease or even death (1 Cor 3:17; 5:5; 11:27–30, 32; 1 John 5:16). One also notes that there could be a forfeiture of rewards on the part of those already believers, though not a loss of salvation: 1 Cor 3:15; 10:4–5. First John 2:28 warns delinquent believers of being shamed in the presence of Christ at his coming, likely due to a loss of reward and acclamation from the Savior.

Rewards Later

It is not surprising that the Reformers had a fear of the idea of eternal rewards for obedience; after all, they had been striving to overcome the misunderstanding of salvation by works, laboring to avoid the connotations of humanly achieved righteousness. Kuyper observes wisely: "Lest Rome's earning of good works enter by the back door, . . . the promised rewards are suffered to lie in deathly silence, and no small portion of the stimulus to godliness—given us by the Scriptures in the rich and manifold promises of reward—is blunted."[115] Following the Reformers, since the eighteenth century, the concept of rewards has been largely neglected by Protestants also. The problem apparently was that in the Reformers' thinking, "reward" was equated solely with "eternal life" and little else, which

---

113. This negative counterpart of blessing, God's discipline and chastisement of his children when they fail to walk with him, is also promised in Scripture: in the OT, in Deut 1:31–36; 4:23–28; 5:11; 6:14–15; 7:9–10; 8:19–20; 11:16–17, 26–32; 27:12–26; 28:15–68; 30:17–18; 31:15–32:43; etc.; and in the NT, in 1 Cor 5:1–13; Gal 6:7; 1 Tim 6:9–10; Titus 3:9; Heb 12:5–11 (quoting Prov 3:11–12; also see Prov 15:5), 15–17; 13:17; 1 Pet 3:7; 4:17–19; Rev 2:5; 3:19; etc.

114. But there is a gross disproportionality: God does not discipline me for every sin that I commit, or at least, punish me to the extent I deserve. Even this is grace!

115. Abraham Kuyper, *E voto dordraceno: Toelichting op den Heidelbergschen Catechismus* (4 vols.; Amsterdam: J. A. Wormser, 1892–1895), 2:377 (my translation from the Dutch). Of the coming judgment of believers for rewards, the Bible is clear: Matt 6:1–4; Rom 14:10–12; 1 Cor 3:13; 4:5; 9:24; 2 Cor 5:10; Col 3:22–25; 2 Tim 2:5; Jas 5:7–11; 1 John 2:28. The actual content of the rewards is uncertain, though it is possible that it involves the privilege of ruling with Christ: Ps 2:8–9 and Rev 2:26; 3:21; 1 Cor 6:2; Col 3:23–24; 2 Tim 2:12. "Treasure" in heaven is mentioned in Matt 6:1–4, 16, 19–21; 19:21, 29; 25:21; Luke 12:32–33; 1 Cor 4:5; 1 Tim 6:17–19; 1 Pet 1:6–7; 2 Pet 1:10–11; as also are "crowns": 1 Cor 9:25–27; Phil 4:1; 1 Thess 2:19; 2 Tim 4:6–8; Jas 1:12; 1 Pet 5:1–4; Rev 2:10. There are also likely to be degrees of such rewards commensurate with degrees of faithful obedience demonstrated by the child of God: Matt 25:20–25; 1 Cor 3:12–15.

rendered obedience leading to "reward" (= eternal life) untenable. While eternal life is certainly a gracious reward contingent upon faith, the biblical evidence points to the innumerable blessings of God, both now and later, for his children, many of them contingent upon a walk with God, the "obedience of faith" (chapter 3).[116]

It is also likely that the Reformers construed merit in a legal sense, the gaining of which was supposed to put God under obligation to dole out corresponding rewards. But of this concept of deserved merit, the Bible knows nothing. Matthew 20:1–16, with the parable of the vineyard workers, points out that there is no mathematical or contractual tendering of rewards (or discipline for misdeeds) from God's side. Rather, the reward is entirely a matter of God's love and grace (and his discipline, a matter of his justice and mercy), completely up to his own sovereign purpose, and absolutely his alone to offer according to his divine prerogatives.[117] There is no question that these blessings of obedience, the products of God's grace now and in eternity, are not commensurate with the deeds of the child of God. This grace is overwhelming, and disproportionately magnificent compared to the feeble obedience his children exhibit; it is this disproportionality that makes it *all* grace. And therein lies the genius of Luke 17:10: the blessings that abound as a result of obedience are clearly not deserved, as in creating a forensic obligation upon God. Neither can they be deserved when it is God's grace through his Spirit that empowers the child of God to obey in the first place. Yet, that should not neutralize the fact that God's pleasure in the faithful obedience of his children is visited upon them, just as his displeasure is, for disobedience. The Scriptures assert that faithfulness is a duty owed to God by his people. As such, then, faithfulness is not contractually reimbursed by reward, but God in his sovereign grace, who chose to empower such faithfulness, also chooses to reward it.[118]

In this context, 2 Pet 1:5–11 is enlightening. Peter exhorts the saints to ap-

---

116. For the "blessing" of salvation from eternal damnation, the only "obedience"/"work" is to believe in Christ as Savior (John 6:29; Eph 2:8–9 distinguishes faith from works). But for the blessing of abundant life now, and rewards in eternity, perseverance towards Christlikeness is called for (2 Cor 5:10). See Joseph C. Dillow, *The Reign of the Servant Kings: A Study of Eternal Security and the Final Significance of Man* (Hayesville, N.C.: Schoettle, 1992), 43–110, 135–45, for an excellent accounting of the OT and NT concepts of "inheritance" and "rewards."

117. Ibid., 529–30.

118. Also see Matt 24:45; 25:23; 1 Cor 4:2; and Rev 2:10, which endorse the faithfulness of the believer as a criterion for rewards.

ply all diligence and "supply" (ἐπιχορηγέω, *epichorēgeō*, 1:5) moral excellence, knowledge, self-control, perseverance, godliness, brotherly kindness and love" (1:5–7)—i.e., faithful obedience. In reward, God promises that entrance into the eternal kingdom of Christ will be richly "supplied" (also ἐπιχορηγέω, 1:11) to them. In light of Peter's address to those who are already believers, this is, no doubt, a reference to rewards that will be "supplied" to the faithfully obedient, "if these [the qualities listed in 1:5–7] are yours and are increasing" (1:8), i.e., if they are "supplied" by the believer. Thus the supply of obedience by the believer is reciprocated by the supply of reward by God. The verses preceding this section, 1:3–4, make it clear that faithful obedience is empowered by God's grace: "His divine power has bestowed on us everything pertaining to life and godliness." Even the goal for this gracious empowerment to obedience and godliness is noted—"that you might become partakers of the divine nature," conformed to the image of Christ (1:4). Indeed, this was what man was created for (see below).

Summary: Divine Demand and Human Obedience

Scripture seems clear about the fact that God offers incentives for obedience—positive (rewards/blessings) and negative (discipline/loss of blessings). Preaching, while based upon, and fully cognizant of, the sovereign work of God in sanctification, should not neglect human responsibility and the believer's filial duty of faithful obedience unto God. Rather, preaching serves to bring the children of God into alignment with the divine demands of the sermonic text. And in being so aligned, they inhabit God's ideal world, living by its precepts, priorities, and practices—practical (progressive) sanctification. On the other hand, to assert that God's delight is entirely contingent upon positional sanctification is dangerous, for then it also implies that ongoing sin in the life of the believer does not cause God any displeasure. Preachers must take Paul's words to heart: "We have not ceased praying for you and asking that you may be filled with the knowledge of his will . . . , so that you may live worthily of the Lord, to please him in all respects, bearing fruit in every good deed, and growing in the knowledge of God" (Col 1:9–10). As the specifics of the pericope are attended to and preached weekly, with its divine demand being brought home to the audience, lives of listeners are being changed so that, by the gracious operation and empowerment of the Holy Spirit, fruit is borne and God is pleased as they become more Christlike. To this issue of becoming more Christlike we will now turn our attention, and on that final note this work will conclude.

Christiconic Interpretation

Bryan Chapell emphasizes the "Fallen Condition Focus" of every text of Scripture—"the mutual human condition that contemporary believers share with those to or about whom the text was written that requires the grace of the passage for God's people to glorify and enjoy him."[119] He suggests that this focus of any biblical pericope be the driving thrust for a sermon on that text. Thus the burden of the expositor is to discern this "Fallen Condition Focus" in every text preached—essentially a corrective approach. Yes, humankind *is* indeed fallen and in need of correction. But divine demand, as seen in this work, transcends the fallen state of humanity: for instance, Adam and Eve, pre-fall, were subject to divine demand (Gen 1:16–17, 28–30); the divine demand for praise is one that even unfallen beings have to obey (Ps 148:2; Isa 6:1–3), just as restored humanity will one day do (Rev 4:8–11; 5:9–14); likewise, angels serve and obey God (Ps 103:20–21), and redeemed humans will do so as well in the New Jerusalem (Rev 22:2). Thus not every divine demand is a reflection of the "Fallen Condition." Divine demand in Scripture will need to be met even in the sinless, unfallen environment of heaven, for divine demand is the call of God for his people to align themselves with the precepts, priorities, and practices of his ideal world. So while it is appropriate to consider each biblical text as addressing a facet of the incompleteness of mankind and its falling short of divine glory, this work suggests that there is a better way to understand what biblical pericopes are doing: each pericope is portraying, not merely a sin-influenced *failure* on the part of mankind, but what it means to *fulfill* a divine demand. In other words, the text does not point out a sinful depletion; it indicates what a sinless repletion looks like. This section expands the argument that the text displays not just the *failure of man*, but the *fulfillment by Man* of divine demand.

Jesus Christ and Divine Demand

Since only one Man, the Lord Jesus Christ, perfectly met all of God's demands,

---

119. *Christ-Centered Preaching*, 50.

120. Satan was unsuccessful in tempting Christ to sin (Matt 4:1–11), and Jesus claimed to be doing, always, what pleased the Father (John 8:29; 15:10). To Christ's question, "Which one of you convicts me of sin?" there was no response (John 8:46). Even Pilate assessed him not guilty (John 18:38). Also see Acts 2:27; 3:14; etc., where Christ is referred to as the "Holy One"; as well, Rom 8:3; 1 Pet 1:19; 2:22; 1 John 2:1; 3:5.

260 PRIVILEGE THE TEXT!

being without sin (2 Cor 5:21; Heb 4:15; 7:26[120]), one may say that each pericope of the Bible is actually portraying a facet of Christlikeness, a segment of the image of Christ: what it means to fulfill the particular divine demand in that pericope after the manner of Christ. Thus, fulfilling that divine demand is part of what it means to be Christlike, and the Bible as a whole, the plenary collection of all its pericopes, canonically portrays the perfect humanity exemplified by Jesus Christ, God incarnate. So much so, the *world in front of the text* may even be considered to be an "image" (εἰκών, *eikōn*) of Christ, portraying the impeccable Man, the only One who has fully met divine demand, the only One who has completely inhabited the ideal world of God, being perfectly aligned with its precepts, priorities, and practices.

Now we can make a conceptual addition to the intermediate element in the triadic scheme of "facets of meaning" that was introduced in chapter 1 and further developed in chapter 2. The plenary *world in front of the text* (the synthesis of all the world segments projected by individual pericopes) or the integration of the theologies of the various pericopes of Scripture is, in effect, a composite image of Christ. Each pericope, then, portrays an aspect of that image, a facet of Christlikeness.[121] Thus, in fulfilling the divine demand, text by text, a believer becomes progressively more Christlike as the divine demands of pericopes are sequentially met. Such a reading of the text that sees each pericope as projecting facets of Christlikeness I call *christiconic* interpretation.

FACETS OF MEANING		
Original Textual Sense	World in Front of the Text Pericopal Theology Image of Christ	Exemplification

God's design for his children is that they look like his Son Jesus Christ in his humanity (Rom 8:29; 2 Cor 3:18; Eph 3:19; 4:13–16; Col 1:28; etc.). That is God's ultimate plan for mankind: Rom 8:29 describes the final state of the predestined child of God—"to be conformed to the image [εἰκών] of his Son."[122] Philo was

---

121. The depiction of Christlikeness in every pericope is not a backdoor admittance of a christocentric hermeneutic, for it is not an *explicit* depiction of Christ that is being discovered in the pericope, but rather an *implicit* one—the image (εἰκών) of Christ.

122. "He [Christ] it is who is the spotless image. We must try, then, to resemble Him in spirit as far as we are able . . . to be as sinless as we can. There is nothing more important for us than first to be rid of sin and weakness and then to uproot any habitual sinful inclination" (Clement of Alexandria, *Paed.* 1.2).

on the right track: "[T]he proper end [τέλος]" of man's existence is "conformation to the likeness of God [θεὸν ἐξομοίωσιν, *theon exomoiōsin*]" (*Opif.* 144). This is likely to be a process that begins with conversion and extends into the eschaton: a "growing conformity to Christ here and now" of believers, as well as their final glorification.[123] Christ himself is the image (εἰκών) of the Father (2 Cor 4:4) as John 14:9 also implies: "By means of this image the Lord showed Philip the Father. . . . Yes, he who looks upon the Son sees, in portrait, the Father" (Ambrose, *Exposition on the Christian Faith* 1.7.50; also see Col 1:15 and Heb 1:3). Since Christ, the Son, is the image of the Father, the end-point of Rom 8:29 is the progressive conformation of believers to the likeness of God.

God's goal is to restore the *imago Dei* in man that was his at creation, but was defaced in the fall (Gen 1:26–27; 9:6; Matt 22:20 and parallels; 1 Cor 11:7; Jas 3:9), so that, finally, mankind may "share his holiness" (Heb 12:10). "Paul says that we are transformed into the image of God by the gospel. And, according to him, spiritual regeneration is nothing else than the restoration of the same image" (Calvin, *Commentary on Genesis* 1:26).[124] Hughes notes that by faith, upon justification, the divine image is freely *imputed* to the believer. Through the operation of the Holy Spirit, in sanctification, that image is increasingly *imparted* to him or her. Extending Hughes's alliteration, I might add that finally, in glorification, the image is *impressed* upon the Christian "in unobscured fulness, to the glory of God throughout eternity."[125] Therefore, as far as sanctification is concerned, the NT unhesitatingly points to Jesus as a model: Matt 9:9; 10:38; 11:29; 20:26–28; John 13:15; Rom 15:1–3, 7; 1 Thess 1:6; Eph 5:2; Phil 2:5; 1 Pet

---

123. C. E. B. Cranfield, *The Epistle to the Romans* (International Critical Commentary, 2 vols.; Edinburgh: T. & T. Clark, 1979), 1:432. So also Joseph A. Fitzmyer, *Romans: A New Translation with Introduction and Commentary* (Anchor Bible 33; New York: Doubleday, 1993), 525, who asserts that Christians are "continually transformed or metamorphosed" into the image of Christ. As Jewett notes, "Christ's destiny [is] to restore the image of God to a fallen human race" (Robert Jewett, *Romans: A Commentary* [Minneapolis: Fortress, 2007], 529–30). The conformation of man to the likeness of Christ in the eschaton is explicitly noted in Phil 3:21; 1 John 3:2; etc.

124. In fact, to be conformed to the image of Christ is a grander outcome that transcends the situation antecedent to the fall: from "being able not to die" (*posse non mori*; in the image of Adam) to "not being able to die" (*non posse mori*; in the image of Christ). This also reflects the transformation from "being able not to sin" (*posse non peccare*; characteristic of the image of Adam) to "not being able to sin" (*non posse peccare*; characteristic of the image of Christ). See Peter Lombard, *The Four Books of Sentences*, 2.19.1; Augustine, *Corrept.* 33.

125. Philip Edgcumbe Hughes, *Paul's Second Epistle to the Corinthians* (NICNT; Grand Rapids: Eerdmans, 1962), 120.

126. However, this is not to claim that Jesus is *only* a model, an εἰκών. It is because he is incarnate God and the Savior of mankind that he can be, among other things, a model to this race.

2:21–3:7; 1 John 2:6; 3:16; etc.[126] Interpreting biblical pericopes in this fashion, to discern the divine demand that moves God's people closer to Christlikeness and the εἰκών of God's Son, is the essence of christiconic interpretation.

In sum, 2 Tim 3:16–17 asserts that "all Scripture is profitable" to render every person mature (i.e., Christlike); thus, every preaching text (pericope) irrespective of size bears a divine demand that must be met by a child of God. Only the Man, Jesus Christ, is perfectly "adequate" (ἄρτιος, *artios,* 3:17, positioned in the beginning of its clause for emphasis), completely meeting all the demands of God, in "all Scripture" (3:16). Because he completely fulfilled the Father's will, he is the prototype of the perfect Man, the firstborn. This is the crux of christiconic interpretation: in that he perfectly fulfilled divine demand, every pericope of Scripture implicitly portrays a facet of the image (εἰκών) of Christ, the perfect Man. Thus every pericope of Scripture enjoins Christlikeness, pericope by pericope, facet by facet, "until we all attain to the unity of the faith, and of the knowledge of the Son of God, to a mature man, to the measure of the stature of the fullness of Christ" (Eph 4:13).[127] This is part of what it means to become "partakers of the divine nature" (2 Pet 1:4), a privilege that is consummated in the eschaton. In this life, however, as one progressively conforms to divine demand, pericope by pericope, one gradually becomes more Christlike. This is the purpose of preaching: "We proclaim Him, admonishing every man and teaching every man with all wisdom, so that we may present every man complete in Christ" (Col 1:28).

1 Corinthians 15:49

First Corinthians 15:49 exhorts: "Just as we have borne the image of the earthy, let us also bear the image of the heavenly." Chrysostom takes this bearing of the "image of the earthy" as the doing of evil, and the corresponding bearing of the "image of the heavenly" as the practicing of "all goodness." He claims this is not a matter of future essence or nature as much as it is of current behavior: "Whereas if he were speaking of nature, the thing needed not exhortation nor advice. So that hence also it is evident that the expression relates to our manner

---

127. This behooves the preacher to select, weekly, a portion of biblical text that points to a "bite-sized" facet of Christlikeness; irrespective of size, that slice of Scripture becomes the "pericope" of focus in that sermon. In other words, a pericope is fundamentally any portion of Scripture that bears a divine demand; that demand, having been met by Christ, portrays a facet of his perfect image and points to what it means to be Christlike.

of life" (*Hom. 1 Cor.* 42.2). Such a transformation of the "manner of life" is the process of practical sanctification in this life: "We are to become like Christ . . . which . . . means sanctification. It is God's plan that his people become like his Son, not that they should muddle along in a modest respectability."[128]

Once again, this should not be misunderstood as a sort of lifting up of one-self by one's own bootstraps. Not at all! The gradual conformation to the image of Christ in this life (and the ultimate conformation in the next) is a matter of God's grace—notwithstanding the critical component of human responsibility—and is aided by the indwelling Holy Spirit. The new self that is being renewed according to the image of Christ (Col 3:10) indicates that "Christlikeness is being reproduced more and more in the believer's life"—an ongoing process.[129] This is akin to "putting on Christ" (Rom 13:14), with the "manner of Christ's living" being the pattern for this new life (Col 2:6–15).[130]

2 Corinthians 3:18

Second Corinthians 3:18 declares that "we all . . . beholding as in a mirror the glory of the Lord, are being transformed [μεταμορφούμεθα, *metamorphou-*

---

128. Leon Morris, *The Epistle to the Romans* (Grand Rapids: Eerdmans, 1988), 333. The mood of the verb "bear" in 1 Cor 15:49 is a debated issue: the hortatory aorist subjunctive, φορέσωμεν, *phoresōmen*, "let us bear," is found in 𝔓⁴⁶ ℵ A C D F G Ψ 075 0243 33 1739 𝔐 latt bo and in Clement, Origen, Chrysostom, Epiphanius, Irenaeus [lat], Clement of Alexandria, Gregory of Nyssa, Cyprian, and Jerome—an extremely significant array of witnesses. So also Tertullian (*Marc.* 5.10): "He [Paul] says, *Let us bear*, as a precept; not *We shall bear*, in the sense of a promise—wishing us to walk even as he himself was walking, and to put off the likeness of the earthly, that is, of the old man, in the works of the flesh." The UBS GNT⁴ prefers the future indicative, φορέσομεν, *phoresomen*, "we shall bear" (attested in B I 6 63 9450 1881 *al* sa and in Gregory Nazianzus—a more geographically narrow distribution). According to Fee, "the UBS committee abandoned its better text-critical sense here"! See Gordon D. Fee, *The First Epistle to the Corinthians* (Grand Rapids: Eerdmans, 1987), 787n5. Collins notes that rhetorically, Paul concludes each of his proofs and his perorations in 1 Cor 15 with an exhortation (15:34, 49, and 58); he too, therefore, prefers the subjunctive (Raymond F. Collins, *First Corinthians* [Sacra Pagina 7; Collegeville, Minn.: Liturgical, 1999], 572). In any case, even if the future indicative is meant in 1 Cor 15:49, it is certainly a process that commences this side of the final resurrection. "The process that begins in this life comes to its final consummation at the moment of the resurrection when our bodies experience their complete transformation and the rest of our ultimate transformation is also achieved" (Roy E. Ciampa and Brian S. Rosner, *The First Letter to the Corinthians* [Pillar NTC; Grand Rapids: Eerdmans, 2010], 825). And Schreiner: "The transformation into the image thus begins in this age . . . but is completed and consummated at the resurrection" (Thomas R. Schreiner, *Romans* [BECNT; Grand Rapids: Baker, 1998], 453).

129. F. F. Bruce, *The Epistles to the Colossians, to Philemon, and to the Ephesians* (NICNT; Grand Rapids: Eerdmans, 1984), 146.

130. James D. G. Dunn, *The Epistles to the Colossians and to Philemon: A Commentary on the Greek Text* (NIGTC; Grand Rapids: Eerdmans, 1996), 221.

metha, present passive indicative] into the same image from glory to glory, just as from the Lord, the Spirit."[131] That this is an act of "the Lord, the Spirit" is explicitly stated. And it is another way of stating that "Christ is formed [μορφωθῇ, *morphōthē*]" in the believer (Gal 4:19). Thus there is both a present and future aspect to this transformation. As Bruce declared, on Rom 8:30, "[s]anctification is glory begun; glory is sanctification completed."[132] The present phase is clearly not an instantaneous transformation, but a gradual one, empowered and enabled by the Holy Spirit ("the Lord, the Spirit"). Even this role of the Holy Spirit has its ground in the redeeming work of the Second Person of the Trinity. Part of what has been accomplished by Christ's work on our behalf is the forgiveness of sin: "There is therefore no condemnation to those who are in Christ Jesus" (Rom 8:1), i.e., for those who have placed their trust in him as their only God and Savior, the issue of eternal life is not contingent upon keeping divine demands—salvation is not by works (Eph 2:8-9; Titus 3:5-7). Moreover, because of Christ's completed work of atonement, the Holy Spirit can now indwell every believer (Jesus is the sender of the Spirit: John 14:16; 15:26; 16:7), enabling him/her to live in obedience, empowering the Christian to walk with God in a manner pleasing to him, day by day (and pericope by pericope) conforming him/her into the image of Christ (e.g., Rom 8:29). Or to use another metaphor, pericope by pericope, God is graciously inviting mankind to live by his demand (2 Tim 3:16-17)—i.e., to live in the *world in front of the text,* aligning oneself to the precepts, priorities, and practices of God's ideal world.

Preaching and the Image of Christ

"It is the destination of all the children of God 'to be conformed to him'" (Cal-

---

131. The only other uses of μεταμορφόω, *metamorphoō* ("change"), in the NT are in the accounts of Jesus' transfiguration (Matt 17:2; Mark 9:2) and in Paul's appeal to believers to be transformed in accordance with the moral will of God (Rom 12:2). "The heavenly glory with which He was then transfigured is the heavenly glory with which those who are His are even now being progressively transfigured" (Hughes, *Paul's Second Epistle to the Corinthians,* 118n18). "The phrase ἀπὸ δόξης εἰς δόξαν [*apo doxēs eis doxan*] is idiomatic for a glory 'seen' initially in the world, within history, in and through the gospel, in relationship with that 'glory' which will be revealed eschatologically and which will be infinite and eternal" (Paul Barnett, *The Second Epistle to the Corinthians* [NIGTC; Grand Rapids: Eerdmans, 1997], 208n52). While the NAS, KJV, and NKJV have "from glory to glory," the NIV and REB have "with ever-increasing glory," and the NET, RSV, and NRSV, "from one degree of glory to another."

132. F. F. Bruce, *The Letter of Paul to the Romans: An Introduction and Commentary* (Tyndale NTC; Grand Rapids: Eerdmans, 1989), 168. So also Margaret E. Thrall, *A Critical and Exegetical Commentary on the Second Epistle to the Corinthians* (2 vols.; Edinburgh: T. & T. Clark, 1994), 1:286: "The divine nature as expressed in Christ as God's image is progressively expressed also in those who are transformed into the same image."

vin, *Institutes* 3.8.1). And it is the Holy Spirit that enables arrival at that termi-
nus: "The Spirit of God maketh the reading, but especially the preaching of the
word, an effectual means of enlightening, convincing, and humbling sinners; of
driving them out of themselves, and drawing them unto Christ; of conforming
them to His image, and subduing them to His will" (Westminster Catechism,
155). That glorious transformation, at least on this side of life, happens through
the textual agency of Scripture and by the divine power of its Author, a gradual,
pericope-by-pericope conformation to Christlikeness. In this monumental
metamorphosis into the image of his Son, God has co-opted preachers to play a
significant role, notwithstanding the fact that both people of God and preachers
of God are enabled "not by might nor by power, but by my Spirit" (Zech 4:6).
Each pericope is an instrument that is geared to moving believers one step closer to Christlikeness. Since in this conception, every biblical pericope portrays a
facet of the image (εἰκών) of Christ that man is to be conformed to, this model
of biblical interpretation for preaching is labeled *christiconic*.

The divine demand of a pericope, such as Gen 22, shows what it means to
fear God (Abraham's positive example). In christiconic interpretation, this example of the patriarch is actually depicting a facet of Christlikeness: part of what
it means to be Christlike is to fear God after the fashion of Abraham. Likewise,
a negative example of a biblical character, such as David in 2 Sam 11–12 (see
chapter 2), projects a divine demand regarding reverence for God and the recognition of evil as reprehensible to him. In christiconic interpretation, this, too, is
part of what it means to be Christlike.

In such an interpretation of the text, the image of Christ portrayed in Scripture is not exhausted by the Gospels, or even by the entire NT. Rather we need
the complete canon to picture the character of Christ—the One, and only One,
who fully met divine demand; it is through the entire corpus of sixty-six books
that we learn what it means to be Christlike, through every pericope in both
Testaments. Each pericope depicts a facet of Christlikeness, even the ones that
deal with particular characters in Scripture.[133] In other words, to employ the
narratives and characters of the OT for ethical purposes, as the text demands

---

133. In the christiconic conception of the text, each pericope portrays one facet or another of the image of
the perfect Man, Christ. This is not to deny his deity. However, it is his humanity, not his deity, that
humans are called to emulate, enabled by the Holy Spirit. It is to the image of his perfect humanity that
mankind is being conformed, and it is that image that man will one day bear (1 John 3:2). Therefore,
the preaching thrust of every pericope in the Bible is to move us closer, pericope by pericope, to that
canonical image of Christ.

in its theology, *is* to preach Christ. The christiconic approach thus respects the integrity of OT pericopes and seeks to discover what their authors are *doing* with what they are saying; the interpreter is not necessarily constrained to seek recourse in the NT to explain the OT. What the author is *doing* with what he is saying points to what aspect of each character is exemplary and what is not, i.e., what is Christlike and what is not. In other words, the protagonist of all Scripture is actually Jesus Christ. Everything worth emulating about a biblical character (as it is projected in the theology of the pericope) is a facet of Christlikeness; everything that must be abandoned is the negative image of Christlikeness. Therefore the role of each pericope is to demonstrate an aspect of Christlikeness, and to the extent one obeys the divine demand in a given pericope, to that extent one has become more like the perfect Man, Jesus Christ. And it is in aligning ourselves with this image, obeying the divine demand in each pericope, that God's purpose for his people is being fulfilled: to be "conformed to the image of his Son" (Rom 8:29).[134]

Imitation and Image

Because believers have already found new life in Christ, because they now have the Holy Spirit's empowerment, because they are now God's children, because they are impelled to live for God's glory, therefore they can now seek to obey the specifics of divine demand in each pericope that is preached. And in doing so pericope by pericope, they become progressively more Christlike. Ong observes that though centuries of Christendom have seen myriad discussions on the "imitation of Christ," Jesus is never found calling in the Gospels for anyone to *imitate* him. Rather, quite frequently, the command is to *follow* him. This, despite the fact that both in Koine and in classical Greek, the verb μιμέομαι (*mimeomai*, "imitate") was commonly employed and undoubtedly accessible

---

134. The *world in front of the text* may, therefore, be considered a theologically thick description of Jesus Christ, the one who fulfilled the Father's will—the demands of the projected world. Appropriating the theology of scriptural pericopes and indwelling the projected world is to participate in the drama of God's economy by which the Holy Spirit conforms readers to the image of Christ. See Kevin J. Vanhoozer, *The Drama of Doctrine: A Canonical-Linguistic Approach to Christian Theology* (Louisville: Westminster John Knox, 2005), 229.

135. Walter J. Ong, "Mimesis and the Following of Christ," *Religion & Literature* 26 (1994): 73, 74. The "imitation" motif is more explicit in Paul—the imitation of Paul himself, or of Paul as he imitates Christ: 1 Cor 4:16; 11:1; Phil 3:17; 4:9; 1 Thess 1:6; 2 Thess 3:7–9. Eph 4:32–5:1 calls upon believers to imitate God the Father. In fact, God's children have a mandate to "be perfect, as your heavenly Father is perfect" (Matt 5:48). Also see Heb 6:12–15; 13:7, for exhortations to mimic the saints of God, not to mention the litany of the "great cloud of witnesses" in Heb 11 that Christians are implicitly asked to imitate. Jesus, however, remains the ultimate model: Phil 2:5; 1 John 2:6; 3:16; 1 Pet 2:21; etc. That, of course, is not to deny that Jesus Christ is more than a model. But for the sanctification purposes of preaching, the focus is on his perfect humanity that mankind is called to conform to—to the εἰκών of Christ (Rom 8:29).

to NT writers—"their nonuse [of this verb] appears to be a matter of choice."[135] Ong explores the contrast between imitation and following. The former suggests "something purely mechanical and/or derivative," whereas the latter highlights the truth that "[a] follower necessarily meets with some situations or conditions in fact quite different from those encountered by the person whom he or she is following. This is patent if 'following' means coming along behind the one being followed—perhaps even at an interval of many miles or days or years." Ong goes on to explain:

> By "following" Christ, a person participates in the life of Jesus not simply by reduplicating the historical life of Christ, as the term "imitation" would suggest, but by entering into his or her own life so as to make it an extension of Christ's life. These considerations seem to make it significant that the term *imitate* or *imitation* . . . does not appear in the Gospels or the rest of the New Testament in what Jesus is reported to have asked of others in their relationship with him.[136]

This is precisely the preaching thrust of christiconic interpretation. What is called for is not slavish duplication, but sensitive application of the theology of the pericope (the facet of Christlikeness depicted therein) to the widely varying situations of God's people across the globe, across millennia, across cultures (see chapters 1 and 2). Pericopal theology tells us *what* Christ looks like; the homiletical imperative in the sermon tells us *how* specifically we can look like him in our own particular circumstances. Such an "imitation" is not a means to salvation, but the fruit thereof, made possible by the grace of God and the power of the Holy Spirit. As Augustine put it: "Man who might be seen was not to be followed; but God was to be followed, who could not be seen. And therefore God was made man, that he who might be seen by man, and whom man might follow, might be shown to man."[137]

Christiconic interpretation and preaching is Trinitarian in conception and operation. The text inspired by the Holy Spirit depicts Jesus Christ, the Son, to whose image mankind is to conform. In so conforming, the will of God the

136. Ibid., 74, 75.
137. Augustine, *Serm.* 371 ("De Nativitate Domini, III [c]"), PL 39:1660 (also cited in Aquinas, *Summa* 3.1.2). See E. J. Tinsley, "Some Principles for Reconstructing a Doctrine of the Imitation of Christ," *SJT* 25 (1972): 47.
138. Or: The agenda of God the Spirit in Scripture is to reveal the perfect, divine-demand-fulfilling life of God the Son, so that when applied by believers in the power of the Spirit, the kingdom of God the Father will have "come" as his will is done "on earth as it is in heaven." Of course, the final arrival of this kingdom in all its fullness and glory will occur only in the eschaton.

Father comes to pass and his kingdom is being brought about.[138] In other words, the Holy Spirit employs the inspired text and empowers believers to live in more Christlike a fashion, thus aligning them to the will of the Father. "The biblical story, situated in the context of the church's worship, does just this: it fills out and specifies what the kingdom (*telos*) of God's people looks like, and thus articulates the *telos* of virtue for citizens of the city of God. It shows us the kind of people we're called to be," i.e., the εἰκών we are to conform to—that of Jesus Christ.[139] Thus, the preaching of Scripture is not for the purpose of imparting information, but for transforming people by the power of the Holy Spirit—the changing of lives to conform to the image of Christ, by the instrumentality of God's word. Week by week, sermon by sermon, pericope by pericope, habits are changed, dispositions are created, character is built, and the image of Christ is formed. "In Christ man sees what manhood was meant to be. In the Old Testament all men are the image of God; in the New, where Christ is the one true image, men are image of God in so far as they are like Christ. The image is fully realized only through obedience to Christ; this is how man . . . can become fully man, fully the image of God."[140] Thus, *christiconic* interpretation.[141]

SUMMARY: THE *AQEDAH* AND CHRISTICONIC INTERPRETATION

Particularly for OT passages, how does pericopal theology relate to Jesus Christ and the Rule of Centrality that calls on the interpreter to focus hermeneutical activity *upon the pre-eminent person of Christ and his redemptive work that fulfills the will of the Father in the power of the Spirit*? In answer, this chapter first introduced a test case, the pericope dealing with the *Aqedah*, Gen 22. Traditional views were examined, especially the typological and RH views that locate Jesus Christ explicitly in the text. The theological hermeneutic proposed in this work was applied to this narrative passage and the theology of the pericope was

---

139. James K. A. Smith, *Desiring the Kingdom: Worship, Worldview, and Cultural Formation* (Grand Rapids: Baker, 2009), 197.

140. D. J. A. Clines, "The Image of God in Man," *TynBul* 19 (1968): 103.

141. If the congregation recognizes God's goal of conforming his people into the image of his Son, the preacher may not need to rehearse these conceptual details in every sermon except to state, for instance, when preaching 2 Sam 11–12, that *part of what it means to be Christlike is* to have reverence for God. Rather, I would spend pulpit time drawing out the pericopal theology from the text, substantiating it, illustrating it, and then applying it specifically into the lives of God's people. A periodic exposition of the christiconic concept in the life of a church would, no doubt, be useful, say, in an adult Bible study, small group gathering, or Sunday school class.

detailed (the "Comprehensive Theological Focus").

Christocentric interpretation was then explored and evidence was adduced against finding Christ explicitly in every pericope: the biblical text itself employs exemplars for deriving ethical imperatives and detailing moral instruction; it has not been the universal practice of the church to handle every text in a redemptive-historical fashion; and leaning on apostolic hermeneutics for support, it was shown, did not make for a strong case for christocentric preaching. The standard biblical passages offered in support of such an interpretive operation were also examined (Luke 24:13–27, 44–48; 1 Cor 1:22–23; 2:2; 2 Cor 4:5): none of them renders substantive aid to the RH method of preaching. In contrast, this work has shown that divine demand in each pericope necessitates human obedience—not legalism, but the obedience of faith, an operation of grace (see chapter 3). The value of such obedience and the incentives for such submission to divine demand now and in the hereafter were discussed. Finally a procedure for interpretation consonant with the Rule of Centrality was proposed: *christiconic* interpretation. God's goal for his children is, ultimately, to conform them into the image (εἰκών; Rom 8:29) of his son, the Lord Jesus Christ, the only one who perfectly exemplified "faith-full" obedience. He alone fulfilled divine demand. Thus every pericope points to a facet of the image of Christ; to that facet God's people are to conform, in the power of the Holy Spirit. Pericope by pericope, as facet after facet of the image of Jesus Christ is portrayed and applied, God's people are being molded into Christlikeness, a process to be consummated on the last day. In preaching in this fashion, with this theological hermeneutic, the text inspired by the Holy Spirit that depicts Jesus Christ will have become life in the people of God, and the will of the Father will have been done, his kingdom will have come!

CONCLUSION

Now may the God of peace who . . .
brought back from the dead . . . Jesus our Lord,
equip you in every good thing to do His will,
working in us what is pleasing before Him,
through Jesus Christ, to whom be glory forever. Amen!

HEBREWS 13:20–21

This work has attempted to provide the preacher with a bridge to cross the gap between the ancient text and the modern audience, a gap that is the consequence of textuality and its distanciation. In sum, a theological hermeneutic has been essayed, with pericopal theology as the intermediary across the chasm between Scripture and sermon, between text and application. It was proposed that preachers adopt a christiconic interpretation of biblical texts, a hermeneutic that respects both the specificity of the passage as well as the canonical depiction of Jesus Christ as the perfect Man, the only one to meet divine demand fully and completely. The Christian's responsibility, then, is to move towards Christlikeness by being aligned to the divine demand in each pericope, thus conforming to the specific facet of the image of Christ in that text.

Summary of Chapters

Chapter 1 considered general hermeneutics, in particular the *world in front of the text*, a function of the pragmatics of the text. This world projection enables application of the text at points distal to its origin in time and space. Texts that function this way are "classics": they are perennial and extend their influence into the future; they are plural and have potential for generating a wide variety of application; and they are prescriptive and have a normative character. The Bible, too, in this reckoning, is a classic, but of a different kind: it is divine discourse. As such, it also calls for a special hermeneutic for its interpretation: a set of six Rules of Reading were offered, rules that have superintended the reading of Scripture in the last two millennia.

Chapter 2 focused on the much-neglected textual unit of preaching—the pericope. This slice of the canon depicts a segment of the plenary world that the canon projects, the *theology of the pericope*. God's people are called to align their lives with the precepts, priorities, and practices of this slice of God's ideal world: pericopal theology thus forms the intermediary between text and audience, enabling valid application. The analysis of 2 Sam 11–12 demonstrated the process for discovering pericopal theology: the interpreter must look *at* the text, not *through* it, privileging the text. Preaching is thus "two-step" in this conception: from text to theology, and from theology to application. In fact, this double stepping is valid not only for biblical interpretation, but for the interpretation of any classic intended for future application; analogous moves in legal interpretation were also discussed in chapter 2.

Chapter 3 examined the issue of divine demand in the theology of the pericope—what God would have his people be and do: in other words, how one may be aligned to the precepts, priorities, and practices of God's ideal world. Divine demand was examined in the genre of OT law; it was established that this law was applicable to every Christian, in every place, in every time—*theologically*, i.e., by the employment of pericopal theology and the rationale of law integral to this theological entity. God expects his children to fulfill their filial responsibility to him, to be holy as he is, a demand that is the consequence of an already existing relationship with him: relationship precedes responsibility. The discharge of such responsibility is the "obedience of faith."

Chapter 4 analyzed Gen 22, the account of the *Aqedah*, a text frequently interpreted in a christocentric manner. Arguments mustered in support of such interpretation were evaluated and found wanting. A more substantial hermeneutic was offered as an alternative, one that respects the specifics of the text in the elucidation of its theology and the divine demand, and that valorizes obedience as bringing pleasure to God and resulting in his blessing.[1] Emerging from this hermeneutic was the proposal for a *christiconic* interpretation of the text: the only one who has fully met divine demand is Jesus Christ, and the canon portrays a plenary image (εἰκών, *eikōn*) of this perfect Man, with each pericope depicting a facet of this image. Indeed, this is the goal of God, that his children be conformed to the image of his Son (Rom 8:29), as pericopes are sequentially exposited and applied. Preaching is, therefore, a Trinitarian operation: the text inspired by God the Spirit portrays God the Son, into whose image the people of God are being transformed; thus the will of God the Father comes to pass.

In sum, since relationship precedes responsibility, and since God in his grace has initiated that relationship with his children through Jesus Christ, believers have a filial duty to obey divine demand and to be as holy as God is. This is achieved not by one's own resources for one's own glory and meritorious gain (= legalism), but in the power of the Holy Spirit, graciously gifted to his children by God, with the acceptance of forgiveness in Jesus Christ for failure to meet divine demand (= obedience of faith). Such a "faith-full" obedience is the process of practical sanctification, the gradual movement towards Christlikeness (conformation to the εἰκών of Christ). In this operation, the pericope plays a key role, for it depicts a facet of the image of Christ specific to that text (i.e., the theology of the pericope and the divine demand therein). For valid application to be made from the biblical text, the preacher must therefore discern the pericopal theology and bring it to bear upon people's lives with relevance.

Over a century ago, Benjamin Jowett declared that "[t]he true use of interpretation is to get rid of interpretation, and leave us alone in company with the author."[2] God's word is for God's people; the preacher is a necessary mediator between word and people, but only so that readers/hearers and author may, at some point, be left alone together. A sermon on a particular pericope, then, needs to exposit what the author is *doing* with what he is saying—the theology of the pericope, i.e., the facet of the image of Christ. Once this theology is exposited, and guidelines for specific application of that theology into the lives of God's people are provided, the preacher would do well to "leave [them] alone in company with the author."

---

1. Not the blessing of salvation (justification), of course; that is obtained by grace alone, through faith alone, in Christ alone.

2. "On the Interpretation of Scripture," in *Essays and Reviews* (7th ed.; London: Longman, Green, Longman, and Roberts, 1861), 384.

A Historical Afterword

While this work has touched upon a number of issues on the capacious canvas of the Christian's spiritual life—practical sanctification, obedience of faith empowered by the Spirit, attaining to the image of Christ, pleasing God, obtaining rewards—the essence of the theological hermeneutic embraced here concerns the approach to the biblical text employed in preaching, the pericope.[3] Rather than look *through the text* for elements behind the text (text = plain glass window), this work urges the interpreter to look *at the text* for elements in it that point to the ideal *world in front of it* or, if you will, the plenary image of Christ (text = stained glass window). The interpreter must *privilege the text*!

Unfortunately, for the longest time, the plain glass window metaphor has reigned supreme in most circles of Christendom: "[T]heologians exchanged the desire to give voice to the text itself for the attempt to read *through* the texts," Grenz and Franke complained. "Despite the well-meaning, lofty intentions . . . to honor the Bible as scripture, their approach in effect contributed to the silencing of the text in the church."[4] Looking through the text, using the text merely as a window to elements *behind* it, the text itself and the agenda of the author (what he was *doing* with what he was saying) have been given short shrift. Moreover, most Bible scholars and theologians have not been coming to Scripture with the eye and heart of a preacher; therefore the pericope has been neglected as a textual unit of theological value, and the goal of life transformation—usually a pastoral concern—has tended to be subjugated to other academic interests. As a consequence, preachers have been left in the lurch, a lament echoed by Barth regarding commentaries generated by academics:

> My complaint is that recent commentators confine themselves to an interpretation of the text which seems to me to be no commentary at all, but merely the first step toward a commentary. Recent commentaries contain no more than a reconstruction of the text, a rendering of the Greek words and phrases by their precise equivalents, a number of additional notes in which archaeological and philological material is gathered together, and a more or less plausible arrange-

---

3. Needless to say, this hermeneutic is not only applicable for the endeavor of preaching, but also for any transaction with the Bible intended to culminate in application, whether it be group Bible studies, Sunday school classes, or even one's personal devotional time with Scripture.

4. Stanley J. Grenz and John R. Franke, *Beyond Foundationalism: Shaping Theology in a Postmodern Context* (Louisville: Westminster John Knox, 2001), 63.

ment of the subject matter in such a manner that it may be made historically and psychologically intelligible from the standpoint of pure pragmatism.[5]

In all of these erudite analytical exercises, the theology of the pericope—what the author is *doing* with what he is saying in that pericope for the edification of God's people—has generally been disregarded.

At the risk of simplification, permit me to attempt a historical explanation of how this situation may have developed. For ease of apprehension, I shall divide the current dispensation into four eras: antiquity (100–500 C.E.); Middle Ages (500–1500 C.E.), Reformation era (1500–2000 C.E.), and the contemporary age (2000 onward). While this is quite a bold and broad reduction, I believe it helps one see where the focus of biblical interpretation has been for the most part, in each period.[6]

ERA	APPROACH & GOAL
Antiquity (100–500)	Truth handed down in tradition: *defense*
Middle Ages (500–1500)	Truth given out by the church: *dogma*
Reformation Era (1500–2000)	Truth traced through the canon: *deliverance*
Contemporary Age (2000–current)	Truth found within the pericope: *duty*

Antiquity (100–500 C.E.)

In the early days of the church (broadly the first five centuries of this era—antiquity), during and soon after the days of firsthand witnesses of Jesus Christ and his apostles, the basis for doctrine was the *regula fidei* ("rule of faith"), perpetuated by the authority of the Church Fathers and Councils (*truth handed down in tradition*). The rule of faith governed what would be read as Scripture and what would not (and, later, how Scripture itself would be read) in the days before the canon was finalized.[7] That the rule had an apologetic function is clear, serving

---

5. Karl Barth, "Preface to the Second Edition," in Karl Barth, *The Epistle to the Romans* (6th ed.; trans. Edwyn C. Hoskyns; London: Oxford University Press, 1933), 6.

6. Exceptions to these generalizations can, no doubt, be made. Nonetheless, the point that theologians and preachers are children of their age remains valid. Circumstances, need of the time, and state of the art determine, to a great extent, the hermeneutic for preaching.

7. In fact, the *regula fidei* "paved the way for the dogmatic formulations in the Nicene Creed." See T. F. Torrance, *Divine Meaning: Studies in Patristic Hermeneutics* (Edinburgh: T. & T. Clark, 1995), 76.

as a benchmark for orthodoxy; thus its predominant role was *defense*.[8] So much so, Tertullian recommended that the Scriptures be read only by those who have the rule of faith. Those who did not share this rule, Tertullian condemned as heretics, for

> all doctrine must be prejudged as false which savors of contrariety to the truth of the churches and apostles of Christ and God. It remains, then, that we demonstrate whether this doctrine of ours, of which we have now given the rule, has its origin in the tradition of the apostles, and whether all other doctrines do not ipso facto proceed from falsehood. We hold communion with the apostolic churches because our doctrine is in no respect different from theirs. (*Praescr.* 21)

So also Irenaeus, employing the *regula fidei*, countered the Gnostics, for "[t]he Church, though dispersed through out the whole world, even to the ends of the earth, has received from the apostles and their disciples this faith" (*Haer.* 1.10.1); for Irenaeus, the "rule of faith" alone was the key to correct interpretation.[9] For most of the first five centuries of the church, biblical interpretation focused upon this apologetic function, discriminating between truth and falsehood. This was *truth handed down in tradition* for the purpose of *defense*.

Middle Ages (500–1500 C.E.)

The rhetoric of the Middle Ages was characterized by fragmentation: many of the major texts of rhetoric had virtually disappeared (much of Cicero) or had survived only in bits and pieces (much of Quintilian). This led to the disappearance of an intellectual tradition and a stifling of knowledge creation.[10] All of this was naturally reflected in the preaching of the church. Essentially, medieval interpreters "subordinated scholarship ... to mysticism and propaganda."[11] On medieval biblical interpretation and preaching, historian Old writes:

---

8. Eric F. Osborn, "Reason and The Rule of Faith in the Second Century AD," in *The Making of Orthodoxy: Essays in Honour of Henry Chadwick* (ed. Rowan Williams; Cambridge: Cambridge University Press, 1989), 57–58; and Lewis Ayres, *Nicaea and its Legacy: An Approach to Fourth-Century Trinitarian Theology* (Oxford: Oxford University Press, 2004), 39.

9. Kathryn Greene-McCreight, "Rule of Faith," in *Dictionary for Theological Interpretation of the Bible* (eds. Kevin J. Vanhoozer, Craig G. Bartholomew, Daniel J. Treier, and N. T. Wright; Grand Rapids: Baker, 2005), 703.

10. Brian Vickers, *In Defence of Rhetoric* (Oxford: Clarendon, 1998), 214. His chapter is titled "Medieval Fragmentation" (ibid., 214–53).

11. Beryl Smalley, *The Study of the Bible in the Middle Ages* (Oxford: Basil Blackwell, 1952), 358.

Medieval preachers tried very hard to take their exegesis seriously, but they faced formidable problems. By the year 500 Jesus and his disciples had become figures of long ago and far away. . . . With the fall of the Roman Empire and the barbarian invasions, the New Testament—and in fact the whole Bible—was becoming very difficult to understand. It more and more became a book of mysteries that could only be solved by mystical contemplation. . . . The language barrier also contributed to the difficulty in understanding the Scriptures. How can one do grammatical-historical exegesis when almost no one west of the Adriatic Sea could read Greek, let alone Hebrew? True expository preaching was almost impossible. No wonder the conscientious preacher found allegorical exegesis attractive.[12]

And so preachers in the Middle Ages expounded on the multiple senses of Scripture: historical/literal, tropological, allegorical, and anagogical. This "layered" hermeneutic was crystallized in a distich, famously, but perhaps mistakenly, attributed to Nicholas of Lyra (ca. 1270–1349):

Littera gesta docet	The letter shows events;
Quid credas allegoria	What to believe, allegory;
Moralia quid agas	Moral, what to do;
Quo tendas anagogia	What to strive for, anagogy.[13]

Treatises of preaching in the Middle Ages had a field day with this fourfold layering of meaning; even words were organized and tabulated according to the different senses they had. For instance, Jerusalem stood for a city, the church, the soul of one aspiring to eternity, and the life in heaven where God is revealed.[14]

Not only did preaching acquire this esoteric trend, it also became quite exclusive. As Roberts notes, "The distinguishing mark of most early medieval

12. Hughes Oliphant Old, *The Reading and Preaching of the Scriptures in the Worship of the Christian Church* (7 vols.; Grand Rapids: Eerdmans, 1998–2010), 3: xv–xvi.

13. It has also been attributed to John Cassian (ca. 360–435), among others, though perhaps Guibert de Nogent (ca. 1053–1124) was the earliest to give it voice. See his *A Book About the Way a Sermon Ought to Be Given* (trans. Joseph M. Miller, "Guibert de Nogent's *Liber quo ordine sermo fieri debeat*: A Translation of the Earliest Modern Speech Textbook," *Today's Speech* 17 [1969]: 46). Hugh of St. Cher, *Postillae in Universa Biblia Secundum Quadruplicem Sensum* (thirteenth century), taught: *Historia docet quid factum, tropologia quid faciendum, allegoria quid intellegendum, anagoge quid appetendum* ("History teaches what has been done, tropology what is to be done, allegory what is to be understood, anagogy what is to be desired") (cited in Harry Caplan, "The Four Senses of Scriptural Interpretation and the Mediaeval Theory of Preaching," *Spec* 4 [1929]: 287).

14. See Miller, "Guibert de Nogent's *Liber*," 46.

278 | PRIVILEGE THE TEXT!

preaching was that it was essentially preaching by clerics for audiences of clerics." Rhetoric in the Middle Ages was, after all, only a theoretical skill split from
actual practice and utility; it had lost sight of the audience, and remained closeted
in the enclaves of "experts."[15] Complicating an already cryptic style of interpretation, the Scriptures came to be heard only in the liturgical context, which
itself became ceremonial and symbolic. With time, the reading and preaching
of the Bible became secondary to the liturgy, with preaching almost disappear-
ing.[16] In the Middle Ages, then, essentially, the magisterium became the authority dispensing *dogma* (*truth given out by the church*).

Reformation Era (1500–2000 C.E.)

After the Middle Ages, in the days of the Reformation, the Bible was literally
brought to light again. Translated into the vernacular, preached systematically
and regularly, and mass produced and widely distributed with the arrival of the
printing press, the Bible finally got into the hands of the common man. Naturally, the thrust was now on the soteriological truths of Scripture, long subdued
in the bleakness of the medieval period. In fact, a chapter in a book on the
historical interpretation of the Bible is titled: "Concentration on the Bible's Saving Function during the Reformation."[17] Johnson is right when he declares that
the "concern that every *Christian* sermon expound its text in relation to Christ
and his saving work is solidly rooted in the Reformation and the Protestant
heritage that is its legacy."[18] Thus the period from 1500–2000 C.E. focused on *deliverance*; Scripture interpretation was the domain of biblical theologians who
traced themes through Scripture (*truth traced through the canon*)—primarily
the themes of redemptive history.

---

15. Phyllis Roberts, "The *Ars Praedicandi* and the Medieval Sermon," in *Preacher, Sermon and the Audience in the Middle Ages* (ed. Carolyn Muessig; Leiden: Brill, 2002), 44; Vickers, *In Defence of Rhetoric*,
225–27.

16. Old, *The Reading and Preaching of the Scriptures in the Worship of the Christian Church, Volume 3*, xvi.
Part of the problem also was the burgeoning of the liturgical calendar and the reckoning of feast days.
This necessarily relegated *lectio continua* as a dispensable operation while *lectio selecta* thrived (i.e., specific texts read for each of the innumerable special days). "While patristic preaching was characterized
by an emphasis on regular expository preaching that went through one book of the Bible after another,
medieval preaching was characterized by a predominance of festal preaching . . . following the liturgical
calendar" (ibid., xvii).

17. Jack B. Rogers and Donald K. McKim, *The Authority and Interpretation of the Bible: An Historical Approach* (San Francisco: Harper & Row, 1979).

18. Dennis E. Johnson, *Him We Proclaim: Preaching Christ from All the Scriptures* (Phillipsburg, N.J.: Presbyterian and Reformed, 2007), 49n49.

This focus on redemption, after several centuries of confusion as to what it took for sins to be forgiven and salvation to be gained, was not only appropriate, but epochal. However, such an exclusive focus on biblical theology that monopolized preaching, centering it upon RH themes, had a singular weakness: it was insufficient to equip the children of God "for every good work" (2 Tim 3:17). Essential it was for salvation, but inadequate for sanctification. Almost every sermon tended to be either evangelistic or a recitation of salvation benefits, without much attention to the specifics of the pericope, its theology, or its demand for life change. As was noted in chapter 4, this legacy continues to thrive in modern times with the popularity of RH interpretation and preaching.[19]

Contemporary Age (2000–current)

This compartmentalization of eras—antiquity, Middle Ages, and Reformation—is not to imply that the church has no use for *defense*, *dogma*, or *deliverance* in the contemporary age. Yet for the last two millennia, a somewhat blinkered focus on one or more of these has stifled ecclesial scholarship and pastoral proclamation, particularly the furtherance of our understanding of what it means to live a Christian life in accordance with the divine demand of each pericope in Scripture. Scholars have tended to operate with larger tracts of the biblical text and have been inclined to remain in the realm of biblical and systematic theology, analyzing language and history and geography and "what actually happened" (*behind* the text). All of this is at a conceptual distance from the specificity of a pericope and its utility to change lives for the glory of God. Long's pungent criticism is apropos:

> [C]onscientious biblical preachers have long shared the little secret that the classical text-to-sermon exegetical methods produce far more chaff than wheat. If one has the time and patience to stay at the chores of exegesis, theoretically one can find out a great deal of background information about virtually every passage in the Bible, much of it unfortunately quite remote from any conceivable use in a sermon. The preacher's desk can quickly be covered with Ugaritic parallels and details about syncretistic religion in the Phrygian region of Asia Minor. It is hard to find fault here; every scrap of data is potentially valuable, and it is impossible to know in advance which piece of information is to be prized. So, we brace ourselves for the next round of exegesis by saying

---

19. My limitation of the Reformation era to the end of the twentieth century is quite arbitrary.

that it is necessary to pan a lot of earth to find a little gold, and that is true, of course. However, preachers have the nagging suspicion that there is a good deal of wasted energy in the traditional model of exegesis or, worse, that the real business of exegesis is excavation and earth-moving and that any homiletical gold stumbled over along the way is largely coincidental.[20]

What has been generally offered to preachers by academia over the generations are products of a hermeneutic of excavation—the turning over of tons of earth, debris, rock, boulder, and gravel: a "shotgun" style of exegesis that yields an overload of biblical and Bible-related information not particularly useful to move the preacher closer to a sermon. Sorely needed by preachers are commentaries that do exegesis in a unique fashion, geared explicitly and precisely to arrive at the *theology* of each pericope of a given book of the Bible. For it is only after arriving at this intermediary point of textual theology that a preacher can proceed to a sermon generating valid application that is both authoritative and relevant.

In sum, what is painfully lacking—by way of commentaries and homiletical aids—is an understanding of the theology of each pericope, demonstrably discovered, prominently laid out, and explicitly stated, so that the reader can apprehend the thrust of each pericope and see how the argument of the author is developed pericope by pericope to achieve the author's theological goal.[21] There needs to be more looking *at* the text, than looking *through* it. The burden of this current work has therefore been to exhort interpreters to *privilege the text* for the purpose of arriving at pericopal theology and its divine demand. Only then can valid application be arrived at; only then can life-change be achieved, in the power of the Spirit, for the glory of God. In this operation, the key figures are (or ought to be) pastors and preachers, the mediators of the interaction between the people of God and the word of God—the leaders of congregations shouldering the (human) responsibility of growing the flock more and more into Christlikeness, sermon by sermon, week by week.

---

20. Thomas G. Long, "The Use of Scripture in Contemporary Preaching," *Interpretation* 44 (1990): 343–44.

21. A commentary with this campaign plan has been attempted by the author: *Mark: A Theological Commentary for Preachers* (Eugene, Oreg.: Cascade, 2012). This is not exactly a preaching commentary, in the usual sense of providing illustrations and quotes and such. Rather it is a "theology-for-preaching" commentary, i.e., a work that seeks to undertake an extremely focused interpretation of the text to develop the theology of the pericope sequentially through the Gospel of Mark. Employing this theology, preachers may then proceed to craft a sermon specific for their particular audiences. In that sense, it is a *theological* commentary, based as it is on the theological hermeneutic proposed in this work.

In the contemporary age, rhetoric has begun to bloom and language philosophy has matured; the fields of pragmatics and relevance theory are rapidly producing fruit, not to mention the abundance of two millennia of biblical scholarship to reflect upon. Perhaps one could also say that the issues of the last several centuries have, at least to some extent, been settled in this age. The confluence of all of these developments, I think, has led to a renewed focus on preaching, on the pericope, and on life transformation of God's people for God's glory. While the church always *defends*, proclaims truth (*dogma*), and preaches *deliverance*, it may well be that in the present new era, the emphasis should be on the filial *duty* of the child of God to demonstrate "faith-full" obedience to the *truth found within the pericope*. Homileticians are on the vanguard of this advance, and rightly so: "We proclaim Him, instructing every man and teaching every man with all wisdom, so that we may present every man mature in Christ" (Col 1:28). May there be more of that Pauline ilk, laboring for God's glory!

BIBLIOGRAPHY *of* MODERN WRITINGS

Ackerman, James S. "Knowing Good and Evil: A Literary Analysis of the Court History in 2 Samuel 9–20 and 1 Kings 1–2." *JBL* 109 (1990): 41–64.

Adam, A. K. M., Stephen E. Fowl, Kevin J. Vanhoozer, and Francis Watson. *Reading Scripture with the Church: Toward a Hermeneutic for Theological Interpretation.* Grand Rapids: Baker, 2006.

Aichele, George. *The Control of Biblical Meaning: Canon as Semiotic Mechanism.* Harrisburg, Penn.: Trinity, 2001.

Allen, Woody. "The Scrolls." Pages 135–40 in *The Insanity Defense: The Complete Prose.* New York: Random House, 2007.

Allison, Gregg R. "Speech Act Theory and Its Implications for the Doctrine of the Inerrancy/Infallibility of Scripture." *Philosophia Christi* 8 (1995): 1–23.

Altieri, Charles. "The Poem as Act: A Way to Reconcile Presentational and Mimetic Theories." *Iowa R.* 6.3–4 (1975): 103–24.

Andrews, James. "Why Theological Hermeneutics Needs Rhetoric: Augustine's *De doctrina Christiana.*" *IJST* 12 (2010): 184–200.

Auerbach, Erich. *Mimesis: The Representation of Reality in Western Literature.* Translated by Willard R. Trask. Princeton: Princeton University Press, 1953.

Austen, Ben. "What Caricatures Can Teach Us About Facial Recognition." WIRED Magazine, July 2011. No pages. Cited June 3, 2012. Online: http://www.wired.com/magazine/2011/07/ff_caricature/all/1/.

Ayres, Lewis. *Nicaea and its Legacy: An Approach to Fourth-Century Trinitarian Theology.* Oxford: Oxford University Press, 2004.

Badenas, Robert. *Christ The End of the Law: Romans 10.4 in Pauline Perspective.* JSNTSup 10. Sheffield: JSOT Press, 1985.

Bailey, Randall C. *David in Love and War: The Pursuit of Power in 2 Samuel 10–12.* Sheffield: JSOT, 1990.

Balserak, Jon. "Luther, Calvin and Musculus on Abraham's Trial: Exegetical History and the Transformation of Genesis 22." *RRR* 6 (2004): 361–73.

Barker, William S., and W. Robert Godfrey. *Theonomy: A Reformed Critique.* Grand Rapids: Zondervan, 1990.

Barnett, Paul. *The Second Epistle to the Corinthians.* NIGTC. Grand Rapids: Eerdmans, 1997.

Barr, James. "A New Look at *Kethibh-Qere.*" Pages 19–37 in *Remembering All the Way . . . .* Vol. 21 of Oudtestamentische Studiën. Edited by B. Albrektson. Leiden: Brill, 1981.

Barth, Karl. *Church Dogmatics, II/2: The Doctrine of God.* Translated by G. W. Bromiley. Edited by Thomas F. Torrance and G. W. Bromiley. Edinburgh: T. & T. Clark, 2004.

_____. *Dogmatics in Outline.* London: SCM, 1966.

_____. "Preface to the Second Edition." Pages 2–15 in *The Epistle to the Romans,* by Karl Barth. Sixth edition. Translated by Edwyn C. Hoskyns. London: Oxford University Press, 1933.

_____. "The Strange New World within the Bible." Pages 28–50 in *The Word of God and the Word of Man.* Translated by Douglas Horton. London: Hodder and Stoughton, 1928.

Barton, John. "Approaches to Ethics in the Old Testament." Pages 114–31 in *Beginning Old Testament Study,* by John Rogerson, John Barton, David J. A. Clines, and Paul Joyce. London: SPCK, 1998.

_____. *The Spirit and the Letter: Studies in the Biblical Canon.* London: SPCK, 1997.

Basevorn, Robert de. *Forma praedicandi.* Pages 231–314 in *Artes Praedicandi: Contribution a L'histoire de la Rhétorique au Moyen Age,* by Th.-M. Charland. Paris: Libr. Philosophique J. Vrin, 1936.

Bauckham, Richard. "Reading Scripture as a Coherent Story." Pages 38–53 in *The Art of Reading Scripture.* Edited by Ellen F. Davis and Richard B. Hays. Grand Rapids: Eerdmans, 2003.

Beck, John A. *God as Storyteller: Seeking Meaning in Biblical Narrative.* St. Louis: Chalice, 2008.

Beckman, Gary. *Hittite Diplomatic Texts.* Atlanta: Scholars, 1996.

Bergen, Robert D. "The Role of Genesis 22:1–19 in the Abraham Cycle: A Computer-Assisted Textual Intepretation." *CTR* 4 (1990): 313–26.

Bernstein, Moshe J. "Angels at the Aqedah: A Study in the Development of a Midrashic Motif." *Dead Sea Discoveries* 7 (2000): 263–91.

Bertman, Stephen. "Tasseled Garments in the Ancient East Mediterranean." *Biblical Archaeologist* 24 (1961): 119–28.

Billings, J. Todd. *The Word of God for the People of God: An Entryway to the Theological Interpretation of Scripture.* Grand Rapids: Eerdmans, 2010.

Black, C. Clifton. "Rhetorical Criticism." Pages 256–77 in *Hearing the New Testament: Strategies for Interpretation.* Edited by Joel B. Green. Grand Rapids: Eerdmans, 1995.

Blaising, Craig A., and Darrell L. Bock. *Progressive Dispensationalism: An Up-to-Date Handbook of Contemporary Dispensational Thought.* Wheaton: Victor, 1993.

Block, Daniel I. *Judges, Ruth.* NAC 6. Nashville: Broadman & Holman, 1999.

_____. "Tell Me the Old, Old Story: Preaching the Message of Old Testament Narrative." Pages 409-38 in *Giving the Sense: Understanding and Using Old Testament Historical Texts.* Edited by David M. Howard and Michael A. Grisanti. Grand Rapids: Kregel, 2003.

Bloomfield, Morton W. "Allegory as Interpretation." *NLH* 3 (1972): 301–17.

Booth, Wayne C. *The Company We Keep: An Ethics of Fiction.* Berkeley, Calif.: University of California Press, 1988.

Bowald, Mark Alan. *Rendering the Word in Theological Hermeneutics: Mapping Divine and Human Agency.* Aldershot, U.K.: Ashgate, 2007.

Brennan, Joseph P. "Psalms 1–8: Some Hidden Harmonies." *BTB* 10 (1980): 25–29.

Briggs, Richard. *Reading the Bible Wisely.* London: SPCK, 2003.

Bright, John. *The Authority of the Old Testament.* Nashville: Abingdon, 1967.

Brooks, Phillips. *Lectures on Preaching, Delivered before the Divinity School of Yale College in January and February, 1877.* New York: E. P. Dutton, 1877.

Bruce, F. F. *The Canon of Scripture.* Downers Grove: InterVarsity, 1988.

_____. *The Epistles to the Colossians, to Philemon, and to the Ephesians.* NICNT. Grand Rapids: Eerdmans, 1984.

_____. *The Letter of Paul to the Romans: An Introduction and Commentary.* Tyndale NTC. Grand Rapids: Eerdmans, 1989.

Brunner, Emil. *The Divine Imperative: A Study in Christian Ethics.* Translated by Olive Wyon. Philadelphia: Westminster, 1947.

Bucer, Martin. *Martin Bucers Deutsches Schriften.* 14 vols. Edited by R. Stupperich. Gütersloh, Germany: Mohn, 1960–1975.

Buttrick, David G. *Homiletic: Moves and Structures.* Philadelphia: Fortress, 1987.

_____. "Interpretation and Preaching." *Int* 35 (1981): 46–58.

Candler, Peter M. *Theology, Rhetoric, Manuduction, or Reading Scripture Together on the Path to God.* London: SCM, 2006.

Caplan, Harry. "The Four Senses of Scriptural Interpretation and the Mediaeval Theory of Preaching." *Spec* 4 (1929): 282–90.

Carmichael, Calum. *The Spirit of Biblical Law*. Athens, Ga.: University of Georgia Press, 1996.

Carmichael, Deborah Bleicher. "David Daube on the Eucharist and the Passover Seder." *JSNT* 42 (1991): 45–67.

Carson, D. A. "Of First Importance (part 1): Eight Words That Help Us Preach the Gospel Correctly." No pages. Cited on August 8, 2011. Online: http://www.preachingtoday.com/skills/themes/gettinggospelright/offirstimportance1.html.

_____. "Unity and Diversity in the New Testament: The Possibility of Systematic Theology." Pages 65–95 in *Hermeneutics, Authority and Canon*. Edited by D. A. Carson and John D. Woodbridge. Grand Rapids: Baker, 1995.

The Catechism of the Catholic Church. Second edition. New York: Doubleday, 2003.

Chafee, Zechariah. "The Disorderly Conduct of Words." *Columbia L. Rev.* 41 (1941): 381–404.

Chapell, Bryan. "Application without Moralism: How to Show the Relevance of the Text." No pages. Cited on May 1, 2002. Online: http://www.preachingtoday.com/skills/themes/application/200203.25.html?start=3.

_____. *Christ-Centered Preaching: Redeeming the Expository Sermon*. Second edition. Grand Rapids: Baker, 2005.

Childs, Brevard S. *Biblical Theology in Crisis*. Philadelphia: Westminster, 1970.

_____. *Introduction to the Old Testament as Scripture*. London: SCM, 1979.

_____. *Isaiah*. Old Testament Library. Louisville: Westminster John Knox, 2001.

Chirichigno, Greg. "A Theological Investigation of Motivation in Old Testament Law." *JETS* 24 (1981): 303–13.

Chisholm, Robert B. "Anatomy of an Anthropomorphism: Does God Discover Facts?" *BSac* 164 (2007): 3–20.

Ciampa, Roy E., and Brian S. Rosner. *The First Letter to the Corinthians*. Pillar NTC. Grand Rapids: Eerdmans, 2010.

Clark, David K. *To Know and Love God*. Wheaton: Crossway, 2003.

Claude, John. *An Essay on the Composition of a Sermon*. 2 vols. Third edition. Translated by Robert Robinson. London: T. Scollick, 1782–1788.

Clements, Ronald E. "History and Theology in Biblical Narrative." *HorBT* 4–5 (1982–1983): 45–60.

Clines, D. J. A. "The Image of God in Man." *TynBul* 19 (1968): 53–103.

Clowney, Edmund P. *Preaching and Biblical Theology*. Nutley, N.J.: Presbyterian and Reformed, 1977.

_____. "Preaching Christ from All the Scriptures." Pages 163–91 in *The Preacher and Preaching: Reviving the Art in the Twentieth Century*. Edited by Samuel T. Logan. Phillipsburg, N.J.: Presbyterian and Reformed, 1986.

_____. *Preaching Christ in All of Scripture*. Wheaton: Crossway, 2002.

Coats, George W. *Genesis: With an Introduction to Narrative Literature*. FOTL 1. Grand Rapids: Eerdmans, 1983.

Coleridge, Samuel Taylor. "The Friend: Section the Second, Essay IV." Pages 448–57 in *The Collected Works of Samuel Taylor Coleridge*. Edited by Barbara E. Rooke. London: Routledge & Kegan Paul, 1969.

Collins, Raymond F. *First Corinthians*. Sacra Pagina 7. Collegeville, Minn.: Liturgical, 1999.

Cosgrove, Charles H. *Appealing to Scripture in Moral Debate: Five Hermeneutical Rules*. Grand Rapids: Eerdmans, 2002.

Cowley, A. E. *Aramaic Papyri of the Fifth Century B.C.* Oxford: Clarendon, 1923.

Craddock, Fred B. *As One Without Authority*. St. Louis: Chalice, 2001.

_____. *Preaching*. Nashville: Abingdon, 1985.

Cranfield, C. E. B. *The Epistle to the Romans*. International Critical Commentary. 2 vols. Edinburgh: T. & T. Clark, 1979.

_____. "Has the Old Testament Law a Place in the Christian Life? A Response to Professor Westerholm." Pages 109–24 in *On Romans and Other New Testament Essays* by C. E. B. Cranfield. London: T. & T. Clark, 1998.

Crotty, Robert. "The Literary Structure of the Binding of Isaac in Genesis 22." *ABR* 53 (2005): 31–41.

Crouzel, Henri. *Origen*. Translated by A. S. Worrall. Edinburgh: T. & T. Clark, 1989.

Cullman, Oscar. *The Early Church*. London: SCM, 1956.

Cunningham, David S. *Faithful Persuasion: In Aid of a Rhetoric of Christian Theology*. Notre Dame: University of Notre Dame Press, 1991.

Das, Andrew A. *Paul, the Law, and the Covenant*. Peabody, Mass.: Hendrickson, 2001.

Daley, Brian E. "Is Patristic Exegesis Still Usable?" *Communio* 29 (2002): 185–216.

Daube, David. *Law and Wisdom in the Bible: David Daube's Gifford Lectures, Volume 2*. Edited by Calum Carmichael. West Conshohocken, Penn.: Templeton, 2010.

_____. *The New Testament and Rabbinic Judaism*. London: Athlone, 1956.

Davies, P. R., and B. D. Chilton. "The Aqedah: A Revised Tradition History." *CBQ* 40 (1978): 514–46.

Davis, Dale Ralph. *The Word Became Fresh: How to Preach from Old Testament Narrative Texts*. Ross-Shire, U.K.: Mentor, 2006.

Dillow, Joseph C. *The Reign of the Servant Kings: A Study of Eternal Security and the Final Significance of Man*. Hayesville, N.C.: Schoettle, 1992.

Dorsey, David A. "The Law of Moses and the Christian: A Compromise." *JETS* 34 (1991): 321–34.

_____. "The Use of the OT Law in Christian Life: A Theocentric Approach." *EvJ* 17 (1998): 1–18.

Duggan, Michael W. *The Covenant Renewal in Ezra-Nehemiah (Neh 7:72b–10:40): An Exegetical, Literary, and Theological Study.* Atlanta: SBL, 1996.

Dumbrell, William J. "Genesis 2:1–17: A Foreshadowing of the New Creation." Pages 53–65 in *Biblical Theology: Retrospect and Prospect.* Edited by Scott J. Hafemann. Downers Grove: InterVarsity, 2002.

Dunn, James D. G. *The Epistles to the Colossians and to Philemon: A Commentary on the Greek Text.* NIGTC. Grand Rapids: Eerdmans, 1996.

_____. "'The Law of Faith,' 'the Law of the Spirit' and 'the Law of Christ.'" Pages 62–82 in *Theology and Ethics in Paul and His Interpreters: Essays in Honor of Victor Paul Furnish.* Edited by Eugene H. Lovering and Jerry L. Sumney. Nashville: Abingdon, 1996.

_____. *The New Perspective on Paul.* Revised edition. Grand Rapids: Eerdmans, 2005.

Eco, Umberto. *The Limits of Interpretation.* Bloomington, Ind.: Indiana University Press, 1990.

Eliot, T. S. *Four Quartets,* "East Coker." In *Four Quartets.* Public Domain.

Erickson, Millard J. *Christian Theology.* Grand Rapids: Baker, 1985.

Falk, Ze'ev W. *Religious Law and Ethics: Studies in Biblical and Rabbinical Theonomy.* Jerusalem: Mesharim, 1991.

Fee, Gordon D. *The First Epistle to the Corinthians.* Grand Rapids: Eerdmans, 1987.

Fitzmeyer, Joseph A. "The Interpretation of Genesis 15:6: Abraham's Faith and Righteousness in a Qumran Text." Pages 257–68 in *Emanuel: Studies in Hebrew Bible, Septuagint, and Dead Sea Scrolls in Honor of Emanuel Tov.* Supplements to Vetus Testamentum 94. Edited by Shalom M. Paul, Robert A. Kraft, Lawrence H. Schiffman, and Weston W. Fields. Leiden: Brill, 2003.

Fokkelman, J. P. *King David (II Sam. 9–20 & I Kings 1–2)*. Vol. 1 of *Narrative Art and Poetry in the Books of Samuel*. Assen, Netherlands: Van Gorcum, 1981.

Fowl, Stephen. *Engaging Scripture: A Model for Theological Interpretation*. Malden, Mass.: Blackwell, 1998.

_____. *Theological Interpretation of Scripture*. Eugene, Oreg.: Cascade, 2009.

Fowler, Robert M. *Let the Reader Understand: Reader-Response Criticism and the Gospel of Mark*. Minneapolis: Fortress, 1991.

Frei, Hans W. *The Eclipse of Biblical Narrative: A Study in Eighteenth and Nineteenth Century Hermeneutics*. New Haven: Yale University Press, 1974.

Frye, Northrop. *Anatomy of Criticism: Four Essays*. Princeton: Princeton University Press, 1957.

_____. *The Educated Imagination*. Bloomington, Ind.: Indiana University Press, 1964.

_____. *The Great Code: The Bible and Literature*. New York: Harcourt Brace, 1982.

Gadamer, Hans-Georg. *Truth and Method*. Second revised edition. Translated by Joel Weinsheimer and Donald G. Marshall. London: Continuum, 2004.

Gamble, Harry Y. *Books and Readers in the Early Church: A History of Early Christian Texts*. New Haven: Yale University Press, 1995.

_____. *The New Testament Canon: Its Making and Meaning*. Philadelphia: Fortress, 1985.

Garlington, Don B. *Faith, Obedience and Perseverance*. WUNT 79. Tübingen: J. C. B. Mohr (Paul Siebeck), 1994.

Gathercole, Simon J. *Where Is Boasting? Early Jewish Soteriology and Paul's Response in Romans 1–5*. Grand Rapids: Eerdmans, 2002.

Geertz, Clifford. *The Interpretation of Cultures*. London: Fontana, 1993.

Gemser, B. "The Importance of the Motive Clause in Old Testament Law." Pages 50–66 in *Congress Volume: Copenhagen*. Vol. 1 of Vetus Testamentum Supplements. Leiden: Brill, 1953.

Gibbs, Raymond W. "Nonliteral Speech Acts in Text and Discourse." Pages 357–93 in *The Handbook of Discourse Processes*. Edited by Arthur C. Graesser, Morton Ann Gernsbacher, and Susan R. Goldman. Mahwah, N.J.: Erlbaum, 2003.

Goethe, J. W. *Conversations with Eckermann (1823–1832)*. Translated by John Oxenford. San Francisco: North Point, 1984.

Goldingay, John. *Approaches to Old Testament Interpretation*. Leicester, U.K.: InterVarsity, 1981.

Goldsworthy, Graeme. *Gospel-Centred Hermeneutics: Biblical-Theological Foundations and Principles*. Nottingham, U.K.: Apollos, 2006.

_____. *Preaching the Whole Bible as Christian Scripture: The Application of Biblical Theology to Expository Preaching*. Grand Rapids: Eerdmans, 2000.

Green, Gene L. "Lexical Pragmatics and Biblical Interpretation." *JETS* 50 (2007): 799–812.

Greene-McCreight, Kathryn. "Rule of Faith." Pages 703–4 in *Dictionary for Theological Interpretation of the Bible*. Edited by Kevin J. Vanhoozer, Craig G. Bartholomew, Daniel J. Treier, and N. T. Wright. Grand Rapids: Baker, 2005.

Greenhaw, David M. "As One *with* Authority: Rehabilitating Concepts for Preaching." Pages 105–22 in *Intersections: Post-Critical Studies in Preaching*. Edited by Richard L. Eslinger. Grand Rapids: Eerdmans, 2004.

Greidanus, Sidney. *The Modern Preacher and the Ancient Text: Interpreting and Preaching Biblical Literature*. Grand Rapids: Eerdmans, 1989.

_____. *Preaching Christ from Genesis*. Grand Rapids: Eerdmans, 2007.

_____. *Preaching Christ from the Old Testament: A Contemporary Hermeneutical Method*. Grand Rapids: Eerdmans, 1999.

Grenz, Stanley J., and John R. Franke. *Beyond Foundationalism: Shaping Theology in a Postmodern Context.* Louisville: Westminster John Knox, 2001.

Grudem, Wayne. *Systematic Theology: An Introduction to Biblical Doctrine.* Grand Rapids: Zondervan, 1994.

Guest, Stephen. *Ronald Dworkin.* Stanford, Calif.: Stanford University Press, 1991.

Habermas, Jürgen. *Justification and Application: Remarks on Discourse Ethics.* Translated by Ciaran Cronin. Cambridge: Polity, 1993.

Hamilton, Alexander. "The Federalist No. 34: Concerning the General Power of Taxation (continued)." *Independent Journal* (January 5, 1788). No pages.

Hamilton, Victor P. *The Book of Genesis, Chapters 18–50.* NICOT. Grand Rapids: Eerdmans, 1995.

Hare, R. M. *Freedom and Reason.* Oxford: Clarendon, 1963.

_____. *The Language of Morals.* Oxford: Clarendon, 1961.

Hauerwas, Stanley. "The Self as Story: Religion and Morality from the Agent's Perspective." *JRE* 1 (1973): 73–85.

Hays, Richard B. *The Moral Vision of the New Testament: A Contemporary Introduction to New Testament Ethics.* New York: HarperCollins, 1996.

Heath, Chip, and Dan Heath. *Switch: How to Change Things When Change Is Hard.* New York: Broadway, 2010.

Hess, Richard S. "The Book of Joshua as a Land Grant." *Bib* 83 (2002): 493–506.

Hirsch, E. D. *The Aims of Interpretation.* Chicago: The University of Chicago Press, 1976.

_____. "Meaning and Significance Reinterpreted." *CI* 11 (1984): 202–25.

_____. "Past Intentions and Present Meanings." *Ess. Crit.* 33 (1983): 79–98.

_____. "Transhistorical Intentions and the Persistence of Allegory." *NLH* 25 (1994): 549–67.

_____. *Validity in Interpretation*. New Haven: Yale University Press, 1967.

Holmer, Paul L. *The Grammar of Faith*. New York: Harper and Row, 1978.

Holmes, Oliver Wendell. "The Use of Law Schools." Pages 28–40 in *Speeches by Oliver Wendell Holmes*. Boston: Little, Brown, and Company, 1934.

Hood, Jason. "Christ-Centred Interpretation Only? Moral Instruction from Scripture's Self-Interpretation as Caveat and Guide." *SBET* 27 (2009): 50–69.

Hubert, Friedrich. *Die Strassburger Liturgische Ordnungen im Zeitalter der Reformation*. Göttingen, Germany: Vandenhoeck and Ruprecht, 1900.

Hughes, Philip Edgcumbe. *Paul's Second Epistle to the Corinthians*. NICNT. Grand Rapids: Eerdmans, 1962.

Huizenga, Leroy Andrew. "Obedience unto Death: The Matthean Gethsemane and Arrest Sequence and the Aqedah." *CBQ* 71 (2009): 507–26.

Hunter, James Davison. *To Change the World: The Irony, Tragedy, and Possibility of Christianity in the Late Modern World*. New York: Oxford University Press, 2010.

Illyricus, Matthias Flaccius. "The Rule for Becoming Acquainted with the Sacred Scriptures." In *Clavis Scripturæ Sacræ*. Bibliopolæ Hafniensis, 1719.

Janzen, Waldemar. *Old Testament Ethics: A Paradigmatic Approach*. Louisville: Westminster John Knox, 1994.

Jeanrond, Werner. *Theological Hermeneutics: Development and Significance*. London: SCM, 1994.

Jensen, Alexander S. *Theological Hermeneutics*. London: SCM, 2007.

Jewett, Robert. *Romans: A Commentary*. Minneapolis: Fortress, 2007.

Johnson, Dennis E. *Him We Proclaim: Preaching Christ from All the Scriptures*. Phillipsburg, N.J.: Presbyterian and Reformed, 2007.

Johnson, Luke Timothy. "Imagining the World Scripture Imagines." *Modern Theology* 14 (1998): 165–77.

Johnstone, Keith. *Impro: Improvisation and the Theatre*. London: Methuen, 1981.

Jonsen, Albert R., and Stephen Toulmin. *The Abuse of Casuistry: A History of Moral Reasoning*. Berkeley, Calif.: University of California Press, 1988.

Jowett, Benjamin. "On the Interpretation of Scripture." Pages 330–433 in *Essays and Reviews*. Seventh edition. London: Longman, Green, Longman, and Roberts, 1861.

Kaiser, Walter C. "Leviticus 18:5 and Paul: Do This and You Shall Live (Eternally?)." *JETS* 14 (1971): 19–28.

_____. "A Principlizing Model." Pages 19–50 in *Four Views on Moving Beyond the Bible to Theology*. Edited by Gary T. Meadors. Grand Rapids: Zondervan, 2009.

_____. *Toward an Old Testament Theology*. Grand Rapids: Zondervan, 1978.

Kalimi, Isaac. "'Go, I Beg You, Take Your Beloved Son and Slay Him!' The Binding of Isaac in Rabbinic Literature and Thought." *Review of Rabbinic Judaism* 13 (2010): 1–29.

Kant, Immanuel. "The Conflict of the Faculties." Pages 233–328 in *Religion and Rational Theology*, by Immanuel Kant. Translated by Mary J. Gregor and Robert Anchor. Cambridge: Cambridge University Press, 1996.

Kant, Laurence H. "Restorative Thoughts on an Agonizing Text: Abraham's Binding of Isaac and the Horror on Mt. Moriah (Genesis 22): Part 2." *LTQ* 38 (2003): 162–94.

Kass, Leon R. *The Beginning of Wisdom: Reading Genesis*. New York: Free Press, 2003.

Kaufman, Gordon D. *An Essay on Theological Method*. Third edition. Atlanta: American Academy of Religion, 1995.

Kelhoffer, James A. "The Witness of Eusebius' *ad Marinum* and Other Christian Writings to Text-Critical Debates concerning the Original Conclusion to Mark's Gospel." *ZNW* 92 (2001): 78–112.

Kelly, J. N. D. *Golden Mouth: The Story of John Chrysostom—Ascetic, Preacher, Bishop.* London: Duckworth, 1995.

Kelsey, David H. "The Bible and Christian Theology." *JAAR* 48 (1980): 385–402.

_____. *The Uses of Scripture in Recent Theology.* Philadelphia: Fortress, 1975.

Kessler, Edward. *Bound by the Bible: Jews, Christians and the Sacrifice of Isaac.* Cambridge: Cambridge University Press, 2004.

Kierkegaard, Søren. *Fear and Trembling.* Translated by H. Honig and E. Honig. Princeton: Princeton University Press, 1983.

Knapp, Steven, and Walter Benn Michaels. "Against Theory 2: Hermeneutics and Deconstruction." *CI* 14 (1987): 49–68.

Knoppers, Gary. "Ancient Near Eastern Royal Grants and the Davidic Covenant: A Parallel?" *JAOS* 116 (1996): 670–97.

Krabbendam, Hendrik. "Hermeneutics and Preaching." Pages 212–45 in *The Preacher and Preaching.* Edited by Samuel T. Logan. Phillipsburg, N.J.: Presbyterian and Reformed, 1986.

Kuruvilla, Abraham. "The *Aqedah*: What Is the Author *Doing* with What He Is *Saying*?" *JETS* 55 (2012): 489–508.

_____. "Book Review: *Preaching Christ through Genesis*, Sidney Greidanus." *JEHS* 8 (2008): 137–40.

_____. *Mark: A Theological Commentary for Preachers.* Eugene, Oreg.: Cascade, 2012.

_____. "The Naked Runaway and the Enrobed Reporter of Mark 14 and 16: What Is the Author *Doing* with What He Is *Saying*?" *JETS* 54 (2011): 527–45.

_____. "Pericopal Theology: An Intermediary between Text and Application." *TrinJ* 31NS (2010): 265–83.

_____. "Preaching as Translation *via* Theology." *JEHS* 9 (2009): 85–97.

_____. *Text to Praxis: Hermeneutics and Homiletics in Dialogue.* LNTS 393. London: T. & T. Clark, 2009.

Kuyper, Abraham. *E voto dordraceno: Toelichting op den Heidelbergschen Cate-chismus.* 4 vols. Amsterdam: J. A. Wormser, 1892–1895.

Ladd, George Eldon. *I Believe in the Resurrection of Jesus.* Grand Rapids: Eerd-mans, 1975.

Lakoff, George, and Mark Johnson. *Philosophy in the Flesh: The Embodied Mind and Its Challenge to Western Thought.* New York: Basic Books, 1999.

Lawlor, John I. "Theology and Art in the Narrative of the Ammonite War (2 Samuel 10–12)." *GTJ* 3 (1982): 193–205.

Lawton, Anne. "Christ: The End of the Law—A Study of Romans 10:4–8." *TrinJ* 3 (1974): 14–30.

Lessig, Lawrence. "Fidelity and Constraint." *Fordham L. Rev.* 65 (1996–1997): 1365–434.

_____. "Fidelity in Translation." *Texas L. Rev.* 71 (1992–1993): 1165–268.

_____. "The Limits of Lieber." *Cardozo L. Rev.* 16 (1995): 2249–72.

Levin, Michael. "What Makes a Classic in Political Theory?" *Pol. Sci. Q.* 88 (1973): 462–76.

Levinson, Stephen C. *Pragmatics.* Cambridge: Cambridge University Press, 1983.

_____. *Presumptive Meanings: The Theory of Generalized Conversational Impli-cature.* Cambridge, Mass.: The MIT Press, 2000.

Lévi-Strauss, Claude. *The Savage Mind.* Chicago: University of Chicago Press, 1966.

Locher, Gottfried. *Zwingli's Thought: New Perspectives.* Leiden: Brill, 1981.

Long, Thomas G. "The Preacher and the Beast: From Apocalyptic Text to Sermon." Pages 1–22 in *Intersections: Post-Critical Studies in Preaching.* Edited by Richard L. Eslinger. Grand Rapids: Eerdmans, 2004.

_____. *Preaching from Memory to Hope.* Louisville: Westminster John Knox, 2009.

_____. "The Use of Scripture in Contemporary Preaching." *Int* 44 (1990): 341–52.

_____. *The Witness of Preaching.* Second edition. Louisville: Westminster John Knox, 200.

Longenecker, Richard N. *Biblical Exegesis in the Apostolic Period.* Grand Rapids: Eerdmans, 1975.

Lowery, David K. "Christ, the End of the Law in Romans 10:4." Pages 230–47 in *Dispensationalism, Israel and the Church: The Search for Definition.* Edited by Craig A. Blaising and Darrell L. Bock. Grand Rapids: Zondervan, 1992.

Lowry, Eugene L. *The Homiletical Plot: The Sermon as Narrative Art Form.* Revised edition. Louisville: Westminster John Knox, 2001.

Luther, Martin. "Against the Heavenly Prophets in the Matter of Images and Sacraments, Part I." Pages 75–143 in *Luther's Works,* vol. 40. Translated by Bernhard Erling. Philadelphia: Muhlenberg, 1958.

_____. "Concerning the Order of Public Worship (1523)." Pages 7–14 in *Liturgy and Hymns. Luther's Works,* vol. 53. Translated by Paul Zeller Strodach. Revised by Ulrich S. Leupold. Philadelphia: Fortress, 1965.

_____. *D. Martin Luthers Werke: kritische Gesammtausgabe. Weimarer Ausgabe.* 121 vols. Weimar: H. Böhlaus Nachfolger, 1883–2009.

_____. "How Christians Should Regard Moses." Pages 157–74 in *Luther's Works,* vol. 35. Edited by E. Theodore Bachmann. Philadelphia: Muhlenberg, 1960.

_____. *Lectures on Genesis Chapters 21–25: Luther's Works,* vol. 4. Translated by George V. Schick. Edited by Jaroslav Pelikan. St. Louis: Concordia, 1964.

_____. *Luther: Lectures on Romans.* Library of Christian Classics 15. Translated by Wilhelm Pauck. Philadelphia: Westminster, 1961.

_____. "On the Councils and the Church." Pages 3–178 in *Luther's Works,* vol. 41. Translated by Charles M. Jacobs. Revised and edited by Eric W. Gritsch. Philadelphia: Fortress, 1965.

_____. "Prefaces to the Old Testament." Pages 233–333 in *Luther's Works*, vol. 35. Translated by Charles M. Jacobs. Revised by E. Theodore Bachmann. Philadelphia: Muhlenberg, 1960.

_____. "Temporal Authority: to What Extent it Should Be Obeyed." Pages 77–129 in *Luther's Works*, vol. 45. Translated by J. J. Schindel. Revised by Walther I. Brandt. Philadelphia: Muhlenberg, 1963.

MacIntyre, Alasdair. *After Virtue.* Second edition. Notre Dame: University of Notre Dame Press, 1984.

Marshall, U.S. Supreme Court Chief Justice John. *Cohens v. Virginia.* U.S. Reports 19 (1821): 264–448.

_____. *McCulloch v. The State of Maryland* et al. U.S. Reports 17 (4 Wheat.) (1819): 316–437.

Mathews, Kenneth A. *Genesis 11:27–50:26.* NAC 1B. Nashville: Broadman & Holman, 2005.

Mayer, Wendy, and Pauline Allen. *John Chrysostom.* London: Routledge, 2000.

McKenna, U.S. Supreme Court Justice Joseph. *Weems v. United States.* U.S. Reports 217 (1910): 349–413.

McKenzie, Steven. "The Typology of the Davidic Covenant." Pages 152–78 in *The Land that I Will Show You: Essays on the History and Archaeology of the Ancient Near East in Honor of J. Maxwell Miller.* Edited by J. Andrew Dearman and M. Patrick Graham. London: Continuum, 2001.

Metropolitan Police Act 1839. Chapter 47, statute 54, "Prohibition of Nuisances by Persons in the Thoroughfares."

Metzger, Bruce M. *The Canon of the New Testament: Its Origin, Development, and Significance.* Oxford: Clarendon, 1987.

Milgrom, Jacob. "Of Hems and Tassels." *BAR* 9 (1983): 61–65.

Miller, James C. *The Obedience of Faith, the Eschatological People of God, and the Purpose of Romans.* SBLDS 177. Atlanta: SBL, 2000.

Miller, Joseph M. "Guibert de Nogent's *Liber quo ordine sermo fieri debeat*: A Translation of the Earliest Modern Speech Textbook." *Today's Speech* 17 (1969): 45–56.

Moberly, R. W. L. *The Bible, Theology, and Faith: A Study of Abraham and Jesus.* Cambridge: Cambridge University Press, 2000.

_____. "The Earliest Commentary on the Akedah." *VT* 37 (1988): 302–23.

_____. "What Is Theological Interpretation of Scripture?" *JTI* 3 (2009): 161–78.

Mohler, R. Albert. *He Is Not Silent: Preaching in a Postmodern World.* Chicago: Moody, 2008.

Moo, Douglas J. *The Epistle to the Romans.* NICNT. Grand Rapids: Eerdmans, 1996.

_____. "The Law of Christ as the Fulfillment of the Law of Moses: A Modified Lutheran View." Pages 319–76 in *Five Views on Law and Gospel,* by Greg L. Bahnsen, Walter C. Kaiser, Douglas J. Moo, Wayne G. Strickland, and Willem A. VanGemeren. Edited by Stanley N. Gundry. Grand Rapids: Zondervan, 1996.

Morris, Leon. *The Epistle to the Romans.* Grand Rapids: Eerdmans, 1988.

Morson, Gary Saul. *The Boundaries of Genre: Dostoevsky's Diary of a Writer and the Tradition of Literary Utopia.* Austin, Tex.: University of Texas Press, 1981.

Moule, C. F. D. "Obligation in the Ethic of Paul." Pages 389–406 in *Christian History and Interpretation: Studies Presented to John Knox.* Edited by W. R. Farmer, C. F. D. Moule, and R. R. Niebuhr. Cambridge: Cambridge University Press, 1967.

Mudge, Lewis S. "Paul Ricoeur on Biblical Interpretation." Pages 1–37 in *Essays on Biblical Interpretation* by Paul Ricoeur. Edited by Lewis S. Mudge. Philadelphia: Fortress, 1980.

Nussbaum, Martha C. *Love's Knowledge: Essays on Philosophy and Literature.* New York: Oxford University Press, 1990.

_____. *Poetic Justice: The Literary Imagination and Public Life.* Boston: Beacon, 1995.

Nybroten, Arvid. "Possible Vestiges of the *Afikoman* in the Elevation of the *Panagia.*" *GOTR* 43 (1998): 105–27.

O'Donovan, Oliver M. T. "The Possibility of a Biblical Ethic." *TSF Bull.* 67 (1973): 15–23.

Oden, Thomas C., and Mark Sheridan, eds. *Genesis 12–50.* Ancient Christian Commentary on Scripture: Old Testament, vol. 2. Downers Grove: Inter-Varsity, 2002.

Old, Hughes Oliphant. *The Reading and Preaching of the Scriptures in the Worship of the Christian Church.* 7 vols. Grand Rapids: Eerdmans, 1998–2010.

Ong, Walter J. "Mimesis and the Following of Christ." *Religion & Literature* 26 (1994): 73–77.

_____. *Orality and Literacy: The Technologizing of the Word.* London: Routledge, 1982.

Osborn, Eric F. "Reason and The Rule of Faith in the Second Century AD." Pages 40–61 in *The Making of Orthodoxy: Essays in Honour of Henry Chadwick.* Edited by Rowan Williams. Cambridge: Cambridge University Press, 1989.

Ott, Heinrich. *Theology and Preaching.* Philadelphia: Westminster, 1963.

Parker, T. H. L. *Calvin's Preaching.* Edinburgh: T. & T. Clark, 1992.

Patrick, Dale. *Old Testament Law.* Atlanta: John Knox, 1985.

Petrey, Sandy. *Speech Acts and Literary Theory.* New York: Routledge, 1990.

Pfeiffer, Robert H. *One Hundred New Selected Nuzi Texts.* Translated by E. A. Speiser. New Haven: American Schools of Oriental Research, 1936.

Pickett, Raymond. *The Cross in Corinth: The Social Significance of the Death of Jesus.* JSNTSS 143. Sheffield: Sheffield Academic Press, 1997.

Porter, Stanley E. "Hermeneutics, Biblical Interpretation, and Theology: Hunch, Holy Spirit, or Hard Work?" Pages 97–127 in *Beyond the Bible: Moving from Scripture to Theology*, by I. Howard Marshall. Grand Rapids: Baker, 2004.

Poythress, Vern S. "Divine Meaning of Scripture." *WTJ* 48 (1986): 241–79.

———. *The Shadow of Christ in the Law of Moses*. Phillipsburg, N.J.: Presbyterian and Reformed, 1991.

Pratt, Mary Louise. *Toward a Speech Act Theory of Literary Discourse*. Bloomington, Ind.: Indiana University Press, 1977.

Ramm, Bernard L. *Protestant Biblical Interpretation*. Revised edition. Grand Rapids: Baker, 1970.

Ratner, Sidney. "Presupposition and Objectivity in History." *Phil. Sci.* 7 (1940): 499–505.

The Real Book. 3 vols. Milwaukee: Hal Leonard, 2006.

Recanati, François. *Meaning and Force: The Pragmatics of Performative Utterances*. Cambridge: Cambridge University Press, 1987.

Reumann, John. "A History of Lectionaries: From the Synagogue at Nazareth to Post-Vatican II." *Int* 31 (1977): 116–30.

Ricoeur, Paul. *Hermeneutics and the Human Sciences: Essays on Language, Action and Interpretation*. Edited and translated by John B. Thompson. Cambridge: Cambridge University Press, 1981.

———. *Interpretation Theory: Discourse and the Surplus of Meaning*. Fort Worth, Tex.: Texas Christian University Press, 1976.

———. "Naming God." *USQR* 34 (1979): 215–27.

———. "Philosophical Hermeneutics and Theological Hermeneutics: Ideology, Utopia, and Faith." Pages 1–28 in *Protocol of the Seventeenth Colloquy, 4 November 1975*. Edited by W. Wuellner. Berkeley: The Center for Hermeneutical Studies in Hellenistic and Modern Culture, 1976.

———. "Philosophy and Religious Language." *JR* 54 (1974): 71–85.

_____. "Poetry and Possibility." Pages 448–62 in *A Ricoeur Reader: Reflection and Imagination*. Edited by Mario J. Valdés. Hertfordshire, U.K.: Harvester Wheatsheaf, 1991.

_____. *The Rule of Metaphor: Multi-disciplinary Studies on the Creation of Meaning in Language*. Translated by Robert Czerny, with Kathleen McLaughlin and John Costello. London: Routledge & Kegan Paul, 1978.

_____. "Toward a Hermeneutic of the Idea of Revelation." Pages 73–118 in *Essays on Biblical Interpretation* by Paul Ricoeur. Edited by Lewis S. Mudge. Philadelphia: Fortress, 1980.

_____. "Word, Polysemy, Metaphor: Creativity in Language." Pages 97–128 in *A Ricoeur Reader: Reflection and Imagination*. Edited by Mario J. Valdés. Hertfordshire, U.K.: Harvester Wheatsheaf, 1991.

Riggs v. *Palmer*. N.Y. 115 (1889): 506–20.

Road Traffic Act 1972. Chapter 20, statute 195.

Roberts, Phyllis. "The *Ars Praedicandi* and the Medieval Sermon." Pages 41–60 in *Preacher, Sermon and the Audience in the Middle Ages*. Edited by Carolyn Muessig. Leiden: Brill, 2002.

Robinson, Haddon W. "The Relevance of Expository Preaching." Pages 79–94 in *Preaching to a Shifting Culture: 12 Perspectives on Communicating that Connects*. Edited by Scott M. Gibson. Grand Rapids: Baker, 2004.

Rogers, Jack B., and Donald K. McKim. *The Authority and Interpretation of the Bible: An Historical Approach*. San Francisco: Harper & Row, 1979.

Rosch, Eleanor. "Human Categorization." Pages 1–49 in *Studies in Cross-cultural Psychology*. Vol. 1. Edited by Neil Warren. New York: Academic, 1977.

Rosner, Brian S. "'Written for Us': Paul's View of Scripture." Pages 81–106 in *A Pathway into the Holy Scripture*. Edited by D. Wright and P. Satterthwaite. Grand Rapids: Eerdmans, 1994.

Ross, Allen P. *Creation and Blessing: A Guide to the Study and Exposition of Genesis*. Grand Rapids: Baker, 1997.

_____. *Holiness to the LORD: A Guide to the Exposition of the Book of Leviticus.* Grand Rapids: Baker, 2002.

Roth, Martha T. *Law Collections from Mesopotamia and Asia Minor.* Atlanta: Scholars, 1995.

Ryrie, Charles C. *Basic Theology: A Popular Systematic Guide to Understanding Biblical Truth.* Chicago: Moody, 1999.

_____. *Dispensationalism.* Revised edition. Chicago: Moody, 1995.

_____. "The End of the Law." *BSac* 124 (1967): 239–47.

Sailhamer, John H. *Introduction to Old Testament Theology: A Canonical Approach.* Grand Rapids: Zondervan, 1995.

Sanders, E. P. *Paul and Palestinian Judaism: A Comparison of Patterns of Religion.* London: SCM, 1977.

Sauer, Erich. *The Dawn of Word Redemption.* Grand Rapids: Eerdmans, 1951.

Scalia, Antonin. *A Matter of Interpretation: Federal Courts and the Law.* Princeton: Princeton University Press, 1997.

Schauer, Frederick. *Playing by the Rules: A Philosophical Examination of Rule-Based Decision-Making in Law and Life.* Oxford: Clarendon, 1991.

Schneiders, Sandra M. "The Paschal Imagination: Objectivity and Subjectivity in New Testament Interpretation." *TS* 46 (1982): 52–68.

Schreiner, Thomas R. *The Law and Its Fulfillment: A Pauline Theology of Law.* Grand Rapids: Baker, 1993.

_____. *Paul, Apostle of God's Glory in Christ: A Pauline Theology.* Downers Grove: InterVarsity, 2001.

_____. "Paul's View of the Law in Romans 10:4–5." *WTJ* 55 (1993): 113–35.

_____. "Preaching and Biblical Theology." *SBJT* 10 (2006): 20–29.

_____. *Romans.* BECNT. Grand Rapids: Baker, 1998.

Schwöbel, Christoph. "The Preacher's Art: Preaching Theologically." Pages 1–20 in *Theology Through Preaching* by Colin Gunton. Edinburgh: T. & T. Clark, 2001.

Scott, M. Philip. "Chiastic Structure: A Key to the Interpretation of Mark's Gospel." *BTB* 15 (1985): 17–26.

Seitel, Peter. "Theorizing Genres – Interpreting Works." *NLH* 34 (2003): 275–97.

Sidney, Philip. "An Apology for Poetry." Pages 108–48 in *Criticism: The Major Statements*. Second edition. Edited by Charles Kaplan. New York: St. Martin's, 1986.

Simon, Uriel. "The Poor Man's Ewe-Lamb: An Example of a Juridical Parable." *Bib* 48 (1967): 207–42.

_____. *Reading Prophetic Narratives*. Translated by Lenn J. Schramm. Bloomington, Ind.: Indiana University Press, 1997.

Singer, Marcus George. *Generalization in Ethics*. London: Eyre & Spottiswoode, 1963.

Smalley, Beryl. *The Study of the Bible in the Middle Ages*. Oxford: Basil Blackwell, 1952.

Smart, James D. *The Strange Silence of the Bible in the Church: A Study in Hermeneutics*. London: SCM, 1970.

Smith, James K. A. *Desiring the Kingdom: Worship, Worldview, and Cultural Formation*. Grand Rapids: Baker, 2009.

Sonsino, Rifat. *Motive Clauses in Hebrew Law: Biblical Forms and Near Eastern Parallels*. Chico, Calif.: Scholars, 1980.

Spencer, Aída Besançon. "The Denial of the Good News and the Ending of Mark." *BBR* 17 (2007): 269–83.

Spiegel, Shalom. *The Last Trial: On the Legends and Lore of the Command to Offer Isaac as a Sacrifice: The Akedah*. Translated by Judah Goldin. Philadelphia: Jewish Publication Society of America, 1967.

Spinks, D. Christopher. *The Bible and the Crisis of Meaning: Debates on the Theological Interpretation of Scripture*. London: T. & T. Clark, 2007.

Sprinkle, Joe M. *Biblical Law and Its Relevance: A Christian Understanding and Ethical Application for Today of the Mosaic Regulations.* Lanham, Md.: University Press of America, 2006.

Spurgeon, Charles H. "Christ Precious to Believers." No pages. Cited on June 3, 2012. Online: http://spurgeon.org/sermons/0242.htm.

Stein, Robert H. "The Ending of Mark." *BBR* 18 (2008): 79–98.

Steiner, George. "'Critic'/'Reader.'" *NLH* 10 (1979): 423–52.

_____. *Real Presences.* Chicago: The University of Chicago Press, 1989.

Sternberg, Meir. *The Poetics of Biblical Narrative: Ideological Literature and the Drama of Reading.* Bloomington, Ind.: Indiana University Press, 1987.

Stott, John R. W. *Between Two Worlds.* Grand Rapids: Eerdmans, 1982.

Taycher, Leonid. "Books of the World, Stand up and Be Counted! All 129,864,880 of You." No pages. Cited June 3, 2012. Online: http://booksearch.blogspot.com/2010/08/books-of-world-stand-up-and-be-counted.html.

Thomas, W. H. Griffith. *The Principles of Theology: An Introduction to the Thirty-Nine Articles.* London: Longmans, 1930.

Thrall, Margaret E. *A Critical and Exegetical Commentary on the Second Epistle to the Corinthians.* 2 vols. Edinburgh: T. & T. Clark, 1994.

Tinsley, E. J. "Some Principles for Reconstructing a Doctrine of the Imitation of Christ." *SJOT* 25 (1972): 45–57.

Todorov, Tzvetan. "Primitive Narrative." Pages 53–65 in *The Poetics of Prose.* Translated by R. Howard. Oxford: Basil Blackwell, 1977.

Torrance, T. F. *Divine Meaning: Studies in Patristic Hermeneutics.* Edinburgh: T. & T. Clark, 1995.

Tracy, David. *The Analogical Imagination: Christian Theology and the Culture of Pluralism.* New York: Crossroad, 1981.

_____. "Creativity in the Interpretation of Religion: The Question of Radical Pluralism." *NLH* 15 (1984): 289–309.

_____. *Plurality and Ambiguity: Hermeneutics, Religion, Hope*. San Francisco: Harper and Row, 1987.

Treier, Daniel J. *Introducing Theological Interpretation of Scripture: Recovering a Christian Practice*. Grand Rapids: Baker, 2008.

Trible, Phyllis. *Genesis: A Living Conversation*. Edited by Bill Moyers. New York: Doubleday, 1996.

Tyndale, William. "A Prologue by William Tyndale Shewing the Use of the Scripture, which He Wrote before the Five Books of Moses." Pages 1:6–11 in *The Works of the English Reformers*. 3 vols. Edited by Thomas Russell. London: Ebenezer Palmer, 1828–1831.

Vanderveken, Daniel. "Non-Literal Speech Acts and Conversational Maxims." Pages 371–84 in *John Searle and His Critics*. Edited by Ernest Lepore and Robert Van Gulick. Cambridge, Mass.: Basil Blackwell, 1991.

VanGemeren, Willem A. "The Law is the Perfection of Righteousness in Jesus Christ: A Reformed Perspective." Pages 13–58 in *Five Views on Law and Gospel*, by Greg L. Bahnsen, Walter C. Kaiser, Douglas J. Moo, Wayne G. Strickland, and Willem A. VanGemeren. Edited by Stanley N. Gundry. Grand Rapids: Zondervan, 1996.

Vanhoozer, Kevin J. *The Drama of Doctrine: A Canonical-Linguistic Approach to Christian Theology*. Louisville: Westminster John Knox, 2005.

_____. *First Theology: God, Scripture and Hermeneutics*. Downers Grove: InterVarsity, 2002.

_____. *Is There a Meaning in This Text? The Bible, the Reader, and the Morality of Literary Knowledge*. Grand Rapids: Zondervan, 1998.

_____. "A Response to Walter C. Kaiser Jr." Pages 57–63 in *Four Views on Moving Beyond the Bible to Theology*. Edited by Gary T. Meadors. Grand Rapids: Zondervan, 2009.

Vickers, Brian. *In Defence of Rhetoric*. Oxford: Clarendon, 1998.

Volf, Miroslav. *Captive to the Word of God: Engaging the Scriptures for Contemporary Theological Reflection*. Grand Rapids: Eerdmans, 2010.

von Lohmann, Fred. "Google Book Search Settlement: Updating the Numbers, Part 2." No pages. Cited June 3, 2012. Online: https://www.eff.org/deeplinks/2010/02/google-book-search-settlement-updating-numbers-0.

von Rad, Gerhard. *Das Opfer des Abraham*. Kaiser Traktate 6. Munich: Kaiser, 1971.

Vos, Geerhardus. *Biblical Theology: Old and New Testament*. Grand Rapids: Eerdmans, 1948; repr. 1975.

Wallace, Daniel B. *Greek Grammar beyond the Basics: An Exegetical Syntax of the New Testament*. Grand Rapids: Zondervan, 1996.

_____. "Mark 16:8 as the Conclusion to the Second Gospel." Pages 1–39 in *Perspectives on the Ending of Mark: 4 Views*, by David Alan Black, Darrell Bock, Keith Elliott, Maurice Robinson, and Daniel B. Wallace. Nashville: Broadman & Holman, 2008.

Walters, Stanley D. "Wood, Sand and Stars: Structure and Theology in Gn 22:1–19." *TJT* 3 (1987): 301–30.

Warren, Timothy S. "A Paradigm for Preaching." *BSac* 148 (1991): 463–86.

Watson, Francis B. "Not the New Perspective." No pages. Cited July 11, 2010. Online: http://www.abdn.ac.uk/divinity/staff/watsonart.shtml.

_____. *Text and Truth: Redefining Biblical Theology*. Grand Rapids: Eerdmans, 1997.

_____. *Text, Church and World: Biblical Interpretation in Theological Perspective*. Grand Rapids: Eerdmans, 1994.

Watts, James W. *Reading Law: The Rhetorical Shaping of the Pentateuch*. Sheffield: Sheffield Academic Press, 1999.

Weaver, Richard M. *Language Is Sermonic: Richard M. Weaver on the Nature of Rhetoric*. Edited by Richard L. Johannesen, Rennard Strickland, and Ralph T. Eubanks. Baton Rouge, La.: Louisiana State University Press, 1970.

Webster, John. "Editorial." *IJST* 12 (2010): 116–17.

_____. *Word and Church: Essays in Christian Dogmatics*. Edinburgh: T. & T. Clark, 2001.

Wenham, Gordon J. "The Akedah: A Paradigm of Sacrifice." Pages 93–102 in *Pomegranates and Golden Bells: Studies in Biblical, Jewish, and Near Eastern Ritual, Law, and Literature in Honor of Jacob Milgrom*. Edited by David P. Wright, David Noel Freedman, and Avi Hurvitz. Winona Lake, Ind.: Eisenbrauns, 1995.

_____. *The Book of Leviticus*. NICOT. Grand Rapids: Eerdmans, 1979.

_____. *Genesis 16–50*. WBC 2. Dallas: Word, 1994.

_____. *Story as Torah: Reading Old Testament Narrative Ethically*. Grand Rapids: Baker, 2000.

Wesley, John. "Sermon 34." Pages 4–19 in *The Works of John Wesley: Vol. 2: Sermons II*. Edited by Albert C. Outler. Nashville: Abingdon, 1985.

Westbrook, Raymond. *Studies in Biblical and Cuneiform Law*. Paris: Gabalda, 1988.

Westbrook, Raymond, and Bruce Wells. *Everyday Law in Biblical Israel: An Introduction*. Louisville: Westminster John Knox, 2009.

Westerholm, Stephen. *Israel's Law and the Church's Faith: Paul and His Recent Interpreters*. Grand Rapids: Eerdmans, 1988.

_____. *Perspectives Old and New on Paul: The "Lutheran" Paul and His Critics*. Grand Rapids: Eerdmans, 2004.

Wheelwright, Philip. *The Burning Fountain: A Study in the Language of Symbolism*. Revised edition. Bloomington, Ind.: Indiana University Press, 1968.

White, Hayden. "The Narrativization of Real Events." Pages 249–54 in *On Narrative*. Edited by W. J. T. Mitchell. Chicago: The University of Chicago Press, 1981.

_____. "The Value of Narrativity in the Representation of Reality." Pages 1–23 in *On Narrative*. Edited by W. J. T. Mitchell. Chicago: The University of Chicago Press, 1981.

White, James Boyd. "Judicial Criticism." Pages 393–410 in *Interpreting Law and Literature: A Hermeneutic Reader*. Edited by Sanford Levinson and Steven Mailloux. Evanston: Northwestern University Press, 1988.

Wiesel, Elie. *Messengers of God*. New York: Random House, 1976.

Wilken, Robert L. "Melito, The Jewish Community at Sardis, and the Sacrifice of Isaac." *TS* 37 (1976): 53–69.

Wilkins, John. *Ecclesiastes or A Discourse concerning the Gift of Preaching, as it falls under the Rules of Art*. Seventh edition. London: A. J. Churchill, 1693.

Williamson, H. G. M. *Ezra, Nehemiah*. WBC 16. Dallas: Word, 1985.

Williamson, W. Paul, and Howard R. Pollio. "The Phenomenology of Religious Serpent Handling: A Rationale and Thematic Study of Extemporaneous Sermons." *JSSR* 38 (1999): 203–18.

Wittgenstein, Ludwig. "Notes for Lectures on 'Private Experience' and 'Sense Data.'" Edited by R. Rhees. *Phil. Rev.* 77 (1968): 275–320.

_____. *Philosophical Investigations*. Second edition. Translated by G. E. M. Anscombe. London: Basil Blackwell, 1958.

Wolff, Hans Walter. "The Elohistic Fragments in the Pentateuch." Translated by Keith R. Crim. *Int* 26 (1972): 158–73.

Wolterstorff, Nicholas. *Art in Action: Toward a Christian Aesthetic*. Grand Rapids: Eerdmans, 1980.

_____. *Divine Discourse: Philosophical Reflections on the Claim that God Speaks*. Cambridge: Cambridge University Press, 1995.

_____. "The Importance of Hermeneutics for a Christian Worldview." Pages 25–47 in *Disciplining Hermeneutics: Interpretation in Christian Perspective*. Edited by Roger Lundin. Grand Rapids: Eerdmans, 1997.

_____. *Works and Worlds of Art*. Oxford: Clarendon, 1980.

Wood, A. Skevington. *Captive to the Word: Martin Luther: Doctor of Sacred Scripture*. London: Paternoster, 1969.

Wright, Christopher J. H. *Living as the People of God: The Relevance of Old Testament Ethics.* Leicester, U.K.: InterVarsity, 1983.

_____. *Old Testament Ethics for the People of God.* Downers Grove: InterVarsity, 2004.

Wright, N. T. "How Can the Bible Be Authoritative?" *VE* 21 (1991): 7–32.

_____. "The Paul of History and the Apostle of Faith." *TynBul* 29 (1978): 61–88.

Yaguello, Marina. *Language through the Looking Glass: Exploring Language and Linguistics.* New York: Oxford University Press, 1998.

Young, Frances. "The 'Mind' of Scripture: Theological Readings of the Bible in the Fathers." *IJST* 7 (2005): 126–41.

Young, James O., and Carl Matheson. "The Metaphysics of Jazz." *J. Aes. Art Crit.* 58 (2000): 125–33.

Zimmermann, Jens. *Recovering Theological Hermeneutics: An Incarnational-Trinitarian Theory of Interpretation.* Grand Rapids: Baker, 2004.

INDEX of SUBJECTS

Middle Ages, 276–78
moralizing in, 242–43
persuasion and, 138
purposes of, 25
Reformation Era, 278–79
relevance of, 20–21
specification of application in, 60, 109
theological hermeneutic for, 25
transhistorical intention and, 56
two-step process of, 28, 90, 150–51
precepts, 100, 126, 127
prescriptivity, 59–61
principles, 160, 184
principlization, 127–29
principlizing, 60, 109
priorities, 100, 126, 127
privileging the text
the *Aqedah and,* 219
in pericopal theology, 280
with pragmatic approach, 197
thorough exegisis and, 132
See also pericopal theology; pericopes
projected worlds, 43, 46, 54, 64, 109–10, 184
promises, 235, 236, 237
prophecy, 243, 249
Psalms, 243, 247, 249
psoriasis, 59n64

qere (what is read), 77, 78

reader identification, 40
reading of the law, 97
re-creation, 142
redemption, 96, 278–79
redemptive-historical interpretation
on merit in obedience, 253
sermonic themes repetition in, 241
See also christocentric interpretation
referents, 37–39
Reformation Era, 278–79
Reformed approach, Mosaic law, 157–58
Reformers, rewards and, 256–57
regula fidei (rule of faith), 275–76
relationship and responsibility, 189–95, 205–7
relevance, 20–21, 137, 145
reminders/remembrances, 188
responsibility
relationship and, 189–95, 205–7
reminders/remembrances of, 188

of rhetoricians, 137
sermons and, 241
rewards, 253-257
See also blessings/rewards
rhetoricians' responsibility, 137
Riggs v. *Palmer,* 183–84
righteousness, 163, 164, 165, 167, 204
Roman Christians' obedience, 198
rule of faith *(regula fidei),* 275–76
rules
historical uses of, 65–66
of reading, 68–87
role of, 65–68
See also Rules of Reading
Rules of Reading
Applicability, 79–82
Centrality, 84–86, 209, 212, 235
Ecclesiality, 82–84
Exclusivity, 68–71
Finality, 76–79
purpose of, 27, 33
Singularity, 71–76
wide employment of, 67

Sabbath observance, 185
sacrifices, 214, 215, 224–28
sanctification
guidelines for, 162
Jesus model of, 261
law instrument of, 185
obedience and, 205, 258
principles of, 160
Sarah, 222, 223
Satan, 75, 199
scholia, 81
Scripture
Bible as, 65
as classic, 64
covenant renewal from reading, 97–99
inspiration of, 247
multiple senses of, 277
Rule of Applicability and, 79
rules and, 66
testifying to Jesus, 249–50
textuality of, 31–33
See also Bible
Second Temple Judaism, 160, 189–90
seeing, 123
semantic analysis, 48–53, 52

INDEX of ANCIENT SOURCES

INDEX *of* MODERN SOURCES

INDEX of SCRIPTURE

ACKNOWLEDGMENTS

I owe much to many . . .

My family: my father, always on my side, proud, loyal, and affectionate; my brother and his family, quietly confident in my life and work; and my mother, now in a better place, no doubt still cheering for me!

The Morgans, who are there wherever I'm preaching.

My teachers and colleagues at Dallas Theological Seminary, and my doctoral supervisor at the University of Aberdeen, Francis Watson, all of whom taught me the value of diligent analysis, collegial conduct, and godly character, and all of which I'm still assimilating.

My amicable sparring partners in academia, especially Timothy Warren, John Hilber, and Kevin Vanhoozer, who have sharpened my thinking by their own writings, their close reading of several chapters of this work, their thoughtful comments, and their consistent encouragement.

God's people at Northwest Bible Church in Dallas who, for several weeks every summer, have patiently sat through my homiletical offerings, never failing to be supportive.

And my students, aspiring preachers every one of them, without whom none of this would have been. To them I dedicate this book with gratitude.

Through the making of this work, I have been renewed with an enthusiasm for the art and science of homiletics, and compelled by an urgency to research the word, teach the word, and preach the word, for the glory of God. This work, therefore, goes out with the prayer that God the Spirit would empower preachers everywhere to bear fruit in their pulpit exertions as lives are transformed in the pews. And may these intrepid ones themselves be conformed to the image of God the Son, more and more, day by day, as they abound in "faith-full" obedience.

May Thy Kingdom come!

Abraham Kuruvilla
Dallas, Texas

Pentecost 2012